THE TIMES AND APPEASEMENT

THE TIMES AND APPEASEMENT

The Journals of A. L. Kennedy, 1932–1939

edited by

GORDON MARTEL

CAMDEN FIFTH SERIES
VOLUME 16

CAMBRIDGE
UNIVERSITY PRESS

FOR THE ROYAL HISTORICAL SOCIETY
University College London, Gower Street, London WC1E 6BT
2000

Published by the Press Syndicate of the University of Cambridge
The Edinburgh Building, Cambridge CB2 2RU, United Kingdom
40 West 20th Street, New York, NY 1011–4211, USA
10 Stamford Road, Oakleigh, Melbourne 3166, Australia

First published 2000

A catalogue record for this book is available from the British Library

Library of Congress cataloguing-in-publication Data

Kennedy, A. L. (Aubrey Leo), b. 1885.
  The Times and appeasement: the journals of A. L. Kennedy, 1932–
1939/edited by Gordon Martel.
    p. cm.—(Camden fifth series; v. 16)
  ISBN 0-521-79354-8
    1. Great Britain—Politics and government—1936–1945—Sources. 2. Great
Britain—Politics and government—1910–1936—Sources. 3. Great Britain—
Foreign relations—1910–1936—Sources. 4. Great Britain—Foreign rela-
tions—1936–1945—Sources. 5.   Great   Britain—Foreign   relations—
Germany—Sources. 6.   Germany—Foreign   relations—Great   Britain—
Sources. 7. Kennedy, A. L. (Aubrey Leo), b. 1885—Diaries. 8. World War,
1939–1945—Causes—Sources. 9. World politics—1933–1945—Sources. 10.
Times (London, England). I. Martel, Gordon. II. Title. III. Series.

DA20.C15 v. 16
[DA578]
941.084—dc21   00–058533

ISBN 0 521 793548 hardback

SUBSCRIPTIONS. The serial publications of the Royal Historical Society,
Royal Historical Society Transactions (ISSN 0080–4401) and Camden Fifth Series
(ISSN 0960–1163), volumes may be purchased together on annual subscription.
The 2000 subscription price (which includes postage but not VAT is £60
(US$99 in the USA, Canada and Mexico) and includes Camden Fifth Series,
volumes 15 and 16 (published in July and December) and Transactions Sixth
Series, volume 10 (published in December). Japanese prices are available from
Kinokuniya Company Ltd, P.O. Box 55, Chitose, Tokyo 156, Japan. EU
subscribers (outside the UK) who are not registered for VAT should add VAT
at their country's rate. VAT registered subscribers should provide their VAT
registration number. Prices include delivery by air.
  Subscription orders, which must be accompanied by payment, may be sent
to a bookseller, subscription agent or direct to the publisher: Cambridge
University Press, The Edinburgh Building, Shaftesbury Road, Cambridge CB2
2RU, UK; or in the USA, Canada and Mexico; Cambridge University Press,
Journals Fulfillment Department, 110 Midland Avenue, Port Chester, NY
10573–4930, USA.

SINGLE VOLUMES AND BACK VOLUMES. A list of Royal Historical
Society volumes available from Cambridge University Press may be obtained
from the Humanities Marketing Department at the address above.

Printed and bound in the United Kingdom by Butler & Tanner Ltd, Frome and London

For
Elizabeth Le Mesurier [née Kennedy]
&
Claire Heddy [née Kennedy]

CONTENTS

NOTES ON THE TEXT

The complete set of Kennedy journals amount to some 250,000 words (although without transcribing them all it is rather difficult to make an accurate estimate as they are handwritten and the volumes vary in length). The selections reproduced here, covering the period from the beginning of 1932 until the end of 1939, represent something like 90% of the originals for this period and include virtually all materials of political, diplomatic or journalistic importance. Because Kennedy was making the entries by hand, and because he was a professional journalist, he used a considerable amount of shorthand. For the most part his abbreviations and contractions are reasonably clear and easy to read, so it seemed sensible to retain these as much as possible in order to convey the original texture of the journals. Kennedy frequently used underlining for emphasis, to indicate foreign terms or for newspaper titles. I have retained the underlining for emphasis, but have converted all foreign terms and newspaper titles to italics – whether he troubled to underline these or not. There is also considerable underlining done in pencil, which I have ignored as it appears that this was done long after the entries are made – most likely in the 1950s when he seems to have considered publishing them.

I have kept the intrusion of square brackets to the minimum, using them only where some confusion might result and when Kennedy's shorthand version has been used only once or twice. The only departures from this rule concern his shorthand for 'the' and 'of'. Almost without exception Kennedy replaced these with '/' and 'o'. It seemed to me that to reproduce these faithfully throughout would have meant very heavy going for readers, as a typical sentence would then have read: 'I hear that / way in which / news of Brüning's announcement to Rumbold about non-payment o reparatns / other day leaked out through / telephone.' Thus, it may be assumed that whenever 'the' and 'of' appear in the text below, these have been expanded from Kennedy's shorthand.

I have supplemented the extracts from the journals with some selections of other materials when these seemed particularly helpful. The most relevant sections of leading-articles referred to in the journal have been extracted and reproduced here, and a relatively complete list of all of Kennedy's leading-articles for the period 1932–9 may be found in the appendix. This list is based on the clippings that he carefully pasted into a series of 'Cutting-Books' (which were located by Claire Heddy under the stairs of her cottage in Somerset while we were searching for any letters that might have survived). Unfortunately, two of these have failed to surface: those covering the periods from January 1932 to June 1933 and for August 1934 to May 1935. Another gap occurs when Kennedy stopped writing leaders between October 1935 and August 1938. For the sake of his health, he and Sylvia took an extended sea-voyage to Asia in the fall of 1935; when he returned he was still not fit enough to take up full-time leader-writing and instead served temporarily as Berlin correspondent for the four months between mid-February and mid-June in 1936. When he returned from this assignment he took his usual summer vacation, resumed leader-writing for September and October 1937 and then decided to resign from *The Times* in order to write a book on Anglo-German relations. After doing some temporary leader-writing in the summer of 1937 and some correspondent work for the newspaper early in 1938, he returned to full-time leader-writing in August 1938, when the clipping-books resume.

Further excerpts have been taken from Kennedy's books, *Old Diplomacy and New* (1922) and *Britain Faces Germany* (1927), along with letters from him to others which are located in the archives of *The Times*, and I wish to acknowledge my debt to both *The Times* and its archival staff for their assistance and permission in utilizing these materials. My greatest debt is to the archival staff of Churchill College, Cambridge, where the journals are deposited.

Every effort has been made to trace all of those referred to in the text, and a brief biographical description is given in a footnote when they first appear. Whenever the people described have written a memoir, autobiography or a piece of contemporary literature that bears upon the themes of A. L. Kennedy diaries I have drawn attention to it at the end of the biographical description.

ABBREVIATIONS

Although Kennedy was usually clear and reasonably systematic in the abbreviations that he employed in his journals, he was not always consistent. In attempting to make the following list as simple and accessible as possible I have not listed every possible variant, but hope that I have made it possible for the reader to check on any abbreviations that may seem idiosyncratic or not readily apparent. Kennedy would, for example, close his abbreviations in a variety of ways; Ramsay MacDonald is variously rendered as 'MacD' 'MacD.' and 'MacD:'. In the list that follows below the punctuation has been removed. Perhaps more confusing is the use of superscript in some cases and not in others, with the superscript sometimes underlined, and sometimes not. Thus, 'negotiations' is variously rendered as 'negot$^{\underline{ns}}$' 'negot^{ns}' and 'negotns'; as the underlined superscript is the form he most frequently employed, that is the form that I have used below. Kennedy always used the same abbreviation for both upper and lower case, for example, correspondent is abbreviated as 'corrspt' while Correspondent is abbreviated as 'Corrspt'; in the list that follows, only the lower-case form is listed – but in cases where this is not true, both variations have been provided: for example 'gd' is his abbreviation for 'good', but 'GD' is his abbreviation for Geoffrey Dawson; 'min' is for 'minutes' but 'Min' is for 'Minister'. Similarly, he would regularly add an 's' to his abbreviations for the plural, thus: 'ambassdr' and 'ambassdrs'; in the list that follows, only the singular is listed; again, whenever confusion might result both variations have been listed: thus, 'pol' is his abbreviation for 'political', while 'pols' is his abbreviation for politics – and both are listed. I have not listed those simple contractions in which Kennedy simply dropped the 'io': thus, 'abolition' becomes 'abolitn' – but I have included 'aboln' as possibly confusing.

Abbreviations used in the journal

aboln	abolition
Abyss$^{\underline{n}}$	Abyssinia
Abyss$^{\underline{nia}}$	Abyssinia
AC	Austen Chamberlain
acc	according
Admrl	Admiral
AE	Anthony Eden
after^{n}	afternoon
afterwds	afterwards
Agrt	Agreement
Am	American
Ambassdr	Ambassador
Ambdr	Ambassador
ambassadr	ambassador
ambssdr	ambassador

Am^{cn}	American
$answ^{d}$	answered
armamnts	armaments
arr^{d}	arrived
$Asst^{nt}$	Assistant
Att	Attaché
Astr	Austrian
batlns	battalions
Bav^{n}	Bavarian
B.B.C.	British Broadcasting Corporation
bec	because
betw	between
bn	been
BN	Basil Newton
Bols	Bolshevik
Brit	British
B-W	Barrington-Ward
Cab	Cabinet
Capt	Captain
c^{d}	could
$Chamb^{ln}$	Chamberlain
Chancllr	Chancellor
circs	circumstancs
cldn't	couldn't
Cmdr	Commander
cmnqué	communiqué
commctd	communicated
commssn	commission
Commssn	Commission
Commtee	Committee
communctd	communicated
communué	communiqué
comnctn	communication
Com^{sts}	Communists
com^{tee}	committee
conf	conference
$cont^{d}$	continued
corrspdnce	correspondence
corrspdts	correspondents
corrspt	correspondent
C^{t}	Count
Czchslkia	Czechoslovakia
Czecho	Czechoslovak
d'Aff	d'Affaires

Delegatn	Delegation
Dep^t	Department
Depts	Departments
diff	difference
diff^t	different
diff^y	difficulty
dipl	diplomatic
dip^y	diplomacy
Disammt	Disarmament
disapptg	disappointing
disarmam^t	disarmament
Disarmnt	Disarmament
disarm^t	disarmament
discussn	discussion
Dismmt	Disarmament
Dis^t	Disarmament
D.M.	*Daily Mail*
D.O.T.	Department of Trade
doz	dozen
D.T.	*Daily Telegraph*
econ	economic
Emb	Embassy
Emp	Emperor
Eng	England
esp	especially
Eur	Europe or European
Europ^n	European
even^g	evening
fdshp	friendship
Feb^y	February
Fhrr	*Freiherr*
Fld	Field
F.O.	Foreign Office
For	Foreign
Fr	French
gd	good
GD	Geoffrey Dawson
Gen	General
Ger	German or Germany
Ger^y	Germany
Gov^t	Government
G^t B^n	Great Britain
H.	House
hdqtrs	headquarters

H.M.	His Majesty
H.o C.	House of Commons
Hung^n	Hungarian
imm	immediately
incl	including
internatnl	international
It	Italy
It^n	Italian
Jan^y	January
Jap	Japan
Japs	Japanese
J^y	July
lav	lavatory
L^d	Lord
Libs	Liberals
LlG	Lloyd George
LlGeorge	Lloyd George
L.ofN.	League of Nations
L^y	Lady
MacD	Ramsay MacDonald
mil	military
mil^{ty}	military
Min	Minister
min	minutes
modificatns	modifications
morn^g	morning
M.P.	Member of Parliament
Nat	National
N.C.	*News-Chronicle*
nec	necessary
necessy	necessary
negotiat^{ns}	negotiations
negot^n	negotiation
negot^{tns}	negotiations
Nev Ch	Neville Chamberlain
Norwgn	Norwegian
opp	opposite
oppos^{tn}	opposition
Parl^t	Parliament
parl^y	paliamentary
P^{ce}	Prince
p^{css}	Princess
PHS	Printing House Square
Pk	Park

pol	political
pols	politics
pop	population
pos	position
poss.	possible
pos^{tn}	position
P.M.	Prime Minister
Pres	President
prof	professional
Prof	Professor
pte	private
pts	points
pub	public
pub^{d}	published
questn	question
RB-W	Robin Barrington-Ward
R.C.	Roman Catholic
re-arm^{t}	re-armament
ref^{d}	received
ref	reference
Reg^{t}	Regiment
rel	religious
repr	representative
RIIA	Royal Institute of International Affairs
Rmanian	Rumanian
Robt	Robert
Rom	Roman
Rum^{n}	Rumanian
S	Sylvia
Sat^{y}	Saturday
SDK	Sylvia Kennedy
Sec	Secretary
sec^{ies}	secretaries
sec^{y}	secretary
Sgr	Signor
sh^{d}	should
shdn't	shouldn't
shld	should
sitn	situation
situatn	situation
Soc	Socialist
Str	Street
Swed	Swedish
tel	telephone

telegraph^d	telegraphed
T.T.	*The Times*
T.U.C.	Trades Union Congress
Univ	University
v.	very
w^d	would
Wed^y	Wednesday
wh	which
wks	weeks
wl	will
wld	would
wldn't	wouldn't
yest^{day}	yesterday
yestrdy	yesterday
y^r	your
yrs	years

Abbreviations used in the biographical notes

actg	acting
AdC	aide-de-camp
Adm.	admiral
Amb.	Ambassador
Asst	assistant
b.	born
BBC	British Broadcasting Corporation
Bd	Board
Bt	Baronet
Chanc.	Chancellor
Chm.	Chairman
Col.	Colonel
C-in-C	Commander-in-Chief
Cmdr	Commander
Con.	Conservative
Conf.	Conference
Corrspdt	correspondent
cr.	created
d.	died
DBE	Dame of the British Empire
Dept	department
dip./Dip.	diplomatic/Diplomatic
Dir.	Director
Div.	Division
Ed.	Editor

Educ.	Education
FO	Foreign Office
for./For.	foreign/Foreign
Gen.	General
for.	foreign
Gov.	Governor
govt/Govt	government/Government
Indep.	Independent
Info.	Information
kt.	knighted
Lab.	Labour
Lib.	Liberal
Ld	Lord
Ldr	Leader
Lieut	Lieutenant
LoN	League of Nations
m.	married
Maj.	Major
mb.	member
MdAE	*Ministère des Affaires Etrangères*
Mil.	Military
Min.	Minister
MP	Member of Parliament
Nat.	National
NSDAP	*National Socialist Democratische Arbeiter-Partei*
PM	Prime Minister
PPS	Parliamentary Private Secretary
Pres.	President .
Prof.	Professor
PUS	Permanent Under-Secretary of State
Pvt.	Private
Rep.	Representative
retd	retired
SA	*Stürmabteilung*
SS	*Schützsstaffel*
Sec.	Secretary
StaatSek	*Staatsekretär*
suc.	succeeded as
U.	University
UN	United Nations
US	United States
U-Sec.	Under-Secretary

INTRODUCTION

Aubrey Leo Kennedy was born in 1885, the son of John Kennedy of H.M. Diplomatic Service. Educated at Harrow and Magdalen College, Oxford, the young Kennedy – who spent his summer vacations at the legations in eastern Europe where his father was posted – dreamed of making a career for himself in diplomacy. However, when he failed to gain entry into the Diplomatic Service upon graduation he embarked on a related career in journalism. In 1910 he joined *The Times*, was sent to Paris as assistant correspondent and, in 1912, to Serbia, then Romania and Albania to cover the wars in the Balkans. His career was interrupted by the war, where he served in Flanders and Italy with the King's Own Yorkshire Light Infantry, the Intelligence Corps and the Scots Guards; he was mentioned in despatches, received the Military Cross and the *Croce di Guerra*. Captain Kennedy was demobilized in 1919 when he rejoined *The Times*.

Kennedy began keeping his journal in October 1919 when, on behalf of *The Times*, he travelled through Czechoslovakia, Austria, Hungary, Romania, Bulgaria, Turkey, Yugoslavia and Greece. Over the course of the next four months he gathered information from which he prepared a report for the newspaper on the future distribution of correspondents in eastern Europe while at the same time submitting – as a 'special correspondent' – articles on the political situation there (few of which were actually published). When he boarded ship in Athens in February 1920 he noted that he was 'heartily sorry to be leaving the last post that I'm visiting for *The Times* on this tour. It has been amazingly interesting. I had no idea at all when I started what a number of really interesting people I was going to talk politics with, what a lot of charming acquaintances I was going to make, in fact what a wholly delightful experience I was in for.' The requirement of eventually producing a report and the usefulness of having a record of his travels, discussions and reflections to refer to seems to have been his motivation in beginning the journal although, unlike many diarists, he never stated explicitly his reasons for undertaking it. The sense of being an eye-witness to fundamental changes in the political structure of eastern Europe and of occupying a privileged position in which he was able to discuss present problems and future possibilities with people such as Masaryk and Beneš, British diplomats and soldiers certainly must have encouraged him to believe that he was 'watching history' being made and that keeping a record of it might one day lead to his writing it.

The habit that began in October 1919 was revived in May 1920

when he was sent by *The Times* to report on the Russo–Polish war and
lasted until he retired from journalism in March 1946. The results may
now be consulted in the twenty-five bound volumes that were given by
his daughter, Elizabeth Le Mesurier, to Churchill College, Cambridge
in 1985.

The Kennedy journals provide a valuable source for students of
journalism, politics and diplomacy in Britain between the wars. They
are not 'personal' diaries in the sense that they do not consist of
intimate reflections or descriptions of his private life – he kept his
feelings about his family and his friends to himself; in fact he sometimes
dictated his comments to his wife, who would then enter them into the
journal on his behalf. Anyone seeking an understanding of his relationship with Sylvia (née Meysey-Thompson) after their marriage in
1921 will not find it in these journals; and their daughters are mentioned
only occasionally in passing. This is a professional and political journal.
Although there are occasional comments concerning insomnia and 'bad
nerves' there are few details concerning these bouts and none in which
Kennedy reflects upon the causes. Therefore, although it seems likely
that he suffered between the wars the consequences of having fought
in the first, this is really guesswork. And while there are occasional
hints of personal ambition – to be a politician, to write an influential
book, to be an ambassador or even foreign secretary – these are far
outweighed by his accounts of conversations with politicians, diplomats
and other journalists.

What Kennedy did reflect on in his journal was the role of *The Times*
in shaping, representing and responding to public opinion. Almost from
the day that he began keeping it he was concerned with how opinion
could be 'managed' by those who were in a position to do so. Reporting
from Warsaw during the Russo-Polish war in the summer of 1920, he
proudly noted that his despatches had made their way to the main
page almost every day for two months. But he was disturbed by the
way in which these were being manipulated by the editors in London,
who were 'undoubtedly presenting my news in such a way as to be
more favourable to Poland than I write it – without actually altering
anything they can do this by leaving out paragraphs, juxtaposing
sentences that were not next each other, putting headlines that don't
really characterize the substance etc.'[1] He put much of this down to
the influence of Northcliffe who he believed was using the newspaper
for the exercise of his own prejudices: against Lloyd George, against
the Germans, against the Bolsheviks. Although Kennedy could hardly
be said to admire any of these, the imprint of Northcliffe's personality
was such as to bring *The Times* into disrepute and thus to deprive it of

[1] Journal, volume 2, 25 August 1920.

its position of influence. He was equally concerned that the government (and its officials) did not appreciate the need to keep the public informed, and to rely upon trustworthy emissaries for this task. When, in 1919, the head of the eastern department at the foreign office refused to provide him with any useful information and complained that he really was not allowed to talk to the press at all, Kennedy noted that this was 'a somewhat antiquated theory' and that they ought to realize 'that a (decent) journalist stands for the British Public – is the go-between between officials & the public.' No less troublesome were those at *The Times* who thought it outrageous that he would consider inviting a foreign office official to give him a lead as to the tenor of an article: 'I don't see why it should be. *The Times* & the Government might occasionally collaborate in the national interest, without forfeiting the right to criticize & condemn each other.'[2]

The selections from the Kennedy journals offered in this volume have been chosen primarily with the aim of elucidating the subtle, complicated and elusive relationship between the government, the foreign office and *The Times* during the period in which the nature and role of 'public opinion' was most controversial: during the heyday of 'appeasement' from the accession to power of Hitler in 1932 to the outbreak of war in 1939. But the first ten volumes of the journal, which cover the period from his 'eastern tour' to 1932 and cannot be included here because of the limitations of space, do contain some interesting materials bearing upon these themes. In Paris to attend the reparations conference in 1921 he worried that an old-fashioned, pre-war reserve on the part of British government officials was preventing them from being more forthright in their dealings with responsible journalists. Thus, when he called in at the Ritz to see Harold Nicolson for some information concerning the Treaty of Sèvres:

He invited me into the next room, where, evidently to his surprise, sat Vansittart. They would not give me a word of information! I did not ask for anything the slightest delicate or confidential, but only as to the accuracy of several things pubd in the French Press this morning (date of the London meeting etc.). Vansittart explained that they had been given the most precise instructions that no information whatever was to be given to the Press by anybody except Ld Riddell. That being so I suppose they had no choice. But it makes the task difficult of anyone who is trying to get the British point of view! Steed goes round to all his French pals & fills *The Times* with a foreign point of view.[3]

[2] Journal, volume 1, 20 October 1919.
[3] Journal, volume 3, 26 January 1921.

Kennedy's belief that there was a pro-French cabal operating against the best interests of British policy would become a persistent complaint throughout the journals. And the impression that the French – then the Italians and eventually the Germans – were cleverer in using opinion as an instrument of national policy dismayed him. 'British public opinion is the greatest force in the world'[4] – but in order to utilize it properly the government would have to change its deeply-entrenched distrust of journalists and journalism.

Kennedy also rendered vivid descriptions of many of those he met. He first encountered Lloyd George at a meeting of journalists at the Crillon Hotel in Paris:[5]

He is not sincere. Not real. He answered anything. He has widely distended nostrils, a curiously smooth skin – a most authoritative impatient air, yet controlled so as to make his manner pleasant. One felt that he had no feeling about anything – no enthusiasm, no conviction, no reverence. One was sure that he wldn't remember a single one of his answers; & given the same questions another night might return quite different answers.

That impression of levity, cynicism, cleverness at the moment - quickness to parry an answer was the greatest – the second thing that struck me was how he answered what he was expected to answer – he took his cue from the audience. [...]

There was the Prime Minister of the greatest country in the world being put questions to, sometimes childish, sometimes of the greatest moment [...] & yet there was not a word of weight in all he said, though he seemed serious sometimes. But plenty of ideas. [...]

There was much of the faux bonhomme in his manner. And a little theatricality. He would throw back his head & move his mouth about after an answer which had made a hit. He would repeat two or three times his last phrase. He waved his cigar-holding hand deprecatingly.

He had plenty of ideas, but didn't mean a word of what he said. Get rid of the little brute is my impression v. strongly, after seeing him at close quarters. He is not worthy of England.

In spite of concluding that Lloyd George was 'a superficial charlatan' he nevertheless fought against the attempts of the editor, Wickham Steed, to attack him in such a way that it would work against the national interest: 'it is more becoming for *The Times*, while giving every consideration to French ideas, to support the British view rather than

---

[4] Journal, volume 2, 7 September 1920.
[5] Journal, volume 3, 27 January 1921.

throw itself rabidly against LlGeorge.[6] Not surprisingly, Kennedy found his position increasingly awkward during the Northcliffe regime. 'Steed told Lewis that he was told to come over here by N. to write snappy anti-LlG leaders in the *Paris Daily Mail*, as he had to during the big Peace Conference! a humiliating occupation for the editor of *The Times*, but Steed doesn't seem to think so.'[7]

Nevertheless, Kennedy's own disillusionment with Lloyd George was so profound that it led him to propose to Steed the idea of writing a book entitled 'From Salisbury to Lloyd George: 50 years of foreign policy 1871–1921.' The fact that the proposed book would fit in with the prevailing prejudice at *The Times* certainly increased the likelihood that he would be given leave to do so. His aim in writing the book, he confided to his journal, was 'to bring out the contrast in the methods of the two men – principle v. improvisation, honesty of purpose v. goalless dexterity, directness v. ambiguity.'[8] The moral of the book would be 'Back to Salisbury' and he aimed to get it published before the next general election.

Kennedy's first book, *Old Diplomacy and New*, concluded with a plea to recognize the necessity of treaty revision.[9] The allies, he argued, had denied to their former enemies the rights that they had proclaimed as having won for all of mankind. In some cases they had denied the wishes of the inhabitants – for example by including the Tyrol in Italy for strategic reasons and in refusing to allow for the possible unification of Austria and Germany; in others they had established frontiers that conformed so meticulously to ethnical distribution as to become unnatural – for example in giving Greece the Thracian seaboard and thus cutting Bulgaria off from the sea, and by amputating Prussia in the east. The assumed 'perpetuity of arrangments made for Germany by her victors in the moment of her prostration' also raised the perplexing question of how the provisions of the treaties could be maintained: 'Who is going to prevent Germany from fortifying Heligoland in twenty years' time should she so desire? Who is going to prevent her maintaining or assembling armed forces, or holding military manoeuvres, within fifty kilometres of the Rhine? These provisions suppose an eternal supervision of Germany's internal affairs, a task which neither the League of Nations nor any group of nations can effectually undertake.'[10]

Nevertheless, his temporary position at *The Times* ended in February 1921, until Steed called him to come round to the office in October:

[6] Journal, volume 3, 28 January 1921.
[7] Journal, volume 3, 30 January 1921.
[8] Journal, volume 3, 2 February 1921.
[9] John Murray, 1922.
[10] p. 311.

'Thought it would be to offer me some post again on *The Times*. Not at all. It was to tell me that he was losing his! On Nov. 18 he will cease to be Editor.'[11] John Walter and Lord Astor had combined to bid for control of the newspaper following the death of Northcliffe; and Walter's first act was to give Steed his notice. Although Kennedy was grateful to Steed, he believed that Walter was right. And he was even more relieved that *The Times* had eluded the grasp of Lord Rothermere, who 'has made the *Daily Mail* more vulgar & blatant & senseless than ever, since he has possessed it – & to have had *T.T.* linked to it under a personality with all the blatancy & none of the genius of Northcliffe wld have been a real national misfortune.'[12] And Kennedy's good fortune was to be reappointed on a permanent basis when Geoffrey Dawson resumed the editorship in January 1923. Soon he was back at *The Times* working under Dawson, writing obituaries, a growing number of leading articles and interviewing politicians and diplomats in order to provide background material on foreign affairs.

He soon took on special responsibility for League of Nations matters within the newspaper and throughout the 1920s attended the meetings of the League Council in Geneva, where his belief in the moral superiority of British policy became more pronounced, particularly in contrast to her wartime partners. A conversation with an official who had been negotiating with the French on Equatorial Africa convinced him that:

They have an unfailing spirit of grasp & grab at every conceivable small advantage. They think never of the general interest, but always of their own. Where the map-boundary gave the French a right over us, to the disadvantage of the natives, they insisted on it every time. Even if it made no real difference to them they insisted on their theoretical rights. Cutting off native villages from their waterholes etc. was nothing to them – whereas we always thought about it, & were ready to sacrifice villages <u>and</u> waterholes to the French, for the benefit of the natives. Result – the French 'scored' all along the line.

Harold Nicolson was saying the same sort of thing about the Italians yesterday, when I had a good talk with him about the return of Venizelos to Greece. It is difficult to deal plainly with them. They snatch every possible advantage – gloss your every sentence, misinterpret yr concessions, & suspect yr motives. They bring the negotiations to the level of chicanery & then outdo us at it.

As one of those who had great hopes for the League of Nations he

---

[11] Journal, volume 4, 28 October 1921.
[12] Journal, volume 4, 14 December 1921.

was soon disillusioned by his own experience of Geneva, where he discovered that old-style political intrigue had a whole new set of possibilities opened up before it. Small states jockeyed for position on the Council; politicians and diplomats vied for cushy jobs in the new bureaucracy; the French offered concessions and bribes in order to forestall the attempts of the Germans to re-establish their international respectability. 'The League is much too much of a purely European affair already,' and he blamed Austen Chamberlain for falling under the spell of the French: 'he seems always to borrow his ideas from others, & in this case he has got them all from Briand. The voice was the voice of Chamberlain, but the words were the words of Briand. He used French arguments all the way through, & spoke sharply of the Germans.'[13] He was too trusting, too gullible: 'A diplomatist's armoury is incomplete if it contains nothing in the way of suspicion as a minor defensive weapon in dealing with foreigners'.[14]

Almost as bad as the milieu of petty political intrigue was the 'Geneva atmosphere' that often led people to get carried away and conceive of grandiose plans for co-operation. As often as not this led ultimately to disillusionment as the plans proved to be unworkable and the enthusiasms temporary. In fact few seemed prepared to undertake the slow and painfully difficult task of treaty revision that Kennedy was beginning to regard as being at the centre of the European problem. When discussing this with Haldane, who criticized France and said it was quite impossible permanently to keep Germany in a state of military inferiority because 'Germans were too hard-working, too progressive and too pertinacious' Kennedy noted that 'I'm inclined to agree with him.'[15] When Beneš privately admitted to him that a rectification of frontiers must come eventually, 'I was immensely relieved' and he rose greatly in Kennedy's estimation.[16] What was needed was a kind of central European Locarno, although Kennedy was quite clear that the British would not be prepared to act as guarantors there – a position from which he never departed and which would become critical in 1938 and 1939.

But when it came to finding a statesman who was big enough to tackle the work of revision, none could be found. Kennedy asked Austen Chamberlain why an early and unconditional evacuation of the Rhineland was not possible, particularly as Chamberlain obviously agreed that it was desirable. Chamberlain's reply, that the French simply would not agree, was revealing: 'He is not a man to shape

[13] Journal, volume 4, 13 March 1926.
[14] Journal, volume 4, 12 August 1926.
[15] Journal, volume 5, 7 July 1927.
[16] Journal, volume 5, 24 September 1927.

events.'[17] Within two years however the Rhineland had been evacuated and, at the 'liberation' ceremonies in July 1930 the German government announced that it would not be satisfied until further steps were taken to restore Germany to the status of full equality with other sovereign states. This included such 'oppressive treaty clauses' as the demilitarization of the Rhineland. When Kennedy discussed the British reaction with the ambassador to Germany he again found official views to be vague and short-sighted. Sir Horace Rumbold insisted that Britain could not allow the abrogation of the demilitarization clauses. If Britain were serious about such a position, Kennedy argued, they should say so firmly and at once. 'But in this case were we really prepared to veto her liberation from the demilitar[iza]t[io]n clauses? If she chose to hold manoeuvres in the Rhineland, tho' forbidden by the Treaty, what could we *do*? Nothing but war would keep Ger[many] from doing it; & the public would never sanction war for such a purpose.'[18] While France and Poland might threaten war and have the law on their side, Britain would, at the most, support them diplomatically. Best then to follow Lord Salisbury's method 'of making up one's mind at the <u>outset</u> when one is prepared to oppose to the last ditch, or not – & frame one's whole policy accordingly.'

Kennedy was becoming increasingly convinced of the need for treaty revision. Although many aspects of Versailles remained valid, those clauses that attempted to create and maintain an unjust system really ought to be expunged – both because the Germans (and other revisionist states) were demanding it and because the British would not be prepared, when challenged, to defend these arrangements by force. While the cost of fighting a modern war made it improbable that a state would undertake a war for the purposes of aggression or aggrandisement, 'what about a minority somewhere or other that is being intolerably oppressed, & feels it simply must rise against its oppressors? in a just cause, that is, with which the outside world wd sympathize.'[19] Equally questionable were those attempts to impose an artificial system on the vanquished, one that was at odds with the political realities: 'Eventually a great nation cannot be kept down by servitudes of this sort imposed on Ger[many] by the Treaty of Versailles.'[20]

Kennedy's opinion of those responsible for guiding British policy was not high. It was difficult to imagine, for example, Austen Chamberlain having the imagination or the daring to initiate fundamental change.

---

[17] Journal, volume 6, 4 June 1928.
[18] Journal, volume 9, 25 July 1930.
[19] Journal, volume 6, 6 Sept 1929. He made this point in a conversation with Venizelos, offering the German minority in the Tyrol as an example of what he meant.
[20] Journal, volume 9, 25 July 1930.

The impression that Chamberlain gave him was 'of niceness, & honesty – with a clear grip of the situation, obtained by diligence & fairness rather than by intuition or a flair for international affairs. He has not got Ld Lansdowne's European outlook, nor Ld Grey's tremendous grasp. In fact he is painstaking, honest, fair & well-meaning, & so safe – not likely, I shld say, to stand out as a great For. Sec^y, but not likely either to let us down. He has the qualities that LlG has not got, & lacks those that LlG has.'[21] Lord Robert Cecil, a very different character, had little more appeal: 'I never know whether to like him v. much or have a hearty contempt for him! He spoke v. pleasantly today, & he's always interesting. Yet there's such a curious detachment & aloofness about him. Does he ever care about anybody?' He struck Kennedy as someone who cared 'more for ideas than human nature, more for institutions than for men.'[22] By 1929 Ramsay MacDonald appeared to Kennedy as 'essentially false. False through and through.'[23]

If prime ministers, foreign secretaries and League advocates were false, unimaginative and inhuman, to whom could one look for the kind of bold rethinking that the situation seemed to call for? Long before Hitler and the Nazis came to power, Kennedy had pondered the role of public opinion. At the conclusion of *Old Diplomacy and New* he had argued that diplomacy now rested more broadly upon popular opinion, that 'the Press is, or should be, the echo of its opinions, and the regular intermediary, in supplement to Parliament and in lieu of it when it is necessary, between the Government and the people, the instrument for the interchange of official and non-official ideas.'[24] And what was the place of *The Times*? 'I often ask myself are we responsible to the Foreign Office or the public. That is, is it our first business to act as policy-maker or to tell the whole truth? I do not think a categorical answer is possible.'[25] At first, his notion of the newspaper acting as 'policy-maker' was seen in the light of the semi-official connection between it and the government, and he did not envision a role for *The Times* independent of the government. But the attitude of officials made this position increasingly difficult: 'There are really some people at the F.O. whose mentality is about 150 yrs out-of-date, going back to the time when the Press was not allowed to listen to H. of C. debates.'[26] Although they sought to manage and to manipulate the

---

[21] Journal, volume 4, 5 April 1924.
[22] Journal, volume 4, 10 December 1925.
[23] Journal, volume 8, 3 September 1929.
[24] pp. 388–9.
[25] Journal, volume 4, 20 Feb 1926.
[26] Journal, volume 5, 30 December 1927. The occasion for this complaint was that the Middle Eastern Department had objected to *The Times* publishing the news from Geneva – or giving it a headline – that Persia had lodged with the League of Nations a protest against Britain concerning Bahrein in the Persian Gulf.

press, they were contemptuous of public opinion; and Kennedy had no doubt that opinion could be more powerful and more sensible than governments and officials. Austen Chamberlain, for example, had dismissed the initiative of Frank Kellogg, the US Secretary of State, to outlaw war as an instrument of national policy, burying himself instead in 'juridical casuistries'. He had only been jolted out of this and moved to action by the force of public opinion – 'not, I regret to say, expressed in *The Times*.'[27]

The privileged position occupied by the newspaper was, in fact, a two-edged sword: it cut both ways. While politicians and officials routinely took its journalists into their confidence – on the assumption that they would act responsibly and do nothing to jeopardize the national interest – this could act as a brake upon the expression of independent opinion. Kennedy explained to a British ambassador in 1929 that, as much as they might wish to, it was not possible for them to dissociate themselves from the Foreign Office because Geoffrey Dawson and Harold Williams had put them in that position. 'Even if we honestly spoke independently the foreign country wld always believe we had done it at the instigation of the F.O.' Kennedy hoped to 'get out of this hamperingly close association'.[28]

In fact, Kennedy remained ambivalent. The privileged access that *The Times* enjoyed was not something that could easily be forsaken in exchange for the advantages of something as intangible as 'independence'. Certainly the Foreign Office had no intention of abandoning the well-established practise of using the newspaper as an instrument of policy. When Robert Vansittart acceded to the position of Permanent Under-Secretary of State at the Foreign Office Kennedy met with him in order to discuss a leading article that he was about to write on Mussolini. Recent bombastic speeches by the *Duce* were the occasion for the article, and Kennedy's first inclination was to produce something 'cheerfully frank'. Vansittart encouraged him to go farther: 'what you ought to say is, there's the head of a modern State, who prides himself on being so up-to-date, and upon my soul he's before the flood in his ideas! War, ships, mistress of the seas, prestige, when did we hear those phrases before, and where? why, in Germany before the war! out of date!'[29] As this seemed to fit in with what he already had in mind, Kennedy welcomed the suggestion – although he did find it challenging to adopt a 'light touch' when writing a leader on a serious foreign question.

This was one of the consistent patterns in Kennedy's relationship

[27] Journal, volume 6, 20 July 1928.
[28] Journal, volume 7, 30 March 1929.
[29] Journal, volume 9, 21 May 1930.

with the Foreign Office: he, or Geoffrey Dawson, would identify the subject of a leading article and then approach officials for information or suggestions. But sometimes the initiative came from the F.O. itself. Not long after this first meeting with Vansittart, Kennedy, receiving a hint that Vansittart would like to have an article in *The Times* on Franco-Italian relations, duly arranged for an appointment to discuss it. It was clear enough what Vansittart wanted – 'a prod to French and Itn dipy to make them get on with their negtns'. Why was the F.O. enlisting Kennedy's help? Because 'he considered the sitn too delicate for the Brit. Govt. (i.e. Henderson) to do anything'.[30] Although Vansittart was not very helpful when it came to suggesting how the article might actually be phrased, Kennedy 'saw what was in his mind' and produced the article as requested. And, he noted afterwards, it seemed to have been successful: 'It was at any rate much appreciated by the F.O., and a week afterwards Briand did make friendly overtures to Italy, Grandi has reciprocated, and the whole atmosphere between the two countries is much better.'[31]

When it was evident that the close working relationship between the newspaper and the government could have such beneficial results, it was difficult to break away and establish the 'independence' that Kennedy had looked forward to. In fact, the government sometimes went well beyond giving hints or throwing out suggestions – as, for example, when Kennedy received a message from Arthur Henderson, the Foreign Secretary, that, prior to a meeting with the German Ambassador, 'it would be a great help if we could have a leader, appearing this morning, pressing Germany to do something towards European rehabilitation. He was himself going to speak to Neurath in the sense that other countries had done much, at the instigation of Hoover to help Germany; could Germany not do just something in return? He thought she could.'[32] Henderson suggested that Germany might postpone the building of a pocket battleship and the idea of an *Anschluss* with Austria during the moratorium year – gestures that would re-assure France and other neighbours of Germany. Kennedy assured him that he agreed with this and would write the leader as requested if Dawson agreed. And so he did. 'I have often before of course had a F.O. lead as to the line they would like to see us take; but I don't remember ever before having had a whole subject & run of the argument suggested to me by the Sec^y of State.'[33] Even the timing and presentation were quite clearly laid down: 'I was particularly asked that

[30] Journal, volume 9, 30 June 1930.
[31] Journal, volume 9, 14 July 1930.
[32] Journal, volume 11, 9 July 1931.
[33] ibid.

the article should appear this morn^g <u>before</u> H[enderson]'s reception of von Neurath, & also not to mention, in this morning's paper, the proposed visit of von Neurath, so that our article might appear to be spontaneous.' Kennedy agreed.

When Sir John Simon succeeded Henderson as Foreign Secretary he indicated that, if anything, he wished to go even further in working with Kennedy than his predecessor had done. At their first meeting Simon began by assuring him 'that I was one of a small group of men he wanted to consult. He said he had no intention of pretending to know more about for. affairs than he did; and so he spent much of our time asking me questions, and sometimes he made notes of my answer.'[34] The issue of the moment was Manchuria, on which Kennedy was relieved to find that Simon was definitely against the use of penalties against Japan. 'I agreed with him, because justice is not all on one side; & no penalties could hope to be effective unless world-opinion were in a large majority behind their application. In this case opinion is necessarily much divided.' But Simon went further, asking Kennedy what line *he* would take, were he attending the meeting of the League Council as British Foreign Secretary. 'At this I was quite taken back. I was surprised & nonplussed. I was there as *Times* man, to get the line of action from him – the politicians are on the stage, we, *The Times*, are in the stalls (*Daily Mail* in the gallery:); & one can applaud or booh, but one has not come to act.'[35] Nevertheless, Kennedy improvised something about not abandoning the standards of international life for which the League of Nations stood, but on the other hand not committing it to do more than it had the power to do. 'We are at any rate all war weary and shall continue to be for a period of years.' Which is how he explained the fact that the country now tolerated as prime minister a man who had been a conscientious objector during the war.

Thus, by the time that these journal selections begin in January 1932, when there was a growing sense that issues of war and peace were again on the agenda of international affairs, that crossroads were being reached where choices might have to be taken between peace and justice, Kennedy believed that he understood the mood of the public. He detested pacifism 'in its extreme form', but 'the very principles which were so abominable and rightly unpopular during the War are in the totally changed circumstances of to-day both reasonable and popular.'[36] As a veteran of the war he was familiar with its horrors, and he regarded aerial bombardment – especially of civilians – as a

[34] Journal, volume 11, 12 November 1931.
[35] ibid.
[36] Kennedy to J.W. Collins, 21 February 1930. *The Times* archive.

new form of barbarism that ought to be outlawed. But he also believed that justice was something that was worth fighting for, and he worried that the League of Nations was structured and had developed in such a way as to focus on the preservation of peace to the detriment of creating an international system based on justice. He saw much that was worthwhile in war and found that it created a bond with those who had undergone similar experiences. Dining with the Yugoslav Minister, for example, he discovered that they had little to say until they realized that they had both fought in the war, then 'we talked hammer & tongs about the tremendous appeal of war – conditions, the fellowship, the contempt for unmanliness, the spirit of devotion, courage & self-sacrifice – not in this rather priggish language, but by instance & anecdote.'[37] He disliked those 'clever writers' who take a sordid view of war:

> They are mostly (like Lytton Strachey in this country) people who did not fight themselves, or who (like Stephen Graham) only went out when they were compelled to. They came in for the tail-end of it, when the first enthusiasm had languished, when there was little of the spirit of 1914–5 left, of great adventure, almost of a crusade. In fact, towards the end the worst side of war was undoubtedly of uppermost – kill the other side, no chivalry left. It was v. different at the beginning. The unprecedented feeling of fellowship & self-sacrifice had much diminished by 1918.[38]

Ultimately, it was the widespread opposition to war that convinced Kennedy that any decision to fight in the future would require the issues of justice to be starkly drawn: winning a war depended upon mobilizing the entire nation, and the nation could not be persuaded to fight for old-fashioned reasons of political advantage and territorial gain.

By 1932 Kennedy had established his position in the 'semi-official' world of opinion-making and policy-formation. He had come to have close personal relations with a succession of foreign secretaries: with Austen Chamberlain, Arthur Henderson and John Simon; he had established good working relationships with a variety of officials, ranging from Ronald Lindsay (by then ambassador in Washington) to Reginald Leeper (of the News Department) to Eric Drummond (of the League of Nations); and he could now count upon the support of his editor at *The Times*, Geoffrey Dawson. By 1932 Kennedy was forty-six years old and had acquired almost twenty years of journalistic experience. He

[37] Journal, volume 6, 20 Sept 1928.
[38] Journal, volume 5, 8 November 1927.

had found his *métier* and was ready to make a mark for himself. He now identified the revision of the Versailles system as being the root cause of most of Europe's problems, at the same time that the disrepute of that system prevented the public from supporting any efforts to uphold it.

In fact Kennedy perceived that it was the short-sightedness of the British and the French governments that was encouraging extreme militarism in Germany. In July 1931 he urged the Foreign Secretary to consider 'the advantage of dishing the Hitlerites by openly stating that the Brit. Govt was in favour of bringing modificatns to the Treaty of Versailles.' Henderson, although replying that he favoured revision, did not think it a favourable moment to say so. 'I fear force may be tried first, if he leaves it too long.'[39] Kennedy suggested an alternative, that he might bring up revision 'informally & unofficially' in *The Times*; Henderson 'smiled & nodded acquiescence'.

Perhaps dishing Hitler was not the best strategy. Kennedy began to wonder whether it might not be a better thing to confront him directly rather than continue dealing with the Brüning government, which always claimed that it could not make any political concessions on international matters because if it did so it would be turned out by the Nazis. 'If the Nazis, therefore, are the people who really count, had they not better be the people in office?' Kennedy had not yet made up his mind, but wondered whether it was really worthwhile trying to buttress Brüning up unless he could demonstrate that he was still really fit for the job and that he was equal to mastering his nationalist and communist opponents. 'Hitlerism seems in one sense to be a sort of national neurosis, and the best way of treating it may be to let it come to the surface and then treat the patient gently but firmly. I do not see that <u>fundamentally</u> their foreign policy can really differ much in practice from that of Brüning.'[40] The essential similarity between the policies of Hitler and Brüning could be located in their opposition to the treaty of Versailles. Although Kennedy believed the terms of the treaty to be fundamentally fair, the manner by which they 'were <u>imposed</u> upon the vanquished' had created a bitterness that had not dissipated. And, in addition to the need for a reconsideration of some of the frontiers as they were drawn in 1919, the issue that stood out as the major legitimate grievance was 'the one-sided disarmament clauses' that had been forced on Germany. As no power could compel Germany *not* to build tanks, submarines and aeroplanes, 'She must gain the right sooner or later. Better give it gracefully than have it wrested. She wouldn't build <u>much</u>, because she can't possibly afford it.'[41]

[39] Journal, volume 11, 13 July 1931.
[40] Kennedy to Norman Ebbutt, 8 October 1931. *The Times* archive.
[41] Journal, volume 11, 13 December 1931.

So Kennedy and *The Times* had begun, by the end of 1931, to promote the possibility of a wide-ranging reconsideration of the Treaty of Versailles that advocates and opponents alike would soon be referring to as 'appeasement'. Geoffrey Dawson had proved to be 'unexpectedly bold in support' of this initiative and Kennedy was pleased to note that there were 'many signs that informed opinion throughout the country is beginning to think that way'.[42] The Foreign Office, however, was 'none too pleased'.

Thus, at the point at which these selections from Kennedy's journal begins, preparations are being made for the forthcoming disarmament conference in Geneva under the presidency of Arthur Henderson, Hitler is on the verge of coming to power in Germany and *The Times* is committed to redressing the wrongs done at Versailles in 1919.

[42] Journal, volume 11, 27 July 1931.

THE JOURNAL

1932

LONDON *13 January* Poliakoff[43] has heard from the French here that the other day, when Simon[44] was receiving the French Ambassdr, M. De Fleuriau[45] said, in regard to the coming Disarm[t] Conference, 'if there is any talk of revising the political clauses, it is war.' To which Simon replied – 'Well, in view of the present division of forces, you oughtn't to have much difficulty.'!

This amazed & rather pleased Fleuriau. He no doubt expected solemn words of deprecation. But it sounds true to Simon's extraordinary open-mindedness & detachment. He never seems to have a prepossession of any sort.

The French like him owing to his love of legality.

I hear that the way in which the news of Brüning's[46] announcement to Rumbold[47] about non-payment of reparatns the other day leaked out through the telephone. The British Embassy <u>telephoned</u> a summary of Brüning's conversation <u>en clair</u>. Either the telephone line was tapped, or a telephonist gave it away. The news leaked both in Berlin & London, so I am inclined to think that telephonists were concerned, a German & a British. Esp: in view of the persons at each end <u>to whom</u> it leaked.

We were informed in *T.T.* Office, so telephoned to O.[ur]O[wn]. C[orrespondent in]. Berlin to enquire if it were true. Ebbutt[48] said

---

[43] Vladimir Poliakoff (1880–1956): Russian journalist; exiled to Britain 1919; with *Daily Telegraph* 1920–24, *The Times* 1924–36; also wrote under pen-name 'Augur'. See his *Europe in the Fourth Dimension* (1939).

[44] John Allsebrook Simon (1873–1954): Lib. MP Walthamstow 1906–18, Spen Valley 1922–40 (Nat. Lib. from 1931); Solicitor-Gen. 1910–13; Attorney-Gen. 1913–15; Home Sec. 1915–16; FS 1931–5; Home Sec. 1935–7; Chanc. of Exchequer 1937–40; Ld Chanc. 1940–5; kt. 1910, cr. Viscount Simon 1940. See his *Retrospect* (1952).

[45] Aimé-Joseph de Fleuriau (1870–1938): entered dip. service 1895; Counsellor in London 1913–20; Min. in Beijing 1921–4; Amb. in London 1924–33.

[46] Heinrich Brüning (1885–1970): Catholic Centre politician; *Reichstag* Deputy 1924–33; Chanc. 1930, & For. Min. 1931; ousted in favour of Franz von Papen (q.v.) 1932; exiled from 1934; Queen's College, Oxford U. 1937–9; Harvard U. 1939–52; U. of Cologne 1951–5. See his *Memoiren 1918–34* (1970).

[47] Horace George M. Rumbold (1869–1941): diplomat; dip. service from 1891; Amb. in Ankara 1920–4, in Madrid 1924–8; in Berlin 1928–33; retd 1933; Vice-Chm. Royal Commission on Palestine 1936–7; suc. 9th Bt. Rumbold 1913; kt. 1917.

[48] Norman Ebbutt (1894–1964): joined *The Times* 1914, returned 1918–37; 2nd Corrspdt, Germany 1925–7, Chief Corrspdt 1927–37; expelled for anti-Nazi reporting, suffered stroke 1937, remained paralysed thereafter.

no, so we did not use the information; & missed a scoop.

19 January   I had a long talk with Henderson[49] this morning, the first time I've seen him since his débacles in Aug. and October.[50] He is a little thinner and looks more worn, older, and quiet. Rather battered in fact, yet spoke quietly and without inveighing against his old colleagues, tho' evidently having strong feelings against both Mac-Donald[51] and Snowden.[52]

He gave me to understand that MacD. to a certain extent pushed him into opposition. Reading between the lines of what he said, as it were, I sh^d say that Henderson wobbled over National Gov^t idea, and that the well-known mutual antipathy of the two men enabled MacD just to give him a slight push which sent him over the wrong side. Henderson's responsibility, however, for giving MacD the chance. H. said that MacD was convinced that he (H.) was scheming for the premiership, which was quite untrue. I said I had no doubt it was untrue – & recalled what he had said to me in Geneva once about never having definitely tried for any of the jobs he had got – but that other people <u>were</u> talking about him (H.) as next P.M., & this had no doubt upset MacD.

H: said that after the Zinovieff letter business in 1924,[53] which MacD: <u>had</u> so badly mishandled (that is generally admitted), & the Labour Party had bn badly beaten, Snowden had asked him to come & see him, & had said to him that a lot of them w^d like him to take the

---

[49] Arthur Henderson (1863–1935): Lab. MP Barnard Castle div., Durham 1903–18, Widnes 1919–22, Newcastle 1923, Burnley 1924–31; Home Sec. 1924; FS 1929–31; Pres., World Disarmament Conf., Geneva 1932–33. See his *Labour's Way to Peace* (1935).

[50] In August 1931 Henderson, in the midst of the financial crisis, opposed MacDonald's policy of cutting unemployment benefits in order to balance the budget. His opposition was instrumental in producing a majority in the Cabinet opposed to the Prime Minister, which led him to submit his resignation to the king. Henderson, who played a key role in bringing down the government then lost his seat in the general election of October.

[51] (James) Ramsay MacDonald (1866–1937): Lab. MP Leicester 1906–18, Aberavon 1922–9; Ntl Lab. MP Seaham 1929–35, Scottish Universities, 1936–7; Lab. Party Sec. 1900–12, Chm. 1912–14, Lab. Leader 1922–31; PM & FS 1924; PM 1929–35; Ld Pres. 1935–7.

[52] Philip Snowden (1864–1937): ILP Chm. 1903–6, 1917–20; Lab. MP Blackburn, 1906–18, Colne Valley, 1922–31; Chanc. of Exchequer 1924, 1929–31; Ld Privy Seal, 1931–2; cr. Viscount Snowdon 1931. See his *An Autobiography* (1934).

[53] During the election campaign of 1924 the Foreign Office intercepted a letter which purported to be from Grigori Zinovieff, the President of the Comintern, instructing members of the British Communist Party to stir up a revolt in the armed forces and in the factories. The F.O. published this letter in *The Times* on 25 October, four days before polling day. The Labour Party, damaged by the suggestion that it was associated with such extremists, lost over forty seats and Baldwin formed a Tory government.

leadership. H: had replied 'Philip, I have spent my life in building up the unity of the Labour Party, & I'm not going to undo it now.' (He seems to have forgotten this maxim in 1931!)

He said that 'his very success (at the F.O.) had been his undoing,' implying that MacD: was jealous; & told me that on the Sunday, when Henderson had not yet resigned, H: had said 'I suppose you remember that somebody will have to be going to Geneva next Thursday,' to which MacD: had replied 'Geneva's not for you'; showing that MacD: knew already he was going to be P.M. again, & had made up his mind that Henderson w^d not be Foreign Sec^y.

I daresay that is true enough. I think Henderson is an absolutely truthful man, tho' he may not always tell one the whole truth, & may be a little bit of a self-deceiver. He said to me 'Believe me, Kennedy, one can be too conscientious for some people.'

What I went to see him about was the Disarmament Conference,[54] so above was all by the way, but v. interesting. I said at one moment 'Well, all the same M^r H:, I think it's a pity you didn't stay on with the National Gov^t & remain Foreign Sec^y – to which he did not answer direct, but gave me some of the information noted above. Altogether I got the impression that if he had stood firm on the right side nobody would or could have turned him out.

He told me that communication between himself, as Pres: of the Conference, & the Brit: delegation w^d probably be made through Sir John Simon, from whom he had had two nice letters.

He is not going to be in the same hotel as the Brit: delegation, but in the Paix (where I almost always go, & have already got my room for Feb:).

20 January   At the Rmanian reception at the Ritz last night Selby[55] told us that Henderson's defeat at Burnley in the General Election by Admiral (?Campbell)[56] [sic] was rendered particularly bitter by the fact that the Admiral was a great drinker, in fact often more or less tight when he was making a speech – & completely beat total-abstainer Henderson H. became a teetotaller (Selby told us) because as a boy it had been his job to carry beer to the men in the works, & it had made a tremendously unfavourable impression on him.

[54] The conference was to begin in Geneva on 2 February.
[55] Walford Harmood M. Selby (1881–1965): entered dip. service 1904; pvt. Sec. to FS 1924–32; Min. in Vienna 1933–7; Amb. in Lisbon 1937–40; kt. 1930. See his *Diplomatic Twilight 1930–40* (1953).
[56] Gordon Campbell (1886–1953): naval ADC to King George V 1928; Rear-Adm. 1928; retd 1928; Vice-Adm. (retd) 1932; Nat. Govt MP Burnley 1931–5. See his *Number Thirteen: being the autobiography of Rear-Admiral G. Campbell* (1932).

Later in the evening I was just getting the chance of a few words with Sir John Simon, when the Turkish Ambassdr brought up his new Counsellor to introduce him to Sir J., who had of course to start talking to him, which he did in passable French and v. pleasantly.

Simon had just said 'I saw a report today on your views of Germany's paying reparations today' – it is quite new to me that my conversatns at the F.O. are reported to the For: Sec^y. I expect that that was Sargent,[57] who had listened particularly attentively to me 2 days ago & seemed to be impressed with some of my ideas. [...]

31 January On Friday had an interesting evening in PHS. I had seen Ld Lytton[58] in the afternoon, & he had told me about his plans for the Manchurian Commssn which is about to set out for the Far East.[59] His plan was to travel via Tokyo – spending about a month there – then Nanking – spending another month there – & finally to Manchuria. They had been given 9 <u>months</u> altogether by the League. I said I thought it seemed a long time, esp: as the Commssn is already rather late in starting. That was about 4 pm. Then at night, as I was writing on Shanghai, were [sic] a violent outbreak had occurred between Japs & Chinese, Ld L. rang me up in the office, about 10.30 pm, to tell me that he had bn in comnctn with Geneva, & had practically arranged with Sir Eric Drummond[60] that he & his Commssn sh^d give up their proposed leisurely itinerary, & travel across Siberia as straight to Shanghai as they could – 'at whatever discomfort to one's self' as Ld L. rather ruefully remarked. Certainly rather different from the Trans-Atlantic & then Trans-Pacific trip they had planned for themselves, but much better, I thought. So I brought the idea into the leader which I was writing that evening amid great confusion of news.[61]

In connexion with this same Far Eastern affair Ronald[62] did rather

[57] (Harold) Orme G. Sargent (1884–1962): entered dip. service 1906; Counsellor FO 1926; head, Central Dept 1928–33; Asst U-Sec. 1933–9; Deputy U-Sec. 1939–46; PUS 1946–9; kt. 1937.
[58] Victor Alexander G. Lytton (1876–1947): Civil Ld of Admiralty 1919–20; U-Sec. IO 1920–22; Gov. of Bengal 1922–7, Viceroy & actg Gov.-Gen. India 1925; Chm. Palestine Potash Ltd, Central London Electricity Ltd, London Power Co.; head LoN mission to Manchuria 1932; suc. 2nd Earl Lytton 1891, kt. 1933.
[59] The commission, chaired by Lord Lytton, had been established by the Council of the League of Nations in December 1931 in response to an appeal by China that Japan had violated its sovereignty following the Mukden incident in September.
[60] (James) Eric Drummond (1876–1951): entered FO 1900; Sec-Gen. LoN 1919–33; Amb. in Rome 1933–9; Chief Adviser on For. Publicity, Ministry of Info. 1939–40; kt. 1916; suc. 16th Earl of Perth 1937.
[61] 'Shanghai,' 30 January 1932.
[62] Ronald Charles Lindsay (1877–1945): entered dip. service 1898; Amb. in Berlin 1926–8; PUS FO 1928–30; Amb. in Washington 1930–9; kt. 1925.

a good bit of work for the Far East in Washington. Stimson[63] was proposing that USA & G^t B^n sh^d both make representatns in Tokyo, & was esp: keen on close collaboratn with <u>us</u>, as distinct from any other European nation. The proposal was telegraphed home by RCL; but the F.O. shilly-shallied & was v. doubtful, & finally on Thurs: (last) sent out wishy-washy instructns, saying that both Govts must first be quite sure they meant the same thing etc:

RCL was v. disappointed, & cabled back to F.O. to say so, & added that he w^d not deliver the message that day, but w^d do so on Friday morning <u>unless in the meantime he had rec^d fresh</u> <u>instructns</u>. The hint was taken, & on Friday morning he was instructed to agree to the Am: proposal for cooperatn.

Of course we ought to work with them in the Far East whenever possible, as it is (at present) in this case. But the F.O. was piqued because the State Dept, as is its wont, had communctd the sense of their proposals to the Press in Washington at the same time as they had sent it to London. They had also added a hint that if we co-operated with them in this, it might make it easier to arrange a remission of some of our debt!

GENEVA *8 February*   On arrival here last night (9.15) for the Disarm^t Conference I went straight round to the Beau Rivage (tho' I am staying at the Paix) so as to get into touch with the British Delegatn – as I wanted to write a stiff message against the new French project, but did not want to if doing so would be in contradiction with Brit. policy or otherwise inconvenient.

I met Sir J. Simon in the hall, & a few words with him showed me that he was against the project, though he doesn't feel inclined to say so. (All these people play for position here, & however much they want to oppose a thing, they don't oppose it openly). I also went on to Temperley[64] (to whom I had sent a message from Paris asking him to meet me if he could in the hotel) & he said he was quite sure the Brit. Gov^t would never accept this French scheme – which w^d transform the League on <u>paper</u> into a super-State, & buttress up the hegemony of France. Really a fantastic notion [...] extreme logic sometimes carries the French into the realm of fantasy. The scheme is absolutely logical, but gets right away from realities. Fancy the Council in charge of an

[63] Henry Lewis Stimson (1867–1950): US politician; Sec. of War 1911–13; Gov-Gen. of Philippines 1927–9; Sec. of State 1929–33; Sec. of War 1941–5. See his *On Active Service in Peace & War* (1948).

[64] Arthur Cecil Temperley (1877–1940): Mil. Attaché at the Hague 1920–4; Military Rep. at LoN 1925–35; Deputy Dir. Mil. Operations & Intelligence, WO 1928–33; head, WO section British delegation to World Disarmament Conf., Geneva 1932–5; retd 1935; mil. Corrspdt *Daily Telegraph* 1935–9. See his *The Whispering Gallery of Europe* (1938).

army! It w$^{\underline{d}}$ get beaten in every battle. Some day we may be able to repose such trust in the impartiality & wisdom of the League that we can entrust it with armed force. At present, no; & discussn of the French scheme w$^{\underline{d}}$ do a lot of harm – bring out all sorts of antagonisms.

Simon had forgotten my name! Called me Russell to his wife. He remembered exactly who I was – *Times* etc – & took me aside & talked about this French scheme – his chief criticism was that it talked a lot about arming the League & nothing about disarmament. He suggested I sh$^{\underline{d}}$ come up to his room with him & see what he was going to say in his speech next day (today), but I c$^{\underline{d}}$ see he didn't mean it, so declined. A bit insincere.

9 February   On Sun: night Simon said a v. nice thing to L^{y} Simon – '*The Times* is the only paper in the world to whom you can speak yr mind openly & know that, while it may colour their messages or views, none of it will be used so as to do any harm.' This was after he had forgotten my name!

To-day I have had long talks with 2 prominent Nat: Socialists of Germany – my old friend Bell[65] & Gen: von Epp,[66] who used to command the Bavarian Guards, & later I believe a Bav$^{\underline{n}}$ Alpine Division. A dapper, military-looking & mil: minded man, whom one cldn't help liking. His main view was v. interesting – Germans are essentially military-minded, & to have abolished conscription is liking taking [sic] away a man's backbone. Conscription was educative, & filled the same sort of place as our public school system, to us. The country has gone to pieces without it. If they, the Nazis, get into power, they will establish a system of labour bat[allio]ns to restore the idea of hard work, obedience & discipline. Bell talked of this as a militia, to be used for defensive purposes. But that did not suit the General, who considered nothing of the sort w$^{\underline{d}}$ be useful from the mil: point of view. He considered one year's service quite insufficient to produce good soldiers. [...]

Bell let out a sentence which showed that he thought Germany w$^{\underline{d}}$ be having a war of revenge in about 20 years' time. But he admits the Socialists in Germany are what he calls '*Französisch gesinnt*' – 'French-minded', i.e. ready for an understanding with France. For him the idea is absolutely abhorrent!

[65] George Bell: Nazi activist; hired by Ernst Röhm in 1932 to procure money for *SA* and divert funds to it from *NSDAP*; established *SA* newspaper, *Der SA-Mann*.
[66] Franz Xaver Ritter von Epp (1868–1947): army officer & Nazi politician; established *Freikorps* 1919; Cmdr, *SA* 1926; *Reichstag* Deputy 1928–33; Gen. 1935; Gov. of Bavaria 1933–45; head, Colonial Policy Office of Reich Leadership 1934–41; Min. of Colonies 1941–5; captured & died during internment 1945. See his *The Question of Colonies* (1937).

He says the Nazis do not object to Hindenburg;[67] but they do object to the people round him – & as H: gets older these people matter more & more. What is v. interesting is that these Hitlerites here are in touch with Brüning – also with Röhm,[68] their military organizer, in Berlin, by telephone. These Germans all work together.

I have bn greatly impressed by the personality of Brüning today. He made a speech at the Disarm.ᵗ Conf: this morning; & this afternoon he recᵈ the international Press. He got far the biggest cheer of the Conf: so far when he had finished speaking, & it was delivered in German, & without any particular rhetoric. But his strong & earnest voice made a great appeal, & his personality seemed to pervade the whole hall in a way that Briand's[69] used to in the old *Salle de la Réformation*. And this afternoon at the journalists' gathering the man made a speech that began v. quietly, seemed eloquent because it was so sincere, & ended up with quite a short but almost impassioned appeal to us all to urge that 'big decisions' shᵈ be taken now before it was too late. He was referring chiefly to the economic situatn of Europe. He is the one man since Briand who seems to be a statesman & have something big about him. (This applies to Venizelos[70] too, but he is now v. old & one seldom sees him).

10 February Had a long talk with Sir Eric D.[rummond] today. He was v. depressed by the Far Eastern affair. He must know how much ground the League has lost over it, & feels it keenly. He looked definitely older poor man. One feels sorry for him, esp: as it comes just at the end of his time. He told me that he was definitely leaving next year. '13 years is enough, I think.' I said 'You're still a member of the English Dipl: Service, aren't you' & he said quite brightening up, 'Yes, I am, & it's a nice thing to be' or words just like that – he must be a bit disillusioned about internationalism & feel really rather pleased at the idea of entering the service of England again.

I had rather an argument with him about keeping in with France.

[67] Paul von Benckendorff und Hindenburg (1847–1934): Gen., rtd 1911; Chief of the Gen. Staff 1916–8; Pres. of the Reich 1925–34.

[68] Ernst Röhm (1887–1934): participated in Beer Hall *Putsch* 1922; head of SA 1930; Min. without Portfolio 1933–4; Min. of Bavarian state govt 1933–4; murdered June 1934. See his *Die geschichte eines Hochverräters* (1933).

[69] Aristide Briand (1862–1932): French politican; eleven times PM; For. Min. 1925, 1926–32; PM 1929; Nobel Peace Prize 1926. See his *Discours et Écrits de politique étrangère* (1965).

[70] Eleutherios Venizelos (1864–1936): Greek politician; PM 1910–15, 1917–20, 1924, 1928–32, 1933; led revolt against Turks in Crete 1935, fled to Paris, where he died.

He is in favour of it still. I say that policy has bn pursued long enough. It produced results so long as Briand was there; now the time has come for us to be *detached* – to stand on our own, & fairly soon to take the lead ourselves.

I think we each persuaded the other a little. I don't want to be anti-French anyway. But the worst of it is, that as soon as one is at all cool, they put one down as an enemy. Gen: Réquin[71] was absurdly cold to me in the *Hotel des Bergues* when I met him in the corridor 2 days ago. We used to be, I thought, good friends. But he stood stiffly upright, when I greeted him, & as I held out my hand, took it stiffly in his left!

Massigli,[72] on the other hand, was perfectly sensible when I met him today, & we had a quite intelligent talk about the possibility of alleviating conditions for Germany.

Drummond, by the way, seems quite to favour my idea of letting Germany build say a dozen tanks, a dozen submarines, a doz mil: aeroplanes. It w^d give them equality of status, & at the same time preserve the principle of limitation.

11 February   Saw Grandi[73] this morning. He was rather tired & had not quite all his usual verve. I tackled him about the proposal in his speech yesterday to 'abolish capital ships.' I said that in England it w^d be thought to take away rather from the practical suggestiveness of his speech, as there c^d be no question at present of the abolition of capital ships. We were have [sic] great difficulties with U.S.A. even to get a reductn of the maximum tonnage.

He answered that he had had to put that in, as a counterpoise to the abolition of submarines, which he proposed, & which Sir J. Simon had proposed too. Submarines were just as invaluable to small countries as capital ships to us. Furthermore, France had proposed transferring capital ships, bombing aeroplanes, heavy artillery etc to the League; so Italy had said no, abolish them altogether.

Moreover these were general ideas & general aims, & he did not

---

[71] Edouard Réquin (1879–1954): French army officer; *Chef de cabinet* to Min. of War 1930–2; Mil. Rep. to LoN 1930; Cmdr 11th Infantry Div. 1932–5, 20th Mil. Region 1936–40; mb. Supreme War Council 1938; Dir. College of National Defence 1939. rtd 1941. See his *D'une guerre à l'autre 1919–39* (1949).

[72] René Massigli (1888–1988): French diplomat; head, LoN Section, *Ministère des Affaires Etrangères* 1928–33, Asst Dir. Political Section 1933–7, Dir. 1937–8; Amb. in Ankara 1939–40; escaped from France 1943; Amb. in London 1944–55; Sec-Gen. *Ministère des Affaires Etrangères* 1955–6.

[73] Dino Grandi (1895–1988): Fascist politician & diplomat; Chief, Fascist Gen. Staff 1921; Deputy *Parlemento* 1921–32; U-Sec. *Ministero degli Affari Esteri*; For. Min. 1929–32; Amb. in London 1932–9; Min. of Justice & Chm. Fascist Grand Council, 1939–43. See his *Il mio paese: ricordi autobiografici* (1985).

suppose for a moment they w$^{\underline{d}}$ be carried through just now.

He said too that he had had difficulties at home, & that, unless he had proposed the abolitn of capital ships, he w$^{\underline{d}}$ not have bn allowed to propose the abolition of submarines & bombing aeroplanes. Their air fleet was the pride of Italy, & he had had a tussle in the Cabinet with Sgr Balbo[74] over that – & Mussolini[75] had come down on his (Grandi's) side.

Seeing all this, I still think Grandi w$^{\underline{d}}$ have made a better effect if he had suggested all these abolitions definitely as distant aims, rather than as immediate subjects for this Conference.

He spoke v. critically of France, & in particular of Tardieu.[76]

I had quite an argument about tanks with Sgr G. Why sh$^{\underline{d}}$ they be abolished? I said that at last the wretched infantryman had found something protective, & now it was proposed to take it away from him. W$^{\underline{d}}$ barbed wire & machine-guns also be prohibited, or not? Grandi's answer was that tanks were what gave the offensive its force, & the whole purpose was to cripple the offensive.

I saw M$^{\underline{r}}$ Henderson (here in this hotel) this afternoon, & had it out with him about tanks. He seemed rather to agree with me; anyhow he said he was not so keen about abolishing tanks as about abolishing submarines. But in regard to abolishing both submarines & warships, he regards a provisional agreement about both to be possible. He does not suggest they can be abolished at once; but a general agreement about their eventual abolition might be reached; & then at the next Conf: a more definite step taken.

He thinks the next Conf: sh$^{\underline{d}}$ be held as soon after the next Naval Conf: as poss. That (the Naval Conf:) is due in 1935.

He seems to have this Conf: well in hand, & is hopeful. He is having all the points of agreement, from the various speeches, classified. He himself suggested that Baker[77] sh$^{\underline{d}}$ write to me from time to time, which

[74] Italo Balbo (1896–1940): Fascist politician; a leader of fascist 'March on Rome' 1921; founder & Ed. *Corriere Padano*; Gen. of Air Force 1928; Min. of Aviation 1929–33; Gov. of Libya 1933–40; shot down by Italian soldiers in Libya 1940. See his *My Air Armada* (1934).

[75] Benito Mussolini (1883–1945): founder & ldr of Italian Fasist Party; Pres. Council of Ministers 1922–6; PM 1926–43; For. Min. 1924–9, 1932–6; head of German puppet regime in N. Italy 1943–5; executed 1945.

[76] André Pierre G.A. Tardieu (1876–1945): French politician; Deputy 1914–36; Plenipotentiary, Paris Peace Conf. 1919–20; Min. of Public Works 1926–8, of Interior 1928–30; PM 1929–30; Min. of Agric. 1931–2, of War 1932; PM & For. Min. 1932; Min. without Portfolio 1934. See his *L'Année de Munich* (1939).

[77] Philip John Noel-Baker (1889–1982): mb. British delegation, Paris Peace Conf. 1919; secretariat, LoN 1919–22; Sir Ernest Cassel Prof. of Intl Relations, U. of London 1924–9; Lab. MP Coventry 1929–31, Derby 1936–70; PPS to FS 1929–31; Sec. of State for Air 1946–7, for Commonwealth Relations 1947–50. See his *The First World Disarmament Conference 1932–33 and Why it Failed* (1979).

w^{d} keep him & me in touch (Noel-Baker is acting as his Sec^{y} here).

PARIS *14 Feb:*   I travelled here from Paris [sic – Geneva] in the same train as Sir J. Simon, & [he] was remarkably friendly. He heard from Allen Leeper[78] that I was in the same coach, so came along to my compartment & had a long talk about Reparatns & Disarmmt, the two chief topics at Geneva. Again he struck me as having a mind of a special calibre, which throws jets of pellucid thought all over the subject, but gives no definite conclusion. This may of course be on purpose. And as before, he was always asking me my opinions. In regard to the French super-national army project, he said 'If I liked, I c^{d} simply annihilate it by criticism' – & he proceeded to do so, merely taking up 2 or 3 points, but showing conclusively how impossible the scheme is. Yet he didn't say 'We can't have it,' or commit himself against it. All the train of his thought, however, was hostile to it. He pointed out many absurdities; & although the L.o N. Union apparently bombards him with requests to consider it favourably, he believes – & I am sure rightly – that public opinion on the whole would not accept it. I certainly have done my best to give him this impression.

(Cont^{d} in London *15 Feb:*)

The problem is to eliminate the French project without making the French Delegate simply dig its toes in about any reductn of armamnts.

In regard to Reparatns Simon gave me in some detail the history of the negot^{ns} in Geneva, esp: the part he himself had played – the usual useful British mediatorial part. He said 'I hope you'll be able to make a song about it in *T.T,* I believe the agreement really is important.' He is singularly candid; yet he is roundabout & inconclusive. He seems to have held out firmly for a multilateral Agreement (as opposed to a bilateral Franco-British Agreement), & to have refused to countenance the inclusion of War debts in the coming discussns in Lausanne. Both excellent points (& in entire accord with our numerous exhortations in *T.T!*)

He confided to me that the French intend to invite the Conference to check the official armaments returns of all countries since 1924! This wl of course make a long delay before getting to business, which is what the French want.

He invited me to dine with him & Lady Simon, & Allen Leeper, at

[78] Alexander W. Allen Leeper (1887–1935): delegate to Paris Peace Conf. 1919–20, to Lausanne Peace Conf. 1922–3; asst pvt Sec. to FS 1920–4; 1st Sec. in Vienna 1924–8; Counsellor 1933.

their table in the Restaurant-car. It was a pleasant & interesting affair. Simon goes in for saying clever things, often amusing too – e.g. 'Nobody has ever succeeded in conquering Russia, not even Napoleon or Winston Churchill' – & he told us how on more than one occasion ideas have come to him in his sleep which have given him the clue in some of his big cases in the Law-Courts. The ideas come with so much urgency that they wake him up. In one instance he had bn so struck by it that he woke up L^y S. & told her; & it had in fact proved to be correct. It was, he said, an inference, therefore the result of 'subconscious ratiocination,' as he called [it].

In the other instance he gave us there seemed to be less inference about it & more sheer intuition. However in neither case was it a dream in the ordinary sense of the word, but the continued working of his mind during sleep. He said it happened to him when he was v. tired & overworked.

L^y Simon seems to be Irish, & is v. downright & different in manner from him. He is v. deferential to her.

At the end of dinner, almost as he was getting up to go, Simon said to me – 'There are still a lot of things I w^d like to ask y^r opinion about. What do you think the Council ought to do? [i.e. in this Shanghai business]. I said 'As little as possible.' So he said 'Then I think you must congratulate us on having bn v. successful! We both laughed, & then I went on to develop my theme a little, & said that it w^d be really disastrous for the Council if it went on meeting & was flouted every time by the Japanese. And now there was a question of the Assembly being called. It really would (I argued) extinguish the authority of the League altogether, in internatnl politics, if the Assembly were convoked in extraordinary session, passed strongly worded Resolutions, & were then absolutely ignored by the Japs. It seemed to me absolutely nec: that dipl: action to follow, such as the recall of ambassadors, sh^d be carefully prepared beforehand, for the event of a Jap: refusal to take any notice of the League's recommendatns. It was also therefore nec: that the Assembly sh^d only be convoked at an opportune moment. I felt v. strongly about all this, so spoke it quickly, & Simon listened closely, & Leeper quietly but audibly assented.

I saw Simon again, in his carriage, just before reaching Paris, & found him disturbed by some news from India he saw in a French newspaper which I had got for him (he is a v. good French scholar, by the way, probably better than Austen,[79] I sh^d think, anyhow as good).

---

[79] (Joseph) Austen Chamberlain (1863–1937): Lib. Unionist MP Worcs. E. 1892–1914 (Con. from 1912), Con. MP Birmingham W. 1914–37; Postmaster-Gen. 1902–3; Chanc. of Exchequer 1903–5; Sec. of State for India 1915–17; mb of War Cabinet 1918–19; Chanc. of Exchequer 1919–21; Ld Privy Seal 1921–2; FS 1924–9; 1st Ld of Admiralty 1931; Con. Ldr 1921–2; kt. 1925; Nobel Peace Prize 1925. See his *Down the Years* (1935).

There was a question, apparently, of sending Brit: reinforcements there. 'Haven't we got enough troops in India?' I asked in some surprise. 'We haven't got enough troops anywhere' he answered at once.

By the way, von Bülow[80] (now head of the German Foreign Office) told me that Brüning reads *The Times* himself every day.

14 March – letter to Norman Ebbutt:[81] *In the leader tonight I do not take quite so confident a view of the ultimate result as one would no doubt be justified in doing, because we are most anxious here to get the French to accept the 'basis of equality' with Germany, and really cease to treat Germans on all possible occasions as a conquered tribe.[82] So we just want to indicate that some of the claims of Germany in regard to external affairs ought to be sympathetically considered, and that the present Government will continue to be fiercely assailed during the next 4 weeks anyhow. Everything possible ought to be done therefore to make the path of its foreign policy as easy as may be. I am interested in the opinion expressed in the message tonight, that National-Socialism has reached its high-water mark. I had rather suspected that. I wonder if there may be another tide?* [...]

24 March   Last Monday I asked if I c^d see Simon, & next day (Tues) got a message telling me to come to the H. of Commons at 3 o'clock. He was going to make a speech on For: Policy in the House; so that is a good moment to see him. He likes looking on me as a bit of pub: opinion, & trying the effect of his speech.

When I came into his room he got up & held out both hands towards me, saying 'I am <u>delighted</u> to see you' – I grasped the right one, & was struck by the limpness of its grip! He wanted to talk about the Far East, straightaway, but I managed to get him on to the Danubian Economic Plan for a while first. He was explicit as to G^t B^n's attitude, & told me he had sent a message that very day to Tardieu telling him he <u>must not</u> keep on giving out the impression that Brit: policy was identified with French. It was not.

Simon is of course very much all things to all men, & Tardieu may genuinely have got the idea that S. was entirely with him after the cordial talk the two of them had in Paris the other day, when S. was on his way back from Geneva.

S. drew a rough outline of the States of Central Europe on the back of a bit of paper & their frontier lines, i.e. Customs barriers, & showed

[80] Bernhard Wilhelm von Bülow (1885–1936): entered dip. service 1911; West European section *Auswärtige Amt* 1925–30, *StaatSek.* 1930–6.
[81] Letter in *The Times* archive.
[82] 'A Battle Well Begun': 15 March 1932.

what he thought might be done & how much sacrifice G^t B^n might make for the sake of general $Europ^n$ improvement – roughly, we w^d agree to the lowering to any extent of the internal Danubian barriers, & thus give the five Succession States advantages for each other over everybody else, even to the loss of our Most-Favoured-Nation treatment; but we w^d insist on coming in on equal terms with the other <u>outside</u> nations – i.e. Germany, Italy & France.

I gave him some of my ideas, & then we went on to the Far East. He defended his policy at Geneva, & read me passages of the speech which he was going to deliver later in the afternoon.

I ventured to differ at one point, & he altered the passage a little accordingly. He made the distinction clearer & sharper between the <u>mediatory</u> & <u>coercive</u> functions of the League. In fact he had distinguished, but not in so many words. It is his habit to qualify almost everything he says. My point was that the mediatorial function excludes the coercive in the same dispute at the same time. One ought to make up one's mind early which course the League is going to adopt, & stick to it. In fact, as I say, Simon did so in this dispute, but he had not, I thought, made the most of his own attitude in his speech. Anyhow he wrote in a sentence about keeping the two functions distinct; & I noticed later that he did deliver it in his speech.

I began my leader on those lines, in sympathy.[83]

Simon spoke severely about Tardieu's plan of arming the League with heavy bombers. He does not like it, & evidently means to oppose it flatly.

He had written an address also about Goethe, to be delivered that night at a reception in the City for the centenary of Goethe's death. He read me extracts from it, showing how some of Goethe's ideas were very applicable to Europe today. He wanted me to commend his address to Geoffrey [Dawson],[84] as he always calls GD – which I accordingly did. But he had already sent a copy to him, I found.

S. is an extremely good man for detail, but at present lacks sweep or vision in foreign affairs. That is a criticism I have heard of him, & I think it is right at present; but in India he showed vision, & so he may also in foreign policy.

I tried to convey to him the other day the conception of an English Minister establishing an <u>economic</u> Locarno in Central Europe, just as an Englishman had been necessary to bring European countries together politically. They will not come together <u>spontaneously</u>. Pressure tactfully applied is necessary, as Austen Chamberlain applied it to Briand &

[83] 'A Vindication of British Policy': 23 March 1932.

[84] (George) Geoffrey Dawson (1874–1944): pvt sec. to Milner in South Africa 1901–5; Ed. *Johannesburg Star* 1905–10; Ed. *The Times* 1912–19, 1923–41.

Stresemann.[85] I mentioned that. Rivalry is a great spur to anybody. (That was when we were speaking about the Danubian federation plan).

25 March We (*T.T*) are having a controversy with LlG[86] over his attitude to Reparations, at the Peace-making & now. (His book has just been pub^d making out that he was always in favour of a lenient attitude). We had a leader written by Coote,[87] called 'Wisdom After the Event,' to which LlG has replied in a long letter practically saying '*tu quoque*' – & of course *T.T.* was in favour of making Germany pay to the utmost. LlG has therefore bn able to quote some sentences from our leaders showing that he & we were much in the same boat. GD in my room in PHS three days ago said – 'The truth is LlG was rattled by Northcliffe[88] – just as I was. If ever I was away from the office for 2 days some bloody man from the *Daily Mail* was sent in & wrote an anti-Hun hate.'

It was of course soon after that that GD resigned – & that is his best justification.

Norton,[89] of the F.O., was here to luncheon yesterday, & seeing my Full-Powers box on the mantelpiece, told me that he had put forward the proposal that the seal of Full-Powers sh^d once more be accorded to Plenipotentiaries in fine silver-boxes. It was this box in our dining-room, which was father's father's, that had put the idea into his head, when he was here to luncheon once before. The idea was negatived. I suggested to him to try again when times were better, & he thought he might.

Ld Curzon[90] I believe bought up all the old ones when he was For: Sec^y – there were about 8 left, & he took the lot!

[85] Gustav Stresemann (1878–1929): German politician; Nat. Lib. Deputy 1907–29; For. Min. 1923–9; Nobel Peace Prize 1926.

[86] David Lloyd George (1863–1945): politician; Lib. MP Caernarvon Boroughs 1890–1945; Pres. Board of Trade 1906–8; Chanc. of Exchequer 1908–15; Min. of Munitions 1915–16; Sec. for War 1916; PM 1916–22; cr. Earl Lloyd-George of Dwyfor 1945.

[87] Colin Reith Coote (1893–1979): Coalition Lib. MP Isle of Ely 1917–22; joined staff of *The Times* 1923–42; *Daily Telegraph & Morning Post* 1942–45, Dep. Ed. 1945–50, Managing Ed. 1950–64; kt. 1962. See his *Editorial* (1965).

[88] Alfred Charles W. Harmsworth (1865–1922): proprietor *The Times* 1908–22; Chm., British War Mission to US 1917; Dir. of Propaganda in Enemy Countries 1918; cr. Viscount Northcliffe 1905.

[89] Clifford John Norton (1891–1990): entered dip. service 1921; pvt. Sec. to PUS FO 1930–7; Counsellor in Warsaw 1937–9; FO 1939–42; Min. in Berne 1942–6; Amb. in Athens 1946–51; kt. 1946.

[90] George Nathaniel Curzon (1859–1925): Con. MP Southport 1886–98; Viceroy of India 1916–21; Ld Privy Seal 1915–16; Ld Pres. 1916–19; FS 1919–24; Con. Leader in the HofL. 1916–24; cr. Baron Curzon 1898, Earl 1911, Marquess 1921.

27 March (Easter Sunday) I see in the papers today – I am on holiday – that the Brit. Gov^t has proposed that the four Big Powers concerned in the Danube scheme – France, Germany[,] It: & G^t B^n – sh^d have a conference in London on the subject in April. I remember now that Simon did throw out this idea to me during our conversatn on Tues: – just by the way, almost. He said 'what would you think of having a Conference of the Four Great Powers concerned first, instead of beginning, as France suggests, with a Conf: of the Five Danubian States themselves?' It was a new idea to me & struck me as a little curious, & I suggested that the two conferences might be parallel – this was on the supposition that they w^d be held at Geneva, where all the Govts w^d in any case be represented at the Disarm^t Conference.

I suspect that one of Simon's motives is to obviate the need for Tardieu to pay a special visit to London, as he threatens to do, or anyhow make the visit far less important. Tardieu is for ever exclaiming that the Entente is re-established & that France & England are working close together – but Simon definitely does not want to be identified with French policy every time.

6 April Yesterday, when I returned to work after my Easter holiday, I went to the F.O., & by good luck ran into Sir J. Simon in the ground-floor corridor, & he said 'can you walk across to the House of Commons with me, & I'll give you the news'. So I went with him, & was struck by the clear, close, detailed way he narrated to me the points of the Tardieu conversatns, even when walking down the street, crossing it & up to just outside his room in the House – such a thing as getting into the lift & setting it in motion making not the slightest difference to the even flow of his narrative. He talked with me – finally walking up & down the corridor near his room in the House – until the moment that the Austrian Minister came up to him. I feel as though, if I had a conversation by appointment with a Foreign Envoy, I should always like a few minutes of quiet beforehand to consider what I was going to say to him. But this consideration never seems to affect Simon. He has an ever-ready mind, like Benesh.[91]

He said 'Tardieu is a curious fellow; he seems to have told the *Temps* what the results of our conversations were before the conversations were ended!'

There is, I think, some rivalry between Simon & MacDonald, just as there was between Henderson & MacD. The truth is that MacD is

---

[91] Eduard Beneš (1884–1948): Czechoslovak politician; For. Min. 1918–35; PM 1921–2; Pres. 1936–8; exiled after Munich agreement; Pres. Czechoslovak National Committee, London 1939–45; Pres. of Republic 1945–8. See his *Building a New Europe* (1939).

frightfully vain, & greatly enjoys playing a leading role in foreign affairs. It seems that on Sunday night after dinner at the French Embassy MacD drew Tardieu & Flandin[92] into conversation with himself, & Simon had rather to force himself in so as to know what was being said. Later however L$^{\underline{d}}$ Londonderry[93] carried off MacD: & the two Frenchmen to Londonderry House, so MacD: got his *tête-à-tête* with Tardieu there. They remained there until after 1 a.m.

Above from Poliakoff, who saw Tardieu afterwards, & is always *au fait* with what goes on inside the French Embassy.

In point of fact I think MacD is probably better than Simon at the broad lines of policy. Simon is an ever-ready opportunist; so between them, if they can work reasonably well together, they ought to conduct our foreign policy very well.

9 April Yesterday I went to the Press reception which the new Am: Ambassador, M$^{\underline{r}}$ Andrew Mellon,[94] held imm: after his arrival in London. He is a curiously (and genuinely) shy figure – a poor frame with a fine head, a passive, hesitating manner, but somehow giving the impression of a reserve of strength. He issued his statement in writing, & was mild in answering questions, but pleasant, sensible & quite shrewd.

He has a far-away look, as if he were v. frail. Good features, & a v. nice smile. Of previous ambassadors I have seen he reminded me in personality most of Mr Kellogg.[95]

12 Apr: On the last day of the Four-Powers Conference I had a message from C$^{\underline{t}}$ Bernstorff[96] asking me if I w$^{\underline{d}}$ care to see Herr v.

[92] Pierre Etienne Flandin (1889–1958): French politician & diplomat; Deputy 1914–41; Vice-Pres. Chamber of Deputies 1928; Min. of Finance 1931–2, of Public Works 1934, of State 1935–6, For. Min. 1936, 1940–41; arrested by Allies, North Africa 1943; judged not guilty of collaboration 1946. See his *Politique française, 1919–40* (1947).

[93] Charles Stewart H. Vane-Tempest-Stewart (1878–1949): Con. MP Maidstone 1906–15; Leader of Senate & Min. of Educ., N. Ireland 1921–6; 1st Commissioner of Works 1928–9, 1931; Sec. of State for Air 1931–5; Ld Privy Seal & Con. Leader in the HofL. 1935; Pres., Northern Counties Area Con. Assoc. 1930–49; Mayor of Durham 1936–7; styled Viscount Castlereagh 1884–1915, suc. 7th Marquess of Londonderry 1915; kt. 1919.

[94] Andrew William Mellon (1855–1937): Sec. of Treasury 1921–32; Amb. in London 1932–3.

[95] Frank Billings Kellogg (1856–1937): Amb. in London 1923–5; Sec. of State 1925–9; author of Kellogg-Briand Pact outlawing war as an instrument of national policy 1928; judge of Permanent Court of International Justice 1930–5; Nobel Peace Prize 1929.

[96] Albrecht Theodor von Bernstorff (1890–1945): Counsellor *Auswartige Amt* 1925–30, Senior Counsellor 1930–3; resigned from civil service in opposition to Nazi regime 1933; imprisoned in Dachau 1940; murdered by *Gestapo* 1945. See *Albrecht Bernstorff zum Gedächtnis* (1952).

Bülow, the head of the German delegation. I said I would v much, so was given an appointment at the Carlton Hotel. He may be the next German Foreign Minister. He is quiet, strong-looking, direct & dry, but kindly. He speaks slowly but firmly & v. clearly, & in extremely good English. He is an expert on economic & commercial affairs, & it is significant of present conditions that that is the type to be chosen for high posts in foreign affairs. (He is already head of the German F.O.).

He is just the opposite of his brilliant, insincere courtier-like uncle, the late P^ce Bülow.[97]

GENEVA *16 April* Having arr^d here last night, I met M^r & Mrs Henderson[98] walking along the lake front this morn^g, & he began to reminisce almost at once, which is what he seems to like doing with me. He told me several interesting things. He said that he had two projects he was keen to carry through when he was Foreign Sec^y. One was to create a 'World Economic Dep^t' at the F.O., with Sir Arthur Salter[99] at the head of it. The other was to have an organization, under F.O. control, to instruct the British public in 'the arts of peace.' I expressed warm sympathy with the first, but none with the second – I said I thought G^t B^n had gone far enough, & other countries ought to catch up. He retorted that there were only 3 countries out of the 64 at this Conference that did not genuinely desire a substantial measure of disarmament. A little later he mentioned Japan & France as being two of them. Whether he meant me to infer that G^t B^n was the third I don't know, but I think he did.

In regard to the Econ: Dep^t idea for the F.O., he told me that he did put it up to the P.M., but MacDonald had replied that what was wanted was an extension of the functions of the D.O.T. The D.O.T. is rather too national for what Henderson was thinking of apparently. But Henderson's internationalism goes too far, I think, for the present stage of the world's development. A little later it will be desirable.

H: also talked a good deal about the Conference held in London

---

[97] Bernhard von Bülow (1849–1929): diplomat & politician; entered diplomatic service 1873; Amb. in Rome 1893–7; FS 1897–1900; Chanc. 1900–09.

[98] Eleanor Watson: m. Arthur Henderson 1888.

[99] Arthur James Salter (1881–1975): Dir. Econ. & Finance Section, LoN 1919–20, 1922–31; Sec-Gen. Reparations Commission 1920–22; Gladstone Prof. of Political Theory & Institutions, Oxford U. 1934–44; Ind. MP Oxford U. 1937–50; kt. 1922; cr. Baron Salter of Kidlington 1953. See his *Memoirs of a Public Servant* (1961).

last July,[100] which he thinks was about the last chance of doing anything big about European reconstruction. I agreed with that, & said that the question of Treaty Revision ought to have been faced then. Well, he said, it _was_ brought up – by Snowden! without previous consultation with him or the P.M. – & both he & MacD: had been astonished at the vehemence with which France had said it c^d not possibly be discussed then. They argued that a big issue like that could not be introduced into a Conference convened for another purpose, that all the signatories of the Peace Treaties w^d have to be there, not only half-a-dozen, etc: etc:

Henderson says he was trying to prepare the ground carefully. He had got the French to agree to the Germans coming to Paris, & then he was going to get the whole lot over to London – but he found that while he was negotiating in Paris MacDonald had of his own accord asked the lot over to London. There seems to have been a terrible & most hampering jealousy betw: MacD: & Henderson all the time. Henderson as good as told me that MacD: had invented the story against him of the statement that Gt Bn's financial position was desperate, which he was supposed to have been [sic] made by Henderson, at a banquet at the French Colonial Exhibition, to M. Laval[101] (then Premier). H: said something to me about MacD: having said it had been tapped on the telephone! This I c^d not quite follow, & hesitated to press him on the point.

H: is a v. tired man just now, & his mind is always running on the (to him) tragedy of his ignominious exit from office last summer. He says he is getting better, but his difficulty is to take enough nourishment. He has 'attacks,' M^{rs} H told me – vomiting attacks I believe.

Luncheon with Noel-Baker, & he confirms that H:'s trouble is some poison that has got inside him, & gives him violent shivering-fits, followed by vomiting, which brings relief. H: had his gall-bladder taken

---

[100] The collapse of Austria's largest bank, the *Credit Anstalt* on 11 May 1931 had produced an immediate financial crisis; the Bank of England advanced £4,300,000 in order to prevent a complete collapse. But the crisis sent a shock wave through Germany, where the *Reichsbank* lost £36,000,000 in the first half of June and the *Danat Bank* collapsed on 13 July. Germany appealed for assistance at a conference convened in London on 20 July, but neither Britain nor the United States were able or willing to assist. France, with gold reserves of £486,000,000 was in a position to provide a loan but was prepared to do so only if Germany agreed to abandon any attempts at treaty revision during the period of the loan. On 21 July the Nazis told Brüning that they would not agree to such a provision and he left London on the 23rd without a promise of assistance.

[101] Pierre Laval (1883–1945): elected Socialist Deputy 1914; Min. of Public Works 1925, of Justice 1926, of Labour 1930 & 1932; PM and For. Min. 1931–2; Min. of Colonies 1934; For. Min. 1934–5; PM 1935–6; Deputy PM & Min. of Info. 1940; For. Min. 1940, 1941–3; Min. of Interior 1942; Deputy Head of State 1942–4; tried for treason & executed 1945. See *Laval parle: notes et mémoires* (1947).

out some years ago, & his doctor here thinks that may have something to do with it. He has now taken the gall-bladder out of a live rabbit, & is watching results.

At luncheon Baker said that the latest *bon mot* he had heard was 'The P.M. & Simon have got on each others' vanities.'

Alec Cadogan[102] was there too, & he & Baker discussed all manner of disarmament schemes, one in particular '*le stockage des armaments.*' By this is meant the storing of heavy arms internationally – i.e. each nation to give up its tanks, long-range guns & bombing aeroplanes which w$^{\underline{d}}$ be warehoused on behalf of the League. Baker quite excited because Paul-Boncour[103] had said in private conversation that he would agree that they sh$^{\underline{d}}$ be stored in equal portions in Italy, Germany & France! Both Cadogan & Baker discussed these ideas quite seriously. Geneva seems to reduce even the most sensible men to puerility.

But how one does run into ideas here all the same. I have not been here 24 hrs yet, & this morn^g, on going to the Secretariat, I met Abraham[104] & had a v. interesting discussion about the relations of U.S.A. with the League – then when I left the Secretariat M$^{\underline{r}}$ & M$^{\underline{rs}}$ Henderson by the lake – luncheon with Noel-Baker & Cadogan, & in the hotel, immediately afterwards, met Dame Rachel Crowdy,[105] who is just back from a long journey in the Far East (where I believe she was on a mission investigating the White-Slave traffic),[106] & she told me a lot of interesting things about Manchuria. e.g. there was a tremendously strong opposition in Japan to the militarist policy. Communism is extraordinarily widespread there. The Emperor at the beginning thought of ordering home the generals for entering Mukden & court-martialling them. But now (temporarily anyhow) the soldiers & sailors have pulled it off. The Japs will stay in Manchuria, there is no doubt, she thinks. [...]

17 Apr: Walked out to M$^{\underline{rs}}$ Barton's[107] for tea, & found there the usual

---

[102] Alexander George M. Cadogan (1884–1968): entered dip. service 1908; Min. in Beijing 1933–5, Amb. 1935–6; Deputy U-Sec. FO 1936–7, PUS 1938–46; Rep. to UN 1946–50; kt. 1934. See *The Diaries of Sir Alexander Cadogan* (1971).

[103] Joseph Paul-Boncour (1873–1972): French politician; Deputy 1909–14, 1919–31; Min. of War 1932; PM 1932–3; For. Min. 1932–4, 1938, of LoN Affairs 1936. See his *Entre deux guerres* (1945).

[104] G. H. F. Abraham: Political Section, League of Nations Secretariat.

[105] Rachel Eleanor Crowdy (d. 1964): Chief of Social Question & Opium Traffic Section, LoN 1919–31; cr. DBE 1919.

[106] This was amended in pencil, substituting 'opium-smoking' for 'White-Slave traffic'.

[107] Victoria Alexandrina J. Barton (d. 1935): granddaughter of P.M. Sir Robert Peel; m. 1887 Mr Daniel Barton (d. 1907); established a *salon* for those attending the LoN at *Villa Lammermoor* on Lac Lemar; nicknamed 'the Queen of Geneva'.

collection drawn from all parts of the globe – except Gt Bn, as our people always go off on excursions on Sundays now, & neglect her. I think she rather feels it. I talked there with Colban,[108] the Norwegian Minister in Paris, & Hugh Wilson,[109] the Am^{cn} Min: in Berne, & several other people. Mr Henderson was there, looking better; we walked back to this hotel together.

He talked a gd deal about the affairs of the Labour Party, as to which he is still being consulted. He told me that MacDonald had 3 weeks ago put out feelers to find out whether he might expect to be welcomed again some day as leader of the Party. I gathered that he had met with no response. Henderson said that MacDonald was now putting it about that he had made no such approaches; & in the meantime he had noticed that Malcolm MacDonald[110] had gone down to speak for the 'Tory' candidate at the bye-election at Wakefield. That, he considered, burned M.M.'s boats for him.

We then talked about foreign affairs & about the way France blocks any real move towards conciliation or disarmament. I said I thought the time had come for us to stand up to France. Henderson seemed doubtful about it. 'As long as they have a Gov^t of the Right, you will do no good by it' he said.

18 April   Had luncheon with Aghnides,[111] who is Chief of the Disarmnt Section of the League, & so put me wise over all the *tiraillements* that are going on behind the scenes here. He says plainly that the French are blocking everything as much as they possibly can. Yet on the whole Germans & others prefer Tardieu to a man like Herriot,[112] because they

---

[108] Erik Andreas Colban (1876–1956): entered dip. service 1903; joined secretariat LoN 1919; Dir. of Administrative Commissions (Saar & Danzig) & Minorities Section 1919–27, Dir. of Disarmament Section 1928–30; Norwegian Min. in Paris 1930, in Brussels 1930, in Luxemburg 1931, in London 1934–42; Amb. in London 1942–6; delegate to World Disarmament Conf., Geneva 1930–2.

[109] Hugh Robert Wilson (1885–1946): entered for. service 1911; Min. in Berne 1927–37; Asst Sec. of State 1937–8; Amb. in Berlin 1938–40; adviser to Sec. of State 1940; retd 1941; delegate to World Disarmament Conf., Geneva 1932–7. See his *Diplomat between Wars* 1941.

[110] Malcolm John MacDonald (1901–81): son of Ramsay MacDonald; Lab. MP Bassetlaw div. of Notts 1929–31; Nat. Lab. 1931–5, Nat. Govt Ross & Comarty 1936–45; U-Sec. Dominions Office 1931–5; Dominions Sec. 1935–8, 1938–9; Colonial Sec. 1935, 1938–40. See his *Titans & Others* (1972).

[111] Thanassis Aghnides (1889–1984): Greek diplomat; Dir.of Greek Press Bureau in London 1918–19; joined LoN secretariat, 1919; Dir. of Disarmament Section 1930–9, U-Sec.-Gen. 1939–40; PUS, Min. of For. Affairs 1942–3; Amb. in London 1942–7; Sec. of World Disarmament Conf., Geneva 1932–4.

[112] Edouard Herriot (1872–1957): French politician; Senator 1912–19, Deputy 1919–40;

know just where they are with him. It seems that the other day there was a private meeting between Drummond, Henderson & one or two others, to see whether they couldn't take the v. practical & concrete American proposals (propounded by Mr Gibson)[113] & make them a definite item in the agenda & go ahead with them. The French w^d not let it go through, however. They c^d not bear the idea that the American proposal sh^d be discussed as an integral American proposal while the French scheme (for a League army) was not to be discussed integrally.

Aghnides likes working under Henderson v. much. He says he's the nicest Chief he's ever had. Henderson sent me a message this morn^g through Noel-Baker to say that he had another of his attacks last night. This was because he had told me yesterday that he was at last really better, & had not had an attack for 10 days – & I was going to say something about it in the paper, & he did not want to mislead me.

I did send something last night, but not too rosy, because Henderson, although he did seem better, is a v. different man from what he was a year ago. Aghnides told me that when he had to go & see him on the Riviera (about January, before the beginning of the Disarm^{nt} Conference) Henderson was literally more dead than alive.

It seems he had a v. bad moment about a month ago too – during the Easter holiday. Mrs Barton told me that yesterday, she having heard it from his doctor. Mrs B. has really been helping Mrs Henderson to look after him here.

19 Apr: I was in the Beau Rivage at 7 this evening when Sir John Simon saw me & said 'Ah, I've got something to say to you; can you wait a bit.' So I said I would & went & talked with L^y Theo: Cadogan,[114] who was also sitting in the hall, until he re-appeared.

He then insisted on my having a vermouth, & took me & Willert[115] along & started off by asking me how I thought the disarmamnt

PM 1924–5, 1932; Pres. of Chamber of Deputies 1925, 1936; Min. of Educ. 1926–8; Min. without Portfolio 1934–6; renounced his *Légion d'Honneur* in 1942 in protest of its being awarded to collaborators; interned & imprisoned 1940–5; Pres. of Republic 1947–53. See *Edouard Herriot: études et témoignages* (1975).

[113] Hugh Gibson (1883–1954): American diplomat; entered for. service 1908; Min. in Warsaw 1919–24, in Berne 1924–7; Amb. in Brussels 1927–33, in Rio de Janiero 1933–7, in Brussels 1937–8; retd 1938. See his *The Road to Foreign Policy* (1944).

[114] Theodosia Louisa Cadogan (1882–1977): d. of 4th Earl of Gosford; m. Alexander Cadogan 1912.

[115] Arthur Willert (1882–1973): joined staff of *The Times* 1906, editorial staff 1909–10, Chief Corrspdt in U.S. 1910–20; head of News Dept & Press Officer, FO 1921–1935; Ministry of Info. 1940–5; kt. 1919. See his *The Frontiers of England* (1935). ·

business was going? I gave him my opinion, & then he went off &
expounded his view of the situation. All this was I think because the
British Delegatn is going to move a Resolution tomorrow, & he wanted
to get my 'reaction'. He didn't seem to have anything actually to tell
me.

But he suddenly saw Mrs Corbett Ashby[116] coming along in full
evening dress, & remembered he was dining with her. So he dashed
off.

I then had a talk with Mrs Corbett Ashby, who seems a nice woman &
desperately keen about the League.

Then in the outer hall I was introduced by Willert to Ld Londonderry, & had a short conversation with him. Most pleasant & very
on the spot. We talked about Hedworth Williamson;[117] & then he asked
me whether it was possible to get cuttings out of back numbers of *T.T*,
as he kept cuttings, & the cuttings of two letters which he & L^{y}
Londonderry[118] had written to *T.T* at different times had got lost. He
gave me details & I promised to get them for him when I got back to
London, if I could.

21 Apr: Sir Thomas Horder,[119] the famous doctor, has arr^{d} here with
the Prime Minister, & I was introduced to him in the Lobby by Willert.
He spoke about the P.M. with remarkable frankness & crispness. I
noted his words directly afterwards. He said – 'People ask me why I
let him do these things (i.e. come to Geneva). I say at 65 you can't
change a man's temperament. At the most you can make him alter his
habits, & that very little. Sir John Simon wanted to prevent him coming
to the Disarmam^{t} Com^{tee}. I said No, he may come. He wants to be
"getting facets," as he says himself. He has done it all his life.'

'It has become part of his nature, I suppose,' I said, & Sir T. Horder
said 'Exactly.' He said disarm^{t} was what MacD was most interested
in, & it w^{d} not do to keep him away from it. I asked whether he was
up to making a speech. 'Well, he may speak' said Sir T. Horder 'but a
sustained effort is what he is not capable of.'

[116] Margery (Irene) Corbett Ashby (1882–1981): Lib. politician; unsuccessful candidate
in seven elections; UK substitute delegate to World Disarmament Conf., Geneva 1931–
5; DBE 1967.
[117] Hedworth Williamson (1867–1942): businessman, landowner & courtier; suc. 9th Bt
1900.
[118] Edith Chaplin (1879–1959): daughter of 1st Viscount Chaplin; m. Viscount Castlereagh (later Ld Londonderry) 1899; founder & dir. of Women's Legion 1915–19; DBE
1917. See her *Retrospect* (1938).
[119] Thomas Horder (1871–1955): physician to King Edward VIII & King George VI;
kt 1918; cr. Baron Horder of Ashford 1933. See his *Fifty Years of Medicine* (1953).

When the P.M. came inside the Com^{tee} hall this morn^g he saw a lot of people he knew & shook hands with many & exchanged a few words with others, incl: Litvinoff.[120] When he had got to the end of the row & was having a few words with Brüning, Henderson (the Chairman) brought his mallet down with a sharp rap & MacD: & Brüning sat smartly down, & the debate went on. One brief moment of sweet imposition of his authority for Henderson!

L^y Londonderry has come here with MacDonald.[121] How much more open these friendships can be now than in the days of Dizzy!

I had a talk with Sir Eric Drummond this afternoon. He looks better now than he did last Feb^y, when he was frightfully worried over the Sino-Japanese dispute, which so diminished the authority of the League. He hopes now that the Lytton Commssn may be able to suggest a solution which w^d be acceptable to China as well as Japan. He looks to Turkey being a member of the League soon, & thinks she ought to be elected to the Council. I mentioned the difficulty of any country being elected that does not belong to a group; & he thought the best way of getting round this w^d be for one country in each of three groups to renounce its right for one year – so for 3 years one seat w^d be available for Greece or Hungary or one of the at present abandoned countries. But that w^d only supply one place for once country – unless the whole process began over again.

Sir Eric told me that the Japs: were v. much above themselves & some of them were openly talking about war against the U.S.A.

22 April   Sir John Pratt[122] was at the same luncheon as I was today (the Abrahams) & he spoke v. freely & rather critically about Sir J. Simon. He said he badgered his Staff quite a lot, had no idea of time or keeping a programme, & wore them all out. Pratt says he has the nature of an artist, or rather a virtuoso who always wants to be in the limelight.

I said I was rather surprised, as he had never seemed to me to be in the least bit fussy, but always remarkably cool. Pratt said that was

[120] Maxim (né Meer Wallach) Litvinov (1876–1951): Russian diplomat; entered FO 1918; Commisar of For. Affairs 1930–9; Amb. in Washington 1941–3; Deputy Commissar for For. Affairs 1946. See his *Notes for a Journal* (1955).

[121] MacDonald, whose wife Margaret had died in 1911, was introduced to Lady Londonderry, a Conservative political hostess, at a Buckingham Palace reception in 1924. He had met her occasionally until 1930 when he spent a vacation with her and Lord Londonderry at their home in the Scottish highlands; after that time they formed a close personal attachment.

[122] John Pratt (1873–1952): Lib. MP Linlithgow 1913–18; Cathcart div. of Glasgow 1918–22; kt. 1922.

his public appearance, but beforehand & in private he was full of nerves. He had seen him leaning back in his chair & complain of 'this fearful nerve-strain.' I don't really see how anybody can be For: Min: nowadays without having that sort of nerve-strain. Pratt admitted Simon's first-class intellectual equipment & that he never missed [the] point.

About the Chinese, whom Pratt knows well, he said 'They can do everything except govern.'

23 Apr: Had an interesting last talk this morn^g with Temperley. He told me that Sir J. Salmon[123] [sic – Salmond] of the Air Force had come out in order stoutly to oppose the abandonment of the right to bomb from the air, which Simon has advocated here. So has practically every other country. It is an inhumane, indiscriminate form of warfare, & if any weapons are going to be abolished, this ought to be – anyhow nationally. One indisputably legitimate use of the air-bomb is the dispersal of an assembling army; & it seems just possible that if ever the League is going to have any sort of force at its disposal, it w^d not be a bad thing for it to have bombing aeroplanes.

I put this to Temperley & he quite agreed.

He is an immense help to me. One of the nicest of men.

BOULOGNE *24 Apr:* In Paris this morn^g I went to see by arrangement M. Barrere,[124] one of the best of France's ambassadors in recent times, & one of Foch's[125] greatest friends. That was why I went. [...]

M. B^{re} ended up by deploring the less good relations that now existed between Fr: & Eng:. I said I thought that the fundamental difference was that we in Eng. thought that the time had about come to forget about the war (politically), whereas it was a far more vivid memory in France. M. B^{re} assured me that within a year or two there w^d be another war! that Germany was secretly armed etc.

I mentioned this also to Ld Tyrrell[126] later, & he said there c^d never

[123] John (Maitland) Salmond (1881–1968): Air Marshal 1923, Air Chief Marshal 1929; Marshal, RAF 1933; Chief of Air Staff 1930–3; Dir. Imperial Airways 1933–9; Dir. of Armament Production, Ministry of Aircraft Production 1939–45.

[124] Camille Barrere (1851–1940): Amb. in Berne 1894–7, in Rome, 1897–1924.

[125] Ferdinand Foch (1851–1929): Commandant, French Army Group, Somme July 1916; Chief of Staff to C-in-C (Gen. Pétain) May 1917; Generalissmo, allied armies on western front April 1918. See *Memoirs of Marshal Foch* (1931).

[126] William George Tyrrell (1866–1947): entered FO 1889; Asst. U-Sec. FO 1919–25, PUS 1925–8; Amb. in Paris 1928–34; kt. 1913; cr. Baron Tyrrell of Avon 1929.

be complete understanding of each other's mentality between a country that had often been invaded & one that had not.

M. B^{re} was charmingly friendly, & invited me to go & see him at Fontainebleau (27 R: de l'Arbre Sec) in Sept, saying he could send his car in to Paris to fetch me.

I had luncheon with Tyrrell at the Embassy, & he was full of his quips & wise comments, but our talk was general a good part of the time, as Mrs Holman[127] was there (his daughter) & a French lady, a sort of companion or sec^y. He said Mr Mellon was the richest & the meanest man in America, & had been sent to Eng: to give him an Old Age pension! Tyrrell also has a v. poor opinion of Hoover.[128] He asked me how Simon was regarded at Geneva. I said clever but insincere, & that foreigners expected sincerity in an Englishman, though trickiness from each other. T: quite agreed. I was delighted to find that he sees a way out of our differences with France both in the matter of Disarmament & of Reparatns which is just what I had in mind in both cases. So one's course seems clear. [...]

LONDON *28 April*   At dinner last night with the Rubido-Zichys[129] Ld Colebrook,[130] who is Lord-in-Waiting to the King (or something akin to that) told me that the King was <u>very</u> pleased with Simon's conduct of Brit: foreign policy at Geneva.

I expect what the King likes is that he takes & keeps the lead.

Leeper confirmed to me the other day that S. is a terrible slave-driver to his own Staff; & makes them fetch & carry for L^y Simon, when she is there!

At the dinner last night I sat with Lady Vansittart[131] afterwards, & she told me how overworked Van: is.[132] He never sleeps soundly now, she said, but always dreams vividly, although he takes digitalis[133] &

---

[127] Anne Holman: m. Adrian Holman (dip. service 1920–54) 1932; marriage dissolved by divorce 1934.

[128] Herbert Hoover (1874–1964): Pres. of U.S. 1928–32. See *The Memoirs of Herbert Hoover* (3 vols 1952–9).

[129] Ivan Rubido-Zichy (b. 1874): Hungarian diplomat; Min. in London 1925–33.

[130] Edward Arthur Colebrooke (1861–1939): Lib. Chief Whip, HofL. 1911–22; permanent Ld-in-Waiting 1924–36; suc. 5th Bt 1890; cr. Baron Colebrooke of Stebunheath 1906; kt 1922.

[131] Sarita Enriqueta Vansittart, daughter of Herbert Ward, widow of Sir Colville Barclay; m. Robert Vansittart (q.v.) 1930.

[132] Robert Gilbert Vansittart (1881–1957): entered dip. service 1902; Counsellor 1920; Sec. to FS 1920–4; Asst U-Sec. & principal pvt. Sec. to FS 1928–30; PUS FO 1930–8; Chief Dip. Adviser 1938–41; kt 1929, cr. Baron Vansittart 1941. See his *The Mist Procession* (1958).

[133] 'digitalis' has been inserted in pencil; originally, a space was left in the journal.

other harmless drugs to help him along. He never gets a holiday.

There is something wrong with a system that gets the head of the F.O. into this state. He never can rest quietly, L^y V: said; [&] must go from one occupation to another.

L^y V. also caused me great surprise by more or less comissioning me to sound Harold Nicolson[134] about returning to the dipl: service. She said Van: thought he was a great loss & w^d welcome him back. To be sure of my ground I asked her whether I should mention this to Harold Nic:, & she said yes. How far Vansittart himself intended all this, I don't know; but unless I hear from him to the contrary in the next day or two I'll mention the matter to Harold. If he should go back, some of his former colleagues (& rivals!) will not, I fancy, give him nearly such a warm welcome as Van:! [...]

By the way, in regard to disarmament, I asked Tyrrell in Paris how we c^d possibly get a compromise with the French; & he said that Paul-Boncour 'here in this room (in the Embassy)' had told him that they w^d be satisfied if the League were supplied with an Air-force. (This was the very idea I had had with Temperley).

5 May   Last night S. & I were invited to a small musical party [...] I had quite a talk before the music began with Ld Londonderry – who had arrived before L^y L & the PM! He talked about the Disarm^t Conference a little & said it had become not a Conference of disarmament but of politics. He seemed rather worried about it, but I think that that is just where it really has the chance of achieving something – a big work of political appeasement by redressing the present inequality of status between France & Germany.

6 May   Last night a musical party at the Czechoslovak Legation, at which A. Fachiri's[135] sister, Jelly d'Aranyi was playing. A large crowd of diplomats, among whom the Italian Ambassdr. I paid my respects to him, but he was stony cold – I was puzzled a moment – & then I remembered! Two days before I'd written an article on Malta dead against the Italian claims there! & pointing out that it was really rather stiff that Italy sh^d complain about our very liberal treatment of the It: language in the island, when it was doing its utmost to obliterate the

---

[134] Harold George Nicolson (1886–1968): entered FO 1909; Counsellor in Teheran 1925–7, in Berlin 1927–9, resigned 1929; editorial staff *Evening Standard* 1930; Nat. Lab. MP Leicester W. 1935–45; PPS Ministry of Info. 1940–1; See his *Diaries & Letters*, vol.1 *1930–9*.

[135] Adila Fachiri (née d'Aranyi) (1888–1962): Hungarian violinist.

German language in the Tyrol, where the pop: is entirely German – quite unlike Malta, where Italian is simply an imported & privileged survival.

20 May   Saw Sir Horace Rumbold yesterday at the Ritz, he being here to take a short holiday while he can. He sees no great hope for Lausanne. Brüning has burnt his boats, & can offer no compromise solution now. And Germany, says Rumbold, is behind him to a man in that.

I got him to talk a little about General Schleicher,[136] the 'mystery' man of the moment in Germany. Evidently a strong & yet supple man. A soldier with political insight. A Monarchist by instinct but not necessarily by policy. Capable of intrigue, & so called an intriguer ('he has possibilities of intrigue' were Rumbold's words).

2 June   Yesterday I had a good talk with Sir Eric Drummond in Norfolk Ho:[use]. He had just been with Sir J. Simon for an hour & a half, & seemed in excellent spirits; so I hope he has got some assurance of getting what he wants when he leaves Geneva – whatever that may be! Head of the F.O., I hope.

I said to him in the course of our talk 'People are always asking me who is going to succeed you when the time comes for you to leave Geneva, & what I say is "Several names will be mentioned & discussed & canvassed, & then they'll come back to your no: 2 M. Avenol".'[137] Sir Eric said that was v. probable, but that Avenol might be black-balled by Germany – & then they'd have to fall back on an Englishman once more! [...]

Sir Eric told me his grounds for hopefulness in the Disarm[t] question, but I do think he rather underestimates the disastrous choice of von Papen[138] & his reactionaries as German Chancellor by Hindenburg.

Sir Eric also told me he was going to try to curtail the session of the Assembly, as suggested in *T.T.*

---

[136] Kurt von Schleicher (1882–1934): entered army 1900; Col. 1926, Maj.-Gen. 1929; Min. of Defence 1932; Chanc. 1932, replaced by Hitler in Jan. 1933; assassinated in Nazi purge, June 1934.

[137] Joseph Louis A. Avenol (1879–1952): French civil servant; Deputy Sec-Gen. LoN, 1923–32, Sec-Gen. 1933–40. See his *l'europe silencieuse (1944)*.

[138] Franz von Papen (1879–1969): Catholic Centre rep. in Prussian legislature 1920–32; replaced Brüning as Chanc. 1932, deposed by von Schleicher, Dec. 1932; conspired to replace him with Hitler, Jan. 1932; mb. of Hitler's cabinet 1933–4; Amb. in Vienna 1934–8; Amb. in Ankara 1939–44; found guilty of war crimes, released on appeal 1946. See his *Memoirs* (1952).

I went on to the German Embassy & saw Bernstorff, & told him what a terrible impression I thought it w$^{\underline{d}}$ make in England, France, Belgium & U.S.A. to make von Papen Chancellor in the place of Brüning. Bernstorff was I think impressed by what I said, he like all Germans not having in the least realized the effect on foreign minds of what they do.

Earlier in the afternoon Leeper at the F.O. had told me what confusion had been caused in Whitehall the other day by MacDonald's conversation by wireless from Lossiemouth with M$^{\underline{r}}$ Stimson in Washington. The F.O. had rec$^{\underline{d}}$ no written report of what had been said. The result had been that the Governments of Gt Bn & U.S. had blundered into this World Economic Conference idea without consulting any other countries – which alway annoys them v. much – & without being at all clear what they propose to discuss, or when, or where.

2 June: to Reed:[139] [...] *Personally, the fall of Brüning appears to me to be a disaster. If the Hitlerites had taken his place one would at least have been able to say that they doubtless represent the biggest trend of opinion in Germany today – but even that consolation is denied one by this Government of the backwoodsmen.* [...]

8 June On Mon: (2 days ago) I went, at GD's suggestion, to see Freiherr v. Neurath[140] at the German Embassy (having got an appointment beforehand). He is in a curious position, not having resigned his ambassadorship, but having been appointed For: Min: in the new German Gov$^{\underline{t}}$.

He is a powerful, brisk man; able, with that bluff German frankness, that still hides something all the time. I caught him out misleading me once. But on the other hand he is frank, & once let out something apparently unintentionally.

He spoke in an anyhow exceedingly interesting way on the recent German crisis which had resulted in the overthrow of Brüning & the instalment of the contemptible v. Papen. It is obvious that Hindenburg was got at, not directly by the East Prussian Junkers & the soldiers, but

---

[139] Douglas Reed (1895–1976): sub-ed. *The Times* 1924–9, Asst Corrspdt in Berlin 1929–35, Central European Corrspdt in Vienna 1935–8; resigned ff *Anschluss* because of his conflict with editorial policy on appeasement; *News Chronicle* 1938–45. See his *Disgrace Abounding* (1939).

[140] Konstantin von Neurath (1873–1956): Amb. in Rome 1921–30; in London 1930–2; For. Min. 1932–8 (when he was displaced by Ribbentrop); Protector of Bohemia & Moravia 1939–43; Gen. *SS* 1943–5; sentenced to 15 years for war crimes 1946, released 1954.

through his son (who acts as his ADC) & his Sec^y General. He was led to believe that Papen was a suitable man, being told he was in the Centre Party (Brüning's Party). So he was, but a traitor working against Brüning all the time. (This was told to me by Bernstorff). v. Neurath told me that Hindenburg had tried in vain to get other people to take on the job before he invited Papen. He also said that Brüning was in a state of absolute nervous collapse, & had been unable to make up his mind about filling up the vacant positions in his Ministry. This I believe to be an exaggeration. The man is tired, naturally, & at the end of a two year's terrific ordeal has gone to bed for 2 or 3 days, no doubt in a state of exhaustion.

When v. N. had been talking to me for about 20 min: the Austrian Minister was announced; so I asked if I might write down some of the things he had told me for publication, & let him see what I had written when he was free again. He said certainly, so I was shown into Bernstorff's room, & there wrote out a statement which he afterwards passed verbatim. I added on my own account (before he saw it, of course) one or two points which he had not actually said to me, but which I believed to be in his mind. These were included in what he passed. One of these was that he favoured the proposal of a world Economic Conference. I pointed this out to him specially, & he guffawed, & said 'Ach, yes, I favour it, but I do not zink anything will come out of it. It is no use. But it is good to say I am in favour of it.' Typical!

The whole statement is said to have produced a tranquilizing effect in the City.

I also put in a bit about Brüning – that he thought he c^d say that Brüning was pleased that he sh^d take on the For: Ministry (he had told me he had consulted Brüning before doing so), & he looked at Bernstorff & said 'yes, zat will have a good effect here,' to which Bernstorff nodded in reply. [...]

9 June   Yesterday even^g GD went to see Macdonald [sic] after his first full day's work on return from Lossiemouth, & found him with a bad headache & his eyes troubling him. A bad lookout!

MacD wants to try to resuscitate the Disarm^t Conference, so is going to Geneva before Lausanne, tho' it can only be for two days. It cannot be more than an exhortation unless the German delegation is there in full strength. I asked Neurath if he cldn't possibly be there when I met him on Monday, but he said it was physically impossible, as he must get back to Berlin & w^d need his few days there to prepare for Lausanne. It seems the P.M. asked him again yesterday, but he gave the same answer.

Yesterday evening in PHS I had suggested a leader on the service of the Customs in Manchuria, & as GD was seeing the P.M. he said he'd ask him how much importance he attached to the question. When he asked him the PM said very much, but he had not bn kept informed of the developments of that question – so he sent across from Downing Str at once to the F.O. asking Vansittart to come across. Van: came, & gave the opinion that nothing could be done until the Lytton Commssn had reported.

Typical F.O. advice. The Lytton Commssn cannot report until about Sept, by which time the Japs will have arranged the matter to their liking. And what has been done out there cannot be undone. The only possibility is to prevent its being done.

So the P.M. left it at that, & we took a feeble line in *T.T.*[141] It seems to me that the time is coming again for more <u>delegation</u> of authority & responsibility. Telephones etc have tended to concentrate authority in the principal; he is now expected to decide everything himself, & even <u>do</u> everything.

11 June   This morn^g first Noel-Baker & then Mr Arthur Henderson spoke to me over the telephone from Geneva. Henderson wanted to get me to come out there to cover the P.M.'s visit – as I had originally intended to do. I had rung up Baker about it from PHS the evening before. It was thought by the F.O., & apparently by the PM, that there was to be a meeting again at last of the General Com^tee of the Disarm^t Conf:, & the idea was that the P.M. w^d take the opportunity to make a big statement & try to push the whole thing forward. So I was going out to write about it. But when I talked to Philip Baker on the tel: I found that he was quite surprised by the idea, & that no meeting of the general Com^tee had been arranged.

He said it w^d be the simplest thing in the world to arrange it, but of course they w^d like to know that the P.M. & Simon really had some helpful suggestion to make. This I naturally could not guarantee. Baker therefore said he'd talk with Henderson & then probably ring me up.

This he did at my house this morn^g about ¼ past 10; & soon Henderson came to the 'phone & spoke to me himself. He said that if the P.M. wanted a meeting he had of course only to instruct his delegation to ask for it. He did not want the Gen: Com^tee to meet & then simply start wrangling all over again over the technical points so long discussed by the experts in the technical com^tee. He w^d however be ready to arrange a meeting of the General Com^tee on the Wed^y if that w^d serve a useful purpose. He w^d in the meantime try to get MacD,

[141] 'The Manchurian Customs': 9 June 1932.

Simon & Herriot to sit on the 'Bureau' i.e. Com^{tee} of Procedure on Tues: afternoon. Then a decision w^{d} be taken – & he suggested I sh^{d} go out.

I have not gone (I actually had a ticket for the Golden Arrow this morn^{g}, by which MacD & Simon are travelling) because, my medium being *T.T.*, I have to judge according to where I shall be in the best position to express views in it. I do not aim at influencing events by being an intermediary, so long as I am on *T.T.*, but by writing articles in *T.T.* It is no use my being at Geneva unless there is something there for me to write about. I had better do what I can through a leader here.

13 June I was rung up by C^{t} Bernstorff this morning. It seems that there has been rather a row in Berlin over Neurath's remark, as pub^{d} in *T.T.*, that Dr Brüning was in a 'state of exhaustion.' So Neurath from Berlin had asked Bernstorff to ask me to say now in *T.T.* that what Neurath had really said was that Brüning was 'tired'. Of course I absolutely refused. In the first place it w^{d} be pretending that we, *T.T.*, had made a mistake, whereas I had in fact read the statement through aloud to Neurath, & had printed it word for word as passed by him. In the second place, Neurath had actually in his conversation with me used much stronger words about Brüning. He had repeatedly spoken of the 'collapse of his nerves,' & I had myself toned this down, in the written statement subsequently passed by Neurath, to 'state of exhaustion'.

I said the most I could do w^{d} be to put into a leading article as soon as possible some phrase about Brüning having 'recovered v. quickly from his temporary fatigue.' Brüning did in fact take to his bed for a day or two, so he must have been very near 'exhaustion'. It seems he is reacting violently against the phrase now.

14 June I heard yesterday at the F.O. that the P.M. had turned out [sic] British agreement to the abolition of bombing-aeroplanes, & that it was at the instigation of Lord Londonderry (who is Min: for the Air). Lord L: has an undue amount of influence over MacDonald through Lady L.

No doubt there are strong arguments in favour of retaining bombers, but all the same it w^{d} be a big thing if all countries c^{d} agree to abolish them, & I c^{d} wish we were taking a strong lead in the matter. Simon has spoken indirectly in favour of abolition at Geneva.

London is of course open to air attack, & vulnerable to nothing else that matters.

It is a dreadful responsibility to take to prevent the abolition of bombing aeroplanes.

17 June At luncheon today Selby told me that when Henderson became Foreign Sec^y there was a bundle of papers at the end of the day waiting for him to go through them. He asked Selby 'Ought I to see these papers myself?'. Selby said 'Well. . .' v. slowly (he repeated his own way); but was interrupted by H:, who said 'Well, if that's how you feel, take them all away & bring me tomorrow only the absolutely essential ones.' Which ever afterwards Selby did. H: then used to initial things freely without reading them, on Selby's advice; but if Selby said, 'you really ought to see the documents in this paper,' Henderson w$^{\underline{d}}$ master them absolutely.

Of course it is Selby's job (as principal Pte Sec^y) to find out how much each master wants to see himself – that's why he was rather hesitant the first time.

Sir J. Simon, he said pathetically 'has no hours'. He just goes on with what he has in hand. He starts early & ends late. If his work takes him on till 10 p.m., he just goes through with it, & then has some supper.

This sort of thing is not popular with his Staff!

Tyrrell used to get through his boxes in 5 mins, Selby said – believing in oral information & in studying movements of pub: opinion by continually seeing journalists. Crowe[142] on the other hand believed in documents, & sat till midnight & later over his red-boxes.

23 June [. . .] Yesterday Hoover made his big proposal for an 'arms cut' of $\frac{1}{3}$ for all nations. I had to give the first reaction to it in this country in a leader, to be followed by a longer one tonight. I a little resented getting a message telephoned from Geneva from Sir J. Simon, asking us not to show 'the slightest embarrassment' over Hoover's proposal. It is a matter of importance that Hoover sh$^{\underline{d}}$ not feel that we are snorting about it, as it has a reaction upon Lausanne i.e. upon debts.

I do not at all mind a hint of his views from the For: Sec^y at any time, in fact I welcome it greatly. But one hates anything that looks like trying to manufacture public opinion. To be of any value the reaction of opinion must be sincere. And I sh$^{\underline{d}}$ have thought a For. Sec^y w$^{\underline{d}}$ have wished to hear its sincere & independent expression of

---

[142] Eyre Crowe (1864–1925): entered FO 1885, Asst U-Sec. 1912–19; Min. at Paris Peace Conf. 1919; PUS FO 1920–5; kt. 1911.

it – tho' at the same time I see & understand his point about the debts.

Anyhow, to judge by Simon's speech at Geneva, I felt more sympathetic towards Hoover's plan than he did.

24 June[143]   On thinking over what I have written above, I have realized that after all a '*Times*' leader is not meant always to be an expression of public opinion, but should more often be an instrument of policy.

Simon came back from Geneva yesterday morning, & I asked if I might see him & was given an appointment at 5.30 at the F.O. When we began to talk he said straight away 'your leader this morning was dead right' & then he added that he hoped we would go on in the same strain, & praise the Hoover Disarmament proposals. Then for about three quarters of an hour he pulled it to pieces & severely criticized Hoover's method of introducing it into the Disarmament discussions, which he indicated was done very hurriedly & largely from electoral considerations. He did say however that Hoover's *démarche* was a great stimulus to the Disarmament Conference – & I took this as a heading for the leader I wrote after leaving him.

Simon seemed a little nettled at Hoover all the way through. I think he felt that he himself (S) was really leading the discussions at Geneva & that they were doing pretty well; & now Hoover was complicating the situation & appearing to take the lead, which he cannot really do from Washington. [...]

A great many of Simon's points I embodied in the leader so I will not bother about them here. But there were some interesting sidelights. For instance he let out that he did not see why capital ships should not be abolished. He looked at me searchingly & enquiringly when he said that, & I remarked that reduction to 25,000 tons was quite enough for the present. Later on I said I thought Hoover was trying to go too fast & that it would be a big result of the present conference if a universal system of limitation were instituted & provision made for the reduction in size of certain weapons. He agreed very heartily 'you are quite right' he said. [...]

He has an extraordinary mind. At one point Selby came in saying that Sir Phillip Sassoon[144] wanted to talk to Simon personally on the telephone. 'Very well put him through' said Simon, & when he took up the receiver to listen to Sassoon I naturally stopped talking. Simon however deliberately asked me to finish what I was saying, (which was a question). He then went on with his telephone conversation with

[143] This entry is in Sylvia Kennedy's hand.

[144] Philip Sassoon (1888–1939): Unionist MP, Hythe 1912–39; U-Sec. for Air 1924–9, 1931–7, 1st Commissioner of Works 1937–9; suc. 3rd Bt 1912.

Sassoon (which was arranging about an aeroplane to take him back to Geneva on Saturday) – And I can only suppose that why he wanted me to finish what I was saying was so that he could think about it while he was talking to Sassoon. I think he has the most subtle & quickest & most complex mind I have ever come across though Wickham Steed[145] & G.D. run him pretty close.

When we began our conversation I said to him 'I appreciate very much your receiving me when you have such a short time & must be so rushed' 'Rushed' he said 'not at all, not a bit' & I'm bound to say that he did not give the appearance of being the least rushed – or tired – though after a very strenuous ten days of negotiation he had been in the train all night, flown over from Paris in the morning, was seeing people all day & going to a Court that night. He had just come from Buckingham Palace when I saw him, & he received Sir Walter Layton[146] the moment that I left.

I wonder how the routine work of the Foreign Office is done in the meantime? Simon seems to be absolutely indifferent to time & circumstance.

9 September: Kennedy to Reed Confidential: *The leading article on the German claim to equality of status which I have written tonight is in substantial agreement with the views of Sir John Simon, whom I saw just before writing it.*[147] *They are however his personal views – actually he let me do most of the talking, but he agreed to this line. He has seen MacD[onald], but the British Government has not yet formulated an official view. Simon confided to me that he was rather upset by the French dèmarche – sending him their draft reply to Germany before it was even finally approved in France. When Fleuriau brought it, he told me, he was careful not to read it before he discussed the matter with Fleuriau. He will take no responsibility for it. He has of course read it since, & described it to me as being 'not good!'.*

'The German Claim'

SIR JOHN SIMON returned to work at the Foreign Office yesterday; and the most urgent matter to engage his attention in the brief interval before he will be going to Geneva is clearly the claim recently put forward by Germany

---

[145] (Henry) Wickham Steed (1871–1956): head of For. Dept *The Times* 1914–18, Ed. 1919–22; afterwards pvt. Sec. to Ld Rothermere; overseas broadcaster, BBC 1937–47. See his *Hitler: Whence & Whither* (1937).

[146] Walter Thomas Layton (1885–1966): Ed. *Economist* 1921–38; kt. 1930; cr. Ld Layton of Dane Hill 1947.

[147] 'The German Claim' 10 September 1932.

for equality of status in armaments ... The moment must soon come when the British Cabinet will have to adopt a definite policy in what has become an urgent matter. To some diplomatic difficulties time brings a satisfactory solution. In this case delay is more likely to provoke an act of impatience which will irretrievably ruin the prospects of the Disarmament Conference. There is a danger that the new ideals of cooperation and mutual forbearance may be lost in a reversion to unchecked competition in armaments, with all that that implies of mutual suspicion, rivalry, and unrest. The time is critical. The principle of the limitation of armaments is at stake ... the whole sense of the Treaty of Versailles is, indeed, against the maintenance of the large disparity between the armaments of the victorious and the vanquished States. The problem that has become urgent is to diminish that disparity be agreement.

There can, of course, be no sort of doubt that the best and most satisfactory method of diminishing it would be to decrease the armaments of the victorious Powers ... But the course of the Disarmament Conference has shown beyond any possibility of doubt that certain countries are definitely unwilling at the present moment to make really drastic cuts in their armed strengths ... the leaders of many important countries have a feeling of responsibility to their own citizens which forbids for the present the hasty or indiscriminate abandonment of arms; and the sense of insecurity in Europe is in no small measure due to the activities of wide sections of the German people, who openly boast of their military instincts, and to the defiant speeches of one of the leading members of the Nationalist Government which is putting forward the claim to equality. Germany cannot properly demand the equal rights to which membership of the League of Nations undoubtedly entitle her unless she intends to be a loyal member of the League and to abide by the doctrines for which it stands. If some reasonable proof can be given that Gemany really intends to do her part in promoting her ideal of European solidarity, it should be possible to agree to her possession, in a limited degree, of all those weapons which other countries retain. ...

9 September   Lunched yesterday with a member of the F.O. who shall be nameless (even here), who said that he thought Simon was the worst For: Sec^y he had ever had anything to do with − because he lacked conviction & a policy. The criticism may be true. For one thing, we have had v.[five] For: Sec^{ies} lately; & for another, Simon's qualities & extreme cleverness make him more suitable for the work of a diplomatist than of a directing For: Sec^y.

I heard yesterday that Lothian[148] is arguing that he & his Liberal

[148] Philip Henry Kerr (1882–1940): journalist & statesman; Ed. *Round Table* 1910–16; pvt. Sec. to PM 1916–21; Dir. of United Newspapers Ltd 1921–2; sec. Rhodes Trust 1925–39; Chanc. Duchy of Lancaster 1930–1; Parliamentary U-Sec. India Office 1931–2; Amb. in Washington 1939–40; suc. 11th Marquess of Lothian 1930, kt. 1940. See his *The Issues in British Foreign Policy* (1938).

colleagues sh$^{\underline{d}}$ clear out of the Cabinet, which is essentially Tory. I hope his view won't prevail. There is more national work for the National Govt to do. It may before it expires become wholly or nearly wholly Conservative. But I fear that if it becomes so too early the revulsion to Socialism will be very great at the General Election. Also for the outside world it w$^{\underline{d}}$ be much better that the Govt sh$^{\underline{d}}$ continue to represent all Parties.

10 September   Yesterday Sir J. Simon returned to the F.O. from his v. short holiday at St Andrews. I put in to Ronald,[149] his Sec^y, for a meeting, & S. asked me to come at 6. S was still feeling holiday-ish, & began by saying 'Well, I don't think I've anything to tell you; what do you think about this German claim to arms equality?' Given an opening in this way, I went ahead, & developed my idea of a policy – namely, that we must go all out for limitation. Serious reduction of armaments is out of the question at the moment. That is the snag of Hoover's proposals. They propose too much. Even the principle of limitation is endangered by this German demand – which, if refused by the French, may lead to a renewal of unrestricted competition. That w$^{\underline{d}}$ increase unrest & suspicion everywhere. To salvage limitation sh$^{\underline{d}}$ be the immediate purpose of Brit: policy.

This I said with the idea of getting a definite policy into Simon's mind, remembering the remark of my F.O. friend, & also my own previous experiences with S.

He listened closely & said he agreed.

We then discussed methods.

I said I thought Italy must be brought in; but I hoped that British policy w$^{\underline{d}}$ be put forward firmly & clearly. He agreed about Italy. [...]

13 September   I had luncheon today with Temperley, who was extraordinarily full of interesting information, even for him.

The P.M. & Simon do not get on at all well, & the latest row is over this German claim to arms equality. When Bernstorff was saying to Simon the other day that he understood that the Brit. Govt was favourable in principle to the German claim, Simon cut him short, & said he had no right to assume that. But MacD: had said that both to Brüning, at Stimson's villa outside Geneva, & to v. [on] Papen at Lausanne – so naturally Bernstorff had the right to assume it.

[149] Nigel Bruce Ronald (1894–1973): entered diplomatic service 1920; pvt. sec. to PUS 1927; asst pvt sec. to FS 1929–34; 1st Sec. 1930, Counsellor 1934; Asst U-Sec. 1942; Amb. to Lisbon 1947–54; kt 1946.

When both MacD: & Simon were at Geneva, Temperley says it was ocularly visible how ill at ease Simon became – & no wonder; because MacD: was all the time finding out what people were thinking of Simon! He used Sir Thomas Horder a good deal for this purpose. Horder had come in & sat with Temperley for $\frac{3}{4}$ hour questioning him about Simon; & had done the same with Cadogan. Cadogan had given nothing away (tho' he doesn't think much of Simon). Not so Sir Eric Drummond. Temperley had a meal with Sir Eric at which one of the P.M.'s Sec[ies] was present (Ralph Glyn[150] I think he said); & when this Sec: sought an opinion about Simon he got it hot & strong, Drummond not mincing his words. Of course to any League man Simon is taboo, for he has no convictions & little sincerity. Temperley says that when he puts the F.O. policy before the Cabinet he does it in a tentative & diffident manner, almost apologetically. In regard to air bombing, for instance, about which Simon does really feel rather strongly, he gains dialectical points over L[d] Londonderry (not v. difficult) & then gives in to him.

In regard to German armaments – immediately after the Armistice, & even before Peace was signed, a big German armaments firm packed up all its machinery, & even some castings, & sent them down the Rhine in barges into Holland; & has since set them up there! Similarly Krupps designing dept: transferred its designs to Sweden, & has set up in business there; & a clever German chemist has set up a gas factory in Russia – he has discovered a gas which can be used for commercial purposes, but by a simple change he can produce mustard tear gas, for use in war!

As for the German equality claims, T: sees the only possible solution along the same lines as I do – granting the Germans the right to make samples of the forbidden weapons – so as to be on an equal footing. Actually we cannot prevent them by force – so it is best to give them the right by agreement & try to control the numbers – which may be possible now, but will not be later.

Of the German demand[s] the one which the French like least is that for a militia – & this is a demand which Temp: regards as reasonable. There are a number of semi-private armies in Germany, & the Govt wants to have one which will attract the German youth away from the others. The French of course regard this as the thin edge of the wedge of conscription.

Another request which the French detest is the right for the Reichswehr to enter the Rhineland in case of riots etc.

[150] Ralph George C. Glyn (1885–1960): Coalition Unionist MP, Clackmannan & E. Stirlingshire 1918–22; Unionist, Abingdon div. of Berkshire 1924–53; PPS to PM 1931–5; Ld Pres. 1935–7; cr. 1st Baron Glyn 1953.

I hear (not from Temperley that MacDonald is really a v. sick man.

19 September   Had a talk with Palmstierna[151] this morn^g, who as usual was full of interesting pol: gossip. He has good sources of information from Berlin, & says that the majority of the Cabinet there are in favour of getting out of the L.o N. & re-arming. Neurath (the For: Min.) would prefer to stay in the League, but he does not count for an enormous lot, & is anyhow just as 'Nationalist' as the rest of them. Palmstierna thinks that Simon & MacD: both dislike v. much dealing with this lot, & do not go ahead with the negotiations about 'Arms equality' because they hope that there may soon be another Govt. A vain hope, I fancy! I quite understand that they do not want the 'militarists' to score a success; but if they don't make a partial concession & come to an agreement with Papen & Co., it is possible that these gentry wl snap their fingers at us & take what they want. *A vise la Fin*, seems to me a good motto for diplomacy – & in the end what power is going to prevent the Germans from re-arming as they like? We can't do it – therefore make a bargain while we can, & preserve the principle of limitation.

   I believe Communism alone will prevent the re-armament of Europe. [...]

20 September   It seems that Simon said to Leeper[152] this morn^g (this is Leeper's own account) – 'I want to see some one from *The Times*. Who is there?'! Leeper took the broad hint, & said he thought I had gone to Geneva, but that there was Graves.[153] So Simon told him to send for Graves, who must have bn astonished, but no doubt delighted to go, & S. poured out to him a justification of his policy (or lack of policy) in the matter of the German claim to arms equality.

   This reason [sic] of this strange manoeuvre of Simon's is that my last leader[154] was slightly critical of him. He therefore wanted to get another leader tonight supporting him. Leeper told me it was 'most important'. *The Times* comment w^d, he said, be telegraphed out to the Delegations at Geneva tomorrow morning, & it w^d help Simon v. much with the French if they got the impression that Brit: pub: opinion were

   [151] Erik Kule Palmstierna (1877–1959): Swedish diplomat; Min. in London 1920–37.
   [152] Reginald Wildig A. Leeper (1888–1968): temporary clerk FO 1918; 2nd Sec. diplomatic service 1920–9; returned to FO 1929, Counsellor 1933, Asst U-Sec. 1940; Amb. in Athens, 1943–6, in Rio de Janiero, 1946–8; kt. 1945.
   [153] Philip P. Graves (1876–1953): middle eastern specialist *The Times* 1919–46.
   [154] 'The British Statement': 19 Sept. 1932, p.11.

really behind S. in his attitude. I do not however think Brit: opinion
<u>is</u>.

'The British Statement'

It must frankly be confessed that the present German Ministry, which is less
sensitive to foreign opinion than any which the country has possessed since
the War, might have been more impressed by a document that gave clearer
indication of action than this British Memorandum. In its opening paragraphs
the British Government refer to its contents as 'observations' and 'comments';
and the truth is that in this urgent matter – for one party has unfortunately
the power to give it urgency – reasoning and exhortations to patience may
have little influence upon the present rulers of Germany. The practical
matter which the non-German Powers have to decide is whether or not a
system which fundamentally differentiates against Germany and the other
vanquished States is going to be maintained. In this country practically
everybody will agree – and the British Government agree – that the German
claim to equality of status is substantially a good one; and if there were a
real prospect that the next stage of the Disarmament Conference would
result in the total prohibition for all States of capital ships, submarines,
military aircraft, tanks, and heavy artillery it would be a wholly sufficient
answer to Germany to ask her to await the end of the Conference. But the
most optimistic observer of its proceedings hitherto can entertain no such
illusion ... Is it not possible to say now to Germany that categorical
restrictions which are not, within a certain period, imposed upon all by the
Disarmament Convention will no longer be imposed upon her? There is
reason to believe that the Government of Germany would at this time accept
limits in size and in numbers which would keep her armaments below any
corresponding limits that may be imposed upon themselves by the other
Powers. ...

21st After consultatn with Brumwell[155] I did <u>not</u> write the asked for
leader last night. Brum: had been in comnctn with GD, who is still on
holiday in Yorkshire, & GD had particularly commended my leader of
Mon: morn^g [19 Sept.] & its policy; so Brum: did not want to say
anything now that w^d weaken it.

22 *September* Saw Sgr Grandi this morn^g for the first time since he has
become Ambassdr in London. A friendly talk. He said twice he had
found our last 2 leaders on Arms Equality for Germany[156] 'very
interesting' & that he agreed with the views they expressed. Those also

[155] George M. Brumwell (1872–1963): night Ed. *The Times* 1908–22; Asst Ed. 1922–34.
[156] 'Equality of Arms at Geneva': 22 Sept. 1932, p.11.

were substantially Mussolini's views – give Germany equality in principle, but obtain at the same time an assurance that she will not abuse it by starting a competition in armaments. That had been his answer to Schubert[157] in Rome (as I had also heard from Bernstorff – keep within the Treaty, Musso: had said).

Grandi is quieter & more rested looking than when I used to see him in Geneva, but he has developed Mussolini's trick of opening up his eyeballs in such a way that the white shows all round the iris! I told him about next Wed^y's Cabinet, & the critical situation within the Govt, caused by the threat of Liberal secession. So he said he w^d not return to Italy at the beginning of next week, as he had thought of doing. Grandi called me 'my dear Kennedy' & gave me a hint to call him 'Grandi' pure & simple – or at least so I interpreted his parting remark. We shall see. I like him v. much. [...]

'Equality of Arms at Geneva'

The [German demand for equality of armaments] is not legally sustainable, in the sense that no Article or phrase in the Treaty of Versailles explicitly promises equality of armaments to Germany. But numerical equality is not demanded; and the Treaty abounds in indications that there was no intention of maintaining indefinitely the wide disparity of strengths and the differentiation of status that were then imposed. It was certainly intended that the gap should be narrowed, and that all members of the League should be treated on the same footing. In Article 164 of the Treaty, and in a passage in the Allied Note which was sent in reply to German observations on the conditions of peace as first proposed, it was clearly contemplated that some sort of deviation from the establishment laid down in the Peace Treaty might be possible after the entry of Germany into the League of Nations – and she became a member six years ago. The obligation is none the less binding because it is moral rather than legal; and for every reason it seems desirable that the other Powers should now as soon as possible repair the omission of the July Resolution and make to Germany as precise a declaration as possible of their intention to honour their moral obligation. Of their intention to reduce the difference between the armed strengths of the victors and vanquished in the late War there can be no doubt. It was made abundantly clear in the speeches delivered by all the leading delegates during the general discussion in the early days of the Conference. The principle of placing Germany upon the same footing as other States has in fact been implicit in almost every utterance; but it has not yet found its way into the formal phraseology of a Resolution. ...

[157] Carl von Schubert (1882–1947): German diplomat; entered dip. service 1906; U-Sec. *Auswärtige Amt* 1925–30; Amb. in Rome 1930–2.

26 September Harold Nicolson came to luncheon today, just with S: & me; & after luncheon I delivered to him the long delayed message from L^y Vansittart, without however mentioning her name. He responded quite frankly. He said he was just beginning a book on the Peace Conference; & then he wanted to write one on Curzon. That w^d take him till about next autumn. After that he w^d v much like to return to the F.O. – but not to the Diplomatic Service. For one thing his wife would not go to a post abroad.

He said he would not have left (Berlin) if they had bn willing to restore him to the F.O. Now, as long [as] they w^d give him the pay of a Counsellor, & restore him his pension rights, he w^d certainly return, when he has written his books, if he was given the chance. I told him I w^d like to be an ambassador. (when he said he w^d only take an F.O. post. What was in his mind was, I think, that he could not stand the slow gradations through Ministers' posts abroad – but w^d accept an Embassy! He has tried to dodge some of the drudgery).

28 September [...] By the way, Poliakoff, who generally gets hold of the right end of the stick tho' he exaggerates & is biassed, told me yesterday that he had heard that Simon was so upset after reading our leader on Monday morning (19th) on his Memorandum, that he 'had to be bolstered up'. Poliakoff is just back from Paris, where he has seen Berthelot[158] & others, & he must have got his information from them. If true, even partially, I think it shows that such criticism as there was was justified, & that Simon felt he had made a blunder – that is what would have upset him. And I c^d see from the way that Leeper talked to me that S. must have bn much agitated. Also, public opinion is a fetish with Simon.

30 Sept: I hear that in the Cabinet re-shuffle this week Baldwin[159] was in favour of moving Simon to another office – & presumably putting Irwin in his place. But MacDonald demurred. It must come later, no doubt. MacD: likes having a pliant man!

Yesterday Temperley was here at luncheon [...][160] [he] told me a lot of interesting things about the secret re-arming of Germany, & the *dossier formidable* which M. Barrère had talked to me about. On the

[158] Philippe Joseph L. Berthelot (1866–1934): French diplomat; entered *Ministère des Affaires Etrangères* 1895; Sec-Gen. *Ministère des Affaires Etrangères* 1920–32.
[159] Stanley Baldwin (1867–1947): Con. MP Bewdley 1908–37; Financial Sec. to Treasury 1917–21; Pres. Board of Trade 1921–2; Chanc. of Exchequer 1922–3; PM 1923, 1924–9; Ld Pres. 1931–5; PM 1935–7; Con. Ldr 1923–7; cr. Earl Baldwin of Bewdley 1937.
[160] The entry from this point forward is in Sylvia Kennedy's hand.

whole the Germans are avoiding flagrant breaches of the clauses of the Treaty of Versailles, but in the spirit they are breaking them all the time, because to the utmost of their ability they are re-building their military system. They are in particular concentrating on industrial organization, in such a way that it will be possible to manufacture the weapons now forbidden to them in the shortest possible time. In other words they are not building the weapons, but the machinery for the weapons.

5 October I had luncheon yesterday with Ld Lytton who had returned the day before from his mission to Manchuria on behalf of the League (I had met him at Victoria, having had a letter from L^{y} Lytton from Italy). He has a remarkably good intellect, & it is a great pity he has such a tired manner, for otherwise he w^{d} be a first-class man. However for reporting on a situation his qualities do excellently; & his impartiality & honesty give one a v. good idea of what is really going on out there. He convinced me yesterday of two important points – that the 'Manchukuo' govt is a sham, & that the population is almost wholly hostile to it & to the Japanese. So I said that in my leader last night.[161]

Public Opinion and the Lytton Report

Two points the Report makes absolutely clear for the first time – that the Manchukuo Government is a sham, and that the population, which is predominantly Chinese, is hostile to it. The plan drawn up by the Commission would make of Manchukuo a really autonomous State with only nominal dependence, instead of a really dependent State with an only nominal sovereignty.

Some day the Japanese people may come to take the view that the subjugation, and the maintenance in subjugation, of a hostile population, living in contiguity with its parent race, is an unprofitable enterprise. But in the meantime no good purpose can be served by upbraiding Japan, or by making censorious comment upon her recent conduct ... Meanwhile there must be no more compromise over principles, nor need principles be in any jeopardy so long as the State of Manchukuo is not recognised. Its so-called Cabinet is known now to be a collection of ineffective ciphers. The population is certified to be contemptuous of them. It is clear that in working for the ultimate adoption of the Lytton proposals international diplomacy will be working for the welfare of the Manchurians; and Japan herself must certainly in the long run prefer their prosperity to their discontent and hostility.

[161] 'Public Opinion and the Lytton Report': 5 Oct. 1932, p.15.

7 October Luncheon with Philip Noel-Baker yesterday, & then on to the F.O., where I had a heart-to-heart talk with Selby, who has bn the prime mover in the pro-French policy which we have bn criticizing in *T.T.* He seemed to me for the first time to be doubtful of his own policy – so I hope we are having some effect. His argument was largely an apologia.

Noel-Baker gave me his version of the origin of MacDonald's proposal for a 4-Power Conference in London. When Neurath (the Ger: For: Min) was in Geneva for the <u>Assembly</u> & Council – he was 'not discussing' disarmament – Henderson was determined to have a talk with him. Emissaries hinted to Neurath that the former English For: Sec^y w$^{\underline{d}}$ much like to see the former Ger: Ambssdr in London! But the hint was ignored.

So one day when the Council was going to meet at 11 Henderson (who now has nothing to do with the Council) went there early, & paced the corridor by which the delegates had to go in.

He thus intercepted Neurath! 'How glad I am to see you, my dear Minister' etc etc 'Do come & see me.' Neurath c$^{\underline{d}}$ not say no; & paid H: a visit in his hotel. They got on well; & H: proposed a formula which he thought the French might accept, & which he hoped v. much the Germans would too. Neurath said he w$^{\underline{d}}$ consult his Govt & come back to Geneva <u>for the Assembly</u> but co-inciding with the next meeting of the Disarm^t Bureau! Thus Henderson hoped to bring off a Franco-German reconciliation, & a resumption of the Disarm^t Conference.

<u>MacDonald heard of this</u> through Simon – & immediately issued an invitation to France & Ger: (& Italy) to come to London – where <u>he</u>, MacD, w$^{\underline{d}}$ naturally preside!

The jealousy – & I fear hatred – between the two is intense.

GENEVA *9 Oct:* Have heard from 2 sources of the terrific fights & intrigues that have gone on over the proposed modification of the Secretariat – i.e. the dropping of the three posts of Under-Secretary, which are admitted to be superfluous. But it was found to be absolutely impossible to elect a Frenchman (Avenol) to be Sec^y-Gen, unless another Italian & another German were elected to be Under-Secretaries! And they could not very well merely remove the Jap – so three posts at about £3000 a year are kept going on account of national vanities!

10 October Have just had a talk with Henderson, who poor man is feeling hotter than ever against MacDonald. He (H) had arranged for Neurath to come & see him tomorrow here, when he returned to Geneva for the remainder of the Assembly; & Herriot had promised to come from Paris if Henderson c$^{\underline{d}}$ tell him there was a real chance of agreement. Then MacD's sudden invitatn to the Fr: & Ger: Govts knocked all this on the head!

H. was sarcastic about MacD, who when he did come here had made no contribution to the Disarm$^{\underline{t}}$ discussion, but had spent most of his time 'walking round the lake with a lady'. He was 'the only head of a Delegation who had not called upon him (H)'.

When we talked about the guarantees of security which France w$^{\underline{d}}$ be asking, H. was interesting about Locarno. He said the French w$^{\underline{d}}$ be quite satisfied about Locarno if it was interpreted as Austen Chamberlain had originally interpreted it. But no British Govt had given any written endorsement of Chamberlain's interpretation. If the French got that, H: said, they would not expect from us any further guarantees in Europe.

Had a short walk-&-talk with Anthony Eden[162] this morning. His views are sound.

On looking back at my account of Henderson above I feel I have given rather a false impression of my talk with him, for most of it _was_ about disarmam^{t} & the means of bringing it about – it certainly was not all abuse of MacDonald! & he did say other things about MacD, such as how he had asked him whether he would not like to let 'Tommy Horder' have a look at him – MacD. having Sir Thos: Horder here with him last April, & Henderson being then of course in a v. feeble state. He is much better now. And he has got back all his _feelings_. And when he _is_ angry he speaks out.

In regard to the Locarno business, H: told me that during the Naval Conference in London he had worked all one day getting an understanding with the French Delegation about its interpretation, & after 10 at night he went home thinking it was all settled. Next morning he saw in the papers that _nothing_ was settled – & I gather that what he meant was that MacD, hearing of what he had been doing, had undone it all at once! MacD is certainly up to tricks of that sort. Of course in substance MacD may have bn right, for all I know.

Henderson said that when he had been For: Sec^{y} he had come to realize more than ever before the need of time. Time was necessary always for ideas to penetrate & still more for the consequent action to be taken. And so it is to a particular degree with disarmament.

10 October –Kennedy to Geoffrey Dawson: _[The people that Kennedy saw_

---

[162] (Robert) Anthony Eden (1897–1977): Con. MP Warwick & Leamington 1923–57; PPS to Austen Chamberlain 1926–9; U-Sec. FO 1931–4; Ld Privy Seal 1934–5 & Min. for LoN Affairs 1935; FS 1935–8, Dominions Sec. 1939–40; Sec. for War 1940; FS 1940–

this weekend are. . .] making the most inconceivable bargains over their promises to vote for Avenol as the next Secy Gen.! The British Delegation here is v. keen about the British Govt having a strong policy, much on the lines we have advocated, & I have sent a message on those lines again tonight. [. . .]

I feel about Disarmament that the fear of German re-armament might be made into a most potent weapon for jolting the others into really doing something about reduction – i.e. give the Germans liberty to re-arm, but on the condition that they hold that liberty in abeyance for say one year or two years, to let the other countries show if they mean business. One of the main points gained here is that all are talking now much more in Continental terms, & do not expect us to come in beyond Locarno.

BERNE *12 Oct:* I said goodbye to Henderson this morn^g, & agreed with him that it <u>was</u> rather hard to be left out of the Four-Power Conference altogether. Of course, as Pres: of the Disarm^t Conf:, he ought to be invited; but there is the diff^y of him & MacD.

Went on & saw Sir Eric Drummond for a short time. He was in good form. He is v. good at keeping a clear policy thro' the maze of Geneva ideas – tho' his policy, I may say, was precisely that of *T.T.*, & it is possible that his mind had just bn refreshed by reading it! Anyhow he certainly <u>is</u> good at having a line of policy, whatever the intricacies. His weakness may be that his policy sometimes, esp: in semi-personal matters, does seem to be the line of least resistance.[163]

D. was in favour of Lausanne as the venue for the 4-Power Conference. Quite right. But by the papers I see that London & Geneva have bn talked of as the alternatives during the last 2 days. I telegraph^d suggesting Lausanne to GD last night.

D's policy was not <u>precisely</u> that of *T.T.* (as I see I wrote on previous page). He proposed a slight modification – that in effectives & tonnage Germany sh^d, even when her liberty is regained, keep within the Treaty limits, but distribute & dispose of her strength within those limits as she likes. An improvement.

As I left his room I said 'I tell everybody you are the man who ought to direct our policy & be at the head of the F.O. I hope you don't mind.' He chuckled, evidently pleased. We were both in separate doorways by that time, going out, so he said nothing.

That same morning I saw Pierre Cot,[164] a Radical, in the French

---

5, 1951–5; PM & Con. Ldr 1955–7; kt. 1954, cr. Earl of Avon 1961. See his *Facing the Dictators* (1960).

[163] The entry from this point forward was continued at Boulogne.

[164] Pierre Cot (1895–1977): Deputy 1928–42, 1951–8; U-Sec. *Ministère des Affaires Etrangères* 1932; Min. of Air 1933–7; exiled 1942–5.

Delegation, & really keen about disarm[t]. Young, eloquent, & quick in argument. We talked about 'International Dumps' idea – arms stacked in various countries in the charge of the League. To my mind impracticable – but by the time he'd done talking about it there didn't seem any reason left against it! Although useless materially, I believe psychologically some such plan might help.

Pierre Cot <u>would allow</u> small protective tanks to Germany. Drummond said afterwds this was a great advance – he had not before heard his Rad-theoretical mind admit any possible exception to the principle 'no re-armament.'

BOULOGNE *14 Oct:* I had a most interesting day in Paris to-day, long talks with Gen. Weygand[165] & then Ld Tyrrell.

Gen. Weygand doesn't believe in mincing his words. I was astonished at his outspokenness. After I had begun with a few introductory words, in which I mentioned what people were saying in Geneva, '*Genève prépare la guerre*' he said, evidently believing, like Foch, in taking the offensive. He then went on to blackguard the bosch for about $\frac{3}{4}$ hour – almost in a gentle manner, but his words were a sustained invective. He called them *bêtes sauvages* once, & another moment said that France *avait à ses côtés des chiens grundants* – the two growling dogs being Germany & Italy.

'*Je ne désarme pas*' he said. '*Je suis responsable de la dèfense du pays*'.

After he had talked about the 'hypocrisy' of Geneva at the beginning he recapitulated all the German crimes before, during & since the War, & said it was criminal to forget them. When he was out of breath for a moment I said 'Certainly, M. le Général, it is wrong to forget them. But will the time never come when one can forgive them?' He said 'You are quite right. But they must repent first. They have never repented. They are still arrogant against us.' '*Que MM. les assassins commencement est un proverbe français*' he said – & later on in the conversation he said, with a twinkle in his eyes '*Que MM les Allemands commencement.*'

When I talked about the equality in armaments – that is, status – which the Germans are claiming, he hopped about in his chair, & obviously regarded the idea as simply monstrous. Later on he implied that anybody must be a pervert who spoke of the French & the Germans as morally on the same level.

He had an immense belief in British influence. Everybody has just

---

[165] Maxime Weygand (1867–1965): French army officer; Chief of Gen. Staff 1931–5; retd 1935; C-in-C in the Levant 1939, recalled to take command in northern France on 19 May 1940, it was on his advice that Petain sought an armistice with Germany in June. See his *Mémoires* (3 vols 1950–7).

now. And they believe, I am sure, that England will come in on the side of <u>whichever is in the right</u>.

In one point I did get a little encouragement from him. I said 'My ideal w$^{\underline{d}}$ be that every country, like France, sh$^{\underline{d}}$ train their conscripts for only one year. Then we sh$^{\underline{d}}$ be getting near the ideal of a defensive militia.' He accepted this idea, even for Germany. The reason was, I think, because Foch was in favour of that in 1919 – but was overruled by LlG & L$^{\underline{d}}$ Robt Cecil[166] – it sounds too absurd – who insisted on a voluntary long-service army of 100,000 men. 'In this very room' said Weygand 'They argued about it, & F. was forced to give way'.

I also remarked that in practice we could not prevent Germany re-arming, so it was better to control & limit it while we could. He agreed that we cldn't really stop them, but <u>he didn't mind their re-arming</u> – like Benesh (at first).

At the end he said '*Vous attendiez de moi quelque chose de plus intelligent, n'est ce-pas?*' I remained silent, & he repeated the question, so I said something about '*J'espérais quelque chose qui pourrait contribuant à un accord avec l'Allemagne.*' '*Eh bien, mes vues ne sout certainement pas celles de M. Herriot*' he said. [...]

When I went on to Tyrrell, T: told me Weygand was not the man he was – & this I am glad to believe. T: was in excellent form, bubbling with his bons mots. [...]

T: believes the German claim to re-arm to be 'bluff', in the sense that they don't mean to really. I hope he is right. He considers we can accept the new French Security Plan. He attaches great importance to Mr Stimson's latest declaration. 'That was about a Consultative Pact, wasn't it?' said I 'What <u>is</u> the good of a <u>consultative</u> pact?' 'Dope' he said quite earnestly 'All these Pacts are dope'. And he's right. I see it. There's a lot of war neurosis about <u>still</u> – these Pacts are sedatives for the nerves of the nations.

Afterwards he developed the idea of Stimson's no neutrality idea, & how it made it easier for us to come into the French Security Plan & yet not have difficulties with the American navy. He told me I must go & see Norman Davis,[167] who is now in London, & who will probably be Sec^{y} of State in U.S.A. if the Democrats get in.

---

[166] (Edgar Algernon) Robert Gascoyne-Cecil (1864–1958): 3rd s. of 3rd Marquis of Salisbury; Con. MP Marylebone E. 1906–10, Hitchin 1911–23; U-Sec. FO 1915–18 & Min. of Blockade 1916–18; Ld Privy Seal 1923–4; Chanc. Duchy of Lancaster 1924–7; Pres., LoN Union 1923–45; cr. Viscount Cecil of Chelwood 1923; organized the peace ballot of 1934–5; awarded Nobel Peace Prize 1937.

[167] Norman Hezekiah Davis (1878–1944): mb. of reparations & financial commissions Paris Peace Conf.; Asst Sec. of Treasury 1919–20; U-Sec. of State 1920–1; delegate to World Disarmament Conf., Geneva 1932, Chm. of delegation 1933; head of delegation to London Naval Conf. 1935; delegate to Brussels Nine Power Treaty Conf. 1937.

After luncheon he happened to talk about Mussolini. Five years ago he had bn talking to him, & had asked him how long he reckoned it w$^{\underline{d}}$ take him really to establish his regime. 'Ten years' had said M. 'if I can control my extremists'. 'That' said Tyrrell 'showed the greatness of the man'. But his position is difficult now, because Balbo is being too extreme for him, & has ousted Grandi, who stands for sanity. 'Mussolini doesn't shoot' said T: 'And Balbo likes to.' He makes out that Balbo was responsible for the murder of Matteotti.[168]

I told T: about the difficult situation at Geneva, & how the French dominated it, & we did not play the part we ought to. I told him I had had a talk on the telephone about it with GD from the Ritz last night, & GD was rather for keeping out of Geneva. 'Tell him we won't get on by getting out' said T., a good quip, which I must convey to GD.

T: criticized us (*T.T.*) for having criticized Simon in a leader (which I wrote).[169] I defended it. I believe it corresponded with pub: opinion & did jolt France forward a little, for the French Govt pays extraordinary attention to our public opinion. '*Mais ça coûte cher, quelque fois*' said T. (made his position more difficult, I suppose).

He said that last time Simon had come through Paris from Geneva he had arr$^{\underline{d}}$ by aeroplane at 10.30, & had to go to the Quai d'Orsay at 11.30. 'So that gave me just an hour to pump the stuff into him' said T '& then he had $1\frac{1}{2}$ hour with Herriot'. Then he flew on again to London at 2. T: said he was always looking at his watch when he was explaining things. All this seems wrong. A man can't think out a policy like that. Simon is usurping the functions of his ambassadors, & neglecting his own chief duty, which is first to formulate & then to direct a policy.

By the way, when he was talking about Mussolini Tyrrell told me that Oswald Mosley[170] had a terrific dressing down from him when he had bn to see him in Rome & announced his intention of founding British Fascism. Musso: told him it was quite unsuitable for England. This, Tyrrell said, was another example of Musso's big-mindedness.

CALAIS *15 Oct:* (I am writing this from notes made at the time) On the day before I left Geneva – that is on Oct 11 – I had a long talk

[168] Giacomo Matteotti (1885–1924): Italian politician; Sec-Gen. Socialist Party; Deputy 1919–24; abducted & murdered June 1924, after denouncing Mussolini in parliament.

[169] That of 19 Sept.

[170] Oswald Ernald Mosley (1896–1980): Unionist MP Harrow div. of Middlesex 1918–22, Indep. 1922–4, Lab. 1924; Lab MP Smethwick 1926–31; Chanc. Duchy of Lancaster 1929–30; founded British Union of Fascists 1932; imprisoned during WWII. See his *My Life* (1938).

with Benesh, who was more earnest & less lucid than usual, & went on talking for over an hour.

He regards Schleicher as the dominant figure in Europe. He considers that the democratic movement in Germany is suppressed & cannot recover for at least 5 years. Then there may be something like a revolution; but the danger is that Schleicher may in the meantime have militarized Germany & become the accepted master of the nation, like Bismarck – (who was v. unpopular when he began).

Do not let us on any account, he urged, open the door to re-armament. Grant Germany theoretic equality. I asked him how that worked out practically, & a lit[tle] bit argued him out of his position. He had to agree that Germany will in any case make herself some of the forbidden arms – therefore the wisest thing to do is to make a bargain about it while we have the upper hand.

Benesh at first talked as if he w^d rather that the Germans re-armed without any agreement & so put themselves in the wrong. Each side is jockeying to get the other in the wrong. He changed a little later however – tho' probably those are still his real feelings.

He believes that Schleicher desires the failure of the Disarm^t Conference. Certainly true, I sh^d say. B: told me an extraordinary thing about Schleicher – that he had approached him (B) to act as an intermediary to the French General Staff to arrange an alliance between Germany & France – the idea being that then France w^d welcome a strong military Germany!

Benesh favours a new European system in which all bilateral (or other) alliances will be merged, all countries being on a footing of equality & Germany of course included. But what else is the League of Nations? When things are settled like this, he said, England will come in too. I said yes, if all countries were really contented & had not the sense of injustice which they at present have.

Benesh was very earnest throughout this conversation & insisted that Europe was at a turning-point & must take the right road or the wrong one – which must lead straight to Communism. Yet he evidently regards the rise of Schleicher with something very like terror! That is the tragedy. There seems no middle road – unless England can build it. Simon can't. Probably nobody could, but something much bigger is wanted than the diplomatic accommodation at which he excels.

The spectre of a resurgent Germany is scaring central Europe!

21 October –Kennedy to Ebbutt:[171] [...] *There is little enthusiasm here now for holding the Four-Power Conference, but one never quite knows what is in the*

[171] Letter in *The Times* archive.

P.M.'s mind. Simon proposes (this is confidential at present) to draw up a big disarmament plan for ourselves, get it passed by the Cabinet, & go to Paris & Rome with it. I do not personally see v. much hope in this procedure. It seems to me so obvious that what the Germans want is equality of treatment, & here is our Government always thinking it necessary to concoct plans with France before it can move.

My reading of the situation is that we could make quite a good bargain with Germany over armaments now, & one which would be fair to France – but there is a terrible outcry from the pacifists, who have influence with MacD[onald] & Simon, as soon as ever any mention is made of giving Germany a right to re-arm, however nominal. Yet in six months time Germany may refuse a proposition which she would accept now.

I wonder if you agree with this?

We are doing our best to push the Government into taking a strong lead, but Simon is better at keeping an open mind than taking a lead.

21 October   – Kennedy to Geoffrey Dawson Private: [...] *It seems to me that Wigram's[172] letter, & also the memorandum, both illustrate what in my humble opinion is absolutely wrong with British policy at the present moment. They both assume unquestioningly all the way through that what France wants must be accepted by us, & that Germany is simply to be held down indefinitely. There is no suggestion whatever here that we, Great Britain, should have an independent policy, so framed as to be acceptable to both France & Germany by both of them giving up something.*

Germany will remain a seething mass of discontent as long as the rest of us choose to consider Versailles the last word. Versailles was imposed on Germany by force, has never been really accepted by her, & I think never will be.

Germans feel that they have not the ordinary sovereign rights of the pettiest State so long as they are not allowed to administer their own army & their own navy in their own way – within limitations, of course; all countries it is hoped, will agree to limitation.[...]

1 November   Saw Grandi this morn[g]. We discussed the new French Disarm[t] Plan, & Herriot's visit to Spain.

The difficulty for It: about the French Plan is France's proposal to keep a special long-service Colonial force as well as the one-year home conscripts. It: has no Italian Colonial army & does not want to have one. She uses native troops. Also there <u>may</u> be a diff[y] about effectives – are the Fascist militia 'effectives' or not? He himself, for instance, is a

---

[172] Ralph Follet Wigram (1890–1936): entered FO 1919; 1st Sec. in Paris 1924–33; Counsellor, FO 1934–6.

General in the Fascist militia! Would the French count him or not? The militia are intended to defend the <u>Fascist régime</u>. Their training consists of drill every Sunday, & they have no heavy weapons. But, over & above this Reserve of 200,000, there is a volunteer militia of 50,000 which is a standing force & supplements the army; this Italy has offered to count in 'effectives;' but France wants her to count the 200,000 as well

In regard to Herriot's visit to Spain Grandi is worried. He does not like the Spanish proposal to fortify the Balearic Islands, & to make their Moroccan railway of the same gauge as the French African railways, with an agreement (he believes) for French Colonial troops to be carried not only across African but Spanish proper territory (from Barcelona) in the event of a 'League War'. This w^d upset the Mediterranean equilibrium against Italy. French Colonial troops are deliberately intended for use in a European War.

3 November   The Jap Ambassdr Matsudaira,[173] anxious to win sympathy for Japan in Manchuria, & uncertain as to the *Times* Foreign Editorship, invited Graves, Deakin[174] & me all to have luncheon with him yesterday! Quite enjoyable; & then, as we were going away, he enquired tactfully who w^d be going to Geneva to report the Manchurian case when it comes before the Council – & we had to tell him it w^d probably be Casey![175] Even his Japanese impassivity betrayed a tremor of exasperation!

I had quite a good talk with him over disarmament. He says Japan will never agree to the abolition of submarines, tho' she w^d agree to the reduction of their size – but not to the level (250 tons) proposed by G^t B^n. In other respects Japan w^d be ready to make approximately the same naval reductions as G^t B^n – tho' I gather she wants a different ratio to us & U.S.A. than the 5:5:3 of Washington.

6 November   On Fri: night in the office the telephonist rang me to say that 'Mr Henderson from Geneva was on the line, & said that someone wanted him from *The Times*. Trunks had rung them 3 times.' I said it sounded rather strange, as I was sure no one w^d ring up M^r H: without

[173] Tsuneo Matsudaira (1877–1949): entered dip. service 1902; Amb. in Washington 1925–8, in London 1929–36; Min. of Imperial Household 1936–45; delegate to London Naval Conf. 1930; chief delegate to World Disarmament Conf., Geneva 1932.

[174] Ralph Deakin (1888–1952); editorial staff of *The Times* 1919–22, For. News Ed. 1922–52; Special Corrspdt in various countries; Dir. of Reuters 1941–2.

[175] William F. Casey (1884–1957): joined *The Times* 1913; served in Washington & Paris; Special Corrspdt at Geneva & in Spain; Dep. Ed. 1941–8; Ed. 1948–52.

my knowing about it, & I had not done so'. However, I said, if he's on the line, put me through – so I had quite a good talk with Henderson, who I suppose had chosen this method of ringing me up. He evidently was anxious that we sh$^{\underline{d}}$ think well of the new French Plan. He said he thought it ought to give the Disarm$^{\underline{t}}$ Conference 'a fresh start.' He had put the meeting of the General Commssn off until November 21$^{\underline{st}}$, a week's delay, so as to give time to reach some arrangement with Neurath about Germany's return to the Disarm$^{\underline{t}}$ Conf:. Neurath w$^{\underline{d}}$ be coming to Geneva for the special Council (on Manchuria) on 14th. (But this has now bn put off to 21$^{\underline{st}}$).

He told me that Neurath w$^{\underline{d}}$ expect a very definite statement of what the other Powers were ready to do in regard to the German claim for equality of status. He (H:) believed a settlement c$^{\underline{d}}$ be reached in the private conversations; but Neurath was anxious that not too much sh$^{\underline{d}}$ be said about them, as nominally he was coming to Geneva entirely for the business of the Council.

H: & I were in any case entirely in agreement that the first thing to do was to negotiate for the return of Germany to the Disarm$^{\underline{t}}$ Conf: Without Germany the Conf: is lop-sided, even tho' Ger: is already disarmed. Nobody will reduce their armaments unless Ger: is in with them.

Philip Baker wrote to me from the Brit: Embassy in Paris backing the French Plan – & his letter arrived almost at the same time as H:'s tel: call! Baker had bn in touch with Léon Blum[176] (the Socialist leader) & also, of course, Tyrrell.

23 November   I had a long talk with M$^{\underline{r}}$ Mellon this afternoon, in the Amc$^{\underline{n}}$ Emb: From my brief previous view of him & from common report, I expected to find him silent or absent-minded or both. But he wasn't. We talked for over an hour, & although he was slow & stammered slightly, he was easy & interesting. A most distinguished & nice looking man, v. courteous, yet firm. A slight accent.

He talked first of all about his famous visit to England last summer, when he was still Sec$^{\underline{y}}$ to the Treasury, & came over to have a holiday (in France), & see his son at Cambridge. But when he landed, on a Tuesday, he rec$^{\underline{d}}$ a cable from Pres: Hoover, saying that he had come to the conclusion that the financial sit[uatio]n of Europe was desperate, & that he felt that something drastic sh$^{\underline{d}}$ be done about it, & instructing him (Mellon) to make enquiries & advise him before Friday,

[176] Leon Blum (1872–1950): Socialist Deputy 1919–40; PM 1936–7; V-P of Cab. 1937–8; PM & Min. of Finance 1938; interned in Germany 1940–45; PM & For. Min. in provisional govt 1946–7. See his *Peace and Disarmament* (1932).

when he had some engagement outside Washington. That gave M: only 2 full days in London.

He therefore made all the enquiries he could, but without saying he had orders to do so. He came to the conclusion that an immediate moratorium for all war-debts w$^{\underline{d}}$ be best, & cabled his opinion, advising 5 years if possible, otherwise 3, or possibly only 2.

Hoover summoned all Congressmen of both parties within reach, & got their consent to one year. Mellon said (today) that that was not really enough, & he thought Hoover ought to have bn able to get through 2. [...]

M$^{\underline{r}}$ Mellon talked widely about European affairs, also getting me to talk. He wished there had bn some qualifications set up for membership of the L. of Nations! An excellent notion, I said, but who was to be judge of which nation passed the entrance examination! Another idea of his was that the Polish Corridor questn c$^{\underline{d}}$ be solved by modern engineering i.e. by a German viaduct over it, or tunnel under it, joining E. Prussia to the rest of Germany. I said of the two the tunnel, I thought, w$^{\underline{d}}$ be best, because the Poles w$^{\underline{d}}$ be able to destroy the viaduct at any moment. But it's a strange world in which such proposals can be discussed! Frontiers are the trouble – suddenly Europe will recognize that, & abolish them.

6 December I paid my first visit yesterday to Herr v. [on] Hösch,[177] the new German Ambassdr, who has bn 12 yrs in Paris before coming here – & is still quite a young man. Not a grey hair anywhere, even about the temples. The new type of Bosch – pleasant, conciliatory, almost over-civil & pouring pro-German & anti-French arguments into one's ears all the time.

I sh$^{\underline{d}}$ say a good diplomatist. An eager talker – he went on for an hour – marshalling his arguments well, & giving the impression of being very firm behind his conciliatory manner. His arguments were not new, but fresh. [...]

9 December Yesterday I found a visiting-card 'Leopold von Hoesch' left for me at *T.T.* Office, with the corner turned down. A pleasant but certainly calculated politeness.

To-day I had a v. pleasant talk with Sgr Grandi, who kept on calling me 'dear Kennedy', so I ended by calling him 'Grandi'. He was apparently grateful to me for having helped him to score a success at

---

[177] Leopold von Hösch (1881–1936): entered dip. service 1907; Amb. in Paris 1920–32, in London 1932–6.

the beginning of his ambassadorship here. When Sir J. Simon's first Note was pub^d in reply to the German request for 'equality of status' to be granted, I told Grandi that its contents did not correspond to British public opinion. Grandi thereupon urged his Govt to wait. He did not want Italy to reply either in terms similar to us, which w^d not have corresponded to her real views, or in terms which expressed her real views but differed from ours. (Italy just now aims at always taking the same line as us, as far as possible). So better to wait. The Italian Govt did wait, & sure enough Simon's second Note – three weeks ago – struck a v. different note, in harmony with public opinion (as expressed by *T.T.* all along) & also in consonance with Italian views. So then Italy was able to express agreement with British policy.

Grandi thinks that the worst is over, economically, for the countries of Europe. He thinks France is now in as bad a position as any, & the U.S.A. in the worst position of all. A strange paradox!

He is much touched by the way English people are all making him feel at home here.

When we were talking about Disarmament, Grandi told me that Balbo was the only member of the Italian Ministry who w^d never agree to the suppression of aerial bombardment. Mussolini would. And if it ever became a practical proposition Musso: w^d 'push Balbo out' – in Grandi's own words. Grandi said it with a gesture, as if it w^d be quite easy for Musso: – a wonderful tribute to the strength of his position, for Balbo is a formidable & ruthless character (as Tyrrell explained to me.)

13 January   In one of my periodical talks with Leeper at the F.O.
yesterday we discussed the <u>methods</u> of the various recent Sec^{ies} of State.
I said that as far as I had bn able to judge from the outside, Henderson
had bn best at regulating the work he had to do i.e. deciding what he
was to do himself & what c^d be settled by subordinates. Leeper said
perhaps yes, but it had put a great strain on his sec^{ies} – for he w^d <u>not</u>
read papers except the few most important, & his sec^{ies} had to remember
the contents & retail them to him whenever he wanted. Henderson
moreover never wrote a minute himself. He just <u>said</u> the line of policy
he wanted the various Departments of the Office to take in their
different problems.

   Curzon on the other hand used to write many minutes outlining
policy – in his own hand in pencil.

   Simon writes occasional ones.

20 Jan: [...] I was rather pleased the other day at the F.O. when two
junior members of the News Dept, after their usual pow wow with
Leeper, told me that 'once again the line they had to take was that of
the *Times* leader' – that morning's having been mine on Manchuria.[178]

Manchukuo and Geneva

The circumstances of the present dispute are peculiar to the Far East, and
it is wholly unnecessary to assume, because the League is unable to impose
an ideal settlement there by force, that it must always be sterile in action, or
that, because Japan is the country that took the initiative in military
operations, therefore Japan is entirely in the wrong. Certainly her methods
have given rise to justifiable criticism, and it is difficult to reconcile her policy
with the spirit of the international instruments which she herself has signed.
But she acted under great provocation, and the ultimate result of her action,
modified, it may be hoped, by the friendly pressure of other Powers, through
the medium of the League, may be for the benefit of the people of Manchuria,
who already are being paid for the product of their labour in fairer measure
than the rapacity of their previous rulers allowed to them. In any case
neither condemnation nor condonation is necessary from the League. The
future matters more than the past. The League's own Commissioners

[178] 'Manchukuo and Geneva' 17 January 1933 p.13.

pronounced that a mere restoration of the *status quo* would be no solution, even if it had been practicable. The soundest course must be – with the consent of the parties to the dispute, if possible, but if not, without them – to hold up a settlement to the world which will serve as the rallying point of public opinion and the objective of international diplomacy.

28 Jan.[179]   [...] Simon said that though he himself was particularly strong he was beginning to feel the strain of so much work in two places. And he wanted to be present more regularly in Cabinets & in Parliament. He was head of a Party Group, & felt that he ought to help to keep together the National Govt. It would obviously no longer be a National Govt if MᵃᶜDonald & himself & one other (I can't remember whether he said Runciman[180] or Thomas[181] went).

This last remark was probably the motive of his whole conversation, because when I reported it to G.D. in the office, & I also spoke to Coote about it, they both said that Simon's position was becoming insecure. Many of the Conservatives want to get rid of him. G.D.'s idea is that Simon ought to be shifted to another post, MᵃᶜDonald take the Foreign Office, & Baldwin if necessary become P.M.

Simon threw out the suggestion that perhaps I would have a few lines on the arduousness of his work in a leader & G.D. agreed, but said 'We won't have a full leader about it just now'. I wrote about League & Manchuria that night, but it was not convenient to bring in an allusion to him in that connection, so I didn't, & wrote a private note to Simon to explain, saying there would probably soon be a better opportunity. I then wrote about it a few days later.[182]

Simon then talked a little about Disarmament & Manchuria. The world was not static he said & he would not bind himself & his successors never to recognize the State of Manchukuo. [...]

Sir John Simon at Geneva

In all these meetings [the Council of the League on the Anglo-Persian dispute, the preparations for the World Economic Conference, the Disarmament

---

[179] This entry is in Sylvia Kennedy's hand.

[180] Walter Runciman (1870–1949): Lib MP Oldham 1899–1900, Dewsbury 1902–18, Swansea W. 1924–9, St Ives 1929–37 (Nat. Lib. from 1931); Pres. BofT. 1914–16, 1931–7; Ld Pres. 1938–9; Head of Mission to Sudetenland 1938; suc. 2ⁿᵈ Baron Runciman 1937, cr. Viscount Runciman of Doxford 1937.

[181] James Henry Thomas (1874–1949): Lab. MP Derby 1910–36 (Nat. Lab. from 1931); Colonial Sec. 1924; Min. of Employment & Ld Privy Seal 1929–30; Sec. of State for Dominions 1930–5, for Colonies 1935–6. See his *My Story* (1937).

[182] 'Sir John Simon at Geneva': 27 January 1933, p.14.

Conference] the BRITISH FOREIGN SECRETARY has been playing an important part, and it is of course essential that the British Government should continue in all of them to be authoritatively represented. But the question inevitably arises whether it is necessary that the Foreign Secretary should always be present in person. And is it in any case feasible? The normal division of diplomatic work is between the Secretary of State, who directs from the FO – maintaining from his position in London a true proportion between the various questions of the day as they affect British interests – and the envoy on the spot, who executes the Foreign Secretary's policy and interprets the aims and activities of the country where he is accredited. There is the further consideration that with the FOREIGN SECRETARY at Geneva for prolonged periods – as has been the case during the last twelve months – the Cabinet has in his absence to consider problems on which, even if they do not relate directly to foreign affairs, the FO view is required; for it is more true of the FOREIGN SECRETARY than of most of his colleagues to say that his function in the Cabinet is a wider one than the mere representation of his Department. Of course Geneva has by now become a central clearing-house of international affairs, and there is not the slightest doubt that, as things stand, the FOREIGN SECRETARY should personally attend the three regular Councils of the year and part at least of the September meeting of the Assembly. But with Council meetings being drawn out for weeks and even months, and two or three special Assemblies being held during the year, the case is altered. It becomes a question whether British policy would not be more effectively conducted by the FOREIGN SECRETARY staying at home for a great proportion of his time, and thus remaining in closer touch with public opinion, and sending to Geneva an authoritative representative of suitable standing. . . .

18 February Last night Brumwell told me an extraordinary story that is being circulated in the H. of Commons (among its youngest members, I sh$^{\underline{d}}$ suppose) acc: to which I am supposed to have written our leader of 5 or 6 days ago suggesting that MacDonald sh$^{\underline{d}}$ go to the U.S.A. to arrange the preliminaries of the Debt Settlement with Roosevelt.[183] MacD: is supposed to have made the suggestion himself to me at 10 Downing Str.

Of course nothing c$^{\underline{d}}$ be more ridiculously wide of the mark, because I do not know MacD: & am never rec$^{\underline{d}}$ by him. GD sees him a lot, & wrote that particular leader himself.

Possibly it is a compliment that I sh$^{\underline{d}}$ be regarded as the sort of mystery man of *T.T.*, but I do think it shows what a gossipy sort of place the House has become, & what a lot of absolutely inexperienced chattering whipper-snappers there are in it at the moment, with nothing

[183] Franklin Delano Roosevelt (1882–1945): Gov. State of New York 1929–33; Pres. of U.S. 1933–45.

much to do, as there are too many of them (Conservatives). They get hardly any chance of speaking, & a good many were elected almost by mistake at the last election – they stood for apparently hopeless seats & the big National wave swept them into the House.

To-day I had luncheon with Lord Lytton, as usual most courteous & pleasant to argue with. He is rather keener on the League of Nations Union notions that I am, so we differ about the Japs: in Jehol & that sort of thing, but fundamentally we see eye to eye. He has that rare thing in a public man, moral indignation; & we entirely agree about, for instance, the abolition of the bomb. I am v. glad, for I am having an awkward time at present with the opponents of abolition. Ld Londonderry has written twice lately to GD criticizing the views expressed in the leaders I have written.

L^d L: is apparently doing a lot of propaganda & the F.O. are annoyed about it. Most of the permanent Staff are genuinely keen on a good disarmament programme, in which we c^d give the world a lead, but Simon is a poor fighter.

Have had a v. interesting day altogether (tho' it has meant missing going to Hambrook) as this afternoon I went to see Anthony Eden at the F.O. He is just over for 48 hours from Geneva, & I was to have gone to his private house, but he was kept at the F.O., Simon being there (tho' it is Sat^y afternoon) & the two having a talk.

We talked about Disarmament, esp: about the Air & the v. difficult position created by the Air Ministry. 'It is the Home front I'm afraid of' said Eden. He has to go back to Geneva tomorrow with Ld Londonderry & the Chief of the Air Staff – & Philip Sassoon is already there! By the way, he told me that Sassoon had not told him a word about his visit the other day to the German Air Minister, Capt: Göring.[184] Nor had Simon bn told, & apparently Sassoon had avoided the British Embassy. Disgraceful.

Eden was in good form & is a fighter, & a steady sensible fighter. I think we see absolutely eye to eye about disarmament, so I needn't dilate about his views. We both believe that aviation ought to be developed in every way, that any effective control of military aviation is extremely difficult, & abolition almost certainly impossible. There is no harm in trying – but if that fails, we **must** make a dead set against the use of bombs anywhere or for any purpose. It will be retrogression of civilization if we admit that their indiscriminate slaughter is a legal form of war. The bomb must come to be regarded as a dastardly

---

[184] Hermann Göring (1893–1946): Nazi politician; participated in beer hall *Putsch* 1923; elected Deputy 1928; Pres. of *Reichstag* 1932–3; PM of Prussia 1933; C-in-C Air Force 1933–45; Commissioner for the Four-Year Plan 1936; Field-Marshal 1938; Pres. of Gen. Council for War Economy; committed suicide before execution, Nuremberg 1946.

weapon, just as the assassin's bomb is, & proscribed. We both believe that public opinion in most countries, perhaps all countries, if roused & well led, could kill the bomb, & make any country an outlaw that started using it in war.

I personally think the League might have a bombing squadron at its disposal, but we did not come to that point. Anyhow that w$^{\underline{d}}$ have to be later.

Eden said the great thing gained at Geneva at last is, that the French realize that a Convention (Disarm$^{\underline{t}}$) must be concluded which will bring the Germans into it. They must make sufficient sacrifice for that.

He said everybody at Geneva reads T.T. leading articles.

He also said that, if he had the power, he w$^{\underline{d}}$ leave the technical experts behind. Their duty was to prime the Cabinet & the plenipotentiary at home – then the plenipotentiary sh$^{\underline{d}}$ go & meet other plenipotentiaries & come to an agreement, which the experts w$^{\underline{d}}$ have to carry out. As it was, the soldiers, sailors & airmen were interfering with policy the whole time, which was not their business. They hang about at Geneva with little to do, & form a sort of passive opposition to the chief's mission, as in their heart of hearts they are really united against disarmament.

4 March   Had luncheon with Anthony Eden yesterday, he being back on one of his short visits from Geneva. I like him better every time I see him, & it is always satisfactory to find one's self in such close agreement on almost every subject as I do with him.

He told me that he, Alex: Cadogan & Eric Drummond worked out at Geneva, after dining together, a plan of what was possibly now attainable in the way of a Disarm$^{\underline{t}}$ Convention; & he & Cadogan have brought it over, & yesterday morn$^{\underline{g}}$ Eden submitted it to the Cabinet Com^{tee} on Disarm$^{\underline{t}}$. He said that the Conference was in a critical condition, & something must be done to get definite results soon. He believes fairly big results to be just possible – he enumerated categories – submarines, aeroplanes, reduction in numbers – guns & tanks, reduction in sizes – no fresh building or increases anywhere; etc etc: (He told me that now only I & the Cabinet are aware of this plan!)

The immediate result is that MacD & Simon are going to Geneva, probably in a week's time. He (Eden) hopes they will adopt his concrete plan & put it to the Conference complete with figures – but does not know. He fears MacD: may prefer his usual less definite attitude, & try to 'bring people together' without getting their signatures to anything positive.

I proposed that two minor concessions, but important to their *amour propre*, that ought to be made to the Germans, were permission to build (defensive) fortifications & anti-aircraft guns.

Eden thought it a good idea. He told me in regard to the recent Arms Embargo placed on consignments of arms to either Japan <u>or China</u>, that the step had been taken without his being informed – tho' he was representing G^t B^n at Geneva. He had however been consulted beforehand by telephone; & he had given his opinion that it was important to differentiate in manner & method between Japan & China, in view of the recent vote of the Assembly of the League, even if actually in practice it was nec: to prevent arms being sent to either country. That was exactly the point I made to GD. But just as Eden was overruled by Simon, so I was by GD, who took that passage out of my leader[185] (tho' he left in a sentence at the end which was in the same sense, though less precise – I supposing that the earlier ref: was to be left in. GD did not touch it in the typescript, but took it out of the proof after I had gone).

Eden thought it was most important to get <u>figures</u> into the Convention now. The figures he mentioned were – Max: size of Tank, 16 tons. Max: size of mobile land guns, 6"; max. no. of mil: aeroplanes for any one country, 400 (that is well below our present figure, & <u>much</u> below the figures of U.S.A. & France.

The Prime Minister for Geneva

Captain Eden leaves London again for Geneva to-morrow to resume the leadership of the British Delegation; and one of the tasks that await him is to push forward the formation of the sub-committee on the embargo of arms for the Far East. It was a stipulation made by Sir John Simon when he announced the British embargo that international action alone could be really effective. The decision was taken 'pending the opportunity of international consultation.' In that sense it was provisional. If other countries are not prepared to follow the lead which Great Britain has attempted to give the whole position will clearly have to be reconsidered.

8 March   Today I had luncheon with the Prime Minister, through the instrumentality of GD, who asked him if he w^d be able to see me about Disarm^t, before he goes off to Geneva (tomorrow). GD was invited too, but c^d not come. It was at the Athenaeum 1 pm. MacDonald was a bit late, having been kept by a Cabinet Council. Very nicely apologized for it. Very simple & direct in manner, easy to get on with. Asked me if I wanted to wash my hands. I had already; but he asked

---

[185] 'The Prime Minister for Geneva': 4 March 1933, p.13.

me to come along to the lav: with him, & even to go inside! when I stood just outside. Inside were $\frac{1}{2}$ doz: old fellows doing their toilets, & MacD was greeted by several. He chatted easily with them all; & even while performing one of the minor functions of nature kept up a conversation with one of them.

Then he took me into the dining-room & started talking at once about his plans & the position of the Disarm^t Conference. He took a most gloomy view, & actually said he did not expect any success, but that they w^d draw up some sort of Declaration of what had been agreed upon, & then Germany & Italy, if they refused it, w^d have to take the appalling responsibility of failure & of the chaos which w^d follow.

When he explained that his visit to Paris was not to get an agreement, but merely to 'talk things over' with Daladier[186] & Boncour I said it w^d not be so interpreted in Rome. Mussolini I know is furious at this constant Franco-British fraternization & is sulky & is making friends with Hitler.[187] Grandi has just come back from Rome, having bn rebuffed by Musso: He went to try to make It^n policy more conciliatory. But Poliakov went to see him this morn^g, after his return, & found him v. depressed, declaring he had failed. Musso: is playing the prophet of Fascism, with Hitler as his chief disciple. I believe it might just turn the scale if MacD: went to see him, as Austen Chamberlain used to do. That used to keep him sweet. Now he is sour, v. sour. And he has the bad influence of Aloisi[188] round him instead of Grandi.

I tried to flatter MacD, saying Musso: appreciated personality etc, etc: MacD: leaned back from his food & considered the idea, & said 'one mustn't hawk oneself about too much. Paris, Geneva, Washington....Rome'. I answered that this <u>was</u> an exceptional moment. He seems bent on going to Washington as soon as possible. He said he wanted to hold the World Economic Conf. soon, even if conditions appeared unfavourable, because he thought the mere fact that the Conference met w^d have a gd effect – a typically MacDonald view, I thought.

He talked next about the Arms Embargo on Japan & China, & said

---

[186] Edouard Daladier (1884–1970): French politician; Radical Deputy 1919–40, 1946–58; PM 1933, 1934, 1936, 1938–40; Min. of Defence 1938–40; For. Min. 1939–40; attempted to establish a rival govt in North Africa to continue the war but was arrested and imprisoned by the Vichy govt.

[187] Adolph Hitler (1889–1945): Nazi megalomaniac; Chanc. 1933; Head of German State 1934; C-in-C of German Fighting Forces 1938; Personal Commander of army 1941; Supreme War Lord 1942; died in a bunker proclaiming German people had failed him 1945.

[188] Pompeo Aloisi (1875–1949): Italian diplomat; Press Chief, Italian delegation, Paris Peace Conf. 1919; Amb. in Tokyo 1928–9, in Ankara 1930–2; head of cabinet *Ministero degli Affari Esteri* 1932–6; head of Italian delegation, LoN Council 1932–6. See his *La mia attività a servizio della pace* (1946).

he wanted to get that settled up in Geneva first of all. He said he c^d^
give me, if he liked, some astonishing revelations about how some
countries were behaving. One, he said, had appointed a special Com^tee^
to study how, when an arms embargo had been declared against China
on an earlier occasion, it had still been possible to get arms through to
her! This same country was officially proposing to agree to have an
embargo on both China & Japan, while obviously meaning to get
round it clandestinely.

He said in fact that the way several countries were behaving
was disgusting. I said something about this being a bad moment in
international affairs & he agreed that the movement everywhere was
away from international agreement.

Again bringing up the question of seeing Musso: I pointed out that
that w^d^ kill two birds with one stone, as it w^d^ probably have the effect
of getting Hitler to Geneva – if Musso: advised him to go, he w^d^ go.
MacD: fully realized the uselessness of negotiating now with any
German representatives other than Nazis.

He fully expects failure, & then communism in Europe. He was
interesting about communism, saying how easy it was for people
suffering from poverty, depression, hardship etc: to become communist
in sheer despair. He spoke feelingly about that, as if it was a temptation
he had known.

All through our talk today he spoke like a Conservative.

He was so pessimistic however that I said to him at last 'I assume
that what you are really going to try for is agreement, not a Convention
which will merely show up Germany & Italy as the obstructionists'? Of
course he said 'yes, certainly' – & no doubt in public will say so
repeatedly; but it is interesting to know how hopeless he really is. His
mind is clearly turning towards America & world economics, & no
doubt he's fundamentally right in that. Europe must go through a
terrible travail. The visit to Rome might do something though, if only
he w^d^ make it.

At the end he suggested that we might help if we had an article
rather addressed to Germany, pointing out that nobody c^d^ say yet what
she w^d^ not be offered. She must wait until the end of the Conference.
She may get quite a good offer.

On the other hand, he produced a letter from his pocket during
luncheon, the contents of which he made me promise to regard as
confidential, looking earnestly into my eyes as I promised. I suppose
even here I ought not to put down the contents, though they were not
of general importance. But they provoked the remark from me – 'Then
I suppose there is jealousy between Daladier (French P.M.) & Boncour
(his For: Minister); 'A natural jealousy, I think one might say' MacD:
remarked! (Ditto exists, I fear, between himself & Simon).

He struck me as quite distinctly a greater man than Simon. He has lost his fire, though, & is more cautious & calculating, & a manager rather than a creator now. And v. contented. [...]

He accompanied me downstairs from the library at the top of the Club where we had been having coffee, & asked me where I was going. I said 'The F.O. or The Travellers, I'm not quite sure which; but I suppose its rather early for the F.O.' 'Yes' he said with a pleasant smile 'I don't think you'll find many people at the F.O. just now!' (It was 2.20).

I thanked him very much indeed, & he said 'Very glad to have had you' & went off with a pleasant farewell gesture.

Democracy is killing. MacD: has had his freshness knocked out of him by the efforts he has had to make to get where he is; & esp: that last great national election, when he had to stand in his constituency as well as lead the country. Stresemann was literally killed by the exertions he had to make to keep his position in the Reichstag while leading his unwilling country towards conciliation with France.

MacD: spoke all through in a definitely pro-French & anti-German way. He has come <u>full</u> round since 1914–18! I am sure he is <u>very</u> impressionable – & he lives now in the influence of the Londonderry House[189] society in which he moves, & backed by a Conservative majority in the House. He said to me that many young Conservatives had the <u>wildest</u> (that was his word) communist ideas! But he seemed to regard with resignation & almost indifference the almost certain coming, anyhow temporarily, of communism on the Continent. I wonder if, like Palmerston, he likes well the idea of solid conservatism at home, & revolutionary changes abroad! Quite natural really, for we progress smoothly & continuously, they violently & suddenly.

Poliakoff saw Fleuriau yesterday at the F.O. in tears! The poor man had just seen, as he left to come to the F.O., the news of his dismissal, & the appointment of M. Corbin[190] as ambassador in his place. He had seen it on a tape-machine! How brutal a way of dropping an old & faithful servant! [...]

Poliakoff also saw Grandi yesterday on his return from Rome. G: v. depressed, as he has failed to carry his policy of conciliation. He

---

[189] After forming his liaison with Lady Londonderry in 1930, MacDonald became a part of her political, literary & artistic circle, nicknamed 'the Ark' (as 'members' took the names of animals). Following the formation of the National Government in 1931 (with Lord Londonderry as Minister for Air) Londonderry House became a social centre for the new government, and in 1932 the National Labour Party held a major reception there.

[190] Charles André Corbin (1881–1970): entered dip. service 1906; Under-Dir. of European Section *Ministère des Affaires Etrangères* 1924–7; Dir. of Political & Commercial affairs 1927–9; Amb. in Brussels 1931–3; in London 1933–40.

describes Mussolini as becoming unbalanced, & thinking of himself as the Pope of Fascism, infallible, above criticism, & surrounded only by satellites, toadies & flatterers.

10 March   Thinking over my talk with MacD, a curious conviction has come over me – namely that the letter he read out to me (part of it) was from a personal agent at Geneva. He is known to employ this sort of spy. When he took the letter out of his pocket I saw it was not typewritten, but written in a very close hand on small notepaper. He was so v. mysterious about it, & what it contained was not of <u>immense</u> importance – a question of personal support. Yet he seemed most anxious to conceal any idea of the source of this information, made me promise solemnly to regard it as confidential, & when he was reading out the passage, hid the whole letter by making a screen of his free hand, apparently in order that I sh^d not see the handwriting. He did tell me, too, that it was <u>not</u> from a member of the British Delegation.

He was so open all the rest of the time, & suddenly became so clandestine.

I saw Sgr Grandi this morn^g. He looked better, but seemed subdued. He is evidently being left out of things. He indicated that, & said he was a fighter, & did not care about his embassy. However, when I said, I do hope you'll stay here, he said 'So do I'! & added that Europe was going to have a few years of the falsehood of extremes, & then it w^d turn to strong moderate men, like himself & Brüning. He indicated assent.

He told me one c^d not now rely on Mussolini's policy from one week to another. He had two sides, the idealistic & the practical statesman – but when he said idealistic, I think he meant, the man of ideas, an ideologue, was probably the word he had in mind (he has not got quite a mastery of english [sic] yet). He meant that Musso: considers himself the chief prophet of Fascism, & allows himself to be carried away by that idea sometimes.

He made a shrewd remark about France & Germany – 'German policy comes always too early & French policy always too late'.

Referring to our leader yesterday morn^g (on MacD & Simon stopping at Paris on their way to Geneva, & hinting at the possibility of a meeting with Musso: in Northern Italy)[191] Grandi said he had translated it word for word at once, & had it telegraphed to Musso: He was v. complimentary, saying it was worded exactly right, & then going through its points one by one with approval. [...]

---

[191] 'To Geneva via Paris': 9 March 1933, p.13.

By the way, Grandi told me that it took two years, even after all the preliminary fighting to get into power, for Fascism really to establish itself. Then it was turned into a dictatorship largely on account of the rowdiness of its own followers, culminating in the assassination of the Socialist Mateotti. [sic]

He said he thought Mussolini was in a stronger position now than ever before, but that <u>Musso: himself did not</u> seem to think that. Musso: was much more nervous than most people thought about public opinion, he said.

I expect Musso: is really in a very exhausted state, & not quite so certain of himself as a few years ago.

I am glad to say that Grandi does not make eyes at one in the Mussolini manner as he used to when he was Musso:'s right-hand man, & when he & I did not know each other so well as we do now. I call him just 'Grandi' now.

Poliakoff has reason to know that Hitler rings up Musso: every morning just now – & consults him as a disciple his master!

'To Geneva via Paris'

To-morrow's meeting of the British and French Prime Ministers and Foreign Secretaries [in Paris] should be helpful in every way. It could only do harm if it were misunderstood. Already a tendency is noticeable in Italy to be critical of a visit which is interpreted as leaving the Italian Government out in the cold: but it is certain that if the capital of Italy happened to be on the way to Geneva no other visit would more readily be paid. Even as it is, it ought not to be impossible for an occasional meeting to be held at Turin, or Milan, or some other northern town to which the Italian Prime Minister could conveniently come. It is not the fault of anybody that SIGNOR MUSSOLINI does not himself feel able to proceed to Geneva; and nothing would have been more wholly welcome to this country and to all who have the success of the Disarmament Conference at heart than that the head of the Italian Government, as also the head of the German Government, should have been able to attend in person. Since they have decided otherwise the responsibility can only be theirs if there appears to be a taint of one-sidedness in any of the deliberations that are about to be held in Geneva.

13 March At luncheon today at the Travellers Walford Selby was as usual v. discursive, & also as usual said one or two good things – e.g. Simon's weakness is that he doesn't understand the intangible. It doesn't count with him.

Very true, I think.

24 March   At luncheon yesterday Alan Dawnay[192] told me that the P.M., during his speech on Disarm[t] at Geneva, had had a mental fade-out. Actually the room had seemed to recede from him, & when he came-to he found himself still speaking. This was told by MacD: himself to Temperley, who told Dawnay.

I mentioned it to Brumwell in the Office, who told me that it had bn known to happen to him in the H. of Commons too. It accounts for some of those blurred passages that are such a puzzle! [...]

It seems that Vansittart insisted upon the Italian visit being paid to Rome, & not just to a northern resort like Stresa.

The P.M. seems to have had to be pushed & driven all the way! but played up nobly to the best of his ability.

Dawnay also told me that the F.O. want the General Staff to prepare plans <u>only for co-operation with France</u>, in case of a bust-up in Europe. That w[d] be all wrong after Locarno. This is not 1914.

After luncheon, still in The Travellers, I had a short talk with Lothian, who now has quite the appearance of an elder statesman of the Liberal type – & has become, by his own confession, a 'fatalist.' Therefore no good as a man of action.

28 March   I have had a letter from Geneva from Philip Baker, who gives me the inside moves, & he <u>contradicts</u> the confidential information which the P.M. gave me when I had luncheon with him! And in this case I don't see how Philip B: can be wrong. It shows how misleading those secret sort of reports can be. The secret agent always has to be producing something so as to justify his existence.

I had given Philip B: a hint of the 'report' I had heard, without of course giving him any idea of where it came from, not even mentioning to him that I had met the P.M.

29 March   I met David Balniel[193] in the street this morn[g], & he said that Anthony Eden's speech winding-up the Disarm[t] debate in the H.o C. really was v. good indeed, the best a younger Conservative in the Gov[t] has made – 'better than anything of Oliver Stanley's'.[194]

---

[192] Alan Geoffrey C. Dawnay (1888–1938): army officer; Col. 1930; Gen. Staff officer I[st] grade, WO 1931–3; Controller, Programme Division BBC 1933–5; officer commanding Irish Guards 1935–6; army instructor Imperial Defence College 1936–7.

[193] David Robert L. Balniel (1900–75): Con. politician; MP Lonsdale div. Lancs. 1924–40; PPS to Min. of Health 1931–5; suc. 28th Earl Crawford & Balcarres 1940.

[194] Oliver Frederick Stanley (1896–1950): Con. politician; MP Westmorland 1924–45; Min. of Transport 1933–4, of Labour 1934–5; Pres. Bd of Educ. 1935–7, Bd of Trade 1937–40; Sec. of State for War 1940, for Colonies 1942–5.

David said that Simon was jotting things down to himself while Eden was speaking – studiously paying no attention. Jealous, David says. He is also jealous of the P.M., David says. He really is rather a wretched specimen, tho' brilliantly clever. When Simon says anything, as David shrewdly remarked, one always asks one's self <u>why</u> he said it.

4 April   Yesterday GD gave Braham[195] & me luncheon at The Travellers to meet Mr Norman Davis, the American Special Envoy to Europe. He is a broad-faced, sober man, slow in utterance, but giving the impression of grasp, strength & steadiness, with insight. The funny thing was that now & again he reminded one exactly of pictures of Washington!

He repeated very deliberately the American view of the Anglo-Am^{cn} debt – its origin & true nature, also the fact that Americans look upon it as just one item in world difficulties, & also they believe that we are in a better position to pay than they to go without.

He says that Roosevelt is definitely willing to come to a satisfactory arrangement with us, & he & Davis want us therefore to take the line that G^t B^n & U.S.A. between them can set things right, but they must work together. Let <u>us</u> therefore throw debts in as just one of many matters to be settled, & we shall get a good bargain.

He (Davis) himself would like first of all to re-assess all the payments G^t B^n has made to the USA, on the basis of the French payments – that is to say, the payments we have already made w^d count for much more & be spread out over a longer number of years, & the total we have to reach w^d be automatically reduced by many millions of pounds. Then we & France w^d be on the same level as it were, & we c^d all bargain together. This retroactive recalculation w^d however, when all is said & done, only make a <u>mathematical</u> difference – it might all the same be a good basis on which to start negotiations.

Norman Davis was in favour of MacDonald's going to USA now – & we knew Ramsay is himself. But the Cabinet are against it; & it seems that both they & MacD: are deterred by Beaverbrook's[196] campaign against our travelling Premier. This seems to me an extremely silly reason, even if, as is possible, Beaverbrook is representing a fairly widely-held opinion.

---

[195] Dudley Disraeli Braham (1875–1951): journalist; joined *The Times* 1897; head of Imperial & For. Dept 1912–14; Ed. *Daily Telegraph*, Sydney 1914–22; founder & Ed. of *Forum* 1922–4; Ed. *Western Australian*, Perth 1924–30; rejoined *The Times* 1930–45.

[196] William Max Aitken (1879–1964): Con. politician & newspaper proprietor; MP 1910–16; purchased *Daily Express* 1916; Chanc. of Duchy of Lancaster & Min. of Info. 1918; Min. for Aircraft Production 1940–1, of State 1941, of Supply 1941–2; Ld Privy Seal 1943–5; kt. 1911 cr. Baron Beaverbrook 1917.

Davis was to attend a meeting of a Cabinet Com^tee at 2.30 But we were just sitting down to coffee when 2.30 arrived, & GD persuaded Davis to stay on & talk. I thought that was rather a mistake. Two telephone messages came, one from 10 Downing Str, & the other from Mr Davis's Sec^y, asking about him – so it was evidently known that he was lunching with GD.

By persuading him to stay (till 2.45) GD was making him discourteous to the Cabinet, & was also making the Cab: less likely to pay attention to our leaders, I sh^d think, for they w^d by annoyed that Norman Davis preferred staying on with us. And I believe it is really rather important that we sh^d help to persuade the P.M. to go to America, & counter the advice of the rest of the Cabinet & of the *Daily Express*.

Mr Norman Davis has a broad, genial expr[e]ss[io]n, & can see a joke. I liked him.

5 April Yesterday morn^g I went hurriedly round to see the Polish Ambassdr, at the suggestion of Poliakoff. Pol: was there himself, at the Embassy; & telephoned to me that the Ambassdr was feeling strongly about the Rome proposal of a 4-Power Pact; he had been making representatns to Sir John Simon about it the day before; & was in a mood to talk. So I went round. Pol: was right; & M. Skirmut[197] stated at some length his objections to the Rome proposals.[198] He told me about his talk with Simon, & mentioned that Simon had said in the course of it that 'very likely the whole thing w^d come to nothing'. Very feeble, if he really said that. Four-Power conversations & Treaty revision are now the declared Brit: policy, & it is pitiful if Simon is already hedging to that extent.

Simon told GD yesterday that some of Ovey's[199] suggestions from Moscow were so extraordinary that the only thing to do was to recall him, nominally to give information to the Cabinet, & leave Strang[200] in charge of the Embassy. (Strang is a good man). But I must say that Ovey's despatches, pub^d this morn^g, read very well.

[197] Konstanty Skirmut (1866–1949): Polish politician & diplomat; Min. in Rome 1919–21; For. Min. 1921–2; Min. in London 1922–9; Amb. in London 1929–34. See his *Moje Wspomnienia 1866–1945* (1997).

[198] On 18 March 1933 Mussolini – after first getting Hitler's approval in principle – proposed to Britain that Italy, Britain, Germany and France should 'co-ordinate' their policies in European, extra-European and colonial matters, should consider revision of the peace treaties and should recognize the right of Germany to rearm by stages.

[199] Esmond Ovey (1879–1963): entered dip. service 1903; Amb. in Moscow 1929–33, in Brussels 1934–7, to Argentina & Paraguay 1937–42; kt. 1929.

[200] William Strang (1893–1978): entered FO 1919; actg Counsellor in Moscow 1930–2, Counsellor 1932–9; Asst. U-Sec. FO 1939–43, PUS 1949–53; kt. 1943; cr. Baron Strang of Stonesfield 1954. See his *Home and Abroad* (1956).

6 April   Yesterday we (*T.T.*) were definitely informed that MacD: was going to visit President Roosevelt at Washington during the Easter recess – starting in 10 days' time.

The curiously casual sort of way in which these decisions are taken, or seem to be taken, surprises one v. much. There is no doubt that last Mon: – 3 days ago – when I was with Norman Davis & GD at luncheon, Davis did not think there was any immediate prospect of MacD: going. When GD reminded him that we had proposed the visit in *T.T.* 6 weeks ago, Davis said 'Well now that seems to have gone right out of his mind,' & told us about the Cabinet opposition to MacD: going on his travels again so soon, which I have already recorded.

After GD had seen Davis off, he came back to join Braham & me, & I said that now seemed a good moment for reviving the project. GD took Braham aside (B: writes our leaders on America), & that evening Braham wrote the leader putting forward once more the proposal that MacD sh$^{\underline{d}}$ go to the U.S. It was held up 24 h[ou]rs; so in the meantime GD published a word in the political notes saying the idea of the visit was being canvassed again.

The rest of the Cabinet seems to have been against the visit right up to the present moment, but it is clear that MacDonald, though outwardly bowing to the opposition of Hailsham[201] & Co:, clung tenaciously to his desire to pay it. It is also clear now (from our today's message from Lewis[202] from Washington) that the very first person to make the proposal was Roosevelt himself, in his first semi-official talk with Ronald before he (Roos:) was President. Ronald [Lindsay] then imparted it to GD (I presume),[203] & GD anyhow went specially to see MacD (he has told me that) to ask him whether he w$^{\underline{d}}$ support the idea if launched. MacD: said yes, so then GD wrote the first leader on the subject.

It is typical of MacD: to appear to be quite irresolute & then to make up his mind decisively.

I see that my man George Bell has bn murdered by Nazis over the Austrian frontier. Why exactly I don't know, as he was a ferocious Nazi himself, though he had bn Communist once & told me he might become Communist again. I suspect he had a quarrel with the Rosenberg[204] clique, whom he was always running down to me; & the

---

[201] Douglas McGarel Hogg (1872–1950): Con. politician; MP St Marylebone 1922–8; Attorney-Gen. 1922–8; Ld Chanc. 1928–9; Sec. of State for War 1931–5; Ld Chanc. 1935–8; Ld Pres. 1938; kt. 1922; cr. Baron Hailsham 1928, Viscount 1929.

[202] Willmott Harsant Lewis (1877–1950): journalist; Ed. *Manilla Times* 1911–17; Corrspdt in Washington, *The Times* 1920–48; kt. 1931.

[203] ALK has noted in the margin: 'No: see Journal May 11'.

[204] Alfred Rosenberg (1893–1946): Nazi ideologist; joined *NSDAP* 1919; participated in beer hall *Putsch*; Ed. *Völkischer Beobachter* from 1923; founded *Kampfbund für deutsche Kultur* [Fighting League for German Culture] 1929; *Reichstag* Deputy 1930; head, *NSDAP* For.

Rosenberg clique is on top now. Bell w$^{\underline{d}}$ be capable of anything out of spite, & they probably thought it best to put him out of the way.

Our 'hush-hush' people have some story of his having bn murdered because he was in touch with 'a young Englishman' from whom he was trying to get military secrets. That seems an improbable reason for murdering him. He was a terrible tough, anyway, & I'm afraid one can't regard his disappearance as much loss to anyone.

Leeper said at luncheon today that Henderson, when For: Sec$^{\underline{y}}$, could send back very sharp messages to the T.U.C. when it tried to dictate to him on foreign policy.

20 April   Luncheon with Philip Baker yesterday. He confirmed the impression I had already got, that Henderson is getting tired of Disarmament at Geneva, & wants to return & busy himself with the affairs of the Labour Party. Philip B: says he has no ambition to lead the Party, but wants to do properly the work of its Sec$^{\underline{y}}$ & Treasurer, posts which he still holds.

I told Philip I thought this was a great mistake. He ought to see the disarm$^{\underline{t}}$ business through, & hammer away at it, even if it were to last another 2 years. I quite understand how sick they are all getting of it; but in the present state of Europe no actual reduction of arms will be carried out, & even if they rush through a Convention this summer (as Henderson desires), it will remain quite inoperative. It w$^{\underline{d}}$ be no bad thing to spend two years working out a really sound Convention, which w$^{\underline{d}}$ be ready for application when conditions had settled down a little in Europe.

Baker evidently believes the P.M. to be a very sick man, & I can't help suspecting that he & Henderson imagine the Labour Party might get back into power v. soon. I tried to disabuse him. I sh$^{\underline{d}}$ say not for 2 years.

Going on to the F.O. I found that they too are getting sick of the Disarm$^{\underline{t}}$ Conference, & w$^{\underline{d}}$ be only too pleased if its proceedings c$^{\underline{d}}$ soon be brought to an end. Willert entrusted me with a secret memorandum by Cadogan on the subject. I do not agree with it. I perfectly understand their desire to get away from Geneva; but Disarm$^{\underline{t}}$ is a permanent problem.

22 April   Willert tells me that Anthony Eden, who is just back from Tangier, agrees with his & Cadogan's view.

Affairs Dept 1933–45; responsible for training in Nazi ideology within *NSDAP* from 1934; founded Institute for the Investigation of the Jewish Question 1939; hanged for activities as Reich Min. for the Eastern Occupied Territories 1941–5. See *The Memoirs of Alfred Rosenberg* (1947).

I had luncheon the other day with Baron de Ropp,[205] the one political spy I know who seems well worth his keep. He is just back from Germany, & was v. interesting about the internal affairs of the Nazi party. A struggle is beginning between Göring & Goebbels,[206] the extremists, against Hitler, backed by Rosenberg, who are moderates. None of them really knows the world outside Germany, except that Rosenberg knows Russia & the Baltic States well. de R: told me they study *T.T.* minutely themselves, but do not let its views percolate through the German Press, because they are too candid. (I must try to write just favourably enough to <u>Hitler</u> to get him to allow the articles to be quoted in the Ger: Press).

de R: said that the Nazis had got their knife into Ebbutt, metaphorically speaking, owing to his opposition to their movement. He said they w^d not dare to do him any outward visible damage – but that if they were given the chance they w^d certainly get him run over by a motor-car, or otherwise <u>accidentally</u> done in. I must warn Ebbutt, but carefully, because the poor fellow is already much shaken by his experiences. (He is over here in England, resting).

27 April[207] S. & I dined last night with Walford & Lady Selby.[208] Walford had told me some time ago he was kindly going to arrange a meeting for me with Lord Grey,[209] so it was in one way a little disapptg, for I found he had also asked Austen Chamberlain, because obviously A.C. & Grey would do most of the talking, also A.C. would do propaganda for his point of view about Treaty Revision. This was emphatically the case after dinner when the ladies had gone up to the drawing room. We had a most interesting talk; but it was almost a duel between A.C. & myself, with Selby backing up A.C. & Grey making rare interjections, more or less impartial, but usually rather favourable

[205] William de Ropp: former *Times* correspondent in Berlin. A naturalized Englishman of German origins, he succeeded in establishing himself as Rosenberg's principal expert on Britain and saw to it that leading pro-Nazis were invited to Germany. But he was also being paid by Britain, reporting to the Chief of Air Intelligence of the Secret Intelligence Service, Squadron-Leader Winterbotham, whom he supplied with information concerning Nazi political aims and plans. Where his real allegiances lay remains in doubt. See F.W. Winterbotham, *The Nazi Connection* (1978).

[206] Joseph Paul Goebbels (1897–1945): Nazi politician; head of party organization, Berlin 1926, of party propaganda & organization 1928; elected to *Reichstag* 1929; founder & Dir. *Der Angriff* [The Attack] 1927–33; Min. of Enlightenment & Propaganda 1933–45; poisoned his six children, committed suicide 1945.

[207] This entry is in Sylvia Kennedy's hand.

[208] Dorothy Carter; m. Walford Selby 1912.

[209] Edward Grey (1862–1933): Lib. MP Berwick 1885–1916; U-Sec. FO 1892–5; FS 1905–16; suc. 3rd Bart. 1882, cr. Viscount Grey of Fallodon 1916.

to A.C., that is against Treaty Revision at the present moment. For instance, he broke in once to say 'Lord Bryce[210] said of the Treaty of Versailles just after it had bn concluded 'It contains the seeds of a future war' & one might say now, went on Lord Grey[,] that revision contains the seeds of war.'

Personally I simply cannot agree with this last observation of Lord Grey's. Moderate revision is necessary to correct the few exaggerations of the original treaties of peace.

A.C. was a little bit self-important & gave us at enormous length an account of a recent meeting with Signor Grandi which had no very special significance, though briefly put it would have been interesting. This was the first time I had met Lord Grey personally. He has a fine face, saddened by his sufferings. He is so blind as to give almost the appearance of invalidism. He can't see whom he is talking to or what he is eating, & gives a limp, indifferent handshake. There was a sweet, resigned expression about his mouth, but a very blunt use of it when speaking. He was very quiet, but simple & direct whenever he did give an opinion. Once for instance, when A.C. said that he had heard from Tyrrell that it had become possible now that a 'preventive war' might be made by France, on Germany, Lord Grey said at once 'Then in that case we should have to fight on the side of Germany.' A.C. was violently disconcerted, made a sweeping movement with one arm & said 'Never. Never. Germany is always infringing the Treaties' – a rather strange interpretation of Locarno by its author!

I only had two or three minutes at the end of the evening of private talk with Lord Grey, & I managed to ask him the question I most wanted to – was it true that he had never met Bethmann-Hollweg (the German Chancellor in 1914) 'No I never met him' he said 'Do you think it would have made any difference if you had?' I asked. 'Not a bit' he answered. 'I found out afterwards, & I had some suspicion of it at the time, that I was not discussing with the principals at all. Neither Bethmann-Hollweg nor Lichnowsky really represented German policy. The General Staff did. Even the Kaiser was powerless against them. After he had waved his glittering sword, as he did once before, he wanted to draw back. But they wouldn't let him.' [. . .]

In the afternoon, after James Lindsay's wedding I went to The Traveller's to change my clothes & met Lord Tyrrell downstairs. He very nicely came into the bath-changing room with me & we had a short but animated discussion on Treaty revision while I doffed my wedding garments. He made the same remarks to me about being afraid of a war in Europe as he apparently had to A.C. I do not believe

---

[210] James Bryce (1838–1922): Lib. MP Tower Hamlets 1880–5, Aberdeen South 1885–1906; Chief Sec. for Ireland 1905–7; Amb. in Washington 1907–13; cr. Viscount 1914.

for a moment that there will be a serious war in Europe in the near future. There may be the threat of war, mobilization even a declaration of war or some armed scuffles; but I do not believe it will come to real war because the peoples of Europe are sick of war.[211]

I might mention that during our after-dinner talk AC said that he read *T.T.* absolutely regularly every day, & only occasionally other papers; & L$^{\underline{d}}$ Grey said that he had the news in *T.T.* read to him every day – no other paper.

Austen told Sylvia, who sat next to him at dinner, that before a big speech he generally took a few oysters & drank a little champagne. Last night he imbibed quite a lot, as I always noticed he did at Geneva. L$^{\underline{d}}$ Grey also did full justice to Walford's excellent port. I don't usually drink any wine, but caught the infection last night to the extent of having a glass of sherry, two of champagne & two of port.

It was rather touching to see AC shepherding L$^{\underline{d}}$ Grey down & up-stairs, & about the drawing-room. Great political opponents from 1905 to 1914, & now great friends.

4 May I had luncheon yesterday with L$^{\underline{d}}$ Newton,[212] who had just arr$^{\underline{d}}$ that morn$^{\underline{g}}$ from Berlin. He confirmed me in the view that Germany is not dangerous now, & that she is suffering from hysterics – 'Hitler-mad' he called it. Photos: of Hitler all over everything 'Heil Hitler' the usual greeting, even between strangers, young men brandishing sticks, & hitting other people on the head with them if they look like Jews! L$^{\underline{d}}$ N. had a long talk with v. Papen, who made what capital he c$^{\underline{d}}$ out of it at once, to help his own position – he pub$^{\underline{d}}$ his side of the talk at once as an official statement. He also offered to take L$^{\underline{d}}$ N. to see an internment camp, but Rumbold w$^{\underline{d}}$ not agree to his going. L$^{\underline{d}}$ N: was staying at the Embassy, so felt he must defer to R., & he added that he realized that their one idea w$^{\underline{d}}$ be to collect rapidly some sham internees, well fed etc, & then 'photograph him tasting some of their excellent soup with them.'

Selby came & had luncheon with me today. He says our leader of last Saturday had a v. great effect in Germany, 'more than Austen Chamberlain's speech or than the F.O. could have.' The Germans regarded us as friendly, & are much taken aback. They are sending over Rosenberg here to make peace.

Walford S. told me that his father & mother, both over 80, live at

[211] From this point on the entry is in ALK's hand.
[212] Thomas W. Legh (1857–1942): politician & author; Con. MP Newton div. of Lancs 1886–99; Paymaster-Gen. 1915–16; Asst U-Sec. FO 1916; Controller, Prisoners of War Dept 1916–19; biographies of Lords Lyons & Lansdowne; suc. 2nd Baron Newton 1898.

Brighton, & that he often goes down for the weekend − & Fleuriau also has v. often gone to the Hotel Metropole there, for weekends. They have often met there − supped together, & so on. This has all helped to keep up that close intimacy between Fleuriau & the F.O. which has had so much influence on Brit: foreign policy.

At the farewell dinner at the F.O. on the night before, at which Selby has been a guest, somebody had said to him 'This is just like 1912 over again' − a v. true reflection, for among the guests were Tyrrell, L$^{\underline{d}}$ Hardinge,[213] Austen Chamberlain, Winston Churchill,[214] M. Roger Cambon[215] − all so prominent in the years of the Entente Cordiale before the war. Just at this moment, with Nazi-ism triumphant in Germany, there is a distinct hark-back to the pre-War situation.

6 May Am getting a good many bouquets thrown at me after leadering, just now. L$^{\underline{d}}$ Tyrrell wrote that he 'must send me a line of congratulation' after my leader on M. de Fleuriau's departure 'For originality of thought & happiness of expression it would be difficult to surpass it' etc etc.[216] One quite realizes that Tyrrell is retiring himself this year! & possibly he w$^{\underline{d}}$ like to see his name... & a little judicious flattery...but, none the less, it is nice of him to have written as he did.[217] Then tonight Walford Selby has telephoned to me to say that L$^{\underline{d}}$ Grey had written to him (a dictated letter with just a sentence or two written in his own hand at the end), saying that he 'very much appreciated' the leader I had written on Revision, for which I took his speech as text, & also said that he had enjoyed the company at the dinner.[218] 'The conversation was v. interesting, & was good for me.' Grey must be a real good sort.

[213] Charles Hardinge (1858−1944): PUS FO 1906−10; Viceroy of India 1910−16; PUS 1916−20; Amb. in Paris 1920−3; kt. 1904; cr. Baron Hardinge of Penshurst 1910.

[214] Winston Leonard Spencer Churchill (1874−1965): Con. MP for Oldham 1900−04 (Lib. from 1904), Lib. MP Manchester NW 1906−8, Dundee 1908−22, Con. MP Epping (later Woodford) 1924−64; Pres. Bd of Trade 1908−10; Home Sec. 1910−11; 1st Ld of Admiralty 1911−15, 1939−40; Chanc. Duchy of Lancaster 1915; Min. of Munitions 1917−19; Sec. for War & Air 1919−21; Colonial Sec. 1921−2; Chanc. of Exchequer 1924−9; 1st Ld of Admiralty 1939−40; PM 1940−5, 1951−5; Con. Ldr 1940−55; kt. 1953.

[215] Roger Cambon (1881−1970): French diplomat; nephew of Paul Cambon (Amb. in London 1898−1920); entered dip. service 1905; Min. & Counsellor in London 1924−40.

[216] 'Two Schools of Diplomacy': 4 May 1933.

[217] On 24 May ALK crossed out the section from 'One quite' to 'none the less', noting 'I now know that Tyrrell has got an extension for 2 or 3 years.'

[218] 'Peaceful Revision': 27 March 1933.

'Peaceful Revision'

As the meeting of the PRIME MINISTERS of GREAT BRITAIN and ITALY in Rome recedes a little into the distance it is seen to loom up above other recent events as one of the major acts of statesmanship since the War; for it definitely sets Treaty Revision before the diplomacy of Europe and the world as the biggest and most immediate political problem with which it has to deal. What used to be debated only academically or mentioned in the chanceries with bated breath has now to be officially discussed; and it will be a grave misfortune for Europe if, when this pregnant issue has once been raised, the discussion is not carried to some practical conclusion. It had been a commonplace of diplomacy that to open the question of treaty revision would be to set Europe in confusion. It has now been opened; and in spite of the many voices raised in protest their outcry does not sound so loud as might have been expected, partly perhaps because it is drowned in the confusion already existing. The steady growth of European unrest during the last two or three years has in fact made it imperative to analyse and attempt to dure the causes of unrest. The moment is opportune in the sense that further delay, As MR. MACDONALD said in the House of Commons, is only likely to make peaceful remedial action yet more difficult; and if the régime in Germany with which the other Powers will have to deal is considered to be unsuitable because it is almost morbidly nationalist, it must at least be admitted that it is not the fault of Germany that the issue was not squarely faced in the days of HERR STRESEMANN or DR. BRÜNING. The inability of those statesmen to obtain greater satisfaction for Germany has set their reputations in eclipse in their own country. It would be a great miscalculation to suppose that a little further procrastination might bring a moderate leader into power again in Berlin. It would be far more likely to give free rein to a yet fiercer chauvinism than that of HERR HITLER....

7 May Had a short talk with Anthony Eden at Victoria Sta[tion] this morning, by arrangement, he being off to Geneva again, after one of his weekend visits. The Germans are holding up progress on the Brit: Draft Convention on the issue of effectives – in which they are palpably in the wrong. The next question to come up is material – in which the French might easily put themselves in the wrong. So the British Delegation & the Brit: Govt want to force an issue on effectives, so that Germany has either to accept the view of all other countries, or take the responsibility of causing the breakdown of the Conference.

I put to Eden the view that to force an issue now is unwise. Actual reduction of armaments in the present state of Europe is out of the question. 'If by some conjuring trick you bring about a Disarm! Convention now' I said 'Nobody will disarm'.

He agreed.

Therefore, I argued, the best policy is to keep Disarmament going –

keep it alive until Europe returns to sanity, say in 18 months or two years; get a small Commssn to sit & work out a Convention, which can be applied at the opportune moment.

My impression is that our people who go to Geneva are getting so fed up with the place, that they cannot bear to think of this policy of deliberate procrastination!

11 May GD, who was in this morn^g, told me about MacD.'s visit to Washington, that Ronald had got a lot of credit for it. He is supposed to have arranged it; & he certainly managed it v. well. Actually it seems that Mr Roosevelt first informally proposed MacDonald coming himself to Wash:, but no date was even provisionally suggested, & it was supposed he w^d come with other Ministers to pay a formal visit. GD's part was to launch the idea of an _in_formal & _early_ visit – which was adopted.

Two days ago I went to see Franckenstein,[219] the Austrian Minister, who, speaking of the Peace Treaties, told me how galling & humiliating it had been for the Austrian negotiators to be virtually prisoners & definitely under guard all the time of the negotiations. Their communicatns might only be made in writing, & if they wanted a talk it was only allowed along a limited space of the terrace at St Germain (where the Treaty was 'negotiated'), or if they drove out in a car they had an armed escort with them!

We are now paying for this absurd bullying. Hitlerism is one of its results.

On the way through Belgrave Square I met Ld Hardinge (of Penshurst), & we discussed Hitlerism. An opinion he gave differed from what I knew to be Sir Horace Rumbold's – so when I mentioned that, L^d H: said – 'Oh; well I have the highest opinion of Rumbold's opinions. They're always good'. A nice unselfish tribute. I agree, from what I know; but Hardinge's judgment also was exceedingly good when he was in harness.

I had been shown Rumbold's last despatch on Hitlerism at the F.O. Comprehensive & v. damaging.[220] A fine bit of work. Condemns Hitler as essentially militarist in outlook. A year ago militarism was dormant in Germany, said R:; today it is rampant. Hitlerism encourages & exploits chauvinist hysteria, & has a certain cynical contempt

---

[219] Georg von Franckenstein (1878–1953); Min. in London 1920–38; naturalized British subject, 1938; kt.1938. See his *Facts & Features of My Life* (1939).

[220] In his despatch to Simon on 10 May (No. 479) Rumbold reported that the Nazi régime was steadily consolidating itself and showing signs of 'a saner and more responsible attitude on the part of the three leaders, Hitler, Goebbels & Göring.'

for the herd instinct of the German people, which he understands thoroughly.

Yesterday I did what I have never done before – wrote, or rather sketched out, a complete leader in the Foreign Office! I wrote it with the Rumbold despatch in front of me. But as it was necessarily hurried it did not amount to more than a transcription in leader form – & I shall have to re-write it before publication. Moreover it is too scathing for public use. It practically says that propaganda, by which is meant deliberate lying, is a regular weapon of the Hitler regime, & worse even than the diplomatic duplicity of Germans in the pre-War period – which has all emerged indisputably in some of their own memoirs [...]

Before drafting my leader I saw Vansittart for a few minutes. He told me about his talk with Rosenberg, the semi-official Nazi envoy – & I asked him whether he (Van:) had discussed disarmament with him. (The position is as usual critical at Geneva). He said, no, because Herr Rosenberg is not the official repr: of his Govt, & he did not want to cross lines.

Norman Davis (U.S.A.) on the other hand, who saw GD last night, not only saw Rosenberg, but got him to telephone to Hitler afterwards – & a certain détente at Geneva is already noticeable. I am not criticizing Van:, but there are obvious advantages in the easier-going American ways – Davis being an Ambassador-at-Large, & free to talk about anything he likes about anything.

13 May   It seems to be doubtful after all whether Davis accomplished much with Rosenberg. Anyhow the crisis at Geneva was not solved. Still there is a lull & a postponement, & Davis may have had something to do with it.[221]

There has been an incident about a wreath placed at the Cenotaph by Rosenberg – a shocking piece of propaganda – which somebody removed. That night Simon & von Hösch, the German Ambassadr, met at a Court in Buckingham Palace, & Simon, who cannot keep his mouth shut, quite unnecessarily expressed his regret at its removal. Hösch apparently told Rosenberg that same night, & R: telegraphed it to Berlin, & in Berlin next day the papers announced that the Brit: For: Sec^y had called on the German Ambassdr to apologize for the removal of the wreath. If this had bn repeated in the English Press, there w^d have bn questions in the H.o C. about it for certain, & Simon

---

[221] ALK on 21 May crossed out the section from 'It seems' to 'do with it' and inserted 'There has been a great change in the Ger: attitude'.

w^d have had to deny it – because he made no official apology, but only expressed his personal regrets to Hösch. So Wright²²² of the F.O. telephoned round to all the newspapers last night imploring us not to talk about the incident – because a *démenti* (besides being awkward for Simon) w^d v. likely have given the Nazis their chance of recalling Hösch & planting Rosenberg or some other miserable Nazi specimen in his place. So we did not, except the *Daily Express*, which w^d not give any undertaking to Michael Wright.

We shall see if anything comes of it. The *D. Express* publishes it quite quietly.

In the meantime <u>Rosenberg</u> has been recalled, & is to leave tomorrow (Sunday). He told me he was going on Tuesday. His visit has been a washout. Englishmen have no use for propagandists.

'Herr Rosenberg Departs'

[Herr Rosenberg's] glib phrases totally failed to impress the minds of his English hearers, who in any case have an instinctive dislike and distrust of propaganda as a normal instrument of policy. It is true that its German exponents base their elaborate organization upon the propagandist system set up by the Allies in the closing stages of the War, which the Germans themselves are wont in these days to describe as highly successful. But the values of war and of peace are very different.

.... the practice of these methods in peacetime is a deliberate and important method of Nazi policy, which has already produced definite effects on the rather herd-like mentality of Germans, and is still producing them. A special Ministry of Propaganda has converted the newspapers of the whole country into a mouthpiece of National-Socialist doctrine. Arguments officially manufactured by the Minister, HERR GOEBBELS, are repeated upon their pages, and further disseminated over every part of the country by placard and by wireless. The cinemas blaze chauvinistic slogans; the theatres are forced to produce ultra-patriotic plays ... Moreover the revival of the national spirit, which was abnormally depressed, is being deliberately identified with the revival of military strength. Worse still, hatred of the foreigner is being steadily inculcated ... Before talking about good will abroad it would be best to stop the teaching of hatred at home; and before challenging other countries to disarm it would be better to disprove – if it is possible to disprove – that one of the main objects of Hitlerism is to prepare Germany for a war of revenge.

²²² Michael Robert Wright (1901–1976): entered dip. service 1926; FO 1930–6; Paris embassy 1936–40, Cairo 1940–3, Washington 1943–6; Asst U-Sec. FO 1947–50; Amb. in Oslo 1951–4, in Baghdad 1954–8; kt.1951.

'A Challenge to Peace'

Unhappily for the hopes of a new international order, in which arbitration is to take the place of force in the settlement of disputes, the Germany of HERR HITLER has been reinjected with the old Prussian virus. ...

The best hope is that the leaders of Germany should have sufficient sense to realize the hostility felt in other countries not only to this reincarnation of militarism but to the whole method of government which Hitlerism preaches and practises. Opinion in this country has been turned solidly against the Nazis ... It may be hoped that HERR ROSENBERG will have reported by now the genuine revulsion of Englishmen of every party and class from the methods of HERR HITLER's followers – the Jew-baiting, the exploitation of personal enmities, the spying and delation by informers, and the terrible injustices to honourable citizens, which have brought a tragic sequence of suicides by men and women to whom life had become a hideous nightmare. Germany cannot afford to antagonize the entire world. ...

17 May Sir Malcolm Robertson[223] has bn canvassing us (in *T.T.* office) for the Berlin Embassy, which is to be vacated by Rumbold v. soon. Robertson is part German, yet vigorously British – just like Eyre Crowe – & might do well. He spoke well about the present situatn there; & sent us a copy of a letter he addressed to Sir J. Simon, asking to go & see him & talk about the present state of Germany. However, Sir Eric Phipps[224] has just been appointed! So if Simon has any sense of humour – which I fear he has not – he will cordially invite Robertson to come & give his views, which now, no doubt, he w^d just as soon keep to himself!

Had a most interesting talk with Grandi this morn^g. He told me that there was always a conflict in the higher places of Fascism between what he called 'The moderates & the mad' – he being leader of the moderates, & Balbo & Farinacci[225] of the others, with Mussolini 'waving' between the two, as he put it (his English is not v. good yet, tho' graphic). He says he is often tempted to retire from politics, & write a book on Dictatorship. He says it reproduces all the faults of democracy in a concentrated form.

I remarked that there were a lot of people about who c^d write well,

[223] Malcolm Arnold Robertson (1877–1951): entered FO 1898; Min. in Buenos aires 1925–7; Amb. in Buenos aires 1927–9; retd 1930; Chm. of Spillers Ltd 1930–47; Con. MP Mitcham div. of Surrey 1940–5; Chm. British Council 1941–5; kt. 1924.

[224] Eric Clare E. Phipps (1875–1945): entered dip. service 1899; Counsellor in Brussels 1920–2; Min. in Paris 1922–8, in Vienna 1928–33; Amb. in Berlin 1933–7, in Paris 1937–9; kt. 1927.

[225] Roberto Farinacci (1892–1945): *Partito Nazionale Fascista* Sec. 1925–6; captured, executed and hanged 1945. See his *Realtà storicha* (1939).

but v. few who were men of action & leaders, & I hoped he w^{d} not retire.

He believes that if Hitler goes he will be succeeded by men of extremes, like Göring, Goebbels & Rosenberg. He thought the Brit: reaction to Hitler was too hostile.

I explained to him how we felt about him. When I left, he said 'You always give me an impression, so I like to see you very much.'

21 May   Leeper told me the other day that it was all <u>Cadogan's</u> work that figures were got into the British Draft Convention on Disarm^{t}, which MacD: produced at Geneva two months ago. MacD: was against putting in figures; & Cadogan had to go at him again & again.

Very plucky of C:, & it is the figures which give to the Convention its original & most valuable feature. MacD: only consented 24 hours before he had to deliver his speech – so then the Convention had to be completed in a terrific hurry.

The figures give a <u>standard</u> for all future disarm^{t} discussions.

What I wrote at the F.O. from Rumbold's despatch was never used <u>as a leader</u>; but what I read (the despatch) informed all my subsequent leaders on Germany.[226]

14 June   The other day Alan Dawnay had luncheon with me, & was interesting on the subject of specialists, or experts, & their influence on the Disarm^{t} Conference. He says that whenever a big issue is discussed at a Cabinet, the responsible Minister is naturally invited to state his views; & he, being a civilian, naturally says he must ask for expert advice from his Department; & in his Dep^{t} the matter is referred to the specialist, & the specialist naturally makes out a technical & in itself incontrovertible defence of his speciality. This memorandum works its way up again through the Office to the Chief, who, having asked the advice of his Dept, cannot very well throw it all overboard – so, in turns, bombs, submarines, big guns, tanks etc are vehemently defended, each defence on its merits, being irrefutable.

The only way to overcome this difficulty, Dawnay says, is for the Cabinet as a whole to take a strong line – if it does so, Dept's will conform. A lot of high-placed soldiers, for instance, are ready, he says, to abandon large tanks (of course if it is done by all nations), but no official can very well advocate their abolition unless & until it becomes the policy of the Govt.

[226] Between 10 and 21 May Kennedy produced 'A Breathing Space' (13 May), 'Herr Rosenberg Departs' (15 May) and 'A Challenge to Peace' (16 May).

Yesterday evening there was one of those delightful musical evenings which Baron Franckenstein gives at the Austrian Legation, & there I met Herr Dollfuss,[227] the diminutive Austrian Chancellor, who is putting up such a fine fight for Austrian independence against Nazi bullying. He is a vigorous, sturdy, animated little man, with a glint in his eyes – which are slightly protuberant, giving him an appearance of unsteadiness, which the rest of him belies. He gave one a terrific grip when hand-shaking. I had a few words with him in German, his English being poor. I asked him if there was a rapprochement between his country & Hungary – he said yes, pol: & economic relations were excellent. I've always believed this may be the nucleus of building up an economically sound Central Europe – Rubido Zichy's idea.

Grandi was there, & he told me that Italy & Austria were also close brothers, now – at a cost of £2,000,000, he laughingly added – the amount of Austrian loan which Mussolini has agreed shall be taken up by Italy.

Selby had been there at luncheon, Sir J. Simon being also there, – he told me that Dollfuss has <u>informally</u> asked for British non-official intervention on behalf of Austria with Germany. The form this intervention is to take is apparently a leader in *T.T.*! GD is seeing Dollfuss about it this morning. [...]

16 June   [...] A long talk this morn[g] with the For: Min: of Yugoslavia, M. Yevtitch.[228] A nice-spoken, well-groomed man, probably not at all typical of his race! And I kept on thinking of Harold Nicolson's remark about 'affability' in his last book 'Peacemaking' – how misleading the affabilities of diplomacy can be! M. Yevtitch & I seemed to get on v. well – yet really our views were antagonistic. Revision of treaties, 'impossible'. Hungarians a savage & unreliable race, accustomed to be 'seigneurs' & unwilling to resign themselves to any other relationship.

Yevtitch is ready & anxious to work for economic rapprochement, & says that ultimately 'a more general arrangement' might become possible. That is the furthest he w[d] go. I developed my idea that what is wanted is an agreed, as contrasted with an imposed peace, that the Treaty of Versailles was never really negotiated, & indeed did not get beyond the stage of preliminaries, which were then hastily signed. He regarded an agreed peace to be merely '*un idéale*'.

[227] Engelbert Dollfuss (1892–1934): Min. of Agric. & Forestry 1931; Federal Chanc. 1932; murdered 25 July 1934 during unsuccessful coup d'état by Austrian Nazis.
[228] Pavle Yevtitch: Yugoslav Press Attaché in London.

21 June The day before yesterday M. Mazaryk,[229] the Czecho Min: here, invited Sylvia & me to luncheon to meet D^r & Mme Benesh, who are here for the World Conference. B & I had two hrs almost un-interrupted discussion, chiefly on Revision. I put the case for an Agreed Peace. He is against any sort of concession now to Germany or Hungary. I felt that I really had the best of the argument, but of course he is in the position of being able to say *non possumus* – & there is an end of the matter for the present. It may be worse in the end. [...]

B:'s great point was that neither he nor any Little Entente Min. c^d propose Revision & retain his place. Feelings are too strong in their countries & Poland. They are also deeply suspicious of Mussolini, who proposed it first, & who undoubtedly had (& perhaps still has) the hope of disrupting Yugoslavia.

All that B: w^d admit on the constructive side was economic rap-prochement; & when that goes smoothly some general political arrange-ment might be possible – against compensation. B: w^d also draw in Austria & Hungary economically, if possible.

I developed my idea that G^t B^n might be ready to undertake more direct responsibilities in Europe if & when an accepted peace had been negotiated. I quoted Harold Nicolson's book 'Peacemaking' in support of my argument that the Treaty of Versailles was hasty & was imposed – there has been no negotiated peace, except partially at Locarno & for the Turks at Lausanne.

The only time Mazaryk really intervened was to say that he had seen both the P.M. – only for a moment – & 'Malcolm', as he called his son, on the subject of the Four-Power Pact,[230] & that they had explained to him that it didn't really mean Revision. I said I did not think much of statesmanship which talked Revision at Rome & in the House of C., & said it meant nothing in private conversation.

8 July Yesterday I forgot an appointment with Titulescu,[231] a thing I've never done before, I think, & of which I was v. ashamed. His Sec^y rang me up at P.H.S. to remind me, about an hour later – just as I

[229] Jan Garrigue Mazaryk (1886–1948): son of Thomas (1850–1937); Min. in London 1925–38; resigned 1938; Min. of For. Affs 1940–8; deputy PM 1941–5; believed to have committed suicide when communists took control of Czech govt in 1948.

[230] In response to Mussolini's proposals of 18 March 1933, Hitler had declared to the Reichstag on 17 May his unqualified peaceful intentions while at the same time asserting Germany's need for equality of rights on armaments. The Four-Power Pact was subsequently signed on 7 June 1933 on the basis of Mussolini's original proposal, but limiting revision to a reference to Article 19 of the League Covenant and dropping the reference to the co-ordination of policies in the 'colonial' sphere.

[231] Nicolae Titulesco (1882–1941): Rumanian politician & diplomat; Min. of Finance 1920–22; Min. in London 1922–6, 1928–32; For. Min. 1927, 1932–6. See his *Reflectii* (1985).

was settling down to my leader. However I went round to the Ritz forthwith, more to make my apologies than anything else. Tit: was extremely nice about it.

We are in an awkward position, as we are really I think v. fond of one another, & yet differ absolutely over this question of Revision. He almost begged me not to write in favour of it. And yet I am convinced it w^d be beneficial to Europe to get an <u>agreed</u> peace all round. He says he prefers a frank advocacy of revision to that of an agreed peace, because this seems to imply that the present Treaties of Peace were not properly agreed to. <u>They</u> <u>were</u> <u>not</u> – that is my whole point. Never accepted by the nations concerned in their hearts. Other Peace Treaties in the past also have not been, that is true; but at least they were freely negotiated, & in 1919–20 they were crudely imposed.

Titulescu says 'No' to all this, just as Benesh did – & argues, as well he may, that he is broader-minded & more European than most of the people he represents.

Here is an amusing memo: from Poliakoff.[232] The joke is that most of our leaders insisting that the Conference must go on have been written at the instigation of MacDonald! (In the one or two I have written, I have pressed for <u>regional</u> & <u>partial</u> agreements, as being the only ones attainable at present).

9 July Saw Mr Arthur Henderson this morn^g, on the eve of his departure to foreign capitals, on disarm^t business, provided for the first time with full authority to negotiate with foreign governments by the General Commssn of the Disarm^t Conference.

I was glad to find that he does not mean to allow the temptation of standing for the Parl^t to get in the way of his disarm^t work. There is a good Labour vacancy at Clay Cross, & he may be asked to stand – but it is a safe seat, for them, & there is to be a recess from about a fortnight hence until Nov:, so AH evidently feels that he can go on his disarm^t way unperturbed, even if (as clearly he would like) he is re-elected to Parl^t.

---

[232] This reported comments of MacDonald at the 'Steering Committee' of the World Economic Conference: 'and gentlemen I want to say this. I am not a reader of the Press. But, gentlemen, this morning I was waiting for a telephone call. Whilst I was waiting I picked up the Times And gentlemen I found there, in that great newspaper an article, some sentences of which, I think, gentlemen, deserve your attention! (Reads out selected sentences from the Times leader) You see gentlemen what the great national organ has to say about our conference. This is proof that public opinion in this country, gentlemen is deeply stirred by the possibility of an adjournment. The article is accompanied by letters from readers. All in the same sense, gentlemen. I think that we cannot afford to ignore this expression of British public opinion, all the more because it is spontaneous.'

He has diminished strength, & diminished hopes, for disarm^t, but he still believes a useful Convent$^{\underline{n}}$ to be possible.

If he comes back to Parl^t it will be as a private member (not as leader of his Party, he implied).

He was critical of Simon for not having spent more time at Geneva. I said I was ready to criticize Simon for almost everything except that!

AH told me that after a public dinner the other day Winston Churchill had drawn him aside, & in talk about disarm^t, had spoken with the greatest favour of establishing a strict system of supervision of national armaments. To find Winston in agreement with him about anything, H: said with a smile, was a great encouragement!

24 July I have been slack about noting down meetings, but I made some notes on a slip of paper about another v. interesting talk I had with Titulescu before I left London. He was intent on proving to me that the Four-Power Pact did not mean Revision of Treaties. He certainly had a lot to do with negotiation of the Pact; & he & Benesh are in a position to block revision – so there we are!

Tit: showed me drafts & memoranda, which he had in a portfolio, all concerning the negot$^{\underline{n}}$ of the 4-Power Pact, with pencil corrections showing how the texts had been modified & re-modified. He also showed me a secret letter exchanged between the three For: Ministers of the Little Entente, written when the statute of the L.E. was signed, pledging themselves to maintenance of the status quo & against Revision. Benesh wanted to call the Council of the L.E. 'The Supreme Council', but Tit: said 'Absurd, let's call it the Permanent Council.'

There were several modifications of the original draft of the 4-Power Pact in Tit:'s writing. He seems to have had a great [deal] to do with it. It is Mussolini v. Titulescu! And in this case Tit: got the best of it, I am sorry to say. The word Revision has been taken clean out of the Pact.

Tit: also showed me some secret corrspdnce that had passed between him & Gömbös,[233] the Hung$^{\underline{m}}$ P.M. In March last Gen: Gömbös was was anxious to begin talks about Revision. Tit: said he w$^{\underline{d}}$ be pleased to stop in Budapest on his way through, but he w$^{\underline{d}}$ not discuss Revision. G: then asked him if he w$^{\underline{d}}$ agree to discuss the date when discussns on Revision might begin! No, said Tit: again.

Later, in July, Gömbös asked that Hungary sh$^{\underline{d}}$ be allowed, in the Disarm^t Convention, to have an army 10% smaller than the smallest of the Little Entente states. Tit: said to me that this w$^{\underline{d}}$ be impossible.

---

[233] Julius Gömbös de Jafka (1886–1936): army officer & politician; Maj-Gen. 1929, Lt-Gen. 1934, Gen. 1936; elected Deputy 1920; Min. of Defence 1929–31; PM 1932–6.

Tit: feels hotly on this subject of Revision, & I see cannot be moved at present. We had a long, hard but friendly controversial talk.

I have also seen Grandi lately, who was just off to see Mussolini & have a talk about Revision. I talked to him about the attitude of Tit: & Benesh, & he was going to talk to Musso: about it & tell me what Musso: said, but this infernal flight of Balbo looks like detaining Gr. in London. [...]

26 July   I saw poor old Arthur Henderson two days ago, at Transport House, on his return from his European pilgrimage in the cause of Disarm[t]. He seems to have had a certain amount of success – that is to say, Daladier (French P.M.) & Hitler are nearer to each other in pte conversat[n] than they can – or will – admit in public; & Mussolini does want some arrangement. But there are still immense difficulties, which AH sees only too well. I said once or twice that there was really an immense reserve of pub: opinion in every country really favourable to an arms agreement – & what it wanted was a lead & a focal point – & urged AH to make a big public declaration.

AH, when I said this, looked very sad & pensive, & gazed sideways to me without answering – when he did, after a pause, it was a vague affirmative. I believe the truth to be that poor old H: feels done. He told me (earlier in the conversation) that he had had a violent attack of sickness in Rome, on the eve of his departure – had had to lie in his bunk the whole way from Rome to Berlin – 2 nights & a day; & in that condition had to negotiate on arrival. Then he had a terribly long motor drive from Prague to Munich. I said 'You must have been tired when you arrived' 'Tired' he said 'I was ill.'

Again in that condition he had to see Hitler. He said Hitler might have been addressing a crowd out of the window, & not himself at all. 'The grievances of Germany, I suppose?' I asked 'They simply poured forth' said H, making at the same time a gesture with both hands from his mouth outward & downward, as if a fountain were gushing from his lips.

1 August   Had another most interesting talk with Grandi this morning. He is just back from 24 hrs in Rome, where he saw Mussolini, who he says is in most excellent health & spirits. Full of verve; & above all, from Grandi's point of view, he has come right round to G's own policy of conciliatoriness. G: is delighted. He says Musso: has triumphed over Balbo's influence. He wants to work side by side with England in favour of Franco-German entente, as well as Franco-Italian.

Musso: wants to keep Revision alive, but not to push it. (This is just

what Grandi & I were for, so I am v. pleased). In the meantime Musso:
will try to get on with Disarm^t; & Grandi showed me an Italian copy
of a German memorandum (of July 18), stating the German case in v.
moderate language. This he regards as v. encouraging. [...]

Grandi said that Revision had ceased to be a flag waved by Musso
('a red flag to France' I said) & had become a real issue to be
approached cautiously.

I asked Grandi whether he thought Balbo's absence, from Rome, on
his great flight, made a difference to Musso: in for: policy & induced a
moderation which might evaporate with Balbo's return. Grandi said
no, making a comic but v. expressive grimace – corners of his mouth
well down, chin thrust out, shaking his head from side to side & ditto
with the forefinger of his right hand!

5 September How one seems to rush into the middle of news when one
comes back to London from the country! I arrived yesterday morn^g, &
by the evening had heard that the P.M.'s health is wobbling, that he is
suffering from sleeplessness, & that, as usual with him when in a run-
down condition, he is convinced that others are plotting against him &
trying to get him out – that the Conservatives are in fact tired of him.
No doubt there is truth in that – & that is perhaps a reason why he
hobnobs so openly with Londonderry & Hailsham, the two Die-Hards
of the Cabinet, allowing himself to be photoed with them in the garden
at Mount-Stewart, etc.

On the other hand it seems that whereas a few months ago the King
w^d probably not have given a Dissolution if MacD: had retired – but
just allowed Baldwin to take his place – now H.M. w^d insist on a
Dissolution. This naturally makes the Cons: think twice, for they know
they w^d lose a lot of seats. (On the other hand, they will lose more
later).

I did not realize what a lot of influence the King gets from being
able to make a Dissolution a condition of conferring the premiership.
It is a powerful instrument in his hands. He used it with great effect in
the national crisis in 1931, & he seems to me to be showing great
shrewdness in saying now that he w^d insist on a Dissolution (& so a
General Election).

MacD has let us know that he w^d welcome an expression of opinion
from *T.T.* as to whether the Nat.-Govt sh^d continue. That will have to
wait till GD returns from Yorkshire. The long & the short of it will be
that MacD will stay on for the present, but I don't believe in going on
being governed indefinitely by a man suffering from insomnia.

I also heard that Anthony Eden is on a secret visit to France – that
is, he is holidaying in the S: of France, but is to see Daladier & Boncour

in Paris on his way home, on the subject of Disarmament. [...]

6 September At luncheon today Rex Leeper told me that some of the new arrivals in the F.O. start calling other members by their Christian names almost at once, even those who are considerably senior! Naturally heads of Depts are a little taken aback, but do not protest for fear of being thought not modern.

R.L. also told me that it is not the custom to call the head of the Office 'Sir.' At an Embassy or Legation the chief is always called 'Sir;' but the Head of the F.O. not.

I had noticed that Vansittart called Norton (his Sec^y) by his Christian name, Clifford; & Simon called Selby 'Walford' in my hearing. I said to Leeper that I thought this was a mistake. It creates an unbusiness-like & over-sentimental impression. I said I much preferred the custom in the Brigade, where officers may nickname or Christian-name each other as much as they like off duty, but on parade never call each other by anything but their surnames. I go on those lines in P.H.S.

16 September Have had a whole series of Disarmament conversations during the last few days – with Norman Davis on Wed^y, with Eden & Mr Henderson on Thurs: & with A.C. Temperley yesterday. And last night my leader – which is by way of bringing pressure to bear on the French.[234]

I had arranged with Brodribb[235] – now acting Editor – to have it on Sun: night for Monday, the day when Eden begins his conversations in Paris. But Eden (& Cadogan) suggested having it pub^d this morn^g (Sat^y) so as to give it time to 'sink in' in Paris, & Brodribb agreed.

The immediate diff^y is that the French want to set up a Commssn of Enquiry <u>before</u> any Convention is signed, & send it in to Germany to enquire into infractions of the <u>Treaty of Versailles</u>. Other Govts think that this w^d produce an explosion in a country which is already boiling at their treatment since the war. Norman Davis is particularly insistent on the point, Henderson no less so & I wholly agree.

Norman Davis's motto at the moment is 'fairness & firmness' towards Germany. He ended up our talk by saying that we must even now, under Hitler, give them a fair deal, 'but if they show that they are not house-trained, sw–sh—' with a gesture of booting a dog out of the house!

Davis is impressed by Hitler personally. 'He is a <u>good</u> man' he said

[234] 'A Turning Point': 16 September 1933, p.11.
[235] Charles William Brodribb (1878–1945): joined *The Times* 1904; Asst Ed. 1935.

emphatically 'I have never seen such wonderful eyes in anybody's face'.

He assured me that Pres: Roosevelt is still absolutely international at heart. He really means the U.S.A. to play its part in world affairs; but just when he was putting out on the international sea he was caught by the most fearful blizzard, & has had to remain in harbour. [...]

I found Henderson, I am pleased to say, much stronger than 2 months ago. His victory at Clay Cross & the prospect of getting to work again in home politics have bucked him up. He is not the man of 1930 however. He was extremely friendly, & the clearest of anybody about how to get on with Disarmament. He sees however how frightfully difficult it is going to be, & told me flatly that he was not prepared to 'hang on' after Christmas. I had used the expression first. I said it might be necessary just to hang on for even a year or two until conditions became quieter in Europe. 'Well I tell you straight, Kennedy' he said v. energetically 'I am not going to hang on later than Christmas. What are we going to do all the time' he said 'Make speeches? I'm sick of listening to the same people saying the same thing.'

Eden was clearly v. much of the same opinion. He is sick of Geneva. I had a v. pleasant luncheon with him & M^{rs} E, & his Sec^y at the F.O., young Hankey,[236] at the Carlton Annexe. Eden had just got back from France that morning early, having crossed by the night boat from Dieppe. That is not a preliminary I w^d ever care for to a big job, as his is, of trying to get something done at the Disarm^t Conference. Simon is, I gather, cynical about it all now; MacDonald is really keen, but chary of associating himself with another Conference (following the Economic Conference) which may be a failure.

Henderson & he (MacD) are, I fear, still at daggers drawn; & if the thing is a failure MacD: wants it to be Henderson's this time, & not his.

Temperley told me by the way that on the famous night at Geneva when the British Draft Convention was being got into final shape he (Temperley) as well as Cadogan sat up with the P.M. from 10 pm until 1 a.m. putting in the final touches & persuading him to include actual relative figures for the military & air strengths of the different countries – a great achievement.

'A Turning Point'

An accommodating temper in Paris will greatly improve the hope, none too bright˙in any case, that an adequate Convention for the limitation and

[236] Maurice P.A. Hankey (1877–1963): joined Royal Marine Artillery 1895; Sec., Committee of Imperial Def. 1912–38, of Cab. 1919–38; Min. without Portfolio 1939–40; kt. 1916; cr. Baron Hankey of the Chart 1939. See his *Politics, Trials & Errors* (1949).

ultimate reduction of arms will be signed or at any rate initialled before Christmas. The unsettled conditions of Europe are a reason for not making the Convention too ambitious in scope and for not expecting drastic reductions to follow immediately.

.....Before any sort of agreement can be reached, however, it is necessary that all the participant countries should be more or less satisfied with their relative positions; and the fundamental difficulty is the inequality in the positions of two of the three leading States of the Continent of Europe. The Treaty of Versailles left Germany in a position of inferiority relative to France which was not intended to be permanent; and this disparity finds its most obvious and, to German minds, its most painful expression in the respective armed strengths of the two nations. When the forces of Germany were reduced to a minimum after the War her disarmament was quite definitely implied to be a first step to a general reduction; and the failure of her neighbours appreciably to lessen the difference is one of the causes of the present ferment in Germany. The fact has got to be faced that Germany will re-arm.....

22 *Sept:* I find that it was Simon who, off his own bat, made representatns to the American Govt about their building more 10,000 cruisers. He mentioned the matter to Norman Davis here, & instructed Osborne,[237] Chargé d'Aff: in the absence of Ronald, to bring it up in a friendly way to the State Dept. A stupid thing to do, in my opinion. The Americans are entirely within their Treaty rights in building these ships, & unless there was a real chance of stopping them doing it – which seems inconceivable – Simon had better have left it alone. I noticed at the Downing Str: meeting that he blushed furiously when a journalist put a question on the point. When the question was asked there was silence; & I, sitting sideways to Eden, MacDonald [&] Simon in that order – Simon furthest from me – could only see the high rosy dome of the top of his head above MacD's grey locks – & the rosy dome became absolutely scarlet! MacD: finally got him out of it rather nicely by saying that G^t B^n deplored any upward tendency in sizes or numbers of armaments, but we had no grievance etc.

On another occasion MacD: was less happy in one of his explanations. In connexion with the proposed Supervisory Arms Commission he was explaining that the British Govt did not much care for the use of the word 'Control' in that connexion. 'Arms Control' had a rather different meaning in French & in English; in French he said it meant something very rigid, & made a movement with his right hand as if he were banging the lid down on the head of Germans! Of course really it is

---

[237] (Francis) D'Arcy G. Osborne (1884–1964); Min. in Washington 1931–5, at Holy See, 1936–47; kt. 1943.

the other way about – the French word *contrôler* means little more than to 'check' or 'verify'.

8 October   Another of the periodical Disarm[t] crises. Went yesterday morn[g] to see Henderson, who had telegraphed to me from Hastings (where there was a Labour Conference) at Transport House. He was tired after his turbulent Conference, but going pretty strong. I c[d] see that he is being drawn more & more back to home pol[itic]s. He talked to me about 'this great movement;' implied they were impatient to get him back; & repeated his declaratn that he c[d] not go on living at Geneva after the New Year. He said once – 'My word, the Conservatives'll get a rude awakening one of these days.'. He seemed to be absolutely confident that the Socialists are going to get a whacking victory. I think so too.

In regard to Disarm[t] he spoke of a possible compromise between the French desire for a 4-year probationary period – to which the Brit: Govt has adhered – & the new German demand for <u>immediate</u> re-armament within the defensive schedule, & immediate beginning of reduction by others.

We spoke of M[r] Baldwin's speech the day before, also v. strong for a (Disarm[t]) Convention, but the diff[eren][ce] between Henderson's & B's views is this – H: desires & believes in <u>a new international system</u>, with the arms of each country the concern of all, & so on. To Baldwin the Disarm[t] plan is just a common-sense arrangement, convenient to all & saving a good deal of money.

A point that Hend[sn] is keen about is that the new Convention w[d] bring both USA & USSR into the Security Plan which it includes. He is therefore strongly in favour of almost <u>any</u> Convention, rather than a break-up without one.

I went on from Henderson to the F.O., & was horrified at its attitude to the new German proposals. Leeper, evidently speaking from instructions, greeted me with the words that 'the (Disarm[t]) Conference is dead.'! It is clear that Simon preserves little hope (which is natural) & wants to place the blame for failure squarely on the shoulders of Germany. This is also made plain from a speech by L[d] Hailsham yesterday. In other words they are not fighting at all costs to get a Convention through, but diplomatically calculating to put the blame for failure on Germany. This is the same sort of attitude as Willert's to me over Dollfuss the other day. Officially we are by way of backing Dollfuss (both the Govt & *T.T.*), but Willert indicated to me that it might be as well not to back him too strongly, as he might fail, & then we should look foolish. The F.O.'s attitude is, in fact, don't fight hard

for anything if there's any chance of its losing! Very pusillanimous.
None of the elder ones there were at the war.

Leeper yesterday w^d not give me the exact proposals made by P^{ce}
Bismarck[238] when he called on Simon, but tried to rush me into the
conclusion that they were hopeless. This is v. un-English & all wrong.
They ought to give us the facts & let us form our judgment – & I must
say they usually do.

I made the acquaintance of the new French Ambassdr the other
day – M. Corbin. A quiet, good-looking, well groomed man, v.
correct, & competent I sh^d say, but without any special characteristics.
He gave me the arguments in the French Disarm^t case v. clearly. [...]

16 Oct: I heard of Germany's withdrawal from the Disarm^t Conf: &
the L. o Nations on the wireless at Hambrook on Saty night, & felt it
was going to be heavy business writing about it on Sun: night in PHS.
However, GD, who telephoned to me from Cliveden in the morning,
motored to Chequers later & saw the P.M., & came away with a clear
idea of what he wanted *T.T.* to say. He had long talks with me, & also
brought in B-W[239] & Braham – & then wrote down his final ideas in
guiding notes, so my task was much lightened. Simon also telephoned
to us from Geneva.

I sh^d have written a rather different leader from the one GD & I
jointly produced,[240] trying more to discover the fundamental causes of
the breakdown, & to look further ahead. GD however has a day-to-
day mind – essential in journalism – & I see the advantage of confining
one's self to the immediate causes & the immediate effects. On the
other hand I think it is more interesting, on this sort of big occasion,
to try to throw a glance further back & then further forward. In
statesmanship I'm sure that is absolutely essential; in journalism perhaps
less so. A bit of both is wanted in both – perhaps more of the long
view in politics & more of the short view in journalism.

Simon, I think, always has the short view. The sort of thing he does
best is getting up a case which has to be immediately pleaded. He did
brilliantly for us at Geneva in the Anglo-Persian Oil Co: affair. Leeper

[238] Otto Christian von Bismarck (1897–1976): politician & diplomat; grandson of the
German Chanc.; Deputy 1923–7; Counsellor in London 1926–37; Deputy to Head
of Political Dept *Auswärtige Amt* 1937–40; Amb. in Rome 1940–3; Deputy (Bundestag)
1953–65.

[239] Robert McGowan Barrington-Ward (1891–1948): journalist; Asst Ed. *Observer* 1919–
27; Asst Ed. *The Times* 1927–1941, Ed. 1941–8.

[240] 'The Break-Up': 16 Oct. 1933, p.13. Dawson noted in his diary on the 15th: 'a
dreadfully poor leader by Leo K, who cannot write to order & had to be largely rewritten
betw 10 & 12.30.' Dawson Mss 37, f. 151, Bodleian Library.

told me the other day that he only knew the barest outlines two hours before the Council meeting began. He was given all facts & details by the Law Officer of the F.O. & a political member of it, mastered the whole thing at once, & made a brilliant exposition of the British case which didn't leave the Persians one toe to stand on!

28 Oct: Two days ago I had luncheon with the German Ambassadr, alone in the vast dining-room of his Embassy. He spoke freely. Hösch is clearly no Nazi, & hinted to me that he w^d probably soon have to go; but in the meantime he says what he can for the Nazi régime.

He explained a good deal by the misery & − as they consider − humiliation they have been suffering during the last 15 years; & he said that when they talked about '*Zurück zum Frontgeist*' they meant 'back to the spirit of comradeship'. This I can well believe & understand. There was nothing quite like the comradeship of the trenches; & since that time Germany has been torn by faction & moral & social demoralization. They want to get back to the spirit of unity. In the old Germany, & during the War, the army typified that unity. It was (as Gen: von Epp said to me once) the university of the nation.

Marxism, on the other hand, teaches class-hatred. The Nazis therefore, & esp: the best of them, want to destroy the influence of Marxists & Communists.

He assured me, I am sure sincerely, that Hitler wants only defensive arms, & also that he does not want war. I said I was v. ready to believe that, but how about in 5 yrs time? 'Ah, where shall we all be in 5 years' time'? said v.[on] Hösch, 'Who knows what the conditions will be then!' A very significantly evasive answer by an honest man.

He confirmed me in my supposition that German diplomacy had particularly resented the private & secret Anglo-Franco-American talks in Paris with Germany left out, & the outcome of them, which was to set a 4-year preliminary period as a condition before the Draft Convention was to come into operation. Ld Tyrrell had denied to the Editor that this 4-year period was a main contributory cause of driving Germany out of the Disarm^t Conference (as suggested by me in a leader),[241] but von Hösch quite confirmed me in my supposition, as he brought up these grievances without the slightest lead from me. He said it was 'humiliating to German diplomacy'.

He mentioned that when he visited his estate in Saxony, in the industrial part of the country, he had rec^d a deputation, who had greeted him Nazi fashion & ended up with 'Heil Hitler'. He said he recognized several communists among them (or rather his agent did), &

---

[241] 'The Two Cases': 18 October 1933.

that he was sure that if they got the chance later on they w$^{\underline{d}}$ cry with rather more enthusiasm 'Heil Stalin' & 'Heil Lenin'.

MacLachlan,[242] who has bn working in our office in Berlin, also told me that among the elite of the Nazi organization – S.A. & S.S. Corps – there were a lot of Communists.

Early in our talk the Ambassdr made a remark which I found it difficult to take quite as seriously as I sh$^{\underline{d}}$ have – he said 'Germans do not like killing one another' – repeated it twice. They have been at any rate mangling one another for months. However he explained what he meant. The ruthlessness practised on the Marxists etc from the very first was intended to <u>prevent</u> a Civil War – possibly it did. The same idea as the 'frightfulness' which the German leaders advocated & practised at the beginning of the War – only we didn't crumple up, as the wretched Marxists have!

The menu, by the way, was written in French – quite enough in itself to get the unfortunate von Hösch the sack! He is a nice man, & obviously has <u>not</u> got the Nazi mentality. Lord Ponsonby[243] said the other day, unkindly but truly, 'The Germans are always cap in hand or sword in hand'. von Hösch is of the former type – though the description would of course be quite unfair alone, for he is a dignified & courteous man.

5 *November* Have been having a difference of opinion with the F.O. over the Panter case. Panter, the *D.T.* Corrspt in Munich, was arrested on apparently quite insufficient grounds & kept in prison for 9 days. The F.O. & Embassy in Berlin took up the case, & it was presumably their efforts, & public indignation in England, that got him out of prison – for at one time the Reich Govt said it was going to try P: for 'High Treason'. However the German Govt, admitting that they had not sufficient evidence to try P:, let him out of prison only on the condition that he left the country within 48 hours. In fact, having admitted his innocence, they said they'd expel him!

This made me v. indignant, esp: as I felt that if the Germans were allowed to get away with it that the position of every Brit: journalist in Ger: w$^{\underline{d}}$ be made most difficult – even more difficult than at present.

[242] Donald Harvey MacLachlan (1908–71): editorial staff *The Times* 1933–6; Asst Master Winchester College 1936–8; Ed. *Times Educational Supplement* 1938–40; naval intelligence 1940–5; Asst Ed. (for.) *The Economist* 1947–54; Deputy Ed. *Daily Telegraph* 1954–60. See his *In the Chair: Barrington-Ward of* The Times (1970).

[243] Vere Brabazon Ponsonby (1880–1956): Con. politician & businessman; MP Cheltenham 1910, Dover 1913–20; Chm. San Paulo Railway; Dep. Chm. De Beers Consolidated Mines; Gov.-Gen. of Canada 1931–5; Pres. Council of Foreign Bondholders 1936; Chm. League Loans Cmtee 1937; suc. 9th Earl of Bessborough 1920.

The Germans had tried it on the French once, with complete insuccess, [sic] because the French had said at once 'for every one Frenchman turned out of Germany two Ger: journalists will be turned out of France' – & even the Soviet[s] have stood up to the Germans in this matter. So I suggested to the F.O., the moment I heard about the 48 hours' notice, that they sh^{d} say that if Panter were expelled Dr Thost^{244} w^{d} have to leave this country within 24 hours. Th: is a notorious Nazi propagandist, & corrspt of the Nazi paper, '*Völkische Beobachter*'.

It was Willert that I saw, & he got into a regular stew, being unable to make up his mind, having in his typist-secretaries, dictating one thing & then another, & proposing every possible course for the 'guidance' of the Sec^{y} of State, whom he was shortly to see on the matter.

Later he telephoned to me that it had bn decided to enquire of the Ger. Govt the reason for P:'s expulsion.

Next day I saw Sargent about it, who was full of legal & other technical reasons why it w^{d} have bn incorrect to expel Thost out-of-hand.

Of course his reasons were valid, but now & again action is better than reasoning, & the immediate threat of the expulsion of Thost w^{d}, I am convinced, have made the Germans withdraw their order of expulsion to P:, & the position of all Brit: journalists in Ger^{y} w^{d} have bn strengthened.

9 Nov: In the House of Commons 2 nights ago Simon described the Panter case as having been dealt with 'thoroughly & fairly'. [...]

Two days ago (Tuesday) Cadogan was lunching with us, & told me he had just had to arrange meetings in Paris for the next day (Wed^{y}) for Simon with Sarraut,^{245} the new Prime Minister, & Paul-Boncour (Foreign Min:) Next morning these meetings were cancelled, by order, I am told, of the Cabinet. We had suggested in our leader of the same morning that the Brit: Govt w^{d} do better <u>not</u> always to begin its Continental discussions by coming to preliminary agreements with Paris.^{246} I don't know if this had something to do with the sudden change of plans; but there was no other apparent reason.

Yesterday afternoon, in the House, Simon gave some wrong information about Danzig in a supplementary question, so the F.O. rang us

^{244} Hans Wilhelm Thost: sent to London as Corrspdt of *Völkischer Beobacher* 1931; helped found Anglo-German club in Oxford. See his *Als Nationalsozialist in England* (1939).
^{245} Albert Sarraut (1872–1962), French politician & colonial administrator; PM 26 October–23 November 1933, 24 January–4 June 1936.
^{246} 'The Disarmament Debate': 8 November 1933.

up & asked us to suppress the answer, which we did. I suppose anybody might make such a mistake, & take those means to rectify it; but I think Simon is quite the worst For: Sec^y we've had for half-a-century.[247]

Had another v. interesting talk with the German Ambassdr this morn^g. He is the best sort of propagandist for Germany in this country, for he develops his arguments lucidly & moderately, & very readily. He is also a most courteous agreeable man. [...]

19 Nov: There has been a good deal of excitement among the pol: pundits about our two leaders early last week on Disarm^t, giving the German case fully – as learnt by me from the Ger: Ambssdr – & criticising British policy in one or two details – esp: the concession to France of the 4-year 'promissory' period, always called by the French a period of probation (i.e. for Germany).[248]

I have had conversatns with Willert, Leeper, Eden & Sir John Simon himself.

Eden was the only one who made no defence of our policy, but indicated, though he didn't say so, that he agreed with our criticisms of it (this does not mean that either he or *T.T.* disagree fundamentally with Brit: policy).

Eden said that the different Govts were running round the field &

[247] The FO were forming its own impressions of ALK. On 13 November, Reginald Leeper minuted:

'It may be of some interest – as unfortunately it is of some importance – to put on record the views of Mr. Kennedy, the leader writer of 'The Times' on foreign affairs. His views, as stated to me to-day, are briefly the following.

He would not favour any initiative being taken by the British Government towards securing an understanding with France on Disarmament, as he does not think it possible to secure any agreement with France which Germany would accept. He would not therefore like this country to be placed in a position in which she was aligned with France against Germany. He would on the contrary advocate an independent policy, viz., that His Majesty's Government should make a unilateral statement saying how far they themselves would be prepared to go to satisfy Germany's claims as regards armaments. This statement he would accompany by another declaration that His Majesty's Government were prepared for their part to consider all Germany's claims for territorial revision.

I suggested to Mr. Kennedy that his policy might cause some confusion in Europe. For example, it would immediately stiffen the French in their resistance and encourage Germany. It would create the maximum amount of dissention between France and ourselves and would lead to a shimozzle (I avoided the word 'war' out of respect for Mr. Kennedy's feelings) in Europe. 'If so' he replied, 'we should keep out of it.'

I venture to suggest that at a time which is critical for Europe and ourselves the state of Mr. Kennedy's mind has an importance greater than it deserves. Until His Majesty's Government are in a position to take a definite lead I fear that 'The Times' under Mr. Kennedy's influence will not be exactly a helpful element in the situation.

[248] 'A Vote of Censure?': 13 November 1933; 'Herr Hitler's Case': 14 November 1933.

wouldn't take their fences, our Govt included. They ought to jump somewhere & give a lead again.

He talked about 'John' to me, meaning Sir J. Simon – this was no doubt his way of affirming his loyalty to his Chief. Simon, by the way, when talking to me later, referred to Lord Hailsham as 'Douglas'. All this christian-naming seems to me overdone – slushy, in official dealings.

The movement of criticism began to be set really going last Tuesday, when GD was at luncheon with Lady Astor,[249] & met there Ld Lothian, Ld Cecil, Anthony Eden & others, who wanted British diplomacy to give a big lead, in the manner of Ld Salisbury's[250] famous Circular Note in 1878.[251] GD asked me to advocate this in a leader, & I did;[252] & he has followed it up with a short one of his own.[253] The result has been that Sir J. Simon has gone to Geneva once again – taking Anthony Eden with him – to try to get the Disarm^{t} Conference going again. I told both (Simon & Eden) in the talks I had that I did not think this could be done now. A fresh start is wanted. Simon said he would make a strong statement. [...]

Simon's talk with me was a dignified apologia. I sat there while he walked up & down his large room in the F.O. explaining. I felt as if I were the tribunal of public opinion, – he were pleading before it.

One Schwarz, a German who had been a Socialist & is now a National-Socialist, came to the Office on Fri: with a recommendation from Ld Lothian, & I saw him. He had a 'big idea' about Dismmt – shown in the memo overleaf.[254] I believe that after all Hitler & Mussolini may be the men to give the lead.

---

[249] Nancy Witcher Astor (1879–1964): politician; first woman MP; Con. MP Sutton div. of Plymouth 1919–45; wife of Waldorf Astor, she hosted weekend parties at their country home attended by notable politicians and the influential, which gave rise to rumours of the existence of a 'Cliveden set' devoted to promoting appeasement at any cost.

[250] Robert Arthur T. Gascoyne-Cecil (1830–1903): Con. MP Stamford 1853–68; FS 1878–80, 1885–6, 1887–92, 1895–1900; PM 1885–6, 1886–92, 1895–1902; suc. 3rd Marquess Salisbury 1868.

[251] On 1 April 1878, only four days after succeeding Lord Derby as Foreign Secretary, Salisbury had issued a diplomatic circular explaining Britain's refusal to attend the proposed Congress at Berlin. The Russians had insisted on their unilateral right to regard the terms of peace agreed with the Turks at San Stefano ending the Russo-Turkish War as 'final'. As Kennedy later put it in his *Salisbury, 1830–1903* (London, 1953), 'With cogent logic, in terse and virile language...[it] set out the reasons why the Treaty of San Stefano should not be allowed to stand....it produced a galvanic and unifying effect both in this country and in Europe.' pp. 115–16.

[252] 'A British Initiative': 15 Nov. 1933.

[253] 'What is the British Policy?': 17 Nov. 1933.

[254] ALK has inserted a typewritten memo on his conversation with Schwarz at this point:

'Herr Schwarz was a former Socialist journalist on the *Vorwärts*, who has now gone Nazi, declaring that Herr Hitler may prove to be the most effective champion of

23 Nov: Paid a visit yesterday to Grandi, on his return from Rome. He was rather subdued, & appeared to have bn rapped by Mussolini. The last time I saw him he was in great state of elation. He had heard of the shelving of Balbo, & he said he himself was going back to keep in touch with home politics. 'I am a politician' etc. (He is certainly ambitious for a career at home) In the meantime he was going off on his trip to India, the first Ambassdr to the Court of St James's to do such a thing.

Now his trip to India has been postponed, by order of Mussolini, & he observed to me at the end of our talk – 'I want to be Ambassdr here for my 4 years. I want to stay in London.' 'A very good place to be' I said; & we parted as usual v. cordially.

24 Nov: At an interesting luncheon at Ld Newton's yesterday I met Count Bethlen[255] again, now on a lecturing tour in England. I had a long talk with him afterwards. He is working hard for a bigger Hungary. He will not be satisfied I am afraid, with a moderate & sensible

disarmament and a new peace system.

After a longish conversation with Schwarz I do not think this idea can be dismissed as wholly fantastic.

Goebbels has lately coined the phrase that Germany must be *Eine Weltmacht ohne Waffen* (A World-Power without Arms); and Schwarz believes that Hitler is quite likely to lead a sort of crusade on these lines.

The sort of thing that Hitler would do, he said, was to ask that within three months of the signing of a Disarmament Convention there should be 'sample destructions' by other Powers! The International Commission, including German officers, would supervise these destructions, and photograph them cinematographically. They would then be shown on every cinema screen in Germany.

A typically Nazi idea, and brighter than most of them!

In German eyes Geneva has deteriorated. Germans have got into the frame of mind that nothing good can come out of Geneva. It is the home of humbug and intrigue. Schwarz expressed keen regret that Simon had gone to Geneva today instead of adopting the method of the Circular Note which we had advocated in *T.T.*

Among interesting minor points made by Schwarz was that the Boy Scouts and Girl Guides still continue in Germany just as before, only they have been *gleichgeschaltet* like everything else, and made [to] be a Nazi institution, and are supposed thus to be deprived of their foreign origin.

He confirmed to me that the abbreviation 'Nazi' is used as a term of reproach by its enemies, much as 'Tory' is used by Socialists, and therefore it would be appreciated if in serious articles the word 'National-Socialist' were used in full.

An interesting sidelight on Herr Hitler's character was thrown by Schwarz when he told me that Hitler had gone to the opera 'Arabella' meaning to leave after the first Act in order to compose his reply-speech to Daladier on the wireless, but that Hitler had been carried away by the music, had remained to the end of the opera, and had composed his speech between midnight and three in the morning.'

[255] Istvan Bethlen de Bethlen (1874–1947): Hungarian politician; MP 1901–1918; PM 1921–31; died as prisoner in USSR.

rectification of boundaries. he has persuaded himself that the Croats & the Slovenes (& I think Ruthenes) want to return to Hungarian allegiance. He said to me that once changes started they w^{d} have to be big ones. This is playing straight into the hands of the non-revisionists – the Titulescus & others who refuse even to consider the question of revision. 'Force alone can do it' said Bethlen, because the others w^{d} never agree to negotiate. I can quite understand that they w^{d} refuse to do so with Bethlen.

I made one suggestion to him – that he sh^{d} talk about a 'negotiated peace,' & not about 'Revision'. 'Revision' has become a sort of red rag to the Little Entente & others; & in this country the grievance that was almost universally admitted to be real was that the vanquished countries had had no chance of negotiating the Peace Treaties but had had them imposed upon them. Each one was a dictated peace.

He was v. pleased with my suggestion, & said he would work on those lines.

The help we c^{d} give in this country, he said, was to influence France & make her realize that it was worth while keeping Hungary friends with herself & prevent her going over to Germany. [. . .]

28 Nov: At luncheon yesterday L^{y} Theo Cadogan told me that the other day she had sat next to Lord Lloyd[256] at a meal, & he had said to her 'Guess who rang me up while I was shaving this morning.' She answered that she was v. bad at guessing. He said 'Hitler'. And Hitler invited him to come to Berlin to see him, so he has gone there.

Last night in an excellent address on Hitlerism by Robt Bernays[257] who has just come back from Germany – he told us that after his big speeches Hitler was left in a state of exhaustion. Yet he often made several in a day. He travels by aeroplane; & often he goes up directly he has finished one speech, to fly several hundred miles to deliver his next. He reclines at first almost in a swooning condition, hardly capable of talking. When he begins to pick up strength he reads a novel (Bernays mentioned a German translation of Edgar Wallace), & he revives rapidly. On arrival at destination he delivers exactly the same speech over again.

Bernays had heard one of these speeches & gave an excellent

[256] George Ambrose Lloyd (1879–1941): Con. MP Staffs. W. 1910–18, Eastbourne 1924–5; Gov. of Bombay 1918–23; High Commissioner for Egypt & Sudan 1925–9; Colonial Sec. 1940–1; Con. Leader in HofL. 1941; Chm. of British Council 1937–40; kt. 1918, cr. Baron Lloyd 1925. See his *The British Case* (1939).

[257] Robert Hamilton Bernays (1902–45): journalist & politician; ldr writer, *News Chronicle* 1925–9, Special Corrspdt in India 1930–1, in Germany 1933; Lib. MP Bristol N. 1931–45 (Nat. Lib. from 1936). See his *Special Correspondent* (1934).

reproduction of it in brief. He is a gd speaker himself with an excellent voice.

13 December   Had an interesting talk with Grandi yesterday; he never minds talking about himself, & early in our talk he mused aloud 'I wonder if ambassadors are important nowadays'. I said 'I suppose so; but the telephone has centralized everything so much that more depends on the Foreign Minister & less on Ambassdrs than formerly.' This nettled him a little, & he spoke up for his work. He said that he was often able to explain It^n policy to Brit: Ministers, who did not understand as he did the working of Mussolini's extraordinary mind; & he himself was sometimes able to influence Musso: by putting things in his despatches which he knew w^d provoke the desired reaction in Mussolini. 'You w^d be surprised at the things I say in my despatches' he said. Also, of course, he interprets the English point of view to Musso: I said 'probably the English mind is almost as difficult to understand as Mussolini's' – he laughed & agreed. There is a lot, too, in the manner in which instructions are carried out, & we agreed in the end that ambassdrs are still v. important persons!

Actually however I consider that Hösch (whom I saw again this morning) is a better ambassdr than Grandi. Grandi was first-rate as Foreign Minister, both at Geneva &, I fancy, in Rome. Hösch w^d not be particularly good in that way, I sh^d say. He is the model ambassador, & Grandi more of a statesman.

'You cannot prevent or create, as a rule, but you can regulate' was one of the things Grandi said to me when we went on to discuss disarmament. And he was interesting about dictatorships. 'We must get out of our heads all our old ideas about dictators' he said. The new dictator is the representative of the people. He is not against the people. He is against the oligarchy that had got the machinery of govt into its hands.

Moreover Musso: is very susceptible to pub: opinion, he said. He is <u>determined</u> to keep in close touch with it. He tries to inform & influence it, but above all he keeps contact.

'If you think of him as an autocrat' said Grandi, 'think of him as you do of Henri IV.'

Musso: also likes to test the pub. opinion of the world. He is particularly keen just now to get reactions to his idea of a 'reformed' League of Nations.

14 Dec: Had a good talk with Simon this morn^g, far the most genuinely cordial I've ever had with him. He began by mentioning the evening party at Adila Fachiri's the other evening, at which we met & he suggested my coming to see him – & when Sylvia had a v. bright short talk with him. He asked me if I liked music, & I said 'yes, without being a connoisseur of it.' he said that that was his position, but he liked going so as to get peoples' reactions to it! 'It is v. <u>interesting</u> to me psychologically' he said 'I like going there as I like going to the Zoo' – to see specimens, he meant apparently! I laughed at this & said that wasn't at all the pleasure I got out of it. I liked to be in a world of make-believe & romance, away from work. It was the most refreshing thing in the world. 'Oh, I go to chess for that' he said.

We then had a really interesting pol: talk He told me about the present pos.[ition] of the François-Poncet[258] – Hitler & Phipps – Hitler conversations; & told me that the German suggestions had also been made to Italy & to U.S.A. – & he felt strongly that they [the disarmament talks] must be taken seriously & not squashed, as France w^d like. I strongly applauded this attitude. I then went on to say that we must not be afraid of the word 're-armament.' If a system of general limitation was to be established at all, it <u>must</u> involve a certain restricted increase in German armaments. Rather to my surprise he was delighted at my saying that, & exclaimed 'stout fellow,' or some expression of that sort. He evidently realizes the unfortunate necessity of agreeing to some German re-armament, but quite naturally finds it v. difficult to say so in public. At home there is the L.o. N. Union, & abroad France, & the nations bordering on Germany.

However, we agreed that the first thing was to train pub: opinion towards it; & I mentioned that GD was seeing Vansittart at 12 (I was with Simon 11 to 11.45), & that it w^d be a help if Simon c^d make this point to Van: to make to GD. He said he w^d try to go down & see them both & speak to GD himself – but in the meantime Grandi was waiting – he was kept waiting a quarter of an hour!

Simon told me about his coming journey to Paris & to Capri – Lady Simon is v. keen about birds! & admitted he was staying 2 days in the Embassy in Paris & seeing Boncour. No doubt he will also see Mussolini! tho' he didn't say so.

He went on to talk about the pos: of the Nat-Liberals, tho' I said I did not have anything to do with them on the paper; & then, standing up & about to go, I just managed to get an opinion from him about the representation of the F.O. (about which we had a leader this morn^g)[259] There can <u>not</u> be 2 directors of foreign policy of equal rank,

[258] André François-Poncet (1887–1978): French politician & diplomat; Deputy 1924–31; Amb. in Berlin 1931–8, in Rome 1938–40; arrested by *Gestapo* 1943, liberated 1945; High Commissioner, Allied High Commission in Germany 1949–55; Amb. in Bonn 1955. See his *Fateful Years* (1949).

[259] 'Foreign Policy in the Lords': 14 December 1933.

he said, but there ought to be another Under Sec[y] – there are two at the War Office, why not at the F.O.? But you could not separate Geneva from everything else. I agreed with all this, & said I thought pub: opinion wanted the Principal Sec[y] of State to direct from London. There had been rather an excessive amount of travelling about during the last 2 years. He agreed.

When he mentioned Boncour he said – 'There's a sympathy, even, if one may use the expression between men, an affection between us. The law is a great link.'

When I saw Hösch I suggested that there was no way out of the disarm[t] impasse other than Germany re-arming up to the defensive level, & then challenging the rest of us – are you sincere about desiring a general limitation of arms at the defensive level? v. Hösch evidently liked the idea v. much, tho' he was careful to explain that Germany was not actually re-arming.

17 Dec: On Friday I had a talk with Avenol at the Carlton. The expression used about him by Bruce-Lockhart[260] – 'he has the perfect bed-side manner' exactly describes him. He speaks soothingly about the League. The League is not dead yet. '*Il faut maintenir ses institutions*', '*il faut maintenir ses forces*' etc; & once when I pointed out the difficulties of doing this he merely said with a shrug of his shoulders '*Que voulez-vous. Si elle (la Société des Nations) est dissoute, elle sera dissoute.*' And I don't somehow think Avenol will do much to prevent it. He just makes out the best possible case for the League, arguing well.

He wants reform – if reform be necessary – to come from within; but with the rule of unanimity that is impossible. I left him with the conviction that a rough handling is in store for the League, & if it can stand it it will emerge the stronger.

[260] Robert (Hamilton) Bruce-Lockhart (1887–1970): diplomat, journalist & spy; entered consular service 1911; Commercial Sec. in Prague 1919–22; retd 1922; editorial staff *Evening Standard* 1929–37; Political Intelligence Dept FO 1939–40; Deputy U-Sec. FO & Dir-Gen. of Political Warfare Executive 1941–5; kt. 1943. See his *My Europe* (1952).

1934

2 January   This morn^g I met several diplomats at the Memorial Service for poor M. Duca,[261] cruelly murdered by the Black-guards of Rumania, among them M. Caclamanos,[262] who asked me to come & see him some time; so I went this evening, to try him on the subject of what further guarantee we (G^t B^n) can possibly give to France to persuade her to reduce her armaments. I said, not Art[icle] XVI, of the Covenant, not the Kellogg Pact, which being universal, w^d mean, if we guaranteed it, vague unforeseeable obligatns all over the world – but, an undertaking that we w^d be 'actively interested' if a new Disarm^t Convention were infringed, i.e. if we want a new order, we must be ready to make some sacrifice in its favour.

C. was v. favourable to this idea. 'That is a good idea' he kept repeating. He has political nous & a good judgment, so I am encouraged. [...]

11 Jan.[263]   Sir John Simon received me yesterday in the F.O. at about $\frac{1}{4}$ past 6, at the close of a meeting of the Disarmament Committee of the Cabinet, & we talked till seven o'clock, after which I had to go to the office & write a 1st leader.

Simon was particularly friendly, & told me something of his recent meeting with Musso: in Rome. He said he had found it was best to speak straight out to him. He said also that Musso: saw the big issue & stated it plainly; but Musso: neither works out the details himself nor as a rule does any actual negotiating with the representatives of other countries. He, (Simon,) had to do both these things. He therefore found himself talking at considerable length to Musso: about details. Musso: on the other hand had had handed to Simon directly after he arrived in Rome two sheets of paper on which were the headlines of his proposals in regard to Disarmament & the reform of the League.

The division of labour probably suited both very well. I am reminded

---

[261] Jon Duca (1879–1933): Rumanian politician; Deputy 1907–33; For. Min. 1922–8; PM 1933; assassinated by student fascist in December 1933, shortly after his government had been elected and dissolved the Iron Guard.

[262] Demetrius Caclamonos (1872–1949): Greek diplomat; entered dip. service 1907; Min. in London 1918–35.

[263] This entry is in Sylvia Kennedy's hand.

of a criticism I remember reading in the old days of Joe Chamberlain.[264] 'He thinks in headlines'. Now-a-days most statesmen don't think in headlines enough – except Musso: & Hitler. Of Hitler Simon told me that Phipps (our new Ambdr in Berlin) had said that it was a waste of time to put before him a flawless argument logically presented. All that Hitler was interested in was results. What could be done?

In a general way what Simon had to say was that the present regular diplomatic communications & personal contacts had justified themselves. It is no use going back to Geneva (for Disarmament) for the present. Nor is it any good making a dramatic declaration of British policy. British policy is being recorded week by week in dispatches to Berlin & Paris; & if the present Diplomatic negotiations break down these will be published & there will in addition perhaps be a fresh statement of policy in the form of a circular dispatch or otherwise. It had however been decided by yesterday's Cabinet Commtee that the usefulness of the diplomatic method had not yet exhausted itself. I agreed with all the above points of Simon & wrote accordingly.

We also agreed that equality (for Germany) is the real issue at present; & I asked him frankly what, if any, further guarantee Gt Britain could give to France if she disarmed down to the defensive level. Simon said his proposal was as follows–

Part 1. (Security) of the Draft Convention provides for consultation between the principal powers the moment that the Kellogg Pact is violated. He was ready to propose that a violation of the new Disarmament Convention should produce the same immediate consultation. That meant, said Simon, that the U.S.A. & ourselves should be able to come in together – a very important point. On the other hand the French are asking for '*Guaranties d'exécution*'.

20 Jan: Two nights ago dined at the German Embassy, & there made the acquaintance of the present Pce Bismarck, who is Counsellor of Embassy. I took to him v. strongly. He has great political talent, & we had a most interesting conversation on the present state of the Disarmt negotiatns, speaking with complete frankness to one another after about 2 mins: I told him the best thing that cd happen wd be that Germany shd re-arm to the defensive level, whatever other countries might say – & then Hitler wd have the opportunity for a great gesture. Now, he wl be able to say to the rest, here we are defensively armed! Do you really wish for all-round limitation at that level? If so, come down to it. If

---

[264] Joseph Chamberlain (1836–1914): Lib. MP 1876–85; Lib. Unionist MP & ldr 1885–1914; Sec. of State for Colonies 1895–1903; father of Austen & Neville.

not, we're sorry, but we'll have to build ourselves also the big offensive weapons – tanks, guns, bombers etc. Suppose you just for a start destroy a few of your big tanks & aeroplanes. We $c^{\underline{d}}$ have the process cinema'ed & circulated in Germany (Schwarz's idea). That will make a great impression on our people.

Bismarck was much taken with the idea, & said he $w^{\underline{d}}$ expound it in Berlin, where he was going at the end of the week (today).

We agreed that psychology counts more than logic in international affairs.

I had also some good talk with Hösch. I noticed that he had 2 longish separate talks with me, & hardly any words with Norton, Leeper & others (juniors) of the F.O. – except Wigram, whom no doubt he knew in Paris.

6 February   My conversatns with Grandi usually contain some general discussion which is interesting, & to-day we talked about the power of England to mould a school of statesmanship. I believe that English traditions encompass politicians & turn them into statesmen. I gave LlGeorge as an example of an alien temperament which has never responded to treatment – he remains Welsh, & has missed great statesmanship, which at one time seemed within his reach.

Grandi said that he had found England a mistress hard to approach. Once you got to know her, however, she held you. He has in fact now become acclimatized. He wants to stay on. [...]

Musso: at one time thought of making G. leader of the Fascist Party, & Grandi asked for a senatorship. Musso: however told him he was too young. G. repeated his conviction about himself 'I was, I am & will be a politician'. Even now he evidently regards his embassy as an interlude – for by 'politician' he means 'home politician.'

He told me that Italy was strongly against Austria's appeal to the League (in the quarrel of Dollfuss with Germany), & had made its view quite clear to Austria. I was pleased, as I said that was my view (as expressed also in *T.T.*), but the F.O., though sharing it, had not the courage to make it known to Austria. 'The policy of Pontius Pilate' said Grandi 'washing your hands'. This was rather stiff.

9 Feb: A long talk with Arthur Henderson this morn^{g} at Transport House. One thing about him is, that unlike Simon he goes straight for the big issue – & we discussed at length the feasibility of $G^{\underline{t}}$ $B^{\underline{n}}$'s adhering to something like the famous old Protocol for stabilizing Europe & the world.[265]

I agreed that some day, if the Collective Peace system is ever to be established, we must commit ourselves to some extent; but I cannot agree with H: that our commitment ought to be absolute & automatic.

He told me one thing that I had forgotten, & that is that the Protocol (of 1924) was not to come into force until a disarmament scheme had come into force. An important proviso, which Henderson insisted upon.

I told H. I was glad he was hanging on & keeping the Disarm[t] Conference in being. Oblivious of what he had said to me on an earlier occasion ('Well, you'll have to get somebody else to hang on') he said he did not mean to leave it at the moment when it was in difficulties.

He was as usual critical of the Brit: Govt. I admitted faults in 1932 (in the Disarmt Conference). He gave me a hint that he w[d] like to go with Anthony Eden on his forthcoming European tour.

15 Feb: Have seen Eden & Simon during the last 2 days. Anthony Eden asked me to come & see him before he went off to the European capitals, & we went through the points that might be made in bargaining negotiatns in Paris & Berlin. Italy we both thought w[d] give no trouble. In fact we really saw eye to eye on all points, as we usually do. He told me Hitler had bn v. cordial & they were going to have two meetings in 2 days. I told him my idea that Hitler sh[d] rearm up to the defensive level, & then challenge the rest of the world to come down to it – the only hope of an agreement, I believe.

In Paris the important thing will be to get some reductions, actual & visible – & we (G[t] B[n]) in return must commit ourselves a little bit further even than the last Memorandum – i.e. we must undertake to do something – not merely to consult with a view to possibly doing something.

Afterwards we spoke a little about the BBC & Vernon Bartlett's[266] retirement, which was cheered in the H. of Commons the other day, showing in my opinion that V.B. is in closer touch with pub: opinion

[265] The Protocol, which Britain had refused to sign in 1924, had attempted to use arbitration and conciliation to remedy the defects contained in Article XV of the Covenant of the League. The proposal was that signatories might resort to war only in the case of resisting acts of aggression or acting in agreement with the Council or the Assembly of the League. All disputes were to be submitted to and settled by the World Court, and before and during the court's proceedings states would be barred from increasing their armaments or effectives in any way.

[266] Vernon Bartlett (1894–1983): journalist & broadcaster; *Daily Mail* 1915–17, *The Times* 1919–22; Dir. London office, LoN 1922–32; broadcast regularly on for. affairs 1928–34; For. Dip. Corrspdt *News Chronicle* 1932–54; Ind. MP Bridgwater 1938–50. See his *Nazi Germany Explained* (1933).

than the present H.oC. I can see that Eden & the politicians are jealous of the power of the B.B.C., & Eden hoped that no one man w$^{\underline{d}}$ do the foreign talks in future, but a panel of several.

Eden by the way seemed to think that 2 days in each capital w$^{\underline{d}}$ be quite enough. I sh$^{\underline{d}}$ have thought a week in each w$^{\underline{d}}$ have bn better.

At the opening of the APA house in Arlington Str yesterday I met Sir J. Simon, who drew me aside to inform me that his feelings towards D$^{\underline{r}}$ Dollfuss had greatly changed as a result of the brutality with which the Socialist rising was being put down. He indicated it w$^{\underline{d}}$ mean a modification of Brit: policy.

He further told me that he had bn against Austria's appeal to the League (in respect of Germany) but had not been able to say so publicly. 'Suvich (the Italian Under Sec$^{\underline{y}}$)[267] w$^{\underline{d}}$ tell you that I was the man that tried to dissuade her' he said. The remark is curious & unconvincing. Moreover it followed my expression of dissent from his (public) policy.

22 Feb: Was rather surprised in *T.T.* Office yesterday when I was told by our telephonist that Sir J. Simon was on the tel: & wanted to speak to me – still more so when he told me at the start that he was going to speak about 'Private Armies' in his speech at Glasgow today, & wondered if we wouldn't have a leader about it – because that is a home subject. I thought at first that it must be the German SS & SA troops which he meant, which, as it happens, are actually being discussed yesterday & today by Anthony Eden in Berlin with Hitler, & which I may be writing about. But not at all. It is on the need to suppress these irregular forces at the outset that Simon intends to speak. He developed the idea at some length & I cordially supported his line of argument & said I w$^{\underline{d}}$ report what he said to GD. He said, 'oh I asked for somebody in the Editorial Dep$^{\underline{t}}$,' in explanation of his saying all this to me. I think all the same he must have asked for me personally, as otherwise he w$^{\underline{d}}$ not have bn put through to me. I think he believes that GD wants to get rid of him, so prefers to talk to me.

23 Feb: I spoke to GD about above yesterday, & it seems Simon did ask for GD first, & GD was taken up at the moment & himself

[267] Fulvio Suvich (b. 1887): Fascist politician & diplomat; Fascist Deputy; delegate to LoN 1925–9, 1931–2, Hague Reparations Conf. 1929–30; U-Sec. For. Affairs 1932–6, Amb. in Washington 1936–8; delegate to Stresa Conf. 1935. See his *Memorie*, 1932–6 (ed. by Gianfranco Bianchi, 1984).

suggested he sh^{d} speak to me. But that puts a query against Simon's remark that he asked for 'somebody in the Editorial Dept.' However, a minor matter.

During the last few weeks have had conversatns with Alan Dawnay & Sir John Reith[268] about the reorganization of the foreign affairs work of the BBC, involving probably the creation of a Foreign Dept – which they have not got at present.

They are dropping Vernon Bartlett, mistakenly, I think. He seems to me just the man for the weekly talks, & they will not easily do better. The F.O. however complained about him after his famous talk just after Germany's departure from the League; & lately again he has appeared to be slightly pro-German. The F.O. is very pro-French; & the BBC is very susceptible to influential criticism; so V.B.'s contract is terminated as from the end of next month. The idea after that is to get a series of different talkers, & in the meantime to organize either a Foreign Dept, or a big new News Dept, of which the Foreign w^{d} be one section.

Sir John Reith made rather an impression on me – even though he obviously likes to make an impression on one! A tall, gaunt, broad-shouldered Scotsman, he stalks down upon one, shakes hands, & then says nothing whatever, beyond offering one a cigarette. He moreover accompanied his offer of a cigarette by the remark 'Though I'm a Presbyterian I've cut down my cigarettes to 4 a day from about 40 during Lent.' I said I also tried to do something during Lent. After a pause, he asked me what my views were about taking on work on the BBC. I told him what attracted me about it, stating frankly that the high salary which had bn provisionally mentioned between Alan Dawnay & myself was one of the inducements. On *T.T.* I only got £1200 (he asked me the exact figure), & the continual night-work tired me very much (I have had a good many leaders to write lately on the night's news as it comes in – from France, Austria also the H. of Commons. Very trying, when one does not know what the state of affairs will be at the moment when one's leader will be finished!) I added however that I was by no means eager to leave *T.T.*

We then discussed at great length what might be done in the way of a Foreign News service for the BBC, & keeping closer touch with the F.O.

The idea which I ventured to suggest was that there sh^{d} be one talk

---

[268] John Reith (1889–1971): Gen. Mgr, BBC 1922, Managing Dir. 1923, Dir-Gen. 1927–38; Chm. Imperial Airways 1938–9; Chm. BOAC 1939–40; Min. of Info. 1940, of Transport 1940, of Works 1940–2; kt.1927; cr. Baron Reith of Stonehaven 1940. See his *Into the Wind* (1949).

a week, or one a fortnight, which sh$^{\underline{d}}$ give formally & frankly the govt point of view; &, in addition, a wide & representative variety of talks by men with different &/or antagonistic views. Reith seemed to like the idea. I urged that it w$^{\underline{d}}$ abolish the ambiguity that exists at present – witness V. Bartlett, who was supposed to speak independently, but in fact (tho' not in theory) is being dropped because he annoyed the House of Commons.

Where Reith differed from me was that I suggested that I might be the Govt spokesman on these occasions. I said I was accustomed to go to the F.O., get their views, & interpret them to the public in leaders. Could this not be done – only more closely to the official view – *viva voce* on the microphone?

Reith said that members of the Staff of the B.B.C. never themselves spoke, & that it w$^{\underline{d}}$ be better in every way to get members of the Gov$^{\underline{t}}$ itself to do the speaking. My job w$^{\underline{d}}$ be provide the speakers.

The difficulty about that w$^{\underline{d}}$ be that in regard to Foreign Affairs there w$^{\underline{d}}$ only really be 3 possible talkers – the For: Sec^{y} himself, Anthony Eden, & L$^{\underline{d}}$ Stanhope[269] (now Under-Sec^{y}). I did not make that point at the time to Sir J. Reith, but it still seems to me that what is wanted is an equivalent to Willert, (F.O.), in the BBC. Let him give the country regularly the official point of view; then get as many free-lances, sympathetic & critical, as possible. Three names that occur to me at once are Austen Chamberlain, Noel-Baker, & Bernays (Liberal) – in addition to Vernon Bartlett.

Reith said to me rather pointedly that he didn't want people to come to the BBC just for the sake of getting bigger salaries; he wanted people to come in a missionary spirit. I said, if I came, I w$^{\underline{d}}$ come for both reasons. I <u>was</u> very keen on helping the public to understand foreign affairs; but also at the present moment an increase of salary w$^{\underline{d}}$ be most valuable to me.

It is incidentally v. difficult to combine the missionary spirit with strict impartiality. And the need for impartiality & objectivity was one of the things that both Reith & Alan D: impressed upon me most.

27 Feb: [...] The suggestion that Simon may go to the Home Office has caused a hubbub & has been dubbed by himself 'a pure invention.' It is however generally supposed to have been inspired by Baldwin, with whom GD is v. thick, & who undoubtedly <u>would</u> like Simon to

[269] James Richard Stanhope (1880–1967): politician; Civil Ld of Admiralty 1924–9; U-Sec. for War 1931–4; Parliamentary U-Sec. of State for Foreign Affairs 1934–6; 1st Ld of Admiralty 1938–9; Ld Pres. 1939–40; suc. 7th Earl of Stanhope 1905.

leave the F.O. & be superseded by Lord Halifax.[270] Moreover Baldwin was in with GD recently over the position of Anthony Eden – between them (& my leader) they got him made Lord Privy Seal. So naturally the other papers believe that again GD was 'inspired' to put in his Note about Simon. But in this case he was not.

This morning the other papers contain the information that Simon complained yesterday to the P.M. about the intrigues & political manoeuvres being conducted against him.

I fear that GD <u>is</u> beginning to believe himself a bit of a king-maker. The more <u>influence</u> a journalist gets the more careful he must be to realize that it is influence he wields, not power. He may be prompter or critic, & sit in the stalls or in the balcony, but he is not an actor.

On 7 March, Kennedy officially informed Geoffrey Dawson that he had been offered a post by the BBC to be director of their newly-formed News Department at £2000 a year.[271] Kennedy said that he would prefer to continue with 'The Times', if they would raise his salary to £1800, with 8 weeks vacation, explaining that he particularly wanted the vacation in order to travel, which he believed essential for keeping in touch with foreign countries & with friends abroad. The newspaper acceded to this proposal by giving him a salary of £1500 plus an allowance of £300, along with the 8 weeks.

9 *March*   I saw Anthony Eden again the other day on his return from his European mission (as well as having met him at Victoria & having a few words with him then). He said that Hitler showed mastery of the details of the disarm[t] problem, & did not merely make a speech on the subject, as he formerly did with negotiators – e.g. Norman Davis & Henderson. L[d] Cranborne[272] (who was with Eden in his room in the H: of Commons & had toured with him) said however that at luncheon at the British Embassy Hitler had seemed a very dull & ordinary man.

---

[270] Edward Frederick L. Wood (1881–1959): Con. MP Ripon 1910–25; Pres. of Bd of Educ. 1922–4, 1932–5; Min. of Agric. 1924–5; Viceroy of India 1925–31; Sec. for War 1935; Ld Privy Seal 1935–7; Ld Pres. 1937–8; FS 1938–40; Amb. in Washington 1941–6; cr. Baron Irwin 1925, suc. 3rd Viscount Halifax 1934, cr. Earl Halifax 1944. See his *Fulness of Days* (1957).

[271] Kennedy had already informed Dawson unofficially of the approach from the BBC. Dawson noted in his diary that 'Leo Kennedy is obviously attracted by an offer fr[om] the BBC & I doubt whether an hour's earnest discussion before dinner really shook him. (Reith might have spoken to me before trying to bribe him away).' Dawson Mss. 38 f. 39, Bodleian Library.

[272] Robert A.J. Gascoyne-Cecil (1893–1972): Con. MP Dorset S. 1929–41; U-Sec. FO 1935–8; Paymaster-Gen. 1940; Dominions Sec. 1940–2, 1943–5; Ld. Privy Seal 1942–3, 1951–2; Commonwealth Sec. 1952; Ld. Pres. 1952–7; Ldr in HofL. 1942–57; styled Viscount Cranborne 1903–47; suc. 5th Marquess of Salisbury 1947.

Cranborne made rather interesting observations, & seemed to me to be a shrewd observer. Anthony Eden showed that one of the most valuable results of his trip was that he c^d see just where concessions might be made by the various parties, concessions which w^d never even be hinted in despatches. As usual, we saw eye to eye, & I wrote a leader accordingly.[273]

'The Eden Mission'

The mission seems to have been thoroughly satisfactory within definite limits. The LORD PRIVY SEAL was not commissioned actually to conduct negotiations, but to prepare the next stage of them by collecting and collating the views of the three leading European Governments on the last British Memorandum; and in discharging his task in an exemplary manner he has become the one British Minister who has established personal contact with the principals of each of those Governments. Two of them are dictatorships in which the chief's outlook is all-important; and in the third country a national Ministry has been formed with a new Prime Minister and a new Foreign Minister. The views of M. BARTHOU in particular are little known to the outside world. MR. EDEN must now be able to convey to the Committee, and to his immediate chief, an idea of how the disarmament problem is regarded by the directing minds of Europe. He must know – though obviously nothing under this head can be authoritatively stated – in what direction further concessions are possible from one party or the other. The reactions of the German and Italian Governments to the British Memorandum are understood to have been expressed with frankness and precision. The response of the French Government is still awaited. If it is not received to-day the Cabinet may hesitate to take the question of disarmament at its meeting to-morrow. But the long talks in Paris both on MR. EDEN's outward and on his return journey must at least have provided a general idea of the French mind. Delay favours rearmament; and it might be worth while for the British Government to consider at once the crucial question – which in any case must demand an answer soon – of how far it is willing to go in carrying out its undertaking 'to exchange views as to the steps to be taken for the purpose of restoring the situation' in the event of a proved infringement of the future Convention....

13 March Had another good talk with Bismarck at the German Embassy this morn^g – a sequence to ours in January. [...] we really talked about Disarm^t, & he told the sequel of our Jany talk. When he got to Berlin (to which he was then just going) he was invited to have tea with Hitler in the ? Hof (a hotel I think); & he developed my idea, telling him where it came from – the idea that the only way out of the

---

[273] 'The Eden Mission': 6 March 1934, p.15.

impasse is for Germany to re-arm up to the defensive level, announce it, & challenge the rest of us to come down to that. Hitler, it seems, was delighted. 'Ah, I am understood' he exclaimed; & turning to his entourage he said 'Did you hear that?'

I am v. pleased about that. It is now only a question of timing.

16 March   Yesterday Vitetti,[274] the Chargé d'Affaires of the Italian Embassy, asked me if I w^d come round to see him, & when I went he told me frankly that Sgr Suvitch [sic], the Under-Sec^y for For: Affairs (Musso: being his own For: Min:), had told him to get my opinion on Italian policy towards Austria. Very flattering! The It: Embassy apparently always transmit my leaders home more or less verbatim.

Vitetti is a v. nice little man, a quick talker, full of good arguments.

17 March   I have noticed a tendency lately for foreign diplomats to go to the <u>Press</u> Dept of the F.O. They see Willert. Vitetti & Franckenstein have both done it lately. Actually as a *Times* man I rather regret it, because I have access to the dips:, whereas if they impart their ideas to Willert it is for the purpose of dissemination among the journalists generally. However it is a tribute to the growing influence of the Press.

24 March   There was a general meeting of the Press with Simon at the F.O. yesterday, to hear him talk to us about the latest French Disarm^t Note (M. Barthou's).[275] I was much struck by Simon's depression. The French Note is a badly retrograde one, & that may be a great disappointment, as I am sure he is genuinely keen about disarmament. It is possible also, I think, that he knows that MacDonald has definitely decided to retire, which will make his own position doubtful & difficult. Baldwin w^d drop him, I think.

In his exposition to us Simon was pathetically humble, & kept on apologising for telling us so little, tho' in fact he told us more than is usual on such occasions. He also was particularly friendly to me, & appealed to me once by name for corroboration of an opinion he was giving. He had obviously borrowed one or two of his ideas from our leaders.

[274] Leonardo Vitetti (1894–1973): entered dip. service 1923; Counsellor in London 1932–6; Dir. of Legal and Cultural Affairs *Ministero degli Affari Esteri* 1936–1943; mb. Italian delgation to LoN, the International Court of Justice and the London Naval Conf.

[275] Jean Louis Barthou (1862–1934): French lawyer & politician; Deputy 1889–1922; Senator 1922–34; Min. of Justice 1922, 1926–9; For. Min. 1934; assassinated 1934.

At the end he called to me – calling me 'Kennedy' without the 'M^r' for the first time! – & I went up & had a little private talk with him, though Vernon Bartlett & Gerotwohl[276] joined in. He begged us not to damn the French Note too heartily, as then the negotiatns might come to an end altogether. He is sound in his views, but weak.

29 March   Yesterday I had a long & intimate talk with Hösch. I like him v. much. We went frankly into the question of Hitler's not merely re-arming Germany up to the defensive level, but also announcing the *fait accompli*. He likes the idea, but thinks it premature. He declares that Germany is making every necessary preparatn to produce defensive weapons & transform the Reichswehr into a short-service force, but has not actually re-armed above the Treaty level in any respect. I rather doubt that, but of course he cannot admit that they are treaty-breakers until Hitler announces it.

I said it was curious that the principles which triumphed in a war were often vindicated by the vanquished rather than by the victors. In 1830 it was the beaten French who stood for liberalism & free parl^y institutions; & & [sic] now it is Hitler who is really championing the ideas of the future.

GENEVA *9 April*   Had a long talk on Disarm^t this morn^g with Arthur Henderson, & found myself for the first time completely differing from him – on the point of the Disarm^t Convention being universal or regional. He sticks absolutely to the universal idea; I say the only hope is a regional limitation plan. Now that it is generally accepted that there must be application of penalities for infringement of the Convention it seems to me to be particularly necessary to have regional understandings limiting the possible sphere of action of each country. Henderson indicated that if that line were adopted the Conference as at present constituted must come to an end & a new beginning made (without himself). All the Resolutions etc: so far passed are of course, as he said, universal in force; & legally & juridically no doubt his view (& the French) is right; but not practicable. Germany has the initiative, & is not at Geneva.

Henderson is becoming more & more anti British Gov^t, & his views are biased accordingly. He for instance criticized Simon for not coming to this meeting of the Bureau, & said that if he had, Barthou & Norman Davis & probably Suvich w^d have come too. But the meeting is only

---

[276] Maurice Alfred Gerotwohl (1877–1941): journalist; Diplomatic Corrspdt and ldr writer on for. affairs, *Daily Telegraph* 1919–35.

likely to last one afternoon, & to adjourn; & Anthony Eden was given Cabinet rank for just this sort of occasion; so why <u>should</u> Simon come?

Altogether Uncle Arthur is becoming a little pernickety. He charged me with having sneered at him, because in a recent article I said he was 'punctilious'! I hotly denied that there was any opprobrium in the term, which I understood to mean 'having a sense of duty'. He assumed that I had got the information which I gave in that article 'from Simon & Eden,' whereas in fact, as I told him, I got it from the League of Nations Office (which is most friendly to him).

An interesting admission he made to me was that <u>any</u> British Gov^t w^d have to keep a free hand to equalize our air armaments to those of France.

Later I saw Abraham, one of the acute brains of the Secretariat & a nice, sensible fellow. He accepts the idea of regional agreements, & does not think they w^d dish the League, even tho' not negotiated at Geneva. What must kill the League in the long run is the continued absence of important countries. At present however Japan is keeping in the closest touch with everything that is going on here, keeping a special Staff at their Consulate to do so. Russia shows signs of wanting to do so too; & Germany has said she will consider the question when disarm^t has been settled. Japan, unlike Germany, still has her members of the Secretariat & she pays her subscriptions.

One of Abraham's good points was that the League is <u>not</u> a substitute for diplomacy.

Later I saw M. Avenol, the Sec^y-General, who spoke as usual in an amused half-cynical but really serious spirit about the League & Disarmament. He pleased me by saying that *The Times* leaders on Disarmament had bn '*intéressants, mais très intéressants, et substantiels*'.

He is ready to compromise on the question of regional v. universal agreements within the framework of a general Convention. He is moderate in all things.

Mr Henderson by the way reverted to the old Protocol (of 1924) & bitterly regretted that it had bn rejected by G^t B^n. He maintained that if it had bn accepted everything w^d have bn much easier since. 'Too late' was not only true of what was done in the War; it was just as true of what was done in peace.

I think the Protocol was 'too early.' Something of the sort may be possible later in the century.

Abraham, by the way, made a remark to me which was typical of the League mentality. 'If Peace & Justice are in conflict' he said 'we choose peace.' They are men of goodwill, but not of grit.

11 Apr: Had two talks with Anthony Eden yesterday, one at the end of the morning & one after the afternoon meeting of the Bureau. Very genial, as usual. In the morn^g he had just seen Henderson & then Massigli, & had talked to Simon on the telephone in the F.O. Henderson had thrown out to him the suggestion that the Brit: Gov^t sh^d take on the re-casting of the Draft Convention, but he had forthwith declined. He had then telephoned to Simon, & Simon had confirmed his decision. Simon, it seems, had read my message in *T.T.* & had been 'v. interested' & had concurred with the observation that 'it was not altogether clear why Mr Henderson sh^d contemplate handing over the task to an individual Govt.' Actually Eden & I both [see] Party manoeuvres in it. The 'world' Conference looks like failing, & Henderson being now an M.P. in Opposition, w^d much rather that the blame sh^d fall on the Brit: Gov^t than on himself as Pres:. In any case I think Eden did well to turn down the proposition at once. In our evening talk we agreed that much the best chance of agreement was by local or regional arrangements between the countries immediately affected. Henderson, in his talk to me yesterday, had <u>insisted</u> on the necessity of a <u>world</u> Convention – that was what the Conference had been called for, & he himself could have nothing to do with local agreements which moreover established only limitation & not reduction.

Henderson made the interesting admission to me that 'any Party' in G^t B^n w^d have to see to our Air Defences; implying, I thought, that even the Labour Party w^d not agree to our permanent inferiority to France in that respect.

Aghnides (who as Chief of the Disarm^t Section of the L. of Nations works in v. closely [sic] with Henderson) admitted to me this morn^g confidentially that he had noticed a difference in Henderson since he had become an M.P. again.

Aghnides believes in regional agreements, & says that quite obviously the all-important thing is for the great European Powers to come to an understanding between themselves. The smaller Powers anyway have not got much in the way of heavy armaments. He also agrees that in the Air the thing to go for is the abolition of bombing except as a police measure with the sanction of the League of Nations.

Had luncheon with the Sec^y-General. A very different affair from the gatherings under the Drummonds. No ladies – except one French lady, a journalist – all extremely informal & casual & people not even bothering to talk v. much. I sat next to Avenol, & he developed his idea of a General & Universal Conventn containing just the main principles, & then groups of nations to negotiate definitive agreements within those principles. This seems to me the best way out, so I spoke on those lines to Henderson later when I went to say good-bye to him – he leaves tonight. He does not like it. He still believes in the professions people make here in favour of all-round reductns & hopes for a substantial world Convention. On the other hand he did speak about the possibility of having to 'close down' the Conference – the first time I've heard him. He wants to bring matters to a climax in the summer, & give an account of his stewardship to the Assembly in September. We had quite a cordial good-bye.

12 Apr: (In train between Geneva & Dijon)[277] I had two good talks this morn^g before leaving Geneva with Benesh & Titulescu. Benesh was as spry as ever, & when I went to him at 9.45 he was already just finishing with somebody else. He has an intensely clever face. He talked about the future of Austria, the recognition of USSR by the Little Entente, & Disarm^t. He was as usual circuitous & comprehensive about Austria. He stands for its independence. He wants it to become the protégée neither of Germany nor Italy. He does not like the new Italian plan (an Italo-Austro-Hungarian economic understanding), & gave me the interesting information that in addition to the public agreement there is a private one, which is of an anti-Czech character commercially & which goes much nearer to creating a Customs Union than the pub^d declarations indicate. He says that Czech & Italian industries are not really very much in competition, & eventually he believes the Little Entente States will come into a general scheme with It: & Hungary – & Germany of course cannot be kept indefinitely out. Mussolini has said that he does not want to keep the Little Entente out – that he is even preparing the way for their collaboration. Benesh takes him at his word. But there will be an awkward moment when Benesh reveals his knowledge of the secret arrangements – he says he has them all in detail.

But Italy must not try to dominate Austria politically. In this connexion he told me an interesting thing. When Musso: was elaborating his plan Hitler sent for the Yugoslav Minister in Berlin & declared to him emphatically – 'Never Mussolini or a Hapsburg in Vienna,' saying that Germany w^d do <u>anything</u> & <u>everything</u> she could to prevent that.

I said that we supported the Italian plan in *T.T.*, because I considered that Italy <u>was</u> working for the strengthening & independence of Austria, & a beginning must be made somehow. Benesh said he agreed that a beginning must be made, & was willing to allow Mussolini the credit for that. Then he made the reservatns recorded above.

He pointed out that Austrians are still proud esp: towards Czechs & Italians, whom they formerly dominated.

In regard to Disarm^t he was not unduly optimistic & in a general

---

[277] This entry is in pencil.

way approved my idea of a universal Convention of the simplest description, containing leading decisions stated in broad terms, & then the negotiation of separate practical agreements within those terms by groups of nations. He saw difficulties, of course, but was inclined to agree that it offered the best hope now. He admitted to me, by the way, for the first time that Henderson was over-optimistic.

He raised one curious difficulty in regard to our proposal to guarantee only the disarm^t Convention but not frontiers. Then, he said, a country will attack first & arm above its level afterwards! Typically Central European! He said something to me about C. European politics being absolutely different from British.

Curiously enough Titulescu a little later said much the same thing in a different way. 'There is intrigue & lying in European politics' he said 'but you (British) don't go in for it, & I don't either.'

Dear Titulescu came into his sitting-room in his night-garb (11.30 am) as I had sent up to say I had to leave for Paris directly. He wears brown bags to sleep in apparently, several pyjama jackets, & over them a sort of Chinese cape. He looked more than ever like a Mongol! but spoke with his usual friendliness & frankness. He told me about the Little Entente negotiations for the 'normalization' of relations with USSR (the King of Yugoslavia is an obstacle, but will probably come round).

Actually there was agreement between USSR & the three Entente States that recognition w^d come & resumption of normal relations, but negotiatns in respect of Security & Propaganda might take another 6 weeks or two months.

Titulescu himself raised the question of the revision of the Treaties, which I rather avoid with him now, as our views are opposite. However, he having brought it up, I just marked off a little bit off the edge of the table where we were sitting & said 'couldn't you alter just a little bit of frontier?' 'To suppress a frontier is easier than to change it' he answered – get rid of the economic barriers & political frontiers won't matter. But the Hungarians refused their economic offers.

PARIS *13 Apr:* Have bn having interesting talks this morn^g with Tyrrell & Gen: Weygand. T: declared to me he was much better than he had bn for some time; but he seemed tired. That may however be the natural depression caused by his forthcoming departure & the end of a long career. He did not speak quite with that epigrammatic crispness which when he is in good form is such a delight; but I was v. glad to get his views on French politics external & internal.

I started by telling him my impressns of Geneva, & he agreed with my conclusion – try for a <u>very</u> <u>general</u> universal Convention, &

particular & more detailed limitation agreements between groups of States. I said agreements for 'limitation & reduction', but he said, no, limitations only, nothing else can be achieved now.

He hoped that in *T.T.* we w^d stamp on the German plea that they are in danger on account of security. Their neighbours, he said, are *beati possidentes*, & not the least likely to attack. They are gorged (the fact remains however that Germany is most vulnerable).

We must get some Convention, he said, & Doumergue[278] & his Cabinet realize it (all except Tardieu). Economy demands it; & competition in arms w^d be terrible for France for other reasons. It w^d mean an extension of the period of service; & the peasant w^d loathe that. Germany has a dictatorship, & is not hampered by Parl^y questions & opposition to expenditure. Germany is highly industrialized; & a master of dissimulation.

L^d T: firmly believes that Germany is not merely arming fast (all know that) but that she has no intention of stopping. Hitler, he considers, is in the position of the Kaiser before the War – an amiable & really well-meaning man, but in the hands of others stronger than himself. He is the mask.

All through Tyrrell thought of this Germany as the Germany of 1904–1914 over again. That is where he & I differ. I believe it is a new Germany – with of course many – even most – points of resemblance, but a few big differences. One is that this regime is essentially neo-Socialist. They have the post-War outlook, & do not like the Junkers who ran Imperial Germany.

Incidentally, Tyrrell showed that he doesn't really believe in economic sanctions. I had said that I doubted their utility, as they were so slow in their effect. 'Yes' he said 'they are only the dope we have used to bring our people (British) out of isolation'. Typical of T:'s methods. One step at a time for the British. The French go straight to the logical conclusion.

Turning to internal affairs L^d T: said the three reforms Doumergue wanted to carry out before he resigned were

1. Change the electoral law so as to abolish the Second Ballot with its pacts & bargains
2. Give Pres: & P.M. the right to dissolve the Chamber
3. Deprive Deputies of their right to initiate legislation involving national expenditure.

He thinks Doumergue can last a year if he wants to.

[278] Gaston Doumergue (1863–1937): French jurist & politician; served in many posts before First World War; Pres. of Senate 1923–4; Pres. of Republic 1924–31; PM 1934.

As he spoke of the corruption of the French Press I mentioned that I had recently heard that Briand had subsidized journalists in large measure, which had upset me – but Tyrrell said he had had them paid for articles in support of his <u>policy</u>, whereas other politicians paid them to crack themselves up.

Then I went on to Gen: Weygand. He was v. frank, & entirely anti-Geneva. He does not want a Disarm^t Conventn, unless it brings France a British guarantee of Security. Almost every suggestion of the Disarm^t Conference was for him *'une plaisanterie'*. If I mentioned such a thing as the proposed distinction between defensive & aggressive weapons it was *'encore une plaisanterie'*. He had no use for Locarno; & in the course of our conversatn he produced a Hitler knife – one which I believe Chiefs of Boy Scouts & those sort of people carry on their belts in Germany – unsheathed it & showed me on the blade the slogan *'Blut und Ehre'*.

I did not show myself unduly impressed, & might have answered that at least *'Blut u. <u>Ehre</u>'* is a good deal better than Bismarck's *'Blut u. <u>Eisen</u>'*. Gen: W: is still making plans to beat the Germans. To him the War was the real thing, & almost everything that has happened since unreal – he said this (the second sentence) in so many words.

I began (as I had with Tyrrell) by giving my impressions of Geneva, & the conclusns I'd come to. When I said I thought the full Conference might be able to draw up just a few general principles to be adhered to by all Countries, he at once asked, *'lesquels?'* So I gave three–
No military training for home service to be extended beyond one year;
No more of the heaviest engines of destruction to be made (guns, tanks etc)
Bombing from the air to be absolutely prohibited.
He said in principle he had no objection to make; but in practice it w^d be impossible for France to tie herself just yet to a maximum of one-year service. The coming years, till 1940, are her 'lean' years, with fewer youths than usual growing to military age – so he wanted to increase the period of service to two years if possible, so as to have enough men to cover the defence of the frontiers.

In regard to heavy weapons, he said making limitations about them was like trying to stop a tank with a spider's web – nations w^d break through them, & he did not believe in the efficacy of supervision.

I was however greatly cheered to find that he agreed absolutely about aerial bombing. *Ce n'est pas la guerre;* he said, *c'est la barbarie.*

He said aerial bombing was pure destructiveness, & w^d never win a war against a nation of spirit. A nation c^d not be conquered unless it was occupied (or on the verge of being occupied, he no doubt meant – for Germany was not occupied in Nov: 1918).

All through his main point was to argue in favour of a Franco-British alliance (Foch's idea). A British guarantee of execution (of a new Convention) w$^{\underline{d}}$ not satisfy him. He wanted a guarantee of Security, that is, the equivalent of an alliance. When I mentioned Locarno he pulled out a typewritten sheet of its essential terms, to show they were not good enough for France.

At the end he explained that he was giving me purely his personal views, & not for publication. I said, I suppose they are not necessarily the views of the Government? 'No, they are not' he said '*mais je pense qu'il y a un membre du gouvernement qui pense comme moi.*' I imagine he referred to Marshal Pétain,[279] of whom there was a signed photograph on the wall behind him. [. . .]

LONDON *17 Apr:*   During a talk which I had with Grandi this morning he informed me that he was commissioned by Sgr Mussolini to thank me personally for the leading article I wrote on March 19 entitled 'The Rome Protocols.' It was an explanation of Italian policy in Central Europe; & Grandi said that Mussolini considered that it put it so clearly & fairly that it had converted public opinion here [London] to an understanding of it.

Very nice, but I do not want to get too many commendatns from foreign potentates! [. . .]

19 Apr: B$^{\underline{n}}$ Palmstierna, the Swed: Min:, rang me up specially this morn^{g} to tell me that he considered that he c$^{\underline{d}}$ be satisfied that that [sic] the Germans <u>are</u> making bombing aeroplanes. This of course is most important.

25 Apr: I met Sgr Suvich twice yesterday, first at the It: Embassy at luncheon, & then in his rooms at Claridge's for a talk. He is affable but not impressive, conciliatory rather than directive. He has nothing of Grandi's energy & force of ideas. It looks as if our parable in *T.T.* of Tarquin & the tallest poppies had bn only too true; & this is the sort of man Musso: likes to have round him rather than Grandi or Balbo. [. . .]

---

[279] (Henri) Philippe Pétain 1856–1951): army officer; C-in-C in 1917, retd 1934; PM following collapse of French army June 1940; subsequently head of state of regime based at Vichy; convicted of treason ff. liberation; death sentence commuted to life imprisonment.

26 Apr: Had a particularly interesting luncheon yesterday with GD (at his house) to meet Sir George Clerk, the new Ambssdr in Paris, the other guest being Philip Lothian. Lothian & I had a great argument about the possibilities of international sanctions, & security for France. He has big views & is a good arguer. Sir George Clerk made the impression of a most sensible person, also extremely smart & a charmer. I liked v. much one of his remarks – 'Willie Tyrrell has been first-rate at expounding the French view to the British Gov^t; what I have got to try to do is to explain the British view to the French Gov^t.' And then he added '& now, you, gentlemen, tell me how I'm to do it.' To which Lothian replied 'Be yourself, George, you're a good enough Briton'. We laughed & agreed, & I think Sir G. Clerk was pleased.

At night a splendid reception for the formal opening of the new Italian Embassy. Met lots of people. Had a short significant talk with P^{ce} Bismarck, from which I drew the uncomfortable inference that he w^d be rather pleased if (as seems likely on the surface) the present disarmament negotiatns completely broke down. Not from any of his words, of course, but from his tone – & I've no doubt that many people behind Hitler share that feeling.

4 May Yesterday at the F.O. Leeper actually talked to me about the danger of Germany attacking us! 'Fantastic' I said. 'Facing realities' said he. 'Fantastic' I repeated. But we are good friends, so our equanimity survived this exchange.

The F.O. – esp: Vansittart – are furious at our (*T.T.*) having suggested off our own bat that this country sh^d take the lead in getting Hitler's proposals for Disarm^t accepted – nailing Germany down, in fact. The F.O.'s one idea is that if the Disarm^t negotiatns break down we must be found on the side of France – a thoroughly defeatist attitude. By bold leadership we c^d even now pull off a restricted Agreement of some value. France w^d follow our lead eventually.

The day before I had seen v.[on] Hösch, who was off next day to Berlin, to which he had bn summoned by telephone by Hitler. We went over recent developments, & he said the Ger: Gov^t was much puzzled what to do next. I said 'stick to Hitler's policy. Even if France threatens & says she will out-arm Germany, never mind – re-arm up to the defensive level, & then stop.' He said it w^d be difficult to stop, if the countries round went on increasing. I said I thought it was vital that Germany sh^d stop at the defensive level.

11 May   Had an extremely good talk with von Ribbentrop[280] this morn^g. He is the personal envoy of Hitler. Hitler not only never travels out of Germany, but never has been out of Germany & Austria in his life – except in the War. Ribbentrop has travelled a good deal, speaks English perfectly, & is most presentable. So Hitler (so Ribbentrop told me) has chosen him to be his *alter ego* in the Disarm^t question.

It seemed to me he c^d not have chosen a better man. We got on v. well. Within 5 min: we were on a footing of confidence; & I developed to him at length my idea of what Hitler might do to further disarmament. A speech about the (time of the) beginning of the next meeting of the General Commssn of the Conference, giving the half-a-dozen points about which there is substantial agreement, & proposing that they sh^d be embodied in a brief Convention. This w^d establish the principle of Regulation, & be a beginning. I told him how important I thought it was that Hitler sh^d come forward not merely as the champion of German rights – which he has done all the time – but as a pioneer in Europe. We spoke for over an hour about this. Ribbentrop seemed favourably impressed. I said frankly that I wished my (the British) Gov^t would have championed the idea; but I had put it to them (in leaders) & they preferred to follow the lead of France, (whose one idea is to keep Germany down).

R: says he often has luncheon with Hitler, & then they go for a walk afterwards, & on one of these Hitler had said to him 'I want to be friends with England for 500 years.' I laughed at this expression, which rather took R: aback, as he seemed to think I doubted Hitler's seriousness! He also mentioned an episode that had happened to Hitler in the War, in which the gallantry of four English gunners had tremendously impressed him; & Hitler had told R: 'I felt after that that I wanted to be friends with that people.'

When I left Hösch yesterday in the hall, I remember saying to him 'I believe there <u>will</u> be a Disarm^t Agreement; it is common sense' – & tonight here (Hambrook) I have heard practically those words on the wireless – spoken by Ribbentrop to an interviewer, & now broadcast. Whatever the origin of them, R: said, I think, just the right sort of thing & the right amount, acc: to what I've just heard.

24 May   Long talk on Disarm^t this morning with Arthur Henderson,

---

[280] Joachim von Ribbentrop (1893–1946): Nazi politician; elected to *Reichstag* 1933; deputy of German govt on disarmament questions 1934; Amb. Extraordinary 1935; ldr of German delegation in LoN Council 1936; *Gruppenführer SS* 1936; Amb. in London 1936–8; For. Min. 1938–45; hanged at Nuremberg for conspiring to wage aggressive war. See *The Ribbentrop Memoirs* (1953).

who remains serenely determined to go on with the Disarm[t] Conference, tho' most people think it can accomplish nothing. He told me one or two interesting things about Barthou. In spite of official denials, Barthou <u>had</u> drafted a much more conciliatory reply to Simon's timid advances last month than that which was actually despatched. But it seems he had a hint from the Gov[t] that the Cabinet w[d] not regard it favourably, as Tardieu & Herriot had agreed to make an uncompromising anti-German stand, taking the German Budget figures as their reason or pretext. So Barthou re-drafted his reply to Simon before he presented it to the Council of Ministers – thus being able technically to state with truth that his draft had bn accepted & that the Gov[t] was united. Barthou denied emphatically that there had bn any division of opinion to our Corrspt in Paris (Cadett),[281] & he afterwards made a public denial.

Henderson did well to find this out from Barthou. As he put it to me he had 'cornered him' – for Barthou also denied to H: at first that he had changed his mind.

H: was particularly friendly. He suggested a possible way of bringing Germany back to the Conference, which I agreed to try out in *T.T.*, & he will canvass it at Geneva.

H: has v. much come round to my point of view, which I put to him at Geneva, & which then he refused – that is, that <u>reduction</u> is not possible now, & the best thing we can get is regulation – a short Agreement under a few main heads, securing the points which have emerged in the discussions as important & substantially agreed upon by all.

He had had a talk with the German emissary v.[on] Ribbentrop, & seemed to look forward to a turn of the tide in the autumn. Till then we must hold on.

26 May   Had an interesting talk with Michael Huxley,[282] himself of the F.O., who said how easy it was for permanent officials to get imbued with one particular view – pro-French, we were thinking of – & go on in the same groove never changing, or being in real contact with public opinion – because being kept hard at it in the Office, & outside it never being supposed to talk shop.

And such officials, he said, can have much influence. They always have the ear of the Sec[y] of State – who himself sometimes is a rushed &

[281] Thomas T. Cadett (1929–40): joined *The Times* 1924, Corrspdt in New York 1927–9, in Paris 1929–40.

[282] Michael Heathorn Huxley (1889–1979): entered dip. service 1922; resigned 1935; recalled to FO Sept. 1939, served until 1945; Ed. *The Geographical Magazine* 1945–55.

harassed individual, who has no instinct at the job he has bn allotted in the Cabinet, & has to rely on these same officials.

At the F.O. at present holding important positions are Vansittart, Sargent & Wigram, who are strongly pro-French. All have spent much time in Paris, & none, I think, in Berlin.

30 May   Two days ago had yet another talk with v.[on] Hösch, who mentioned almost casually in the course of the conversatn that if the terms of the German Memorandum of Apr: 16 were accepted, Ger: w^d return to the Disarm^t Conference at once. I felt this to be v. important, but he was surprised at my surprise. 'Why, doesn't everybody see that' he asked. I said no, I thought not. He asked why people hadn't taken the German Memo: more seriously. I said, well, speaking absolutely frankly, it is that so many people still doubt Germany's good faith. He seemed to understand, & said nothing.

I urged that Hitler sh^d bring out in a broadcast speech how simple it w^d really be to get Germany back to Geneva – to the Disarm^t Conference, not the League. In the meantime I've got our Berlin office to send a message on the point, & I backed it with a leader last night.[283] All pretty hopeless, I'm afraid. One's suggestions, when they are taken up, become action with a time-lag of about 3 months! By then the position has changed, & something rather different is needed.

'The German Case'

It must naturally be repugnant to some of them [the other countries participating in the disarmament conference] that a member of the Conference should make an impatient exit and then state conditions for its return. But it has at least to be admitted that impatience was quite comprehensible for a country in the position of Germany, which had already waited fifteen years for that 'initiation of a general limitation of the armaments of all nations' which it had been told to expect at Versailles. And there is the further consideration that the terms proposed by Germany for her return are moderate and reasonable.

In claiming equality of rights HERR HITLER has not asked for immediate numerical equality. He is content that other nations should maintain for five years a large superiority both in numbers and in categories – for they would not start abolishing even the heaviest armaments during that period, and Germany would not build any weapons which other countries undertook eventually to abolish. Complete supervision would be established, and would cover the para-military forces. These proposals might perfectly well form part of a first Disarmament Convention. At a moment when there is great

[283] 'The German Case': 30 May 1934, p.13.

confusion in the Conference the countries assembled at Geneva might do worse than draw up a brief Convention embodying the points made in the German Memorandum....

31 May A sharp controversial talk with Leeper at the F.O. yesterday, he having been formally charged by Vansittart to complain of my article in *T.T.* that morning 'The German Case', & to say that no purpose seemed to be served by our discussing Disarmament together any further. I asked what the F.O. (i.e. Vansittart's) policy was, & was given to understand that it was bringing pressure to bear on Germany (but how?), telling her to stop re-arming, & ultimately very likely forming an alliance with France. I said that I could not agree with that policy, which was a continuation of that which had brought us to the present impasse. Further I did not think public opinion w^d ever agree to an alliance with France, (though I personally realize that there may be much to say for at any rate a temporary alliance).

Last night, when Simon's speech at Geneva came in, I saw to my surprise & pleasure that Simon had v. largely taken <u>our</u> line & not Vansittart's. I sh^d think V: would be furious.

Leeper again tried to terrify me with the notion that Germany was preparing to invade us by the air. He spoke of Germans as an uncivilized nation (an echo of Vansittart, I imagine).

1 June Yesterday the P.M. had luncheon with the board of *T.T.*, & afterwards GD told me that he (GD) had said something about Simon having made a gd speech at Geneva the day before, & MacDonald answered 'Yes, it's the speech he ought to have made years ago.'

Very true – but why didn't MacDonald see that he made it? MacD could command Simon at any time.

GD also gave me back the copy of my memorandum on Disarmament of March 1933, of which I had then given a copy to the P.M. It was a simple statement of attainable ends; & if the Gov^t had adopted that policy instead of producing its ambitious scheme of 96 Articles, I believe it might have achieved an Agreement. As GD gave it back to me yesterday, just after seeing the P.M., it may be that he showed it to him. He also gave me back another of my Memoranda. He bade me keep them v. carefully as they were v. 'valuable' & might come in useful again.

6 June Yesterday at the F.O. Leeper admitted that Simon, in his concluding speech at Geneva, had spoken on the lines advocated in

T.T. & <u>not</u> on the lines advocated by the F.O. So all that storming of Leeper & Vansittart last week has been stultified. A pitiful exhibition.

Leeper added that he c^d now no longer give a line of policy to journalists. Our foreign policy, he said, 'is a series of honeymoons.'

10 June   Saw Eden this afternoon on my return from the country, he having returned from Geneva yesterday morn^g (& gone off to Warwickshire to make a speech last night, back again & on the telephone this morning early). He is pleased at the outcome of Geneva, compared to what the position was a week ago, & has reason to be. He says Barthou is trying to qualify to be Doumergue's successor, & Piétri[284] is marked out to succeed Barthou, & that would be an excellent change. Fundamentally, there is no great improvement; but as Eden said in his speech last night, there is 'a further chance' of it now.

A.E. read out to me a passage from a note he had received from Simon, commending him on his work at Geneva since he (Simon) left in brief epigrammatic phrases, neatly worded.

16 June   An extremely intimate political talk with v. Hösch on Thursday. He had bn in telephonic comnctn with Berlin, & was anxious to make clear to me the German view of Litvinoff's proposed 'Eastern Locarno Pact.' The *Wilhelmstrasse* is against it, as to them it seems merely a disguised military alliance against Germany – & in a v. interesting confidential letter I have just had from Temperley from Geneva he tells me that he suspects the object of Gen: Gamelin's[285] stay in Geneva was to draft a military pact with Russia. 'I cannot believe that Gamelin has bn spending two weeks here for nothing' he writes 'Chiefs of Staff are busy men'.

Hoesch always puts his points extraordinarily clearly & in such a way that one remembers them without effort.

We talked about Sir J. Simon at one time, & he said he knew that Simon's cross-examination of foreign diplomats was sometimes <u>cruel</u> – the more he found them weak in their replies, the more he pressed them!

---

[284] François Piétri (1882–1966): Dir-Gen. of Finance in Morocco 1917–24; Deputy 1924–42; Min. of Colonies 1929–30, of Finance 1931–2, of Defence 1932, of Colonies 1933, of the Navy 1934–6; delegate to London Naval Conf. 1930; Min. to World Disarmament Conf., Geneva 1932–4; Amb. in Madrid 1940–4. See his *Més années d'Espagne* (1954).

[285] Maurice Gamelin (1872–1958): French army officer; Army Chief of Staff 1931–5; Inspector-Gen. of the Army and V-Pres. of the War Council 1935–7; Chief of the Gen. Staff 1938–9; Generalissimo of French Land Forces 1939–40; interned by Vichy regime 1941, interned in Buchenwald 1943–5, freed by US troops May 1945.

Excellent for a barrister, but less good in diplomacy!

Hoesch said he himself took care to know his subject well when going to see Simon. As a matter of fact, he always seems to me to have every fact at his finger tips & to be able to marshal it as wanted.

I developed my idea of re-stating Locarno in terms of the air, of which he approved.

He said he had pressed my previous idea – a re-statement of the German Disarm^t proposals by Hitler at the beginning of the last session of the Disarm^t Conference – & had much regretted it had not been taken up by Hitler. He thought it w^d have done good. [...]

11 July [...] I saw Simon yesterday at the F.O. Quite a casual meeting, but useful to me, as little was known about what had happened between him & Barthou. He prided himself on G^t B^n still having great influence, in spite of what all the critics say. Barthou was <u>most</u> anxious, he said, to get Brit: support for his Eastern Locarno project. I did not say that <u>of course</u> Britain always counts immensely – but some For: Sec^{ies} know how to use that influence constructively & others don't!

In this case however Simon does seem to have modified Barthou's original idea & in the right direction – i.e. prevented it from being so one-sided as it was going to be. Simon was v. delighted because Barthou seemed so keen to make up for his rudeness at Geneva. 'Very repentant', Simon said. It was the least one c^d expect! He considers that now his relations with Barthou are excellent.

Simon is always cordial at greeting, cold at parting. I noticed it particularly yesterday.

He referred back to the leader in *T.T.* written by Braham Tuesday 3rd, entitled 'Medieval Methods' – about the Hitler putsch. He called it 'a historic bit of writing'; but he had bn much upset by a sentence at the beginning which acquiesced in the Nazi claim that 'law & order' reigned throughout the Reich. As a tremendously keen upholder of the methods of law & justice he c^d not bear to see it accepted that law could be administered by political murder.

There <u>are</u> one or two things that this cold-blooded man is really earnest about – one is liberty of the subject, another is the maintenance of civil justice, & another, I would say, is disarmament. He <u>is</u> keen about disarm^t, & he is a good diplomatist – but he is lamentably lacking in directive power, foresight & opportune action.

15 July [...saw] Eden, whom I found with M^{rs} E: & Hankey (his Sec^y). E: was debonnair & jolly & slightly cynical about Barthou's new Pact – but he (Eden) is in earnest all right at heart. Everybody who has been occupied with Disarmament for the last $2\frac{1}{2}$ years must get an occasional feeling that he is assisting at a diplomatic comedy.

12 September   I met Dr Brüning the German ex-Chancellor, yesterday, at luncheon with Deakin. A fine man. Clear-cut, strong face, with a gentle & courteous manner, & a most pleasant & humorous conversationalist. One felt that what he really minded about the present German regime was that it is degrading humanity, not merely Germany, but humanity. One can see that he loathes Hitlerism, & can't bear that it sh^d be taken to represent Germanism. He made a sort of appeal to me twice – once immediately after luncheon, & again just as he was leaving – almost making a little speech, to the effect that the world's humanism was being dragged down in many places – look at America, he said – that what was wanted was a revival of belief in justice & liberty, that Hitler was not Germany, that one ought to distinguish between the rights of Germany & the methods of Hitler. (I do try to do this in *T.T.* But of course the French & F.O. view is that it is a mistake to make any concessions to Germany while Hitler is in command).

The moment we met D^r Br: & I had quite an interesting little talk about German regional patriotism. Still v. strong, he says. There is great variety among Germans. And a Republic does not appeal to them. They want a <u>figure</u> as rallying point. Hitler is trying to supply it. But Br: does not think he can take the place of an emperor. He agreed with Deakin that in the last resort Hitler might invite Kaiser Wilhelm to come back – but that w^d indeed be a course of desperation, & w^d not last.

Br: threw many interesting side-lights on recent events, & Church,[286] who was with him, gave some ghastly descriptions of men released from concentratn camps, beat, grey-haired & broken, tho' they had gone in in the prime of life. Br: concurred, & said 'Yes, even those who are at liberty will not be able to do any more political work'. Church also told us about the Crown-Prince's Pte Sec^y, who had bn seized on the night of June 30 & put into a v. small sort of cellar with two other men, & <u>never allowed to budge from it</u> for 3 weeks. They were treated worse than dogs, food being thrown into them. The place of course became filthy. The Crown Prince dared not do anything for his Sec^y. Only when he was released he sent him some caviare & champagne!

[286] Archibald George Church (1886–1954): Lab. politician; MP E. Leyton 1923–4; Wandsworth Central 1929–31; PPS to Sec. for War 1929–31.

The object of the Nazis is to degrade their opponents – but they are degrading themselves. Torgler[287] the Communist leader, is probably dead, or else only half-alive in his cell – & he was acquitted in the Reichstag fire trial!'

Br: thought the Weimar Republic idea was never well suited to Germany.

Hitler's mind, he said, is that of a gramaphone. He can & does repeat word for word what he has bn told, or read. He can turn himself on & run on automatically.

Gen: Schleicher's mistake had been to spend his birthday with the French Ambassdr & his wife (M. & Mme François-Poncet). Frau von Schleicher was there too. It was in a *Schloss* in the country. Certainly a rather unusual way for an ex-Chancellor to spend his birthday – & it cost him his life.

Hindenburg was surrounded by untrustworthy people. Br: gave as an example that he had a conversatn once with Hind^{bg} in which he pleaded for Schleicher to be retained in his post. Then he found out afterwards that Meissner,[288] Hind's Sec^y, had told Schleicher that he (Brüning) had criticized Schleicher to Hindenburg.

Br: distrusted the published figures of the plébiscite which approved Hitler as Führer the other day. He said he knew that many of them were faked. I did however get the impression that Brüning disliked Hitler & hitlerism so intensely that he might be exaggerating the opposition to it in Germany. The difficulty for people of great faith – as Br: is – is often not to believe what they want to believe.

He gave us one particularly interesting touch about Hind^{bg}, which was that after he went to Neudeck from Hanover he acquired a sort of inferiority complex towards the country gentlemen by whom he was surrounded! At Hanover he had been the much respected ex-soldier, but a townsman; & when he went to E. Prussia & found himself among the Junkers long-settled on the land, knowing all about it & v. strong-minded, he half-unconsciously tried to imitate them & live up to their traditions, & thus became too susceptible to their views.

It was of course these Junkers who were responsible for getting Brüning dismissed, through Col: Hindenburg, the Fld-Marshal's son.

[287] Ernst Torgler (1893–1963): Deputy, *Reichstag* 1924–33; arrested February 1933 for complicity in setting Reichstag fire; acquitted, kept as prisoner 'for his own protection' until 1935, when he was expelled by Communist Party; in 1940 made clandestine radio appeals to foreign communists on behalf of Reich Propaganda Ministry.

[288] Otto Lebrecht E. Meissner (1880–1953): Ministerial Dir. & Head of Presidential Chancery 1920–3; *Staatssek.* 1923–45 & Chief Presidential Officer 1934–45; Min. of State 1937–45; arrested 1945; acquitted of war crimes 1949. See his *Staatssekretär unter Ebert, Hindenburg, Hitler* (1950).

Br: thinks that v. Papen is in danger of his life. At Vienna he will be comparatively safe, but impotent.

Church said he had seen people scrambling together outside the newspaper kiosks to get hold of *T.T.*. Sometimes he had seen copies torn in the process. Brüning said he knew of cases where tenements combined to take in a copy, which was passed round.

Our circulation has lately risen by 7000 copies in Germany!

19 Sept: Bismarck came & had luncheon with me yestrdy. I like him well, he having a passion for & an understanding of politics. He of course knows his grandfather's career by heart, & evidently thinks of him as a guide – which is unfortunate sometimes. For instance yesterday, when we were talking about Eur: pols: after the fall of Bismarck, B: said, the mistake was that France was no longer kept isolated. I turned on him at once, & said do for goodness sake not [sic] let's have that ideal nowadays. Let all countries work in cooperation, & not try to keep each other isolated. There must no doubt be rivalry, but why can't it be rivalry in the advance of culture & in civilization. I don't think that's a mere vain aspiratn, I ended, do you? He said no, he hoped we w^d come to that; but as long as <u>injustices</u> persisted there c^d not be real cooperation.

He told me the interesting thing about his grandfather, that at the end of his time he was afraid Germany had taken on too much. 'And he may have been right' added young B: 'She did have a bigger position than she could hold.' But he regards the Treaty of Versailles as the most unfair Treaty in history. He says the Polish corridor question is only shelved, not settled.

He suddenly asked me what people in England really think of Germans just now? What would you say? I said, well that depends on whom I'm talking to. He said 'Quite openly'. So then I said, well I think most people w^d say you were not quite civilized & not quite normal. 'Not quite normal' he exclaimed 'Is that all!' I said all that 'Heil Hitler' struck us as quite eccentric. He explained by the German passion for having a hero & master etc & our conversation proceeded quite amicably!

19 October   Yesterday after luncheon here Willert told me he considered that I had more influence than the head of the Foreign Office (Vansittart)! I record this in no spirit of boasting. Willert may be entirely wrong. But at least he is head of the News Dept: of the F.O., gets on well with Vansittart, & did not say it in a spirit of flattery. He is in fact v. blunt, not a flatterer. In any case it was nice to hear it; & to-day I had a long talk with Craigie[289] at the F.O. about coming naval conversations; & he was very sore because the Japanese Admiral, Yamamoto,[290] has been talking at large to the Press on the Japanese proposals. Personally I think this is wise – he is taking the public into his confidence, & putting his case as favourably as possible. However it is naturally annoying to Craigie, who is our chief negotiator, & who has heard nothing whatever officially about what the Jap: proposals are! A strange position. But again, Yamamoto prefers public opinion to official secrecy.

Of course in a way it is to my interest – by which I mean to the interest of *The Times* – that the Brit: Gov^t should <u>not</u> do that – because Craigie sees me, & I do not think he sees anybody else of the Press at all – so we score. [...]

23 Oct: At lunch in Hampstead yesterday with Prof: Geyl[291] (Dutch) I met a clever Dutch Jew journalist D^r van Blankenstein,[292] For: Ed: of the '*Nieuwe Rotterdamsche Courant*'. An active-minded well-informed man, who travels about Europe a good deal; & whether on his travels or in Rotterdam writes an article for his paper practically every day (telephoned to Rot: if he's abroad). I do envy his industry. But it must be much easier to write every day if

1. One can choose one's subject without any <u>close</u> connexion to the daily position
2. One has not any sort of 'national institution' responsibility
3. One is not likely to be very much quoted in other papers at home & abroad.

7 November   Had luncheon yesterday with Lothian, whom one had known a bit as plain Mr Philip Kerr, & who has since blossomed out as a Marquess, also 'Earl of Ancrum', as I learned from family portraits in his flat. The part of an 18th century nobleman suits him v. well. He

[289] Robert Leslie Craigie (1883–1959): entered FO 1907; Asst U-Sec. FO 1935–7; Amb. in Tokyo 1937–41; interned 1941, repatriated 1942; rep. on UN war crimes commission 1945–8. See his *Behind the Japanese Mask* (1945).

[290] Isoruku Yamamoto (1884–1943): naval Attaché in Washington 1926–8; Chief of Aviation Dept, Imperial Navy 1935; Vice-Navy Min. 1936–9; C-in-C Combined Fleet 1939–43; Adml 1940; directed attack on Pearl Harbour 1941.

[291] Pieter Geyl (1882–1966): Prof. of Dutch History & Institutions, U. of London 1924–35; Prof. of Modern History, U. of Utrecht 1936–58; arrested 1940, interned Buchenwald 13 months, in Netherlands until 1944.

[292] Marcus van Blankenstein (1880–1964): joined *Nieuwe Rotterdamsche Courant* 1906; Ed. *Vrij Nederland* (Free Netherland) in London during WWII; Chief Ed. *Voice of the Netherlands*.

has a good presence, tho' a trifle portly, a fine intellect, cultured tastes & an extreme interest in politics. As with Bismarck (the present one, I mean) one gets into a keen political discussion within 2 minutes of meeting. He takes a long-term view, & is better at general policy than the next step, but is acute, remarkably well informed, & has met everybody. He is just back from the U.S.A., where he had a good talk on Anglo-American-Japanese relations with Pres: Roosevelt. His (K's) opinion is that we shall have to stand up to Japanese ambition some day just as we had to German ambition – & the sooner the better. [...]

10 Nov: [...] I met Admrl Dickens[293] at luncheon with Robin B-Ward on Thursday. He is Director of Naval Operations (I think) at the Admiralty – & he gave me to understand that the Admiralty are most indignant at a phrase I used in a leader on the Naval Conversatns to the effect that the function of submarines was the destructn of the enemy's commerce. The submarine people are angry, he said!

I admire their spirit! No doubt they do not consider it their function at all. A nation of sportsmen – but

1. We w^d have little foreign commerce to destroy in any war except with USA
2. For other nations our commerce is far our most vulnerable point.

Yesterday I met Admrl Yamamoto, the Jap: Naval delegate. He & I & an interpreter sat for some time more or less in silence, the Admrl looking depressed & worried. He was v. reticent on purely naval questions; but gradually we switched to general questions connected with sea-power in the Pacific – fortifications & the integrity of China – & he warmed up considerably; & we had a really v. interesting talk. We ended by being v. frank with one another, & I said that although public opinion would, I thought, acquiesce in Jap: numerical naval equality, it w^d not acquiesce meekly in Jap: inroads into China proper. Because we had take[n] Manchukuo lying down, I said, it did not follow that we w^d do the same if Japan tried to oust us from the Yangtse valley. I was speaking simply 'in the name of public opinion,' & the Admrl seemed interested & drew me on to a lot of other questions. He declared to me that Japan would maintain the two principles of the Open Door & Equality of Opportunity in China, that Japan was in

[293] Gerald Charles Dickens (1879–1962): Naval ADC to King George V 1931–2; Dir. Naval Intelligence 1932–5; Commander reserve fleet 1935–7; Vice-Adm. 1936; retd 1938; kt. 1937. See his *Bombing & Strategy* (1947).

favour of non-fortificatn in the Pacific, & had not fortified & was not fortifying the Mandated islands – giving a lot of reasons, such as their unsuitability to be fortified naval bases. I saw Craigie later in the afternoon, & he was very interested in the Admrl's declarations. He thought it w^d be a good thing if they were pub^d. I said I did not know how far they were meant to be confidential; so I telephoned to Kato[294] at the Embassy last night, & he has rung me up this morning to say that the Admrl has no objection to his ideas being pub^d, tho' they are personal to himself, & that sh^d be made clear. I must get them into the paper next week. [...]

15 Nov.:[295] [...] Yesterday morning I was rung up by Willert saying that there was great agitation at the F.O. on account of a para: I had got in that morning's paper on the visit of Herr von Ribbentrop. The French Embassy was apparently indignant about it & this of course was more than the F.O. c^d bear. All I had said in the news note was that Herr von R. who is Hitler's special envoy for disarmament, had expounded the nature of German re-armament to Eden & Simon in his two talks & had assured them that there was nothing aggressive in the German purpose. This was what Hoesch had told me the day before.

According to Willert however this made it appear to the French as if we – the British Govt: were tacitly agreeing to German re-armament (to a defensive level.) Eden therefore officially denied that this had been the purport of the conversations in the H. of Commons in answer to a question, which I expect was specially arranged. The conversations were said to have had only a general character – but Ribbentrop is officially entitled only to speak on disarmament & he had about an hour each with Eden & Simon!

It looks as if once more fear of French disapproval were paralyzing our diplomacy. Simon himself has spoken in favour of partial & controlled German re-armament. However I may hear more about this to-morrow as I am seeing Ribbentrop in the morning.

Nov: 16[296] I saw Ribbentrop this morning in his room in Brown's Hotel & had an animated hour with him. He began by tackling me straight away on the subject of the news note in '*T.T.*'. It was not

[294] Sotomatsu Kato (b. 1890): Counsellor in Washington 1929–32, in London 1932–5; Min. in Ottawa 1935–7, Manchukuo 1938–9, at Large 1939–40; Amb. in Paris 1941–4.
[295] This entry is in Sylvia Kennedy's hand.
[296] This entry is in Sylvia Kennedy's hand.

correct he said. They had not talked about German re-armament; & he & Eden had agreed that they would both say that they had only had a general discussion. He said 'Did Hoesch tell you that we had talked about German re-armament?' I said 'Yes, but he had not told me word for word what I had written down. We (Hoesch & I) had had a general conversation & he had told me the sort of thing you (von R.) were commissioned to say, & I took full responsibility for the wording of the note (I rather got the impression that von R & Hoesch are rivals. I hope that Ribbentrop is not trying to supplant Hoesch.).

Von R. explained to me that the point was v. important to him as his relations with Eden depended on trust, & if it was thought that he (Von R.) had gone back on their private arrangement it would hamper the whole of his future relationship. He told me he was lunching with him to-day, so I undertook to explain the full circumstances in which I had written the note & actually did so at the end of our talk by telephoning to Hankey at the F.O. from Ribbentrop's room.

I went on to say what a pity it seemed to me to be that they had not discussed more fully what was the real fundamental problem in Europe. I showed sympathy with the German view in this matter, in the claim for equality of status, & said I did not think there would be any appeasement till it was reached. [...] I regretted he had not discussed it with Eden, & said that he being the Special Commiss[ion]er for Dismmt it was difficult to imagine what he <u>had</u> talked about during his hour's conversation. He rose to this & said 'Well I will tell you confidentially Mr Kennedy.' He then began to pull faces & walked up & down the room two or three times & said 'Well we talked about two things. The Church (which I did not believe)[297] & how to find a basis to resume negotiations on Disarmament.' <u>That</u>, is what I am sure was the real reason for his visit & what they talked about.

He said it was very difficult & he proposed to go to France very soon. He expressed keen regret at the way British diplomacy always drew back whenever the French objected. I developed my idea that it would be much the best way if Hitler would proclaim openly to all the world when Germany had got her defensive armaments & challenge other countries to come down to the defensive level. R. considered the idea a lot, but spoke at some length about the increase of armaments in some countries between April 16th (when Hitler made his offer) & the present moment. He implied that what Germany now wants is something more than defensive weapons. Hoesch had practically told me the other day that Germany was now making bombing aeroplanes; & when I talked about them (not mentioning H of course) R. did not

---

[297] 'which I did not believe' has been crossed out and replaced by 'I think he did at least mention this'.

deny their existence. I put in a plea for bombers only being used collectively & internationally or for police purposes. We had then been at it an hour & R. asked me to come back in a week's time & discuss the matter further.

So I telephoned then & there in his presence to Hankey & left.

19 Nov: Simon rec^d the Press at the F.O. this morn^g to tell us about the Anglo-Am-Jap Naval conversatns. A remarkably frank exposition. As usual we – G^t B^n – are between the two & can please neither.

Simon was, I thought, indiscreetly candid; but quite fluid about policy. No definite line at all. Difficult to have one in this case, no doubt. He can't even say we are mediators, because that annoys the Americans! After the general talk I had a few words with Simon, & said I wished we could agree to drop the formula of 5–5–3 which annoyed the Japs so much, as it appeared to me that, just as he (Sir J. Simon) had said once about <u>German</u> armaments, it was a case of either re-armament by agreement or re-armament without it. He agreed, but said, we can't persuade the Americans to take our view.

20 Nov: After thinking over Simon's talk yesterday I felt that all the same a naval policy <u>should</u> be possible for G^t B^n – namely, to cut out the ratio, keep what can be preserved in the Wash: Treaty, & begin work on a new Treaty next year. That was all <u>indicated</u> by Simon, but not stated as a policy.

By the way, Simon astonished us assembled journalists yesterday by beginning the proceedings by reading out passages (or rather translating them) from a French skit on modern politics! It was about a *député* on a weekend visit to his constituency, & all his tricks to get votes. Simon tittered towards the end of his reading. It was really quite queer.

After luncheon I went to the Jap: Emb, to see Kato – & Matsudaira came in, & he & I had quite a good talk, Kato leaving the room. I told Mat: as much as was permissible of what Simon had told us in the morn^g; & he in his turn told me that the Jap: Govt was <u>committed</u> to the Jap: people to denounce the Wash: Treaty. Japan, he said, w^d be ready to declare it had no <u>intention</u> of building up to the same maximum as G^t B^n & the USA, but it w^d not <u>give an undertaking</u> to that effect. [...]

Later 8 pm. I am just back from seeing Simon (he asked me to come & see him at the H. o C. as I couldn't do luncheon) – & what he wanted was to put himself right about his last speech in the House on the Traffic in Arms, which was a flop. He is going to speak again, probably the day after tomorrow; & he went through the points he intends to make, to see if I approved, apparently.

I did not pretend of course to guarantee him the approval of *T.T.*.

He was much puzzled how far to admit himself wrong in his first speech; also, should he advocate an enquiry, into the Traffic?

I explained to him what I thought people didn't like in his first speech, & advised that he sh^d make a point of getting more control of the trade for the Gov^t – something on the lines of the Electricity Board. Also the element of private profit was what people didn't like. I thought he had made a mistake in attributing partisan motives to the Labour Party in the last debate – they may have wanted to score off the Gov^t, no doubt; but there was also real indignation, which was shared by the public. He took this very well. He said he saw he had made a mistake.

He ended the conversation with 'Let us keep in touch.'

23 Nov: Simon duly stood up in his white sheet in the H. of Commons yesterday, recanted his speech of a fortnight ago, & made constructive proposals on the lines indicated to me for a restricted enquiry into the whole question of the private manufacture of arms & the traffic in them. He also made the points I had suggested, such as getting 'effective national control'. The recantation went down well in the House, & he is much praised in the Press this morn^g – so our collaboration worked out well, & I hope it will continue. We have exchanged letters since our talk, on the subject of the regulation of arms in France – on which he put me right.

24 Nov: I had a v. cosy luncheon with v. Ribbentropp [sic] in his room at Brown's Hotel yesterday. We went over the whole ground of Anglo-Ger: relations, with particular regard to Disarmament. I see that what is in his mind is to get German re-armament blended with a new system of non-aggression – some sort of collective system. This tallies well with what I urged upon him in the spring, & urged again yesterday – Hitler coming out as the champion of a new order in Europe. I believe there is a chance of it. Whatever else Hitler may be he is a man of new ideas. Germany may yet lead in an acceptable plan of arms limitation.

von R: is afraid of Russia. He says their air armaments are terrific.

von R: told me all his plans, & what he had been doing here – after luncheon one day he had found himself sitting on a sofa between Austen Chamberlain & Bernard Shaw! – & at the end of our talk we very carefully drew up a note of his visit which I was to put in *T.T.* on the morning of his departure i.e. next Tuesday. However just after I had got down here (Hambrook) for the weekend, I had a telephone call from his Sec.[y], saying that R: had doubts about it, & asking that I sh[d] not publish anything before we had had a further talk about it on the telephone. [...]

28 Nov: I saw Ribbentrop yet again on Mon: before he left (on Tues: morning). It was chiefly about the form of note in the paper in which I could announce his departure. He fusses unnecessarily about those things. But he again invited me with insistence to fly to Berlin to see Hitler, & named 'the first half of January' as the time. Later he hinted that big events might be expected then in regard to disarmament. I infer that Hitler intends to repudiate Part V of the Peace Treaty; but Ribbentropp [sic] has in mind that he sh[d] simultaneously propound a collective system for Europe. I warmly supported this idea. Hitler has a new mind, & might pull it off, unless he himself crashes.

There has been a great hoorroosh & agitation in Cabinet circles here over disarmament during the last 24 hours, because the electorate, as they hear in the Putney bye-election, is getting fed up with the dilly-dallying of the Gov.[t] in this matter.[298] The Cabinet has never really bn united upon it, Hailsham & Londonderry being obstructionists, & Simon so timid. A bold policy of limited collective responsibility might still win them respect, as I tried to impress on GD this morn.[g] Simon was to have gone to GD's house at 9.45 this morn.[g] but cried off at the last moment, & GD came round here to me. He is seeing Stanley Baldwin & Simon this afternoon. SB is pretty sound, but does not apparently see or anyhow admit that a collective system is calculated to <u>diminish</u> the armed strength of each individual nation, & not increase it.

I saw Norman Davis, the American Naval delegate, yesterday – a shrewd old man, whatever people may say, & one who makes his point, though he takes a long time to do it.

29 November – Kennedy to Norman Ebbutt[299] *I saw Ribbentrop two or three times during the three weeks he was in London, & of course got the impression from him that what Herr Hitler desires is first to establish German defensive equality, & then to announce it. But he would like to couple the announcement with a simultaneous declaration in favour of resuming cooperation with the Western*

[298] In the bye-election of 28 November 1934 the Conservative candidate's share of the vote dropped from the 81.6% at the general election to 54.7%; the Labour candidate's rose from 18.4% to 45.3%.
[299] Letter deposited in *The Times* archive.

Powers. Ribbentrop is himself particularly insistent on this point − that it would be best to think out carefully as definite a plan of cooperation as possible before making the announcement. I am looking forward to seeing what you tell us tonight.
[. . .]
Parliamentary opinion is fast facing the fact that none of us will get any forrader until Germany has got practical equality. I am wondering how France will take it. Baldwin, v. wisely I think, coupled the recognition of German rearmament with a firm statement that we should never allow ourselves to be outstripped in the air, & that should help the French to swallow the pill. I rather wish myself that the British Government would come out with a strong statement about Locarno having complete validity in the air; which would mean that if any country started playing monkey tricks the other signatories would all be entitled to retaliate in kind.

30 Nov: Had a lively $\frac{1}{2}$ hour with Grandi this morn^g. He told me a lot about Musso:'s meeting with Hitler at Venice last summer. H: was a <u>great</u> disappointment to M. M: had thought too highly of him at a distance; after a close-up he thought (said Grandi) even too badly of him. In any case he sets no store by him now. He c^d not get him to discuss a question properly. Hitler went off at a tangent & broke the thread. He made speeches. The 'last shock' (as G. put it) was on the third day of the meeting, when Musso: found that H: knew nothing of what the world was saying about their meeting, & did not seem to care even what his own country (Germany) thought about it. This is in complete contrast to Musso:, who always keeps pub: opinion, domestic & foreign, before his mind. Musso: is a more practical man than Hitler. He also found that Hitler did not really have a grasp of foreign affairs. His talk was 'mean' (Grandi's word − I imagine he had in mind the Italian *mesquino*).

Grandi is a profound believer in Locarno. 'I am a maniac about Locarno' he said.

6 December   [Yesterday. . .] Sir J. Simon asked me (unexpectedly) to go & see him at $\frac{1}{2}$ past 5, & informed me that the Brit: Gov^t was going to send troops as police into the Saar. [300] This was clean contrary to

[300] The Saar had been placed under the administration of the League of Nations in the Treaty of Versailles, with 'full and absolute' possession of the coal mines given to France in compensation for the destruction of its mines. A plebiscite was scheduled to be held fifteen years after the Treaty came into force. Germany agreed to pay France 900 million francs to recover ownership of the coal mines there (if she did not pay the price agreed by a panel of experts, the territory would be acquired by France regardless of the vote). Britain, Italy, the Netherlands and Sweden agreed to send in an international police force under a British general to supervise the plebiscite. On 13 January 1935 90% of the inhabitants voted in favour of returning the district to Germany.

every assurance he (Simon) had given in the H. of Commons, & even yesterday afternoon he answered a question in the negative, when he was asked by Mander[301] if there had bn any request for Brit: troops there.

Simon was at his worst. He crawled. He was obviously aware of his *volte face*[302] which had in fact, tho' I didn't know it at the moment, bn brought about by Eden in Geneva in consultation with Laval that v. afternoon. Eden's policy is perfectly sound, but it is rather pitiful that the Brit: Govt sh^d have come to it in this way. Actually of course there is a reason for changing – Laval has succeeded Barthou. Simon in our talk yesterday said 'Because Laval isn't Barthou, thank God'; & he added that we sh^d get something in Disarm^t through Laval before long. Simon's mistake was in not insisting much earlier on the international & police character of keeping order in the Saar, & not being ready to do our bit.

Later in the evening he telephoned to me in *T.T.* Office to give me the news that Hitler & Neurath had already bn approached by us in Berlin, & 'did not disapprove' of the taking over of the policing by foreign & non-French detachments. I told him we were supporting the British move & he thanked me warmly 'for your help'.

A wretched man.[303] He was intent all the way through[304] in getting credit for a policy which he had v. little to do with.

---

[301] Geoffrey Le Mesurier Mander (1882–1962): Lib. MP Wolverhampton E. 1929–45; kt. 1945. See his *We Were Not All Wrong* (1941).

[302] The section following 'volte face' to 'this way' has been crossed out, with the marginal note 'incorrect 23.1.35' made alongside.

[303] This sentence has been crossed out in pencil.

[304] The section from here to the end of the sentence has been crossed out – in ink – and replaced with 'on getting support for a policy which he was terrified to think might be violently criticized.'

10 January   Had a short but v. interesting talk with Simon yesterday evening. [...] he told me that after the recent H. of Commons debate (in which German re-armament was freely talked about by both Simon & Baldwin & not condemned) Simon told Phipps to explain privately to the German Gov^t that this did <u>not</u> imply that G^t B^n would condone unilateral denunciation of the Treaty.

11 Jan: Simon must indeed have spoken to the Ger: Ambassador of his Saar proposal then & there; & what is more, he must have sent instructions that same evening to Phipps, in Berlin, to sound the Ger: Gov^t in that sense.

That did not give *The Times* much chance of making the suggestion! &, worse luck, the *D.T.* got hold of it somehow, & referred to it next morning (yesterday, 10th) so we were dished.

Simon realized this, for Leeper telephoned to me this morn^g, to say that Simon had written to him from Paris, & had referred specially to this incident, & had said 'Kennedy kept faith with me. I don't know where the leakage (to the *D.T.*) occurred'.

In point of fact of course it was Simon who had himself rather misled me, as he distinctly implied that he was leaving it to *T.T.* to throw out the suggestion that Germany sh^d attend at Geneva for the League decision about the Saar, whereas it was made at once by himself – & so we missed the news!

In point of fact the Germans rejected the proposal outright, as I told Simon I thought they would. He agreed that they might, but considered that the proposal was still worth making & its rejection w^d put them in the wrong. [...]

19 Jan: [...] Two days ago I had a talk with Grandi, who is just back from sport in the snow, & looks better than I have ever seen him. He combines courtesy & geniality with a v. stimulating manner. He has the knack of making his interlocutor (me anyhow!) feel clear-headed & eloquent!

Memorandum on Conversation with Signor Grandi: *[...] Referring to the trouble in Abyssinia he said that when Italy argued that the three European countries, Italy, France & Great Britain, ought to present a united front towards people like the Abyssinians, she had in mind not only the question of prestige but also the question of trade in arms. He said that if Abyssinia looked like having trouble with Italy there were always British & French arms firms offering to supply the Abyssinian Government. Jibuti became an entrepôt of arms. He admitted the legitimacy of it but said that naturally it was the sort of thing that caused irritation.*

Speaking of the European situation he said he really thought things were going much better now & we must all keep up the pressure. He thought much the best way of bringing Germany in would not be via Geneva, but quite informally with the other great Powers. The French would like to insist that Germany must reappear at Geneva; but if we took that attitude towards Hitler he could make his terms for returning; whereas if the other Powers just had an informal meeting to discuss European affairs & invited Germany to join them it would obviously be greatly to the interest of Germany to do so. I said, where do you think they had better meet? & he said without hesitation: London. [. . .]

23 Jan: B-W told me yesterday that he had heard on unimpeachable authority that Simon had strongly <u>opposed</u> the proposal to send troops to the Saar for police purposes. This is in accordance with his temperament & accounts for his embarrassment when he first spoke to me about it. Yet last time I saw him he said to me 'Just as I was sure public opinion would approve the decision to send troops to the Saar,(!) so I feel it would not like giving a guarantee to defend Austrian integrity. We will have to do something more in the way of commitments in regard to Disarm^t, & we mustn't queer our pitch now over Austria'. With this part I heartily agreed – but I do think that we shall have to take on a fresh commitment in E. Europe if we want to make the Eastern Security Pact a success. [. . .]

25 Jan: Had a lively discussion with the new Polish ambassador, Count Raszcynski,[305] whom I had just met before, once when he was Sec^y here & once in Geneva. He talks freely & frankly & like most Poles has plenty of ideas. We discussed Polish feelings towards the proposed Eastern Security Pact, & the possibility of further Brit: commitments. I told him I thought pub: opinion here was moving towards taking more responsibilities in Europe, & that what seemed possible was a more explicit assertion of Locarno (esp: in the air), & a

[305] Edward Raczynski (1891–1993): delegate to World Disarmament Conf., Geneva; Min. to LoN, 1932–4; Amb. in London 1934–45; actg For. Min. 1941–2; Min. of State in charge of For. Affairs in cabinet of Gen. Sikorski, 1942–3; President-in-Exile 1979–86. See his *W sojuszniczym Londynie* (1997).

guarantee of the <u>new</u> Disarm^t Convention, if it sh^d be concluded. Ultimately we might consider take [sic – taking] some sort of part in the Eastern Security Pact, but not just yet.

Count R: seems to be a curiously casual man for an ambassador. First he kept me waiting some time (no complaint, but he made no sort of apology), & then the Chilean Ambassador was announced during our conversatn, & he kept <u>him</u> waiting perfect ages in the corridor!

HAMBROOK 27 Jan: At tea with Admrl & L^y Fergusson[306] to-day I met Sir Thomas Inskip[307] & had an interesting talk with him about the pol: position. He is in favour of a general election now, if a good excuse can be found for it, & also – a better idea – wants MacDonald to shed members of the Gov^t who have done their bit & bring in new blood. It is what 'SB' (as he called Baldwin failed to do in 1927, & MacD doesn't apparently seem up to doing it now. (I expect Ld Londonderry is the stumbling-block). He says MacD finds it v. difficult to read a document through. He said he didn't see how MacD: could lead another Gov^t, so I threw up my *ballon d'essai* about getting Simon to be the next leader of a Nat: Gov^t. He took it better than most people, agreeing that Simon w^d make a good Chairman of the Cabinet, & that he ought to be taken away from the F.O. anyhow. He said Simon was excellent at the <u>next step</u> – better than at the long view – & also in the presentatn of a case to the public.

Speaking of Hitler he said that he had just met a man who had seen both Hitler & Goebbels in Germany. Hitler <u>alone</u> had talked to him in a most rational & interesting way; but Goebbels had an exciting effect upon him, & Hitler became rather excited under the influence of Goebbel's [sic] mad fanaticism.

Sir T. Inskip said most of the people who were working against the Gov^t on India now were people who had personal grudges against it – Sir Roger Keyes[308] because he had not bn made First Sea Lord,

[306] James Fergusson (1871–1942): naval officer; Adm. 1926; retd 1928; kt. 1920; m. Enid Githa 1901.

[307] Thomas Inskip (1876–1947): Con. MP Bristol Central 1918–29, Fareham div. of Hampshire 1931–9; Solicitor-Gen. 1922–4, 1924–8, 1931–2; Attorney-Gen. 1928–9, 1932–6; Min. for Co-ordination of Defence 1936–9; kt. 1922; cr. Viscount Caldecote 1939.

[308] Roger John B. Keyes (1872–1945): naval officer & politician; Rear-Adm. 1917; Vice-Adm. 1921; Adm. 1926; Adm. of the Fleet 1930; retd 1935; Nat. Con. MP Portsmouth North 1934–43; kt. 1918; cr. Baron Keyes of Zeebrugge & Dover 1943. See his *Naval Memoirs* (2 vols 1934 & 1936).

Duchess of Atholl[309] because her husband had been prosecuted over the lottery business & so on.

31 Jan: Last night Lothian came into the Office, on his return that day from Berlin by air. The day before he had had a $2\frac{1}{2}$ hour talk with Hitler; & on arrival he sat down in the Travellers & wrote a Turnover for us. I held up my leader $\frac{1}{2}$ way through, so as to have a talk with him before finishing it. He is <u>convinced</u> that Germany doesn't want war. Her preoccupation is with domestic affairs; & insofar as she looks outwards it is anxiously towards the East, & not to the West.[310]

2 February   I've had short talks with Lothian again twice, & he gave me his personal impression of Hitler. 'A political prophet' is how he describes him. Rather fanatical, but not wildly so. Full of his creed, which is strange in parts e.g. about race. But that is fundamental. The German race. It must be united, wherever Germans are. And, *per contra*, he does not want to denationalize any other race, like the Poles – which distinguishes Nazi Germany from Imperialist Germany. Also from Mussolini, who has the ancient Roman taste for conquest. Hitler looked well, L: said. They discussed <u>naval</u> armaments, & Hitler said he w$^{\underline{d}}$ agree to Germany having 35% of British strength, & not provisionally only, but permanently. Very important, & we sh$^{\underline{d}}$ make our account with Germany <u>now</u>, & not repeat the mistake of the French & hesitate & hesitate, while the German level of demands steadily rises, like a taxi ticking up. I have put this to the Editor.

About colonies or mandates, L's idea is that Germany might perhaps have something when she shows herself fully civilized again.

6 Feb: We were kept in the dark about this conference[311] until Sunday evening (Feb 3) when Simon rec$^{\underline{d}}$ the Press – though on Saty night Flandin (in spite of solemn undertakings) let it out to Havas. Simon

[309] Katharine Marjory Ramsay (d. 1960): Unionist politician; MP Kinross & West Perth 1923–38; resigned seat following Munich agreement, fought – & lost – by-election as Independent; DBE 1918; m. 8th Duke of Atholl (d. 1942) 1899. See her *Searchlight on Spain* (1938).

[310] Added in pencil: 'Hitler wants peace' & he banged the desk!

[311] On 31 January Laval and Flandin had come to London, the result of which was the Anglo-French communiqué of 3 February which expressed the hope that Germany would co-operate in the proposed Eastern and Danubian pacts and join an air pact (by which each signatory would promise to support a victim of aerial aggression by any of the contracting powers) as a supplement to the Locarno agreements.

gave us a v. good exposé. He has done this job, not Eden this time. But while Simon was explaining it to us Eden rather ostentatiously took a chair from the side of the room & carried it up & planted it down next to Simon & associated himself with him. Eden's appearance has changed a bit. He is harder, more worldly-clever looking, a regular politiciany politician! I used to think he was something better. We heard at the Barings at luncheon yesterday that he gets all cuttings about himself.

Later that evening Simon broadcast his exposé of the Agreement (Anglo-French), for which he was taken to task by Lansbury[312] in the H.oC next day (Monday). I can understand the pique of par-liamentarians, for it is putting public opinion before parl^y opinion to explain it to us & then broadcast before the House has heard anything about it. But I consider Simon was justified because 1. Public opinion is more important than parl^y for a National Gov^t 2. Flandin had blabbed 3. It was a Sunday (on which the Agreement was signed).

Next day in the F.O. I passed one of the messengers who is an ex-Guardsman, & said something like 'well, if we had to fight again it w^d be in the air this time,' to which he replied – 'Yes, I sh^d like another war to come off. It'd wake some of them up. There's some of them wants waking up.'! – a fiery guardsman's reaction to the F.O. atmosphere!

16 Feb: [...] This morning Ribbentrop has rung me up from Berlin to urge that the Locarno spirit sh^d really be shown in the present negotiatns for an Air Convention. Why sh^d they be conducted jointly by G^t B^n & France? I accept his point, & have in fact already made it in this morn^g's leader, which I was able to read out to him. I asked him why the German Gov^t, in its reply yesterday, had not answered the other points besides the Air Convention? He answered that they were v. complicated & that in Germany it was Hitler alone who settled all points; so he was particularly anxious that a British Minister, or better still, two British Ministers, should visit Berlin & talk the whole complex of questions over with him (Hitler) personally.

25 Feb: Last Friday Leeper rang me up in PHS & asked me to come & see him, which I did. I found him in (for him) rather a state of excitement. He had bn having a talk with Simon, & obviously what he

---

[312] George Lansbury (1859–1940): Ed. *Daily Herald* 1913–22; Lab. MP Bow & Bromley div. of Tower Hamlets 1910–12, of Poplar 1922–40; Ldr of Lab. Party and Opposition 1931–5. See his *My Quest for Peace* (1938).

was out to do was to get the Press (he had just bn seeing Gordon Lennox)[313] to support the idea, which has just bn launched, that Simon sh^d extend his Berlin visit – which is now virtually decided on – to Moscow. Leeper was v. keen on the idea himself, saying he thought it w^d be 'a brilliant stroke of diplomacy'. He quoted the same sort of arguments in favour of it as I have bn using in favour of Simon going to Berlin – equality in negotiation, & so on. I did not jump to his idea, & we did not have a leader in favour of it. On the other hand we will not oppose it if Simon decides to go.

Both the ideas of the Air Convention & of the visit to Berlin have bn ours (*T.T.*'s) rather than the F.O.'s & Leeper seemed keen that this time his happy thought sh^d prevail!

27 Feb: There was one of B^n Franckenstein's delightful musical receptions at the Austrian Leg: on Mon: night, in honour of the Chancellor, Schuschnigg,[314] & the Foreign Minister, Baron Berger-Waldenegg.[315] S: & I went with Mrs Dawson.[316] After the concert, downstairs, Austen Chamberlain drew me aside & spoke to me at some length, warning me not to be too friendly to Germany. When I re-stated our (*T.T.*'s) policy to him, he said he 'did not disagree with it,' but he wanted me at least to be critical when they were tactless or showed bad taste – of which he gave me a recent example. Actually I had written a leader re-stating & defending our policy already before coming to the reception, so I was fortunately spared the question of whether to take notice of what AC said or not.[317]

As usual we got on v. well. He asked me to come & see him at any time to talk things over; & I asked him if he w^d sign a photo for me! [...]

2 March 1935   We had the Persian – or Iranian – Minister & his wife to luncheon the other day, & after lunch we levitated him! It went v.

[313] Victor C. H. Gordon-Lennox (1897–1963): journalist; Political Corrspdt *Daily Mail* 1923–9; Dip. Corrspdt *Daily Telegraph* 1934–42; Ed. of weekly *Whitehall Letter*. See his *X-Ray of Europe* (1939).

[314] Dr. Kurt von Schuschnigg (1897–1977): Christian Socialist Deputy 1927–38; Min. of Justice 1932, of Education 1933; Chanc. 1934–8; spent war years in concentration camp; Prof. of Political Science, St. Louis (U.S.A.) 1948–67. See his *The Brutal Takeover* (1938).

[315] Egon Berger-Waldenegg (b. 1880): Min. of Justice 1934, of For. Affairs & Justice 1934–5, of For. Affairs 1935–6; Min. in Rome 1936–8.

[316] Margaret Cecilia Dawson (1890–1969): d. of Sir Arthur Lawley, 6th Baron Wenlock; m. Geoffrey Dawson 1919; a leading London hostess at their home on Regent's Park during Dawson's years as editor of *The Times*.

[317] 'A Pleasant Visit': 27 Feb. 1935.

well – he being a tiny man, he flew up like a feather – & M$^{\underline{me}}$ Ala seemed delighted.

On Thursday I was summoned – for the first time & at the last moment – to a Board luncheon in P.H.S. It was a v. interesting affair. I sat next to D$^{\underline{r}}$ Murray Butler,[318] Pres: of Columbia University & other guests were Hore-Belisha,[319] the Min: of Transport, Lothian & M. Colban, the Norwgn Min. D$^{\underline{r}}$ Butler talked the whole way through luncheon. We his neighbours had nought to do but listen – & his talk was worth listening to. He gave a most vivid description of how Roosevelt had revivified the country on the first day of his presidency by his broadcast – the whole country was despondent, all the banks closed, & nobody seeing a way out – & R: quietly but confidently told them there <u>was</u> a way out. Hore-Belisha did most of what talking there was <u>with</u> him (D$^{\underline{r}}$ B). He (H-B) was v. bright. He has a twinkling expression, which reminded me of Ll-George. Versatile & light-hearted. I had quite a good talk with him afterwards on foreign affairs. He was sound, I thought, & rather amusing – John Walter[320] came up to us in the middle, & H-B said 'Oh, we were just talking about people like Napoleon & Simon who <u>will</u> go to Moscow'. (Simon is by way of paying a visit there soon). [...]

Lothian told me he had sent an urgent note to Simon the night before – S: was leaving that day for Paris – saying that if he went straight on from Berlin to Moscow it w$^{\underline{d}}$ deprive the Berlin visit of 50% of its value; & I am glad to say that Simon is not doing it. Leeper was hotly in favour of it (as recorded).

5 March 1935   Yesterday Simon rec$^{\underline{d}}$ the Press at the F.O., & afterwards drew me aside for a few words. He said he agreed entirely with our leader of that morn$^{\underline{g}}$ which favoured making the visit to Berlin a separate occasion[321] – & moreover still believed in getting the Air Convention negotiated – but it was important that this sh$^{\underline{d}}$ not appear to be done under German pressure so he w$^{\underline{d}}$ like to say <u>before he went</u> to Berlin that he was ready to <u>negotiate</u> that separately, though not to <u>conclude</u> it, till other points were settled too. I reminded him of our

[318] Nicholas Murray Butler (1862–1947): Pres., Columbia U. 1901–45; Pres., Carnegie Endowment for Intl Peace 1925–45; Nobel Peace Prize 1931. See his *Across the Busy Years* (1939).

[319] (Isaac) Leslie Hore-Belisha (1893–1957): Lib. MP Plymouth Devonport 1923–9, Nat. Lib 1929–42, Indep. 1942–5; Min. of Transport 1934–7; Sec. of State for War 1937–40; Min. of Nat. Insurance 1945; cr. Baron 1954. See *The Private Papers of Hore-Belisha* (1960).

[320] John Walter (1873–1968): great-great-grandson of John Walter, founder of *The Times* 1898; Chm. 1910–23.

[321] 'Sir John Simon for Berlin': 4 March 1935.

brief conversatn after he had addressed us on the day of the Anglo-French *communiqué*, when he had given preference to the Air Convention, & he admitted it & said that was still his view. [...]

I hope GD is not going to lose himself in political wire-pulling.[322] That way lies disaster for a journalist. He must exercise his influence through the leader. [...]

I think Simon & MacDonald both feel their positions threatened. They stand or fall together. Simon, I c^d see, did not like having to support increased estimates at all. MacD on the other hand was probably responsible for putting in the anti-German para: which appeared to be singularly tactless on the eve of Simon's visit to Berlin. So, though MacD & S. hang together, I don't know that they work together!

7 March   Yesterday I saw v. Hoesch about the postponement of the visit to Berlin. He told me Hitler really has got a sore throat. He was gassed in the war, & is always nervous lest he lose his voice. He was therefore pleased to have the good excuse for postponing Simon's visit afforded by our *gaffe* in the P.M.'s White Paper on National Defence – putting in a paragraph which attributes the blame for re-armament to Germany.

11 March   Had a telephone message from Horace Seymour[323] this morn^g asking me if I c^d go round & see Simon, so went to F.O. He wanted to talk over the speech which he wl have to make in winding up tonight's important Debate in the H. o C. He read me the principal passage, which amounted to an assurance to this country & to Ger: that he was going to pay his visit to Berlin on the basis of the London Declaratn of Feb 3, which remained 'unqualified', in spite of the rather different tone of the White Paper. He made the usual free use of the words 'Confidence' 'appeasement' 'settlement' etc. I begged him if it were by any means possible to go for something more than an 'exploratory' journey. I brought out the words 'Achievement' & 'Results' as emphatically as I could, & made him think. Why not get on with the Air Locarno? Why not negotiate & initial it? I suggested that in fact it w^d stand, & get the force of an agreement, even if it had only been initialled, because it was really only an amplificatn of Locarno, &

---

[322] ALK clipped an *Evening Standard* article of 4 March portraying Geoffrey Dawson as a political manoeuvrer seeking to throw out MacDonald and to take in Lloyd George.

[323] Horace James Seymour (1885–1978): entered dip. service 1908; Min. in Tehran 1936–9; Asst U-Sec. FO 1939–42; Amb. in Beijing 1942–6; kt. 1939.

nobody w^d denounce it. He agreed, & I can see he is quite keen himself on getting on with it, but is opposed by his own office (Vansittart). I even mentioned Austen Chamberlain, saying his name was linked in history with the achievement of Locarno. This to stir him by rivalry! He was moved, as much as that cold fish can be moved. I could see he w^d like to do it. He said he w^d like to get into it a prohibition of bombing, even if it were only in the preamble (But he admitted the Air Ministry was an obstacle). I said wouldn't it be possible just to put in the preamble something of this sort 'Should any State so far depart from the obligations of civilizatn as to make a bombing attack on another signatory, <u>all</u> the other signatories of the Treaty will be pledged to retaliate in kind.' He thought yes, something of that sort might meet the case. Simon said he <u>would</u> try to 'stiffen up' his speech.

From one or two remarks he let drop I can see he has practically given up hope that Germany will agree to any Arms Convention of Limitation. What a tragic missing of opportunities! They definitely w^d have agreed a year ago.

The only thing to do now is to go for Security. Later, if that is well established, & Socialist Govts come in, some Limitation may be possible. [...]

13 March Am seeing a good deal of the Foreign Sec^y *genus* just now! On Monday Sir J Simon, yesterday Austen Chamberlain, & today I am glad to say Arthur Henderson & M^{rs} H are to come to luncheon.

I went to see AC as a result of our talk at the Austrian Leg: the other night. There is an amplitude about AC's talk. He is never satisfied until he has covered all the points; & as we had necessarily been hurried at the Legation he wanted to amplify what he had said there about the coming European negotiatns.

He had argued <u>against</u> my idea of getting on with the Air Convention first, to the point of initialling it. Now he modified that. He said, yes, get on with it, but make its conclusion conditional upon our getting 'further guarantees' from Germany in regard to Central & E. Europe.

That seems to me a good line – a <u>policy</u>. I wish to goodness Simon had so clear a policy. I couldn't help saying to AC that his speech the night before in the debate on the White Paper (Defence) had expressed the true policy of this country much more clearly than anything said by the Foreign Sec^y. 'Simon has no policy' was one of AC's remarks. He said he did not wish to be unduly critical, & in public he supported him, but he gave me several examples of what he heard had gone on inside the Cabinet, showing how unable Simon was to take a strong line. I said I thought S: himself was in favour of getting on with the Air Convention, as he had always agreed with me on this point. AC however said that he had agreed with him in an opposite sense i.e. a negotiatn of all points must be simultaneous. He was fond of agreeing with people & then making out that he c^d not get on with it owing to opposition. This however is probably the simple truth. S: for instance told me that he had already drafted a preamble for an Air Convention, condemning bombing (about which he consulted me the other day); & personally I am sure Simon, a liberal & a bit of a pacifist, is very genuinely in favour of a new Air Convention & of abolishing bombing; but he is nervous about his position & pitifully weak.

As I said to AC, Simon is not man enough to be ready to resign if his proposals are not accepted. 'That seems to make all the difference to a man's authority' I said. 'Yes', said AC, 'it does. There are 3 classes of Cabinet Ministers – the one who is always threatening to resign. He becomes a nuisance to his colleagues, & his threat moreover loses its force. Another everybody knows has no intention of resigning; & the third does not easily threaten to resign, but means it when he does.'

AC considered that in the debate the night before he had 'bowled a fairly skilful ball' which had got the batsman, Cripps[324] into difficulties, & made him put up an easy catch to point; but Simon, fielding there, had not merely missed the catch, he had run away from it! (by not smashing up Cripps in his winding-up speech, as he could easily have done, Cripps having been forced by AC to declare that the Labour Party w^d have made war with Japan over Manchuria. Simon's excuse, given to me by the F.O. next day, was that he (Simon) wanted to go to Berlin representing all Parties. Rather feeble. No need to represent Cripps, esp: to Hitlerites).

AC told me at great length how he & Norman Davis & others had bn staying at Blickling with Lothian, & Norman Davis had made the usual remark of Americans that we (G^t B^n) had 'let them down' over Manchuria. AC had asked how; & Davis had answered that a proposal had bn made by the U.S. for a meeting of the Nine Powers of the Wash: Treaty, which had bn turned down by the British Gov^t. This seemed so important to AC that he had had enquiries made, when he returned to London; & he learned from the F.O. that what had really happened was that the Japs had proposed a meeting of the 9 Powers but without China – no doubt to get the matter out of the hands of the League; & naturally the Brit: Gov^t had refused to act upon it.

AC had also learned from Ray Atherton[325] that when Davis got back

[324] (Richard) Stafford Cripps (1889–1952): Lab. MP E. Bristol 1931–50; Solicitor-Gen. 1930–1; Amb. in Moscow 1940–2; Min. of Aircraft Production 1942–5; Min. for Economic Affairs 1947; Chanc. of Exchequer 1947–50; kt. 1930. See his *The Struggle for Peace* (1936).

[325] Ray Atherton (1885–1960): US diplomat; Counsellor in London 1927–37; Min. in Sofia 1937–9, in Copenhagen 1939–40; Chief, Div. of European Affairs, Dept of State 1940–3; Amb. in Ottawa 1943–8.

from Blickling he (D) had asked Ray Ath: just what were the facts!! This naturally revolted AC – that a statesman of Davis' repute sh^d make a statement of that sort about the Brit. Gov^t without knowing more about it.

AC does at least take immense trouble to get a thing exactly right.

At the same time, I asked him a question about Abyssinia – why we had agreed with Italy in 1925 that the railway Italy was to build from Eritrea to It: Somaliland sh^d pass to the <u>west</u> of Addis Ababa – & he confessed he had quite forgotten, though he was For: Sec^y when the Agreement was signed. That is perhaps quite natural; but the point strikes me as an important one, & one which may become more important shortly. [...]

14 March   Yesterday Arthur Henderson (& M^rs H) came to luncheon with us. I got him, too, to sign a photograph, & felt that I clinched my friendship with him. I have found him the easiest to deal with of the For: Sec'ies I have known, & we have in common a devotion to the ideal of disarmament.

One curious point that came out of our luncheon talk was that he likes Curzon! Two greater opposites it w^d be difficult to imagine. But obviously he also thinks poorly of Simon, though he confined himself to telling a story against him. He said that at Geneva people said he (S) had spent so much of his life getting convictions for other people that he had got none left for himself! [...]

Coote (our Pol: Corrspdt) was at luncheon too, & he & Henderson had a v. interesting discussn about the next election, esp: what part LlGeorge w^d play. They seemed to think the election w^d probably be in May 1936, & that LlG w^d play a lone hand. That anyhow was H's opinion. I said, doesn't LlG want <u>power</u>, which he might get by coming into the present Nat. Gov^t? H: said 'no, LlG likes <u>playing</u> at politics. He has a wonderful nose for it. He won't come in to the tail end of a Gov^t. He will try to hold the balance after the next election' (that was also C's opinion, tho' I rather think GD w^d like to see LlG come into this Gov^t & revivify it).

H wants to revive the Disarm^t Conference & took me aside in the drawing-room afterwds & we stood by the window discussing how this c^d be done. I was not optimistic for the moment. The best we can hope for is <u>limitation</u> when Ger: has got her equality. H: had the good idea that it still remained for the <u>Conference</u> to accept German equality. It has so far only bn done by the Five Powers. If the Conference formally accepts it that may make it easier for Germany to return to it.

16 March   Took Elizabeth to see Lives of Bengal Lancers today – the best film I have ever seen – & in the News Reel Ramsay MacDonald came on, seated at his desk, & defending the White Paper on Defence. He did it quite extraordinarily well. But of course no word about that disastrous paragraph 12, which has simply killed the European negotiatns. Hitler has gone off in a sulk, & tonight he has announced the re-introduction of conscription in Germany.

19 March   Yesterday at luncheon at the Jap: Emb: the Ambassdr (M. Matsudaira) was amusing about his inaugural radio-telephony talk with Tokyo. It w$^{\underline{d}}$ put ambassdrs much more under the surveillance of their Foreign Offices, he had said; & the Jap: For: Minister had said to him from Tokyo that he quite agreed & that it might in time enable the Govt to dispense with ambassadors altogether! On the other hand, Matusdaira said (to me) that such conversations c$^{\underline{d}}$ never be quite safe from listening-in, & the value of the radio-tel: was much diminished by the fact that the real value of talking, as distinct from despatch-writing, would be to discuss confidential points; & that was precluded by the danger of being overheard. [...]

I saw Count Raczynski, the Polish Ambssdr, this evening, & suggested to him that a way out of the difficulty about an Eastern Security Pact might be to get an Eastern European <u>Air</u> Convention, on the model of the proposed Air Locarno. He said he had not thought of it, but at first sight liked it very much, & he proposes to discuss its possibilities with Eden, whom he is going to see in a day or two, before he (Eden) goes off to Berlin with Simon. He wants to talk over with him what subjects would be suitable for discussion in Warsaw when Eden pays his visit there on Apr. 1; & he seemed glad to have this idea to propound.

Curiously enough it was proposed to us (*T.T.*) in a letter from Paris from P$^{\underline{ce}}$ Henry Ghyka, a Rumanian, which I thought worth publishing, but which so far GD has held up. He does not like ideas to come from dagoes! Anyhow it is a good idea.

Afterwds I went on & saw Vitetti at the It: Embassy – or rather, he was just driving off to the Ritz & took me with him in his car & we had a quick discussion about the Franco-Italian idea that G$^{\underline{t}}$ B$^{\underline{n}}$ & France & Italy sh$^{\underline{d}}$ all be joined in a common protest to Berlin about the introduction of conscription.

We have already protested; but Simon's decision to carry out the visit all the same has led those idiotic Germans to jubilate in the Press about the separation of G$^{\underline{t}}$ B$^{\underline{n}}$ from France, etc: etc:; & there has bn the suggestion that there might be an Anglo-Franco-Italian meeting in Paris or N. Italy in the next few days, before S: goes to Berlin.

I hope Simon won't yield to this. A statement in the House sh^d be enough.

31 March Simon did not yield; but he sent Eden to Paris, on the way to Berlin. All right.

I launched the E. European Air Pact idea in a leader on Fri: morn^g.[326] Last Fri. 29th just as I was sitting down to write my leader on the results of Simon's visit to Berlin, the telephone bell went, & I recognized Ribbentrop's voice – from Berlin! All he wanted to say was that he thought the interpretation in London of Hitler's statement of policy made it appear more divergent from British policy than it really was. I was glad that at least this showed that they are <u>anxious</u> to keep in harmony with us.

I think our F.O. may have mis-interpreted Hitler a little in this way, that Hitler was asked to state German aims, & did so, not as a diplomatist, which he isn't, but as a propagandist. He was not negotiating. He was stating German aims, & did so frankly.

'Debit and Credit'

the proposal [for an Eastern Security Pact] was rejected by HERR HITLER without equivocation or ambiguity. The German objections, however, though intelligible, are not entirely convincing. It may be admitted that HERR HITLER not unnaturally regards himself as a defender of Western institutions against Bolshevism, and cannot therefore contemplate an arrangement which might automatically place him side by side with Russia in repelling the aggression of a third country, and it is easy to understand moreover that he does not desire the help of Soviet troops onGerman soil even against a common opponent; but it should still be possible to arrange for a collective security group in that part of the world in which only those countries that opted for it should bind themselves to mutual assistance … Perhaps a general Eastern Air Convention might be a useful cover for particular defensive agreements. The importance of the air is paramount there, as it is in the West; and some of the objections which Poland is known also to entertain towards the proposed Security Pact might possibly be modified if the general obligation to act were confined to an element which does not involve the occupation of one country by the troops of another, even for purposes of mutual assistance. The first need of civilization in the East, as in the West, is to oppose to the concentration of bombing aeroplanes an overwhelming combination of forces.

[326] 'Debit and Credit' 29 March 1935, p. 17. Dawson noted on the 28th that 'Leo K returned to the European situation on wh. I'd had a talk w S.B. early in the morning, & between us we probably annoyed the F.O. again!' Dawson Mss. 39, Bodleian Library.

1 April A lively talk with Grandi this morn^g. It is curious, but when I talk with Vitetti, I find myself listening to brilliant coruscations, & when I talk with Grandi, I always feel in good form myself! & yet I get as much benefit from talking with Grandi, whose interjections are to the point & authoritative. This morn^g I particularly did most of the talking, as he has bn ill for a month, & wanted to pick up threads. I gave him my impression of the British talks in Berlin & Moscow, & said frankly I had not made up my mind about what ought to be done at Stresa.[327] He said he simply c^d not see either; & we agreed it w^d be easier after full reports had bn rec^d from Anthony Eden about his later visits, particularly Warsaw, where he arrives today. Poland is now one of the balancing States. Italy is so no longer. Owing to her fear of Austro-German union, she has taken – for the time! – definite sides with France against Germany. Then there is her Abyssinian policy, which is making her mobilize for action in Africa & N. Italy at the same time.[328]

Grandi laughed when I said Mussolini was in warlike mood, but he agreed; & added 'you know Mussolini'.

I developed my theme that Brit: policy nowadays usually did the right thing but spoilt it by doing it too late. e.g. It <u>ought</u> to have bn detached & impartial when Germany was struggling for her rights, & ought to intervene decisively on one side or another at a crisis. Instead of that it had done exactly the opposite. When Germany was struggling, & deserving of some little help – esp: under Stresemann & Brüning – Brit: pol: had been consistently pro-French. Now, when Germany has asserted her rights, & is becoming somewhat defiant & aggressive, instead of reassuring France, Simon (not the F.O.) has suddenly become thoroughly impartial, gone to Berlin, & all the rest of it. If he had done this a year or two ago, we might have had agreement by now. Grandi said 'I could not have put it better'. [...]

When we were saying good-bye he said neatly 'The post-war period has ended; the pre-war period is beginning.'!

2 Apr: Last night GD told me he had bn dining where there were a lot of public men – The Beefsteak, I expect – & Sir Ian Hamilton[329] had come up to him & said how grateful he was to *T.T.* for its attitude towards Germany in the present crisis, & that Edward Halifax is also

---

[327] Britain, France and Italy were scheduled to meet at Stresa on 11 April in order to discuss joint action following Germany's repudiation of her obligations under the Treaty of Versailles.

[328] Italian forces had clashed with the Ethiopians along the Somaliland frontier at Walwal on 5 December 1934.

[329] Ian Standish M. Hamilton (1853–1947): army officer; Gen. 1914; commanded Mediterranean Expeditionary Force 1915; kt. 1900. See his *Gallipoli Diary* (1920).

heartily in favour of our policy, & considers the F.O. policy 'disastrous' – not <u>Simon's</u>, who is with us rather than with Vansittart. Rather surprisingly L$^{\underline{d}}$ H: told GD that in the Cabinet Eyres-Monsell[330] was one of those in cabinet who heartily supported coming to understanding with Germany. Probably he wants to pull off a naval agreement. I have bn told confidentially that we have invited the Ger: Gov$^{\underline{t}}$ to send representatives to London for preliminary naval conversations. It is v. exasperating not being able to publish this. We urged some time ago in *T.T.* that, in regard to naval armaments at least, the same ghastly blunder sh$^{\underline{d}}$ not be repeated (as in land armaments) & we drift into a one-sided settlement.

6 Apr: Yesterday I had luncheon with C$^{\underline{t}}$ Szechenyi (at Prunier's) & he told me that nowadays the policy which the F.O. expounded to him was usually not the one which was adopted!

And yesterday evening Reed came into the office, having just got back from travelling round Europe with Anthony Eden – Berlin, Moscow, Warsaw, Prague; & he said that all the way round the various Govts had said to Eden – we are very glad to know what you have to say; but what will your public opinion allow you to do?

7 Apr: I had a sharp 5 min: with Anthony Eden on the telephone this morn$^{\underline{g}}$. He is not well enough to see anybody yet – except the doctor & Sir John Simon – but we went straight to the point – which is, should our policy be to browbeat Germany, or to agree with her? He is in favour of the former. He says, be v. firm with her now, & in 6 months time we'll get a good agreement (about arms, colonies etc). I say, so far, her demands have gone up every six months so far, & I see no reason why the process sh$^{\underline{d}}$ stop – unless we agree with her; & therefore, the sooner the better – e.g. the naval proposals. Hitler asks for 50% of British naval strength. Monstrous, says Anthony Eden. A perfectly good basis of discussion, say I. She <u>is</u> a great Power; why shdn't she have 50% of our naval strength – & next year she'll be asking more – & who will stop her? Stop her <u>now</u>, by agreement.

Eden said that our last leader (The British Role, Apr 4)[331] which he had read in Cologne, had horrified him, & undone the good he might have done on his mission. It looked as if we w$^{\underline{d}}$ always give way to

[330] Bolton Meredith Eyres-Monsell (1881–1969): Con. MP Evesham 1910–35; Whip 1911–21; Civil Ld Admiralty 1921–2; 1st Sec. Admiralty 1922–3; Chief Whip 1923–31; First Ld Admiralty 1931–6; kt. 1929, cr. Viscount Monsell 1935.
[331] 'The British Role': 4 April 1935, p.13.

German demands. I said that was not in our minds; but we had made up our minds (which the Gov^t has not) about what is legitimate & what is not legitimate for Germany to demand, & so far her demands have not exceeded the legitimate. Therefore concede with good grace; but make it clear that excessive demands w^d be met as firmly as Germany was met in 1914.

I said I was sorry if we had impeded him, & that we would certainly be ready to say (in *T.T.*) to Germany that we were by no means prepared to concede anything she might care to ask.

'The British Role'

far too much stress has hitherto been laid on the negative side of HERR HITLER's statements to SIR JOHN SIMON, and that far too little attempt has been made to fix attention on their positive side. It is a matter of common knowledge now that HERR HITLER arrived some time ago at the figure which in his view German armed strength ought to reach in relation to the present strength of his neighbours; but the Berlin conversations seem to have made it clear that he is also willing, having disclosed his figure, to discuss with them a proportionate all-round reduction. It is certain in any case that he is still ready to renounce the construction of any weapons of which other countries are ready to deprive themselves. There seems at least to be an opportunity, therefore, for every country to renounce the construction of, for instance, the largest tanks, or monster guns with a range of more than a score of miles. That in itself would be a gain worth securing; and LORD STANHOPE spoke in the House of Lords last night as if the Government did hope that it might still be secured. HERR HITLER moreover agrees to the international inspection of national armaments. Here again a system is within reach which, whatever its technical difficulties, would certainly have enormous psychological value. HERR HITLER is ready to negotiate an air pact in Western Europe; and the negotiation of an air pact in Eastern Europe may possibly be a proposal worthy of consideration. HERR HITLER has stated the naval demands of his country, which are not exorbitant; and there is fortunately reason to believe that the British Government are alive to the advantage of including Germany in any future naval negotiations. These are all substantial points. They are more. They are constructive proposals. It is the plain duty of this country, and of every country which is seriously working for peace, to exploit to the full every possible point of agreement. Much might have been achieved before if there had not been so ambitious a search for universal remedies. If British diplomacy can exploit and enlarge each single possibility of agreement it will be rendering inestimable service to Europe.

8 Apr: Last night we heard that Anthony Eden had bn ordered by his doctors 4 to 6 weeks' complete rest. He is evidently pretty bad. That may have influenced his judgment when talking to me in the morning, for he seemed almost rabidly anti-German. He did not quite see things in perspective. For instance he spoke of Goebbels' rather fiery speech of last Sat[y] at the Danzig elections, & said that that was the result of the leader in *T.T.* on Thursday morning.[332] Nap: III is supposed to have said once that if it rained in E. Europe it was attributed to him; just now whatever happens in Central Europe is attributed to *T.T.*!

9 Apr: Had a lively talk with Grandi this morn[g]. He is off to Stresa tomorrow, & he expounded to me the sort of thing that might be agreed to – a Five (or six) Power Pact against aggression. Italy, G[t] B[n], Russia <u>and</u> Germany to agree to take action against any one of their number that turned aggressor. Whether we or Germany w[d] agree to <u>take action</u> remains to be seen. Musso: also wants something more done about Austria; & is in favour of a declaratn that Bulgaria, Hungary & Austria are entitled to increase their military strength above the level of the Peace Treaties. I said I thought that w[d] be an excellent start for Art[icle] XIX (reconsideratn of treaties that have become obsolete), which has not yet bn given a chance. Grandi said 'I hadn't thought of that. Yes, it might be linked to Article XIX'.

Grandi said 'Neither Mussolini nor Hitler care much for the League. But what we want is a union of the Five Great Powers – or six, if Poland comes in'. Talking about our (*T.T.*) not resisting German claims, I said that that was because we had made up our minds how how [sic] Germany might in our opinion justifiably get the conditions of peace changed, that were imposed upon her. Quick as lightning Grandi said 'I wish I knew what conclusion you had reached about Austria.' We both laughed, & then I said 'If the Austrian Govt itself opted for some sort of federation with Germany, there w[d] be no violent opposition in this country. If Germany tried to seize Austria that w[d] be quite a different thing.'

10 Apr: My leader of Mon: (Apr: 8 called 'Preparing for Stresa') caused great annoyance to the Cabinet, it seems. MacD: imparted his displeasure to Alan Robbins,[333] & said that he, Runciman & Simon were v. annoyed. R & S were specially mentioned, I am sure, because they were known to be in favour of our policy of still trying to reach an understanding with Germany. In any case it seems the Cabinet

---

[332] 'The British Role'.
[333] Alan Pitt Robbins (1888–1967): editorial staff *The Times* 1909–53; Parliamentary Corrspdt 1923–38; News Ed. 1938–53. See his *Newspapers Today* (1956).

spent about $\frac{3}{4}$ hour – half their morning session – talking about our leader! Their real bother is that they admittedly have no policy, & we outlined one; & this is interpreted by foreigners as the policy of the country. The reasons for annoyance given by MacD were that the leader w^d hamper him at Stresa – I honestly do not see how or why – & that G^t B^n can never agree to the German naval demands – we suggested that we might. Hitler asks 35% of our naval strength. What likelihood is there of our ever settling on better terms! I fear limitation of any sort wl go by the board if our wretched Gov^t can't make up its mind. Simon actually prided himself, in the House of C. last night, on the fact that the Govt had not yet formulated a policy.

'Preparing For Stresa'

A war of which all speak seldom comes; and it is indeed difficult to see at this moment what issue could induce a responsible Government to launch its people, and so the people of other countries, into the ghastly turmoil and destruction of a modern war. The chief danger to peace appears to be that a dissatisfied Government should so successfully obtain its ends by pressure without violence that it may be induced to adopt this method once too often, and provoke – as Germany did in 1914 – a violent and general reaction. But the conditions to-day are fortunately very different from those of 1914. The League of Nations exists, and the Kellogg Pact has been signed; and, even though they are not backed by trustworthy machinery of action, they provide both a standard of international conduct and the mechanism for that instant consultation of which SIR EDWARD GREY felt the lack twenty-one years ago. Moreover, the Treaty of Locarno pledges the Western countries of Europe to action in the event of a flagrant aggression; and it should be supplemented by an air convention without unnecessary delay.

There can be little doubt that at Stresa both the Italian and the French Governments will be concerned to consider every possible means of strengthening the arrangements for combined action in resistance to aggression and in defence of treaty rights....

The British Government therefore will have to make up its mind how far it is prepared to support proposals which have as their general purpose the strengthening of machinery against aggression. There is a movement in France which has abandoned hope of obtaining satisfactory protection from an extended security system, and advocates a triple alliance with Czechoslovakia and Soviet Russia. This would manifestly be directed against Germany, and would receive no support whatever from this country, which remains resolutely opposed to any division of Europe into hostile camps.

....[Hitler] wishes Germany to be regarded as capable of being a Mandatory Power. He is willing to limit arms and war material, and agrees to the international supervision of national armaments. Some of the German demands are high, but there is nothing really incompatible with the agreed principle of equality, reckoned on any fair basis of national size and national needs. For the present there is not the slightest doubt that public opinion expects the British Government, not to take sides, but to work for a general agreement. Unredressed grievances are the most powerful of all the causes of war. Only if they are wholly ill-founded can a negative or partisan policy be justified.

17 Apr: We are getting a great many letters, for & against our (*T.T.*'s) policy towards Germany after her declaration of conscription (March 16). Most for, a few v. abusive ones against. Here is a particularly appreciative one for.[334]

19 Apr: Willert rang me up the other day & said he wanted to have a talk, so I got him to come & have lunch − & he told me he is going off for a journey in Europe, & <u>may</u> want to write an article or two at the end of it. He had seen Vansittart. He felt sure, he said, that what European countries wanted was that <u>we</u> (G^t B^n) sh^d guarantee peace. He w^d like to get his articles, if he wrote them, taken by *The Times*. He is going as an emissary of Vansittart's to prove his case, no doubt about it.

4 May   I don't often talk politics at Lords, but just as I was leaving the Pavilion this morn^g after watching the MCC v Yorks match I ran into Mr Weigall[335] whom I first met after he'd seen Hitler & asked me to go to the Athenaeum for a talk. So we talked about Hitler again; & I see that he evidently keeps in v. close touch with Ribbentrop − whose letters, by the way, our people open! i.e. letters to him, so Weigall told me. He is therefore sending him one by a man called Tennant, who leaves London on the 9th, with messages for Rib: & Hitler. Weigall had

[334] My dear Sir,

I sent a letter to 'The Editor' earlier today on Concessions to Germany. Whether you are able to use it or not, I want to thank you very, very cordially for the noble course you have pursued during this last crisis in European affairs. Your steady, firm but moderate attitude representing the finest traditions of Britain and England is invaluable. With a difference which one need not attempt to define your influence is probably equal to that of a first-rate Minister, and as I read your fine leading articles I think we have found a successor to Castlereagh at last. Be assured that you are on the true road, that you are getting at the hearts, the deepest feelings, of the British people. They have been inarticulate, but your expression of them is giving millions the lead which they have been waiting for.
Yours sincerely,
John Orr

[335] Archibald Weigall (1874–1951): Cons. MP Horncastle div. of Lincolnshire 1910–20; Gov. of South Australia 1920–22; chmn, Royal Empire Society 1932–6; kt. 1920.

bn consulted, & his advice had been 'Follow *The Times*.'!

In the course of our conversatn he paid me the immense compliment of saying 'Was it you who wrote the leader on the 18th?'[336] Nothing could sound sweeter to the ears of a leader writer. The life of a leader is 24 hours – fancy one lingering in the memory for over a fortnight!

'The Geneva Verdict'

The terms of the resolution [by which the League Council condemned the German announcement of rearmament] were in themselves unexceptionable. The scrupulous respect of all treaty obligations must always be 'a fundamental principle of international life.' They are clearly the essential basis of civilized relationships between nations. Nor has any Power the legal right to liberate itself from the engagements of a treaty, or modify its stipulations, unless the other contracting parties consent. The German Military Law of March 16, re-establishing conscription, undoubtedly conflicted with these principles. Legally the German Government has not by its unilateral action conferred any right upon itself – though obviously its own people do not dispute its right; and in practice they are making it effective ... The League itself has always been regarded there as an instrument of the victorious Powers; and our Berlin Correspondent reports that the Geneva verdict again shows it, in German eyes, to be a flexible instrument in their hands.

It is regrettable that no allowance should have been made by a body like the League Council for the special circumstances in which Germany incurred her obligations. It would have enhanced the reputation of the League for impartiality if one voice at least had been raised to recall the manner in which this particular Treaty [Versailles] had been imposed. Germany signed it literally at the point of the bayonet. At the time of signature her representatives made explicit protests that they would be unable to carry out all of its provisions ... Not until MARSHAL FOCH was instructed to be ready to march into Germany within three days did the Germans consent to a Peace in the framing of which they had had hardly any part at alliance The procedure in Paris was a complete departure from recent practice. At all the previous great Peace Congresses of modern times the representatives of vanquished countries, though obviously at a disadvantage, were free to negotiate their treaties article by article. ...

Far different was the treatment of the Germans in 1919. They were not invited to Paris at all for the first months of the treaty-making, and then it was to receive the Treaty already fully drafted. They were allowed three weeks in which to make written comments – which they did energetically – but oral discussion was barred. By dint of their written observations they gained a few points here and there, but no very substantial alterations were made; and, when they signed, they signed, as has been said, under protest. There were a great many circumstances which made it difficult for the

---

[336] 'The Geneva Verdict': p.13.

victorious States to hold the full Peace Congress that was undoubtedly intended; and they made the work of what was meant to be a preliminary conference a race between anarchy and peace. But the facts of the conclusion of the Treaty of Versailles, however little they are remembered by most Governments to-day, are not only familiar to Germans – they are burnt into their minds. Hitlerism is largely a revolt against Versailles; and until this fundamental truth is taken fully into account there will be no real peace in Europe. ...

11 May   Conwell-Evans[337] called on me at *T.T.* 2 days ago. He is a useful acquaintance, & it was nice of him to come – he is a personal friend of Ramsay MacDonald, & knows Germany at first-hand from having been a lecturerer at Königsberg University for 2 years, ending the other day. He is a friend of Ribbentrop's, & has had 2 talks with Hitler.

He is enthusiastic about the policy of *T.T.*, & in a letter I've just had from him actually says 'I greatly admire your work. It is impossible to exaggerate its value. *The Times* is doing more for European peace than the League or any other body at present'.

He is in constant touch with Ribbentrop, & has sent him messages now, before Hitler's big speech on 17$^{\underline{th}}$, about what I suggest – i.e. that Hitler sh$^{\underline{d}}$ initiate air limitatn, & rejoin the League, with, no doubt, certain conditions – or else, build up a new international organizatn on the basis of the Kellogg Pact. But League preferable at present, as the Brit: public believes in it.

The way things are done nowadays is curious. After the famous Anglo-French cmnqué of Feb 3 Hitler wanted to find out what sort of reply w$^{\underline{d}}$ be considered satisfactory in England. He mentioned this to Ribbentrop, Rib: telephoned across the North Sea to Conwell-Evans, C-E asked Lothian, & Lothian asked Simon – & the answer went back through the same chain!

I met Simon yesterday at the reception at the Ritz to Q. Marie of Rumania. As usual the man was thinking of his own position, & went off into a long explanation about his statement, or rather mis-statement in the H. of Commons the other day on the subject of the transferability of Mandates by the League. I said I thought the matter was finished with, but he indicated that it w$^{\underline{d}}$ probably be brought up again.

I had a talk with another Cabinet Minister, Sir Godfrey Collins[338]

[337] T. P. Conwell-Evans (1891–1968): Prof. of English, U. of Königsberg 1932–4; Joint Sec., Anglo-German Fellowship 1934–9; interpreted for Lloyd George during visit to Hitler 1936. See his *None So Blind* (1947).

[338] Godfrey Pattison Collins (1875–1936): Lib. MP Greenock 1910–36 (Nat. Lib. from 1931); Lib. Chief Whip 1924–6; Scottish Sec. 1932–6; kt. 1919.

[...who] attacked me about our policy in regard to Germany, saying that *T.T.* had made things harder for the Gov^t, as we 'had raised Hitler's demands'. I think I effectively refuted this charge. The futility of his own mind's working on the subject was shown by what followed. I said 'After all, limitation can come by agreement & in no other way.' 'Of course, of course' he said, rather impatiently, as if the remark was foolishly obvious. Then I said, 'then let us agree now. Hitler's demands increase every six months. Where shall we be in a year's time?' 'Where will Hitler be' he said. [']He will be in a rotten position compared with us.' His policy, in fact, is to out-build. That is the only alternative to early agreement, & surely agreement is better. [...]

20 May   Coatman[339] of the BBC (who got the post I considered last year) saw GD yesterday, & told him that he had been to the F.O. about Hitler's speech, which H: is to deliver to-day. He had seen Vansittart, & V. had advised him not to be taken in by anything Hitler said, &, even if he was moderate, not to give the speech a good reception. Coatman was surprised at this, even knowing Vansittart. GD called it outrageous, & C: was evidently inclined to agree, & proposes to judge the speech on its merits. Van:, as GD says, is trying to spread an atmosphere of suspicion about the speech even before it is delivered. Any olive branch w^d be poisoned, acc: to him.

20 May   Kennedy to Norman Ebbutt[340] Confidential: *[...] I have never seen Vansittart's memorandum, but it exists all right. I understand that he has mapped out the German programme step by step, showing how Germany will ultimately dominate Europe. The worst of this is, that he cannot bear to allow it to appear that he is wrong; & therefore Germany has to be the villain of the piece, whatever she does: We have proof of rather outrageous attempts by the F.O., under his direction, to rush the public into forming unfavourable opinions of German official utterances.*

24 May   Having put about hostile insinuations against Hitler's speech before ever it was delivered, the F.O. refused, on the day after it had bn delivered, to express any official opinion, on the ground that Baldwin

[339] John Coatman (1889–1963): Dir. of Public Info., Govt of India 1926–30; Prof. of Imperial Economic Relations, London School of Economics 1931–4; Senior News Ed. BBC 1934–7, North Regional Controller 1937–49; Dir. of Research in Social Sciences, U. of St Andrews 1949–54. See his *Magna Britannia* (1936).
[340] Letter deposited in *The Times* archive.

was making a statement that afternoon in the H. of Commons: Warner,[341] however, (of the News Dept) who is a good chap, vouchsafed some informal animadversions upon Hitler's speech! Mostly cavillings & questionings & demands for interpretations. These F.O. people will not see the big thing & go for it.

27 May Have had some telephone talk with Ribbentrop in Berlin over the possibility of a meeting being arranged between Baldwin & Hitler. H: wants it, & B: is not against it. I don't think anything will come of it just now; indeed this w^d hardly be a good moment, as B: is about to become P.M. again, & he had better let Hitler wait a little.[342] In any case Ribbentrop is coming over to London next week for the naval conversatns.

3 June Saw Ribbentrop this morn^g at the Carlton, he having come over for the first Anglo-German naval negotiations. He is now Ambassador-at-large, & evidently his stock is rising. He spoke as though he might discuss other matters besides naval strengths; & I ventured to urge him whatever he did not to try, or even appear to try, to drive a wedge between us & France. That w^d spoil his visit.

von R: told me that <u>he</u> had drafted the German reply to the Anglo-French commnqué of Feb. 3. Officially that was of course v. Neurath's job – but evidently von R: is cutting out von N: as Hitler's adviser on foreign affairs.

14 June Got back from Yorkshire on Wed^y aftern^n, & in the evening was impressed by GD into attacking at once an unctuous manifesto put forth by LlGeorge & a lot of Nonconformist ministers, also Liberals like Gilbert Murray, H.A.L. Fisher, & Lothian! (GD was much upset to see his name!). I only started reading it after 9 p.m., & could not do much writing before 10 – but it was obviously an attempt by LlG to exploit the natural disappointment of idealists in order to hoist himself into power, & we wanted to scotch it at once. He talks of 'union above party or confession' etc, but in reality he is trying to destroy such union as already exists behind the Nat: Gov^t. Baldwin had given a copy of

---

[341] Christopher Frederick A. Warner (1895–1957): entered for. service 1920; FO 1920–3, 1928–1951; Amb in Brussels 1951–5; kt. 1951.

[342] On 16 May Ramsay MacDonald, facing the imminent desertion of his remaining Labour and Liberal friends, which would have reduced him to dependence upon Conservative support, and beset by headaches, insomnia and depression, resigned the premiership. Baldwin was appointed Prime Minister on 7 June.

the document to GD in the evening before dinner. Our regular copy arrived late in the office, & it was pretty clear (confirmed next morn^g) that only the favourable papers e.g. *News-Chronicle* were getting early copies in time to write it up fully. Baldwin had got his copy from Kingsley Wood,[343] who had it from some of his dissenting friends.

I found on my return to PHS from Yorks a letter from Willert, written from the Riviera, after his journey in Europe. He says 'The more I have seen & heard the more I congratulate you & *The Times* on the line you have taken in regard to Germany.' This is most satisfactory, as I am sure Willert started on his journey with rather different ideas in his head. I hope he will report to Vansittart in the sense of his letter to me.

17 June A lively luncheon at my house here today; I'd invited GD to meet von Ribbentrop, & von R:, I'm glad to say, was most eloquent & interesting. His importance is that he is Hitler's confidant & mouthpiece. GD had bn led to underestimate him; but I think he was v. glad to have had the talk. von R's mission is obviously to get on as well as ever possible with G^t B^n & representative Englisnmen. He has done well with the naval negotiations. Now he wants to get on with the Air Pact & to go from London to Paris & talk to Laval about it. We both advised him to talk to Baldwin about it before he goes. He says he will; & he is most anxious to arrange a meeting between Hitler & Baldwin, possibly in South Germany in the autumn. He wants Baldwin to hear H's ideas about Western European solidarity against Bolshevism. I said I thought Baldwin was more a man who would appreciate practical proposals rather than an exposition of ideas.

3 July Had my first contact with Sam Hoare as For: Sec^y yesterday evening.[344] I was writing my leader in my room in P.H.S. when the telephone went, & a voice said 'Is that Mr Kennedy' ('Yes, it is') 'This is Sir Samuel Hoare' – & then he went on to say what had happened in the House of Commons after Eden had made his statement about Abyssinia, & the Brit: offer to Mussolini to give up a strip of territory & a port to the Emperor of Ethiopia if he in his turn w^d give up territory

[343] Kingsley Wood (1881–1943): Unionist MP 1918–43; Postmaster-Gen. 1931–5; Min. of Health 1935–8; Sec. for Air 1938–40; Ld Privy Seal 1940; kt. 1918.

[344] Samuel John G. Hoare (1880–1959): Con. MP Chelsea 1910–44; Sec. for Air 1922–4, 1924–9, 1940; Sec. of State for India 1931–5; FS 1935; 1st Ld of Admiralty 1936–7; Home Sec. 1937–9; Ld Privy Seal 1939–40; Amb. in Madrid 1940–4; suc. 2nd Bart 1915, cr. Viscount Templewood 1944. See his *Nine Troubled Years* (1954). Hoare had replaced John Simon as Foreign Secretary in the Baldwin Cabinet formed on 7 June.

to Italy. The proposal to let some territory go had roused the super-patriots & Hoare was evidently nervous about the attitude we were going to take. I was able to reassure him, having already written a passage saying that the sacrifice w^{d} have bn worth while if it had brought a settlement of the Italo-Abyssinian dispute.[345] Hoare used the words 'gravity of the situation' & 'caution' rather too often in his brief conversation. We want somebody bolder & franker. Still, at the F.O. they tell me he does <u>take decisions</u>, which Simon never did.

(Hoare rang up GD, but he was out, so he asked to be put through to me).

'Mr. Eden's Statement'

It was indeed a bold proposal; and the British Government, in spite of its non-acceptance even as a basis of discussion, were justified in making it by the urgent necessity of preventing a breakdown of the general collective system, which is the obvious outcome of a failure to settle the Italo-Abyssinian dispute. It is understood that the port which it was suggested might be handed over to Ethiopia was Zeila, which is the outlet for one of the trade routes from the Abyssinian interior. It was further proposed that Abyssinian consent should be sought for Italy to acquire extended territory in the Ogaden region, which covers the triangle between Italian and British Somaliland. Great Britain would further have done what she could to promote the establishment of direct communications between the two Italian possessions in East Africa. Even though they have proved abortive, these tentative proposals must at least have convinced the Italian Government that the British interest in the whole matter is the discovery of a reasonable solution, the preservation of peace, and the maintenance of the position of the League of Nations. ...

There can unfortunately be very little question that the Italian leader is determined to get control over a part or the whole of Abyssinia ... In Eritrea and Somaliland she has done what is possible to introduce material benefits and standards of civilization; but she is hampered by a poor strategic position and by the harassing tactics of the Abyssinians, who have an exaggerated opinion of their own prowess as a result of their victory at Adowa some forty years ago and are supposed to want to drive Italy into the sea. They will not allow Italians to penetrate adjacent Ethiopian territory commercially, and are in fact bad neighbours. These views can be understood, and some of them are perhaps justified. But their importance does not entitle Italy to run completely counter to the treaties and other agreements which she herself has signed ... British public opinion views with profound misgiving the Italian policy towards Ethiopia, and will whole-heartedly support the Government in any proposals which they may still consider to have the slightest prospect of producing a peaceful solution.

[345] 'Mr. Eden's Statement': 2 July 1935, p.17.

6 July   Sir Sam Hoare is always asking GD to go & see him. GD says he (H:) evidently considers that Simon made a great mistake in not keeping *T.T.* by his side. Little does he know the effort that Simon made to do so! GD is not v. much impressed by Hoare as For: Sec^y.

Hoare says he has made 'two determined attempts' to get the Air Pact already – so far not much progress.

I had a good talk with Grandi 2 days ago about Abyssinia. Very frank on both sides. He made a good many points, such as that England's enthusiasm for League sanctions over Abyss: was extraordinary considering that we had resolutely refused to undertake any such thing in regard to Austria! I said that Colonial questions touched us more closely than Central European ones, & that, further, we thought Austria w^d very likely wish to have some sort of federation with Germany, so we would not feel at all inclined to prevent her by force.

Ld Allen of Hurtwood[346] sent us a letter the other day, & with the one for publication was a private one, in which he said –

'Would you permit me, as I happen to be writing to you, to say how profoundly grateful I believe every section of British public opinion is to you for the series of leading articles on international affairs which have appeared in *The Times* during the last 2 months'. [...]

14 Jy   Had a conversatn with Avenol at the Hyde Pk Hotel on Fri morn^g (for which I had to tear myself away from the Eton & Harrow match!) He was as usual cool & full of dicta, such as that he didn't know whose difficulties were the greater, Mussolini's or the Negus's (as he called the Emp: of Abyssinia). He considered also that Musso: was making his supreme throw – staking everything; he will be master of Abyss: as well as Italy, or lose alliance.   Avenol has no objection at all to the dipl. neg^{tns} now going on. In fact he welcomes them. But he was quite clear that once the Italo-Abyss. dispute came before the Council again each member-State w^d have to take up a position for or against the sanctions demanded by the Covenant.

Nevertheless, the Cov. has not yet bn infringed. He regrets that the date July 25 was fixed beforehand for the meeting of the Council. A time-table in such cases is not desirable.

Avenol said that if at the Council table G^t B^n gave the lead for action against Italy 'all w^d follow'. Yes, no doubt they'd follow at Geneva, but they certainly w^d not in the Mediterranean!

[346] Reginald Clifford Allen (1889–1939): Sec. & Gen. Mgr *Daily Citizen* 1911–15; Chm. of No-Conscription Fellowship 1914–18; ILP Treasurer & Chm. 1922–6; Dir. *Daily Herald* 1925–30; cr. Baron of Hurtwood 1932. See his *Plough My Own Furrow* (1965).

31 July   Yesterday C.^{t} Dürckheim[347] invited me to lunch with him at Brown's hotel. Much upset about our leader of that morn^g on Germany. I had not written it – having been in the train travelling up from Yorkshire – but agreed with its critical tone, & told Dürckheim we were ready to do <u>justice</u> to Germany, but had no use for Goebbels & Rosenberg, who seemed to be the heroes of the moment after Hitler.

He also wanted to know what were the prospects of Baldwin paying a visit to Hitler. I said, less now than when GD & I discussed the matter with v. Ribbentrop. German stock down a bit, Abyssinia engrossing all attention, & a general election coming on before so very long. A visit to Hitler w^d be a gratuity to the Labour Party. Better wait till after the election.

I repeated this to GD afterwds & he agreed.

2 Aug: Got a message yesterday that Sir Sam Hoare w^d like to see me after his speech in the H.oC. about 6.30, but if he c^d not get away Mark Patrick[348] (his P. Sec^y) w^d see me & give me his '*ipsissima verba*'. I suspected that Hoare w^d not get out of the debate, & knowing Mark P. did not want to go. However GD thought I'd better; & so I did, & wasted about an hour at the valuable time 6.15–7.15 when one wants to be writing. All Patrick had to say was that Hoare's speech had bn absolutely realistic, but without cynicism; & had bn well rec^d. The old-fashioned way of doing things, & most ridiculous. I had some time to wait in the P.P.S's room, beguiled by conversation with a rather pleasant woman under-Sec^y (entirely a lady of society, I sh^d say), & I also was taken up to hear the last part of Sam Hoare's speech, slipping a bob into a Parl^y Bobby's hand – a v. inferior type of policeman, who ought to be abolished.

This morn^g I saw Vitetti, & urged that Mussolini, before he plunges into Ethiopia, sh^d give <u>the League a chance</u>. Let him see first whether the League is not capable of producing or backing a settlement which recognizes the Italian 'need for expansion' which Sir Sam Hoare has admitted. I said that the League <u>must</u> provide a substitute for war, or it w^d certainly perish. He liked the idea, & said he w^d put it to Grandi & hoped it w^d be passed on to Rome.

13 Aug: Had an animated $\frac{1}{2}$ hour's talk with Anthony Eden this morn^g,

---

[347] von Dürckheim-Montmartin; adviser to Ribbentrop on foreign affairs. A specialist on German South West Africa.

[348] Mark Colin Patrick (1893–1942): entered dip. service 1919, resigned 1930; Con. MP Tavistock 1931–42; PPS to FS 1932, to Sec. of State for India 1933–4, to FS 1935. See his *Hammer & Sickle* (1933).

on the eve of his departure for Paris, where he is to hold conversatns with Laval & Aloisi on Abyssinia. He seemed still to entertain some hope of reaching a peaceful settlement. The French definitely do, & quote the Corfu parallel, in which Musso: climbed down. I doubt it, & said so. However of course Eden is right to try, & his line is going to be either...or...that is either you (It:) get big concessions now peacefully, or you refuse & face a hostile Council. 'Keep them (the Italians) guessing about sanctions'. We went over a lot of ground. [...]

My prognostication of events is as follows–

Paris negotiatns fail

We sh^d then imm.[ediately] raise the arms embargo, & allow Abyss: to order what she wants (Italy no doubt too)

Matter referred to Council, which names It: as the aggressor.

Short war

Italian success – 'Adowa avenged.'

Then we sh^d make our biggest peace effort – & should succeed. Good offers to Mussolini, & constant pressure on him through the Council, even if the sanctions are of a negative order – non-assistance.

If Musso still persists in war, we must look out for Brit: interests. We can't have him running amok in the Mediterranean.

Eden said 'Sitting here I often feel we could have more influence if we were better armed. We've only half the navy of pre-War days' – a melancholy reflection on the Collective system, which is supposed to allow each nation to have small national contingents.

We agreed that Mussolini thinks in terms of force & power. [...]

Memorandum of conversation with Eden:[349] *[...] He was convinced that there was a genuine feeling in this country behind the determination of the Government to fulfill its obligations under the Covenant. He thought that Italy still supposed that it was either bluff or selfishness or electioneering on the part of the British Government; and if we (The Times) could do anything to convince them that it was not we should be rendering the Government a great service. If the League machinery collapsed it was obvious that the British capacity to co-operate in Europe must be impaired, and the isolationist movement in this country would gain considerably in impetus.*

SANCTIONS: We discussed what sort of sanctions this country might agree to take, and Eden thought that the best thing we could do at present was to 'keep Italy guessing' – that is to say, he was against the demand of Lord Cecil that an interpretation of our obligations should be made now and in favour of the policy we have advocated. We discussed the possibility of 'passive' sanctions – that is to say, the refusal of help to the agressor. [sic]

At any rate, his policy for the moment, he indicated, would be to give the Italians

---

[349] A typewritten copy of the account rendered to *The Times* inserted in Journal.

*the choice of 'either ... or'; by which he meant getting France and ourselves to say
to Italy: 'Now here you have the chance of considerable economic expansion in and
around Abyssinia, and a tacit admission that your interests are very great if not
predominant there. You can have this without a fight; for as long as you do not
expect political domination the Emperor of Ethiopia will agree. On the other hand,
if you will not take these concessions, the matter must come before the Council, and
the Council, it is certain, will be hostile to your pretensions and above all to your
methods'.*

*I suggested that there was not really very much chance of Italy accepting a
compromise now, but that there might be a very good chance after an initial victory.
I thought that Mussolini was quite determined to 'avenge Adowa' by occupying the
Adowa region of Abyssinia. If he could boast of victory, and if he realised, as he
certainly must, that the victory was only a beginning and that he had long and
wearing guerilla warfare before him, he might at that moment be inclined to accept
a compromise on the lines of that which was proposed by Eden to him at Rome a
couple of months ago, only of course it would have to be still more advantageous to
Italy.*

*Eden rather reluctantly agreed to this. He much preferred the idea of making
concessions to Italy now to making them after a victory; but he did admit that they
might be more ready to accept them in a couple of months' time, if they had had
their victory, than they are now. He was not willing to bring pressure to bear on
Abyssinia to make political concessions, though if the Abyssinian Government did
show any readiness to make them it would naturally help matters. One of the things
that he was nervous about in regard to this coming meeting in Paris was that Italy
and France might combine to make us (Great Britain) bring pressure to bear on
Abyssinia to a greater extent than we were willing.*

*He also agreed that there were British interests in the background, and that
if all peace efforts failed their defence might become a very important matter:
Laka Tana, our position in the Mediterranean, etc., etc. He did not think that
there were any signs at present that Mussolini might run amuck in the
Mediterranean. I said 'What about these conferences with his admirals which
he has been holding rather frequently lately?' and he answered 'Well, it may
be meant to impress us.' [...]*

20 August – Kennedy to Dawson: *Thank you for your interesting letter.
I did find Eden rather more pro-League and anti-Italian than I am; but at
the same time, after all that both Baldwin and Hoare have said, and said
lately in connexion with this Abyssinian crisis, about standing by our obligations
under the Covenant, it seems to me that the British Government simply must
make some tangible effort to get the League in action. What action is of course
really the whole question. It is accepted that in any case it cannot be solitary
action; and personally I rule out measures such as closing the Suez Canal, if
only for the reason that the international Convention which governs its use laid*

it down in the first of its articles that the Canal was always to be open 'in time of war as in time of peace'. And later it says 'The Canal shall never be used for the exercise of the right of blockade'.

What I feel ought to be done as a preliminary is to consult with the American Government and see how they feel about it before we go to Geneva. There would be no harm in allowing it to be known that the consultations were taking place, even though the actual conversations would have to remain absolutely confidential and, of course, non-commital. Armed with this information we should be in a better position to make definite proposals at Geneva.

Those proposals cannot, I feel, in any case go further than restrictive or passive sanctions – that is, all members of the League undertaking not to help Italy in any way – and a tentative list might be drawn up of the commodities which we would agree not to allow to be exported to Italy. There has recently been a sub-committee on this very point at Geneva; and if really coal, oil, cotton, nickel etc., were withheld from Italy, she would not be able to carry on war for very long. Financial help and arms would also of course be withheld.

These measures would be taken by Governments on their own nationals; and therefore do not involve international complications. No blockade. If U.S.A. citizens did transmit these things, it would be a matter between them and their own Govt, not between us and them. I feel we ought to adopt this policy of non-assistance of the aggressor, so long as even two or three of the more important League countries do the same, including France.

All this must of course wait on a decision by the whole Council. The Council must declare who is the aggressor. Then we can discriminate.

I am thinking of writing on these lines, if Brodribb approves. We shall probably have a leader tomorrow night, on the eve of the Cabinet.[350]

1 October – Kennedy to Barrington-Ward: *As the Editor told me he was going to be away tonight I write to you to tell you that the doctor (our mutual friend Ledingham*[351] *examined me today, with I am afraid most unsatisfactory results.*[352] *He says it is nerve-exhaustion, and recommends a long holiday. He did this before earlier this year, but I would not consider the idea then, and now the position is if anything worse: At the moment however I simply do not feel capable of taking on work again, so must at least accept his verdict for the present – and he has agreed to re-examine me with a second opinion in a fortnight's time. In the meantime I am*

[350] 'The Cabinet to Meet': 20 August 1935.

[351] John C. G. Ledingham (1875–1944): bacteriologist; Chief Bacteriologist, Lister Institute, London 1908–30, Dir. 1931–43; kt: 1937.

[352] On 17 September Dawson noted that Barrington-Ward 'rang up to say that Kennedy had now crocked.' Dawson Mss. 39, f. 137, Bodleian Library.

proposing to go up north to see if I cannot get really fit, above all get back to natural sleep, of which I have had none since I went into that nursing-home. In my tired condition that small operation was apparently too much for the nerves of my head. [. . .][353]

---

[353] On 15 October Dawson noted that 'Kennedy looked in, but is clearly nowhere near coming back to work. He had seen Dawson of Penn last week.' Dawson Mss. 39, f. 151, Bodleian Library. Leo and Sylvia then took an extended cruise to the far east, the journal for which may be found in the archive of *The Times*. It is much more of a tourists' travel diary and contains nothing of political or journalistic significance – possibly because having a break from these preoccupations was the main purpose of the journey.

GULF OF SUEZ *16 January*   to Geoffrey Dawson: [The Times' *articles on the Hoare crisis] ... evidently gave faithful expression to public feeling, and I congratulate you on the freshness and vigour with which they are written (I judge them to have been by your own hand). I'll have no difficulty in agreeing to this line of policy; though actually the Hoare-Laval plan doesn't appear to me to have been a reversal of policy so much as a panic amplification of the Eden offer made before hostilities began, and to have been quite unjustified by the present military position. The original Eden proposal of nearly a year ago (which as you remember we approved) still seems to me to have been perfectly sound and to stand as the proper bases of an agreed peace. [...]*

PARIS *31 Jan:* Talk with Sir George Clerk, in the same chairs respectively, & the same room, where I had so many talks with L$\underline{d}$ Tyrrell. Sir G.C. talks rather more in the manner of Austen C than of L$\underline{d}$ T, but at the same time he is *trés diplomate* & steeped in the old diplomacy.

He was, quite naturally, chiefly concerned to explain his part in the recent Laval-Hoare conversations, which resulted in the downfall of Hoare.[354] 'They were too hurried' he said emphatically – one sec$\underline{y}$ drawing up one part of the agreement with a French opposite number in one room, Peterson[355] & another Frenchman in another room, & Peterson having to catch the 8.30 train. Hoare, moreover, tired to the point of exhaustion, & longing to get off to Switzerland.

Moreover, the agreement was only for a <u>tentative basis</u> of negotiation. The whole thing was spoilt by a premature leak in Paris, & the equally premature endorsement by the Brit: Cabinet. The whole thing was a big argument against perambulatory diplomacy by Foreign Secretaries – esp: by tired For: Secretaries! (This part is my comment, not Sir George's).

There were, however, (Sir George said) points that never came out & which w$\underline{d}$ have made the proposed agreement much more palatable to

[354] In the furore that followed the revelations concerning the pact, Hoare resigned on 18 December 1935.

[355] Maurice Drummond Peterson (1889–1952): entered dip. service 1913; Min. in Sofia 1936–8, in Tehran 1938–9; Amb. in Madrid 1939–40; Ministry of Info. & FO 1940–4; Amb. in Ankara 1944–6, in Moscow 1946–9; kt. 1938. See his *Both Sides of the Curtain* (1950).

Haile Selassie[356] – for instance, the famous 'Corridor for Camels'[357] was written (by GD) without the knowledge that it was intended to link up the port of Zeila with the Djibuti railway, at least with a lorry service, but preferably with a branch railway line. To have allowed Abyssinia to build a parallel railway w^d have bn contrary to the 1906 Anglo-Franco-Italian Agrt – betw those Agreements of pre-war diplomacy & the post-war ideas was all the difference between Saul of Tarsus & Paul the Apostle: & they s^d have to be reconciled somehow. But Sir George thinks Mussolini w^d be glad to be helped out. He seemed v. positive about this. Among other people I have found the most varied opinions.

Sir George said that Flandin w^d be a little more favourable to the Franco-Soviet Treaty (of May 1935) than Laval & a little less keen on rapprochement with Germany, about which Laval was in earnest. (However the Sarraut Ministerial declaration is quite satisfactory on this point).

The constant changes of For: Ministers did not seem to bother Sir George. He said that there were shades of difference (as indicated above), but that the fundamental point of Fr policy w^d always be friendship & cooperation with G^t B^n.

He thought the chief count against Laval for the Socialists & Radicals was Laval's lukewarmness towards the Treaty with the Soviets. (Comert,[358] whom I saw later at the Quai d'Orsay, thought that that was the second count, the first being his failure to apply all possible sanctions at once.) In regard to sanctions, the Ambassador thought that the longer they went on the more evasions there w^d be. They were putting a great strain on the *grands industriels* of every nation.

He wanted us (*T.T.*) to note the point that Flandin was 'Anglomane' rather than 'Anglophil' – keen about British clothes & weekends & pheasant shooting, but not a prejudiced Anglophil in politics. [...]

1 February Later yesterday I managed to have a short talk with Titulescu, who is staying in this hotel (Ritz) with K[ing] Carol,[359] who is on his way back from London. Tit. was v. pleased about the King's

---

[356] Haile Selassie (1872–1975): elected Regent of Ethiopia 1916; crowned Emperor 1930; exiled after Italian invasion 1936; returned to Addis Ababa 1941; deposed 1974.

[357] The famous leader by Dawson denounced the Hoare-Laval Plan on 16 December 1935.

[358] Pierre Comert (1880–1964): Corrspdt *Le Temps* in Vienna & Berlin 1907–14; Press Bureau *MdAE* 1916–17; editorial staff *Le Temps* 1918–19; Dir. LoN secretariat 1919–33; Dir. of Press Services *MdAE* 1933–8, Asst Dir. US section 1938–40; emigrated to Britain 1940; Ed. *France* newspaper in London 1944–8.

[359] Carol II (1893–1953): King of Rumania 1930–40; abdicated Sept. 1940.

(Carol's) visit to London, where he (Tit) had fixed up a luncheon & dinner to Eden, Vansittart, Tyrrell & others – 'our club' as Tit called them (they w^d not care for this designation, I imagine). Tit was also v. pleased with the election of Dr Benesh as Pres. of Czechoslovakia.

We talked amicably even on the subject of frontiers! He still will not agree to the moving of a single frontier stone; he says now, 'wash out' (instead of '*spiritualisez*'!) the frontiers economically, <u>but he has advanced a little</u>. His latest idea is that sovereignty might be modified in the districts occupied by an alien community – i.e. no taxes, & some other privileges & special conditions. Make a <u>contented</u> alien population. One of Tit's exclamations when I approached the debatable ground of this subject was 'it is easier to give away Rumania than to give away one village'. We spoke a little of the Abyssinian question. He said Rumania was prepared to put an embargo on oil, but he hoped it w^d not be necessy. He believed that soon Mussolini w^d not be able to pay for imports, so that anyhow foreign firms w^d not supply commodities & goods.

On 10 February Kennedy was examined by two doctors, who concluded that he was not fit for full-time work.[360] *One of them, Dawson of Penn,*[361] *wanted him to take an additional two months' vacation, but Kennedy wd not agree to this; Dawson then asked whether there might be some mission abroad that he cd undertake, which led Kennedy to put forward the idea of a trip to Berlin. Otherwise, Kennedy told Geoffrey Dawson, he would prefer to go on half-pay until he was perfectly fit again.*

Dawson replied that he certainly had no objection to the Berlin idea from The Times' *point of view, & was concerned only that Kennedy would find himself in an anxious & exciting atmosphere where he might be tempted to overwork himself. But Dawson (the editor) wrote to Dawson (the physician), that he had found Kennedy 'so dead set on going to Berlin, & so sceptical of being able to work at home or at half-speed in London, that I have come to the conclusion that it would be best to let him go. He will probably do better work, & recover sooner, if he is allowed to indulge his fancy.'*

[360] On 9 February Dawson noted in his diary that Kennedy had 'turned up again to work' (Dawson Mss. 40, f. 28) but by the 12th was noting that 'At 5.30 I went out to see Ld Dawson about Kennedy & had more talks w the latter on my return. I can see that we are going to lose both him & Graves for some time to come.' ibid., f. 30, Bodleian Library.

[361] Bertrand Dawson (1864–1965): physician; physician extraordinary to Edward VII 1907–10, to George V 1907–36, to Edward, Prince of Wales 1923–37; also served successive prime ministers; Pres. Royal College of Physicians 1931; cr. Baron Dawson of Penn 1920.

LONDON *13 Feb:*   Baron von Kajar,[362] [sic] the German Mil: Attaché, in his slow way argues v. well & v. honestly. He put the German case against France v. clearly at luncheon today, with P^{ce} Bismarck, at B's house.

Fundamentally of course it simply is that France <u>will not</u> admit that Germany is equal to her, if not superior. Kajar argues that ultimately economic facts will inevitably bring Eur. nations much closer together. He instanced that not long ago Prussia was fighting Würtemburg ... & now. Even quite lately a Bavarian Army Corps w^d not take its orders from a Prussian (or Saxon etc) even after the War. (Hitler had levelled that out). When one flies from London to Berlin, he also said, one has to have British, Belgian & German in one's pocket, & sometimes Dutch. That will some day come to be regarded as equally absurd.[363]

16 February – Kennedy to Deakin: *I saw Leeper at the F.O. yesterday morning, & he gave me, for guidance on British policy towards Germany, the following pts –*

1. The problem of raw materials is being scientifically studied. The more it is examined the more complicated it is found to be. For one thing, raw materials come from dozens of places which are not British and not mandated. Countries like Brazil and Holland are closely involved. A mere transfer of territory here and there would do nothing to solve it.

The British Government however will not be satisfied with a mere negative answer. But it may take most of this year to evolve a definite policy. In the meantime it is hoped that Germany will not give trouble. For one thing it is supposed that during the Olympic Games she may think fit to keep reasonably quiet. The Embassy in Berlin do not believe she means to jump the Rhineland.

2. The British Government are still definitely opposed to a policy of Einkreisung. They are not even so keen as they have been supposed to be on the Franco-Soviet Treaty. They have not given it their blessing, as the French like to make out (Simon, of course, was very encouraging towards the original project, but that was something rather different). Recent British Governments have agreed that the terms of the Treaty do not run counter to the Covenant or to Locarno. But they remain detached.

3. Finally, the British Government do not wish to keep Germany in a position of inequality anywhere. They agree that her status of equality must be accepted everywhere in principle and in practice. Leeper admitted, on being questioned, that this ought to apply even to the demilitarized Rhineland zone. What sort of way out

---

[362] Leo Geyr von Schweppenburg (1887–1974): Mil. Attaché in London 1933–7, in Brussels & the Hague 1937–9; commander of Panzer troops in Russia and Normandy 1939–45. See his *Erinnerungen eines Militärattachés: London 1933–7* (1949).

[363] 'When Germany conquered them all!' has been added to this entry in pencil, so it may have been entered much later; on the other hand, the following entry of 19 February continues in pencil, so it is difficult to be certain.

from that manifest inequality was best was a question that was causing them a great deal of thought. They had something in their mind (this he said was very confidential) but it was only an idea at present, and other countries had obviously to be consulted before any hint could possibly be given as to its nature. He would not go further than that.

BERLIN *21 Feb:* A pleasant & interesting luncheon with Herr v. Ribbentrop, Count Dürkheim & a sort of ADC, Herr Thorner, at the Kaiserhof hotel – which used to be Nazi hdqtrs before they achieved office, & where afterwards also Hitler used to go & have tea – until, so von R: told me today, the waiters of the hotel used to sell chairs near where he was going to sit to the women of Berlin! Hitler heard about it, & said he w^d not come any more.

At the lunch today I think I did most of the talking, & von R: has asked me to lunch again with him on Sunday. Ribbentrop is almost too friendly! He has put at my disposal a seat at the opera any night I like![364] Nevertheless, I am determined to remain detached. I love music, & did not refuse; for fundamentally I agree with most of Ribbentrop's views – he is v. moderate & I know that he is keen on bringing France in to any understanding that may be reached between England & Germany. I always mention France. I say, 'we do not throw over an old friend when we make a new one'.

22 Feb: Acc: to Major Breen,[365] whom I met to-day, Ribbentrop is working for an Anglo-German understanding, (on which is to be tacked f[rien]dsh[i]p with France). I must try to find out whether this is really his line of approach. Am lunching with him again tomorrow.

To-day I had a most agreeable luncheon with Basil Newton,[366] the other guest being Major Breen, who is Press Attaché here. He has held the post since 1919, so knows Germany well. A nice Irishman, with the rather sweeping judgments of his race. Basil N showed rather more acumen than I gave him credit for.

It is clear that Germany is making herself absolutely ready to carry on a war – & with extraordinary thoroughness, science & foresight. Particularly she is trying to render herself immune against the effects of any possible Sanctions policy – & for that reason, among others,

[364] Kennedy later noted that this was Göring's box & that he took advantage of the opportunity once, when he found only two other guests using it.

[365] Timothy Florence Breen (1885–1966): Press Attaché, embassy in Berlin 1919–37.

[366] Basil Cochrane Newton (1889–1965): entered FO 1912; Counsellor in Berlin 1930–5, Min. 1935–7; in Prague 1937–9; Amb. in Baghdad 1939–41; FO 1942–6; kt. 1939.

wishes to be entirely self-dependent. This does not necessarily mean she means to make war to achieve some political object. She has learnt many lessons from the last war – & one of them was, that war doesn't pay.

Basil N. had met K. Edward VIII[367] lately, when P<u>ce</u> of Wales, & said he was pleasant & ordinarily intelligent. He (HRH) told Basil he had once spent 6 months in Germany – it must have been when he was a boy. Since the War he has spent 2 hours in Hamburg! on his way back from Copenhagen. He can talk quite fair German. He is regarded, apparently with reason, as slightly anti-French & pro-German.

I fancy he may wish to play a part in international affairs like K. Edw: VII.

23 Feb: Luncheon to-day with von Ribbentrop again, this time at his (very nice) home in Dahlem. After a long meal, which only began after 2, we eventually went into his study, which he has built on to the end of the house, & he held forth about the new (German) religion, which he says is a belief in God, in Christ & in good works, but does not accept Pauline theology – esp: the theory of the forgiveness of sin.

I have certainly noticed that there is still a strong religious feeling in Germany, tho' I don't know its nature. All the churches seem to be very full.

In regard to Jews, von R's main contention was that the Jews must not be allowed to <u>dominate</u>. I think that genuinely what the Germans want is to be unmistakeably top dogs in their own house. They were afraid of Jews getting into key positions. Once they have got them under they may leave them in peace.

A good point of Ribbentrop's, was that $\frac{2}{3}$ of Germans are at an extremely low subsistence level, & most of them were hovering on the verge of communism when they were pulled back by Hitler.

C<u>t</u> Dürckheim told me that Hitler is v. fond of the cinema, but if he is bored by the film he just drops off to sleep. He has bn 3 times to see 'Bengal Lancer'. There he did not sleep! But he can also sleep in a motor or an aeroplane more or less whenever he likes. He is also an architect by instinct. von R: says he understands all about it. He has had a new hall built behind his Chancery, & supervised all the details of its construction.

He has told von R. he will see me.

[367] Edward Albert (1894–1972): Prince of Wales 1910–36; suc. King George VI Jan. 1936; abdicated Dec. 1936; Duke of Windsor 1936–72.

24 Feb: Went to see the Labour Camp at Wuhlsdorf this morn^g (with Herr Stahmer & an official of the Labour Hdqtrs). Every fit German boy has to go to one for 6 months. There are 1300 of them, with about 150 men in each – that is, 2 contingents each year of 200,000.

First I saw the men at work, enlarging a big open drain. There is a lot of sodden ground round Berlin, & the drainage is being improved by this State labour. The men get 25pf: a day (about 3½^d) besides being kept.

I then saw their camp – about 5 km away – from & to which they march at the beginning & end of their work. It is an extraordinarily Spartan existence. They are called at 6 a.m. in winter (5 in summer). 10 min light exercise, then breakfast & tidy up the dormitories. Then an hour's march, with spades over their sh[oul]ders, to the swamps. There, 5 hours' hard work – many were standing in water, with gum-boots on. All vigorously wielding spades or pickaxes, except a few who were cutting & pointing wooden uprights to line the dyke. They looked strong & healthy, but not particularly cheerful.

At the camp – which consisted of 5 well-built wooden huts I saw the weekly list of bills of fare. Very simple food – chiefly brown bread, broth meat & milk. Meat once a day, except on one day in the week which is meatless. Everything beautifully tidy; & every hour of the day regulated. They do have leisure after 7 pm, but even then they are told how to amuse themselves! I saw one fiddle in a locker, & I was told they had singing sometimes, in the evening. In the afternoon they have to play football or to drill!

Men who can stand that can stand anything!

I forgot to say they get every other Sunday off.

The poverty of these people is so crushing. They cannot afford to buy newspapers. One or two suffice for the lot – & of course they listen to the wireless. There is a big hall – that is, one long hut. Here they have afternoon lectures on Nat-Socialism, internatnl affairs, German history, & geography. Hitler has got them, body & soul!

They were supposed to have a library – 'of good books,' I was told, – but they only had v. few, as books cost too much.

There are already some voluntary Labour Camps for girls, & it is expected to become compulsory for them later.

26 Feb: At a pleasant diplomatic luncheon at the Dieckoffs'[368] at

[368] Hans Heinrich Dieckhoff (1884–1952): German diplomat; entered dip. service 1912; Counsellor in Washington 1922–6, in London 1927–30; Chief of Anglo-Saxon Dept, *Auswärtige Amt* 1930–5, of Political Dept 1935–6, actg U-Sec. 1935–6; Amb. in Washington 1937–41, in Madrid 1943–5.

Dahlem (*Am Hirschsprung* 3) there was one non-dipl: man, called Bohle – Ernest William Bohle,[369] a British subject, born in Bradford & educated in S. Africa, who is *Gauleiter* of the (Nazi) Germans residing in foreign countries – he is now of course also a German subject. He is starkly Nazi, but also a bit S-Africanish in his outlook! He has Nazi groups in most foreign countries, but <u>only</u> German subjects – e.g. there are 1,000,000 Germans in Brazil, but only 2000 in his organization, the rest being Brazilian subjects; ditto in Czechoslovakia – the 3,000,000 Germans there are practically all Czech subjects.

Bohle is rather truculent, but quite a decent fellow; he swore that they do no spying whatever! & said anybody who liked c^d go over his office at any time. His job was created because at first when Hitler got into power Germans abroad fought shy of Hitlerism, & an organ had to be formed to convert them. That is a typical German idea, & it is also typically German that now apparently most Germans have become Nazi.[370]

I got the impression that this young man Bohle was treated with particular deference. He was put on the hostess's left, above other men much older than himself. As a Gauleiter, serving immediately under Hess,[371] I imagine a word from him can unseat any ordinary official. There are 29 or 30 Gauleiters only. They are the Nazi District leaders. Above them however in the country are about 12 Statthalters, or Governors.

MUNICH 27 *Feb:* Am just back from a visit to the *Braunhaus*, the Hdqtrs of 'The Party,' where I was shown the 'Senate Room' & also Hitler's private study. It was news to me that H: has a Council Chamber. They are not called Senators now; but it seems that from time to time he calls together any persons of eminence or knowledge in the Party to consult with him. There are about 60 seats, round three sides of the room – 7 at the top side, in the middle of which Herr H. sits. In front of him is a table with two recorders – otherwise nobody is supposed to use paper or write but just to give their opinion & help him to come to a decision. [...] Nobody has the <u>right</u> to come to these meetings, but the Statthalters & Gauleiters & his immediate associates are always

[369] Ernst Wilhelm Bohle (1903–60): b. Bradford raised in South Africa; brother-in-law to Rudolf Hess; apptd *Gauleiter* 1933; head of *Auslandorganizations* (Nazi organization for Germans abroad) 1937–44; sentenced to five years' imprisonment for war crimes in 1949; served 9 months.

[370] A question-mark has been inserted (in ink) between 'most' and 'Germans'.

[371] Rudolf Hess (1894–1987): Political Sec. to Hitler from 1920; Deputy Führer 1932–41; flew to Britain on peace mission, captured and interned; sentenced to life imprisonment at Nuremberg; committed suicide in prison 1987.

bidden. Next door – through the door top left – in H's own study. Very simple, but it was extremely interesting & symbolical to note exactly what he had got by way of adornment. I noted them carefully. 3 Pictures – 2 of Frederick the Great, & one of a war-scene; & a bust of Mussolini; & a death-mask of Fred: the Great. Also on the centre table a vivid little sculpture '*Gefesselte Macht*' – (chained strength) a man's nude figure, v. muscular, crouching & struggling, with his arms bound together behind his back. Immediately behind him, as he sits at his desk, is the <u>print</u> of Fred. the Great, & at his side, the death-mask. On a side wall is the picture of Frederick, & opp: the war-picture – which is a realistic & good one of Germans fighting British at close quarters. [...]

The *Königsplatz* here is v. fine, the big new *Partei-haüser* being in really good style – classical, straight-lined, without unnecessary ornamentation, but giving an impression of simplicity & strength.

The *Braunhaus* has typical 'Kellers' in the basement where the Nazi chiefs, Hitler included, have their beer & sausages. In the corridor I saw a large framed photo: of the '*Lokal*' where H: founded the movement in 1920 & gained his first audience by firing his pistol off at the roof.

This afternoon (with Simpson, our Corrspdt here) we passed the *Bierhalle*, & also the place where he led his *Putsch* 3 years later, when 16 of his men were killed & he only just escaped – lay flat on his face, & slid away, but was afterwards caught & imprisoned. There is also a cartoon of him in prison in the *Braunhaus*.

The 16 men who were shot down are now splendidly commemorated in pillared square buildings in front of the *Partei-haüser*. We spent some time round about there this morn^g, & without cessation men & women were going up into these open pillared monuments & saluting the tombs of the 16 'heroes'. Two soldiers guarded the approach to each monument, in each of which 8 are buried. [...]

3 March Last night went to a Music-hall with C^t Dürckheim, & afterwards we looked into a cabaret in the *Kurfürstendamm* for $\frac{1}{2}$ an hour. I only mention this because the place was so full of Jews & Jewesses. I don't know that there's any special significance in this, but Dürckheim explained to me that what the Nat Socialists want is to exclude the Jews from influencing the national life – either in politics or education. They have every intention of allowing them to earn their living, but they do not want them either to mislead youth in universities or to corrupt public life or to diminish Germanism.

Dürckheim said that when Hitler was sitting with friends he usually was v. silent for the first $\frac{1}{4}$ hour or so, looking rather abstracted, but apparently taking things in. Then he often spoke at great length, looking for the most part with a far away gaze beyond his hearers, but suddenly turning to an appropriate one & looking him straight in the eyes.

Dürckheim also gave me his own story. He was brought up in Bavaria, where his father had a small *Schloss* & property, which had bn in the family for generations. First the inflation & then heavy taxation half-ruined them. & Jew-run banks took up to 50% interest off them. When they were in difficulties about paying the interest the Jews brought them into court; & the judge had to enquire whether the property were properly run.

He took the evidence of the local *bürgermeister*, who was a Socialist, & who said it was badly run. Dürckheim says that actually the family took an immense pride in running it well, as long as they had any money at all to spend on it. However the evidence finished them, & their home was put up to auction.

D: also told me about Hitler, by the way, that when he's in Berlin he sees one of his chiefs almost every day, & has long talks with them.

4 March   [. . .] Dieckhoff told me this morn^g that Hitler does everything by consultatn. He does as little document-reading as possible, but likes threshing a matter out in conversatn & is a good listener.

D: also told me that *Gauleiter* Bohle is having great difficulties in his job with most neighbouring countries, particularly Sweden, Holland & Switzerland, & Czechoslovakia but also Poland. They all object to Germans living in their countries being in any way run from Berlin.

The Fascist Gov^t had the same difficulties, & has had to modify its hold over Italians living abroad. Germany, I gather, may have to do the same.

A nice talk with our Ambssdr here, Sir Eric Phipps, this evening. He is v. quick & knows all the latest news. On the other hand he flies about from point to point, & one doesn't feel one has got anything v. substantial out of a talk with him. He does not seem to me to have the mind of a good negotiator. He does not lead the conversation. Instead, he says good things. He enjoys doing that. And sometimes they are also v. interesting. For instance he said Hitler tells all his friends *en petit comité* that he is determined to make Germany '*Sanktions-sicher*'.

5 March   An interesting pol: talk with von Bülow, the head of the For: Ministry. A quiet, clear-headed man who explains every point with extreme clarity. He explained to me in succession Germany's attitude towards the Danubian problem, the relations betw: his Office & the Office of Herr Bohle's Ausland's Organization (wh: I had just bn visiting), the 'Colonial Lie' (about Ger: being unfit to rule colonies) Hitler's recent interview given to de Jouvenel,[372] the Paris journalist, Hitler's famous 13 Points of last May (of which no other country took any notice), & finally the possibility of Ger's return to the League of Nations.

There must be great pol: talent in the Bülow family. In the Staatsekretär's waiting-room I saw a bust of a von Bülow who had been Staatssekretär in the 80's or 90's; then there was the notorious but brilliant von Bülow, made a Prince by Kaiser Wilhelm, & now this one. I don't know their exact relationships, but was told they were relations.

6 March – Kennedy to Dawson:[373] *[. . .] you mention Jew-baiting. I have of course said to almost every German in the innumerable discussions one has with them that they will never get our friendship – apart from a political understanding – so long as they go on bullying the Jews. But I am afraid that the drive against the Jews is so strongly backed that nobody can stop it for the present. I am sure that Ribbentrop is doing his best in this respect, as he fully understands the English point of view. But to get the Jews into a subordinate position is fundamental in the Nazi creed & Hitler himself is fanatical about it. They realize they must have Jews in Germany! But they are determined not to let them have directing influence either politically or in the Press or on the films, I have been told that even one of Ribbentrop's men was carried off by the Secret Police a couple of months ago because in one of his reports he had made that very point – that Germany would never get the good-will of England unless she changed her attitude to the Jews. I understand now that Germans regard Teutonism as something sacred & something that is vitiated by the immixture of Jewish blood or Jewish influence.*

This Teutonism is quite terrific. I am more impressed by it the more I look into German life. North Germans at any rate dislike the idea of internationalism, & it is going to be remarkably hard to fit Germany into the League of Nations. On the other hand . . . I really do not think there is now much hostility to France – simply rivalry, & an intense belief that they, the Germans, are really the most powerful nation in Europe, as they quite undoubtedly will be in a few years' time. Once they have got the position they feel they ought to have, they may like the idea of a European collective system.

Germany is working steadily & unremittingly towards a Peace which she can accept – an agreed Peace, instead of the Versailles Peace. If we keep that in mind I don't think we need have any war scares. Germany is making herself fit to fight –

[372] Bertrand de Jouvenel (1903–1987): Ed-in-Chief *La Voix* 1928–30; econ. specialist, *La République* 1930–4; Special Corrspdt *Le Petit Journal* & *Paris Soir* 1934–9. See his *La dernière année: choses vaes de Munich à la guerre* (1947).

[373] ALK began the letter by telling Dawson that the work in Berlin suited him very well, that the climate was extremely bracing and that he was feeling much better.

*I've no doubt of that. I've equally no doubt that she is not ready & does not want
to fight now.*

8 March   Heard Hitler's speech in the Reichstag (Kroll Opera House)
yesterday, when he denounced Locarno. A master orator – played on
the audience as he liked, even tho' he read his speech. Looked pale, &
exhausted at the end. May be about his last effort of this sort.

I was embarrassed, being betw: 2 Germans in the Gallery, who were
perpetually (with everybody else) jumping up, holding forth their right
arm, & 'Heiling Hitler.' On the other side of one German was L^d
Riverdale[374] [...] & Lord R. jumped up & saluted with ignominious
alacrity. I did it towards the end, not wishing to attract too much
attention; but refused to budge when Locarno was denounced & when
the 'Horst Wessel' song was sung!'

Black uniformed Special Guards everywhere, inside the building in
squads, & all along the route, 3 deep & more squads, between the
Opera House & the Wilhelmstrasse.

Afterwards I had luncheon at the Embassy, arriving nearly $\frac{1}{2}$ hour
late. However the Ambssdr expected that, knowing I was in the
Reichstag, to which he had refused to go, knowing what was coming.
He, & the French, Belgian & Italian envoys had bn rec^d by Freiherr v.
Neurath before the meeting, & given a memorandum. He is furious
(also Lady Phipps). Says we cannot trust these Germans, & the Stresa
front ought to be re-formed (England France & Italy against Germany).

In the evening went to the first two acts of Fledermaus, which is
excellently given here, for rest & refreshment, then early to bed.

8 March[375]   Had a fierce half-hour with Ribbentrop at the Kaiserhof,
where most of the Nazi Gauleiters were assembled having tea in the
Central Hall. R: knew how strongly I felt about the denunciation of
Locarno. He burst into a long tirade about & iniquities of the Franco-
Soviet Treaty. I replied that wasn't the ground of objection, nor was
the occupation of the Rhineland,[376] though that was obviously not
lawful. What was a crime & a blunder was tearing up Locarno. I

---

[374] Arthur Balfour (1873–1957): industrialist; Chm. Industry and Trade Commission
1924–9, Advisory Council for Scientific and Industrial Research 1937–46; kt. 1923; cr.
Baron Riverdale of Sheffield 1935.

[375] There are two separate entries for 8 March, which are rendered here as they appear
in the journal.

[376] On 7 March German troops re-entered the Rhineland. The pretext for this action
was the Franco-Soviet Pact and its alleged incompatibility with the Locarno agreements,
which Germany now declared nullified.

explained to him that <u>confidence</u> was what had got to be restored betw England & Germany, & if they tore up treaties we c<u>d</u> never believe in their written bond. I did not put it quite so bluntly as that, but he understood, & broke into German, holding forth about the needs of the German people coming before juridical points about treaties. '*Das Leben des Volkes*' occurred once or twice, & said I must see the big issues. I said that in our opinion keeping one's signed word was the biggest issue of all.

I think I rather shook him, & from a hectoring tone he became exceedingly polite.

His theory that the interests of the people justified the overriding of treaties went to the heart of the matter. I said that decent relations between peoples depended upon treaties being kept.

The Germans unfortunately take their desires for rights. Once they have persuaded themselves that something is necessary for their national welfare they seem absolutely blind to all other considerations.

He said he was convinced that British public opinion w<u>d</u> approve what Hitler had done. I said I thought not.

In the morning I had bn to the State Opera House (another Opera house!) for the commemoration of the 'War Dead,' which is celebrated in March every year in Germany. Two days before I had seen Lohengrin in the same building, & this reminded of that – the standards, the 'heiling,' the glorification of a man – Hitler.

When the stage curtain went up we saw about 50 standards (colours) being held by Reichswehr men, immobile on the stage, with a huge Iron Cross, with 1914 on it, embroidered on a curtain behind them. The light turned full on them. Quite impressive. A crowded auditorium, most people in uniform, with a fair sprinkling of old army officers in *Pickelhaubes* [spiked helmets].

In the main box, behind us, all the Ministry & notabilities, con-spicuous among them Fld Marshal Mackensen,[377] a fine old veteran of 86, with an eager, florid face, who spoke to everybody in the box, & apparently made quite a little speech to Hitler when he arrived. H. moves in a dignified way. Rather slowly. He seems to have modelled himself on Hindenburg. Stocky & impassive, not a bit the jack in the box one rather expected. He looked so impassive that he might even have bn drugged. When he made his speech to the Reichstag, though, he gesticulated freely.

In the box, besides Hitler & Mackensen, were Göring, Göbbels, Hess, Rosenberg, Fhrr von Neurath & the rest. The Nazi leaders wore a strained expression, gazing fixedly in front of them – Hitler too.

---

[377] August von Mackensen (1849–1945): entered army 1869; Field-Marshal 1915; rtd 1920.

After Beethoven's Eroica symphony had bn played, Gen Blomberg,[378] the Minister of Defence, made a long speech, in which he coupled those killed in the Nazi movement with the men killed in the War. He also made a polite reference to K. George! & Marshal Pilsudski,[379] who have both died since a year ago. Then '*Ich hatte einen Kameraden*' was softly played – not sung – rather effective. Then *Deutschland Uber Alles*, & the *Horst Wessel Lied*.

Then we went out into the Unter den Linden & saw the march past, Hitler taking the salute. Again grave & easy in demeanour.

The troops did the 'parade marsch' (commonly known as the goose-step) in great style. Sailors & airmen did it too, but not quite so high prancing. Marshal Mackensen did all the rounds with Hitler, & stood at his side when he took the salute. Good for a man of 86!

10 March   The Ambassador told me this morn[g] that v. Neurath was in a very embarrassed state when he (von N) presented him (Sir E. Ph.[ipps]) with the Memorandum denouncing Locarno on Sat[y] morn[g]. He also says that the army was against entering the demilitarized zone, but Göring insisted. The army feared France might retaliate, & they didn't feel ready.

I put it to the Ambssdr that the solution to work for was that Locarno must stand, <u>minus</u> the demilitarizatn clause, which was a carry-over from the Treaty of Versailles. When Hitler denounced the mil: clauses of the Versailles Treaty he expressly said that he respected the rest of the Treaty. Why cannot the same be done about Locarno? <u>Legally</u> it still does stand. It cannot be denounced by one party to it. The Ambassdr admitted he had not thought of that as a solution, but he thought it was a good idea.

Afterwds had a chat with Basil Newton – whom I went to see on a private matter. In his quiet way he shows great insight into the character of these people.

To-night heard Goebbels make the opening speech of the Nazi electoral campaign – there is of course no other Party which is allowed to make speeches or for which anybody is allowed to vote. Nevertheless, an amazing performance. 2 hrs & 10 mins. of first-class oratory, making people laugh & cheer all the way through. So easily did he rouse his audience that he actually made them cheer at the number of children

---

[378] Werner von Blomberg (1878–1946): German army officer; headed German delegation to Geneva Disarmament Conference 1932; Min. of Defence 1933–8; supreme commander of *Wehrmacht* 1935, first General Field Marshal 1936; scandal led to his resignation 1938; died in American detention camp March 1946.

[379] Jozef Pilsudski (1867–1935): Polish army officer & politician; staged *coup d'état* 1926; ruled as dictator 1926–35.

born during the Nazi regime! I laughed, & got a black look from my neighbour! He gave the figures for 1933, 1934 & 1935, & then the total, & said all those children are born into *Nazional-Sozialismus* & not *Marxismus*. Loud cheers!

But most of the speech was *Deutschland über Alles*. Patriotic fervour for $\frac{3}{4}$ of it, the other quarter being an account of what Nat-Socialism had done internally – at one moment he was giving, if I heard right, the mileage of roads built, & still he held his hearers. A good many sarcasms about France, jokes about the League of Nations, & terrific chauvinism about *Freiheit* & *Wehrmacht*, which produced thunders of applause. Twenty-thousand people applauding all at once, in the immense *Deutschlandhalle* which has bn built for the indoor sports of the Olympic games.

At the end, Heils, hands forrard, & the Horst Wessel song followed by '*Deutschland über Alles in der Welt*'. Nobody allowed to leave before the end, Brownshirts standing in front of the exits. And everybody seemed happy to stay, just as they had seemed enthusiastic to come. Middle-aged women <u>scampering</u> up stone stairs to the Gallery, all struggling & chattering together.

There being no Party conflict, the speech more or less <u>had</u> to be chiefly about Germany as a whole. That is one of the most dangerous things about dictatorships – they have to be continually scoring victories for the <u>country</u>. Another terrible danger is, that the people don't have a <u>chance</u> of knowing the truth. Goebbels was most misleading & mendacious about the present situation. <u>Whatever</u> the rest of us do, we shall be put in the wrong in the eyes of the German people, unless we swallow whole whatever Adolf Hitler proposes, allowing him to play skittles with any existing treaties that don't suit him.

Funnily enough, coming up here to my room on my return, the liftman spoke a few quiet words to me to show that he <u>did</u> realize that Germany was breaking a treaty & quite understood why England couldn't back her. This is the first case of an understanding of our objections that I've come across.

By the way, the one passage in Goebbels [sic] speech where he didn't get much response was about the Jews. These extraordinarily contradictory people are kindly individually, brutal nationally.

The microphone arrangements perfect. One c$^{\underline{d}}$ here [sic] every word clearly everywhere in that vast hall – which by the way was bigger than the biggest I'd ever seen before, Santo Anna at Manila, the dance-hall to which S: & I went in December!

Goebbels always seemed quite at his ease, & calm, except when he beat himself up to patriotic fury.

What makes the dictator-patriotism so particularly dangerous with the Germans is that they are a *zielbewusst* nation – they <u>must have a purpose</u>. They cannot just live & let live.

So vast was the hall, that from the far end one c<u>d</u> scarcely distinguish the speaker from the figures behind him. But anywhere one heard him well. (I walked all the way round the gallery, slowly – $\frac{1}{2}$ mile, I suppose) Goebbels has <u>studied</u> the art of oratory, Hitler not.

11 March   Had a most interesting talk with Freiherr von Neurath this morning, – he was friendly & most understanding. I put to him my suggestion that Germany sh<u>d</u> agree that the Treaty of Locarno sh<u>d</u> stand, if other countries w<u>d</u> agree to its modification in respect of the Rhineland clauses. He heartily & frankly accepted the idea, & said he w<u>d</u> work for it, & invited me to come & see him again.

He told me that he had submitted a draft Air Pact last May (to the F.O.) & nothing more had ever bn heard of it. This is of course too stupid.

When he had seen Eden in that same room 2 yrs ago, he told me, he had given him a parting word of advice – 'Build more aeroplanes'! & now, after 2 years, we are doing it. 'You are always rather late!' he said to me.

I am delighted that he says he wl take up the Locarno idea.

12 March   At luncheon today (given by Herr Aschmann,[380] head of the Press Dept of the For: Ministry) I sat next to a banker – of the Dresdner Bank – who was interesting on the subject of Germany's need for raw material. He explained to me why, <u>in present circs:</u>, it was necessary for the raw material to be produced on their own territory, so that they do not have to procure foreign currency in order to buy it. But as far as I can understand, when financial conditions are normal – if they <u>do</u> revert ever to what we've called normal – then it makes no difference where the material is produced, if there are no artificial barriers. In any case, this man wanted all the former German colonies back, & kept on talking about '*unsere kolonien*', which rather annoyed me.

He told me his bank was financing a long railway in China which w<u>d</u> eventually link Nanking with Rangoon.

12 March   – Kennedy to Dawson: *[...] I'm afraid I've found it extremely*

[380] Gottfried Aschmann (b. 1884): entered dip. service 1923; Counsellor in Ankara 1928–32; Deputy Dir. *Presse Abteilung, Auswärtige Amt* 1932–3, Dir. 1933–9; on special duties (political warfare) at the Hague & in Brussels 1939–40.

hard to see the German point of view in this business, but I am addressing myself to the task. I cannot have the slightest belief in the sincerity of certain professions, & no honest & impartial person could after seeing some of our friends at close quarters.

14 March – Kennedy to Dawson: *[...] The people at the head of this show are pure gamblers, & do not care two buttons for the League of Nations, which was thrown in by Ribbentrop as a sop to British public opinion. Moreover they are extremely formidable, and I do not believe for one moment that their ambitions will be satisfied by the settlement which may come out of the present negotiations. One gets indication after indication that they are out for practically the whole programme of Deutschland Deutschland Über Alles, über alles in der Welt! which is sung at every political meeting. That expresses their mentality perfectly truthfully. [...] the most disconcerting thing of all is their utter refusal to admit that any legal or moral objection can stand in their way if once they have made up their minds that national interests demand some new gain. Individually most of them seem honest & placid. In the mass they become ruthless & teutonic, especially with leaders like the present trio, Hitler, Göring, Goebbels.[381] [...]*

I do not believe a single neighbour of Germany's will trust to a bilateral arrangement with Hitler – not even Poland in the long run – unless, of course, we guarantee it through the League of Nations.

No doubt it would be some advantage to have Germany inside the League, but it will not be a panacea & we should not sacrifice too much to it or incur too many commitments.

Please consider whether we cannot advocate a solution on these lines. Neurath would work with us, whether he is here or in London.

We have a strong hold over Germany, inasmuch as she does not at all want to see Locarno going on indefinitely with her out of it. Germans are already starting propaganding [sic] their good faith to me, but from innumerable conversations & observations I am convinced that to them the power of Germany is a holy law which overrides everything else.

14 March Yesterday morn[g] I was taken to see the A.E.G. (*Allgemeine Elektrische Gesellschaft*) outside Berlin. A huge & rather wonderful organization. They took me into the high tension room, where a voltage of 1,500,000 is developed. The lights are turned off, & then the current is turned on into a sort of container of immense strength. The current

---

[381] Kennedy went on to express his hope that Neurath might be posted to London, as he thought his understanding of the British viewpoint was better than Ribbentrop's. Neurath had admitted to him that it was wrong and unnecessary to destroy Locarno altogether, and that he was willing to say that Locarno stands, minus the demilitarization clauses.

shot forth right & left from near the top in forks of light just light [sic: like] lightning, while a terrific pressure vibrated through the air – it reminded me of German foreign policy!

Then I saw bars of copper, heavy & about 20 feet long, which were pressed & pressed & elongated until they become copper wire so fine that its length c^d go round the world! 40,000 kilometres.

A.E.G. cooperate closely with Vickers – industrial co-operatn between business houses seems to be a good deal easier than pol: cooperatn!

A hot talk with Ribbentrop at 1 o'clock today; but we parted friends, I can't help rather liking the man. He began most indiscreetly however by flying out at the Brit: Embassy here & the Ambassdr in particular. I remained absolutely silent. He accused him of being an 'enemy of Germany' – if he had said 'an enemy of the Nazi Party' he w^d not have bn wide of the mark. He also attacked our last message in *T.T.* from here. He then declared that Germany was not a bit afraid of anything the rest of us c^d do, either mil^{ty} or economic. He was in a state of suppressed excitement. He looked pale, & spoke like a man with his back to the wall – nationally, & I think also his personal position must be shaken.

I developed my idea of letting Locarno stand minus the Rhineland clauses, but he was in such a state that he hardly seemed to grasp it. He kept on talking about Hitler's 'big & generous' idea for Europe – it is really partly, or mostly Ribbentrop's idea, & I think he is frightfully upset at its not being taken up.

This afternoon (Sun: 15th) I saw Sir E. Phipps a short time, & told him quite briefly & privately about R's outburst against the Embassy. Sir E. Ph: then told me that he had seen Hitler this morn^g about the invitation to Germany to send an envoy to London. After he had transmitted the Brit: Govt's hope that it w^d be accepted Hitler burst forth into a harangue of 10 min: or $\frac{1}{4}$ hour about *die Ehre Deutschlands* – Sir E. Ph: says he is often like that. Then he said he must consider the question of whether to send somebody or not, & w^d let the Ambssdr know this afternoon.

The Ambssdr also told me that he had bn approached by Rib: & Göring about colonies once, at luncheon in Rib:'s house. They both seemed chagrined when Phipps had to give a definite 'No' to the question of whether negotiations c^d be begun on the subject! It seems a casual method of diplomacy to Phipps to be asked out to luncheon & then asked if he has any colonies to give away!

In his interview with Hit: Phipps had not apparently seen the point that Germany w^d willingly take part in the negotiations, but did not want to be present at the Council to hear herself condemned, which w^d be the first act in the proceedings. I don't think he (Phipps) is a v. good psychologist; & as the Germans notoriously never understand another person's (or country's) point of view it is no wonder that he & they don't get on very well.

March 16 [...] In the morning I had seen Gen: Blomberg. He struck me as a particularly able & a v. nice man. A tall fine fellow – he reminded me of Willie Peyton[382] in appearance – with a genial expression, & great readiness in discussion.

He showed a quick understanding of the Brit. point of view about the infringement of the Treaty of Locarno. He said he thought Hitler had denounced the whole treaty instead of only the Rhineland clauses because he thought it was simpler & more honourable. Peoples' ideas of honour differ, but I expect the General is right. He seemed quite favourable to my idea of regarding Locarno as still valid (apart from the Rhineland clauses) if that w$^{\underline{d}}$ help matters.

He then explained to me with great lucidity what a difference the new Franco-Soviet Pact made to Germany from the military point of view. The peace footing of the Russian army is more than twice that of Germany; & he esp: objected to the Russo-Czechoslovak Treaty. He said he was 'not 100 per cent but 80 per cent sure' that Russian air officers were helping Czechoslovakia & that more aerodromes were being made in Czechoslovakia, showing that Russia w$^{\underline{d}}$ be able to use Bohemia as a jumping off ground.

We went on to talk of disarmament, & he said he thought that after the present trouble was over something might be done, but by gradual stages. The thing to begin with w$^{\underline{d}}$ be the Air Pact, with immediate retaliation in kind. He thought it was imposs[ible] to abolish bombers, tho' something might be done to restrict their activities & their targets. I rather demurred to this, & he admitted there were great difficulties. Then navally, he said, we <u>have</u> got a treaty of limitation; but militarily, he said, we cannot agree to limitation, at any rate of effectives – & again he referred to the Russian strength. I asked him whether restrictions in the sizes of guns & tanks might be imposed. He seemed to think it doubtful, but said the question c$^{\underline{d}}$ be discussed. No doubt that w$^{\underline{d}}$ involve the right to investigate (by an international com$^{\underline{tee}}$), & I don't suppose Germany w$^{\underline{d}}$ agree to that now. Alas, Hitler agreed to it twice over a year & two years ago.

'General Oberst' Blomberg said to me on parting if I'd like to see him again '*ich will Ihnen gern eine halbe stunde schencken* [sic]'. Hauptmann Nolde is his ADC. I sh$^{\underline{d}}$ like to see him again, <u>if</u> I feel there's anything to talk about. He said he w$^{\underline{d}}$ convey my idea about Locarno to the

---

[382] William Eliot Peyton (1866–1931): army officer; Maj.-Gen. 1914, Lt-Gen. 1921, Gen. 1927; C-in-C, Scottish command 1926–30; kt. 1917.

Führer – but of course it is the <u>British</u> Gov[t] that ought to insist that the Treaty of Locarno must still stand, & we're not doing it. We're quite ready to negotiate a new one – by no means the same thing.

He spoke German, & I spoke English – he suggested that at the outset, & we stuck to it.

To him, by the way, the demilitarized zone was the most important feature of the Treaty of Locarno.

16 March   The Mil: Att: here, Col: Hotblack,[383] is a most intelligent & well informed man, & he has given me more evidence that war-training is universal here for body & mind. Also, *Mein Kampf* (Hitler's book) so far from being regarded as out of date, formed the text-book of a *Weltanschauung* examination of S.A. men the other day.

Col: H: thinks that Hitler has become more colonial-minded since seeing 'Bengal Lancer'! which he has now bn to 5 times. He has at any rate ordered the film to be shown free to S.A. troops, with the idea, so Col: H: thinks, of making them think that Germans can do likewise. This may be an exaggeration.[384]

17 March   – Kennedy to Dawson: *[...] Fortunately one or two people like General Blomberg count a certain amount. I saw him this morning – a keen, able & moderate man. He explained in very lucid terms the military dangers to Germany of the Franco-Soviet Pact. He, like Neurath, fully appreciates the bad impression which the violation of a treaty makes in England, which is more than most people do here.*

The Nazi leaders rule this country by force and fraud, and a good many of them would like to dominate Europe by the same sort of methods. I have had a big disillusionment since I came here. I talk to everybody I can, from the Duke of Coburg to liftmen, & my impression is quite definite that if the present regime lasts we shall have the Germany of 1914 to deal with over again.

20 March   Saw 3 more Labour Camps today – 2 men's & one women's, in the neighbourhood of Nauen & Potsdam. The first (mens) was in a

[383] Frederick Elliot Hotblack (1887–1979): army officer; Mil. Attaché in Berlin 1935–7; Gen. Staff Officer, WO 1937–9; Gen. Staff, BEF 1939–40.

[384] On the same day Geoffrey Dawson wrote to Kennedy to say that he was welcome to stay on in Berlin as his presence there was of great importance at the moment. He assured him that he shared his lack of confidence in the Nazi regime, & that the occupation of the demilitarized zone had been a stupid blunder. On the other hand, Britain should now try to get the most out of the professions that had accompanied the German move – whether these were sincere or not.

transformed factory, & therefore the mens' quarters were more solidly constructed than the wooden huts I saw elsewhere. But the general arrangements were just the same – a sentry on guard with a spade at the slope, brought to the present as we entered; mil: discipline throughout – clicking of heels etc. sharp words of command. Complete classlessness, a new thing in Germany. In the old army certain educational qualificatns gave privileges. The men struck me as bright & cheerful – I had not seen them <u>in their quarters</u> on my first visit to a camp, but working in mud. Also, a lot of artistic & humorous talent had bn shown in decorating some of the dormitories, in both the camps I saw today. It is remarkable that the men have energy over to build improvements to their camps <u>after</u> their labour – but they do. And as well as classlessness a great community feeling is developed, I was told.

They have 'parade' spades as well as working spades.

The womens' camp was a v. cheerful place, in an old house built in the time of Fred; the Great, & renovated. It is in a district near Potsdam which has lain waste since the days of Fred: the Great, & is now being settled. Or rather, it was always waste, & Fred: started to people it, & now his work is being continued by Adolf Hitler. The women help the neighbouring settlers in every possible way, with indoor & outdoor work. The settlers arrive penniless as a rule, & have to start at the beginning on what is still poor soil. Their object is that prescribed by Fred: the Great in the words 'Whoever makes 2 ears of corn grow where one grew before does more for the country than by winning a battle' – I'm not sure if I've got it exactly right. The saying was quoted to us by our official who was taking us round. The rooms were less decorated than the mens', but full of patriotic exhortations '*Deutschland D: über alles, über alles in der Welt*', & one which signified 'let all else perish but Germany must survive'. 'We are the soldiers of work' etc etc

There was 35 women [sic], including one Englishwoman. The head of it was a particularly nice woman, & vibrant with energy!

The land all over Prussia is being tremendously improved by this underpaid labour & its productivity increased. Internal trade wl be encouraged & they will be more self-supporting.

One of the most significant talks I've heard since I've bn here was with a nice & v. handsome young fellow who showed us round one of the camps. I told him I thought all this discipline & spirit of service were going to make Germany tremendously strong. He seemed pleased, & said that Germany was so small, & had bn so much bigger! It was always shrinking! He was steeped in the history of *das Erste Reich* (Charlemagne) when 'Germany' included half Europe; & he obviously intended that it sh^d again! England, he said enviously, had expanded from a small island to all over the world – they like to take us as a model in some ways – & he added '*Aber wir machen keinen Angriffskrieg*' (we make no wars of aggression). Shades of Fred: the Great & the leaders of 1914! Yet young Germans <u>really believe this</u> – they are so deliberately misled about 1914, that they think they were then attacked. Hotblack told me it was the same in the army (the younger officers). Amazing.

21 March [...] I believe Hotblack is right in saying that the conflict with the Churches in Germany arises first & foremost from the fact that christianity is by its nature universal & to that extent international, & the Nazis can't stand internationalism in any shape or form.

A nice little talk at 6 p.m. with Freiherr v. Neurath, who gave me an indication of the nature of the German reply to the proposals of the Four Locarno Powers (I've noted them elsewhere). He is extremely hale fellow-well-met, & made jokes about the treaty-breaking & sanctioned Italians acting as policemen for the League on the Rhine, & about M^r. Mac-Donald's obvious hope to preside over one more world-conference before he dies – & the hazier the agenda the better it will suit him, he said!

But he was essentially conciliatory, & said he intended to send an answer to the Locarno Powers Note early the next week.

Ribbentrop, whom, he said 'I have ordered to come to Berlin to report', w^d be going back again on the Monday – today being Saturday – & he w^d send his reply directly afterwards.

23 March So many things have happened I can only just record them for the moment – aeroplane journey to Breslau & back yesterday in Führer's plane, the *Immelmann*. Drives through the streets of Breslau in his car, talks with Ribbentrop, & meeting Himmler,[385] & this morn^g a talk with the Ambassadr here.

And this afternoon I went, by invitation of Himmler, to see the barracks of Hitler's *Leibstandarte*-bodyguard, a regiment of 3 battalions, 2700 men, no soldier less than 6 foot high, & well drilled, corresponding to our Guards. There was a wonderful efficiency about the place. They are all motorized, but trained as footsoldiers as well.

We saw a squad being trained to ride motorbicycles over uneven ground – made especially uneven on purpose. We went through

---

[385] Heinrich Himmler (1900–45): Nazi politician; participated in beer hall *Putsch* 1923; head, Hitler's SS bodyguard 1929; *Reichstag* Deputy 1930; head, Prussian police & *Gestapo* 1934; head, unified political police forces 1936; as Min. of the Interior 1944–5 he ordered systematic genocide in the concentration camps; committed suicide after arrest by British 1945. See *Reichsführer!* (1968).

everything – Ward Price[386] (of the *D.M.*) & I, Himmler, & a fine soldier, Gen: Dietrich,[387] who commanded the Reg[imen]t. Himmler commanded the Reg^t. Himmler commands the whole of the S.S., which includes the *Leibstandart*. We came to the underground shooting gallery, where Himmler challenged us to a match – so Ward Price took him on at revolver shooting, & I at the rifle range – & we both beat him! I got one bull, & quite good other shots. But he shot standing up. I shot first, & rested my elbows on the shelf. Of course standing bolt upright to shoot with a rifle makes it much more difficult, I had not seen it done at a range before.

Finally there was a march past, of one battalion, more or less for our benefit! The men had just detrained from Breslau. They goose-stepped past us in fine style, but I have seen it better done by the *Reichswehr*, & our Guards' march discipline is better.

We had tea in their Club, & talked about military matters. Himmler w^d very much like an exchange of visits with our Guards. I might put the idea to Alan Dawnay.

The barracks & Club are at Lichterfelde.

On manoeuvres one day one of these batlns marched 62 km & sham fought for 5 hrs, of which one in gas-masks, & not a man fell out.

23 March – Kennedy to Barrington-Ward: *[...] We have had a splendid series of leaders on the crisis, most of which, I imagine, have been written by you. I have admired them immensely. The first one of all was the only one from which I dissented. We seemed, in my opinion, to abandon Locarno rather too readily & to jump at the new proposals. That strengthened the hands of the originators of the policy, whereas the direction of foreign policy might possibly have been transferred into the proper hands, had a very firm stand been made at the first moment. However, I will frankly say this, that had I to write the leader before I came here, I should have written on exactly the same lines, only, I am sure, not nearly so brilliantly. Also I realize that it corresponded to public opinion. There will be much to talk about when we meet again!*[388]

[386] George Ward Price (1886–1961): journalist & author; For. Corrspdt *Daily Mail* 1912–44. See his *Extra-Special Correspondent* (1957).

[387] Josef 'Sepp' Dietrich (1892–1966): army officer & Nazi politician; commander of *SS* bodyguard 1928–31; Deputy, *Reichstag* 1930; Lt-Gen. *SS* 1931; Gen., *Waffen SS* 1934; head of *Leibstandarte-SS* Adolf Hitler Regiment; Cmdr, Sixth SS Panzer Army 1939–45; sentenced to life imprisonment for war crimes 1946; released 1955, re-arrested and sentenced to an additional 18 months as accessory in the Röhm purge.

[388] Also on this date – 23 March – Geoffrey Dawson wrote to Kennedy that he was 'delighted to think that you feel strong enough to fly about Germany with the Führer. The messages from Berlin in this evening's papers seem to be reasonably hopeful. It is too early yet, of course, to hear from you. What matters at the moment is not that Germany should accept this or that clause of some rather broad proposals, but that the

24 March   Now to go back to the air journeys with Hitler. I was only asked about 1 o'cl[ock] (by Stahmer) so bolted some lunch & taxi'd off with him to the *Tempelhof* aerodrome, or rather the special *Regierungsflughafen* next door. I was taken to Hitler's aeroplane as soon as he had arrived, & Ribbentrop (to whom I owed the trip) presented me to the little man, who was sitting on the front seat, with a table in front of him. I thanked H: for giving me this opportunity. He didn't understand, as I spoke in English, so Rib translated it, H: holding my hand during the process & smiling in a friendly way, but saying nothing. He did not speak at all on either out or home journey, except to answer one or two remarks that were made to him. H read some typewritten sheets that were laid out on his table (the aeroplane being by this time in the air), passed them over the back of his seat to his ADC on the seat behind him, & then gazed out of window for some time & then dozed off. I was sitting 2 seats behind him, just behind the ADC, & there were about a dozen of us in the plane. Ward Price of the *Daily Mail* was also a guest, & the rest of them were SS men in black uniforms. Himmler, the SS chief, was in an escorting plane, with Stahmer & others.

The name of H's plane is the *Immelman*. He was Richthofen's predecessor. R took over when Immelmann was shot down. There was a photo: of Immelm'n on the front wall in front of H, & another photo of himself on the left front wall.

A quarter of an hour before arrival – on both journeys – H: was roused by being tapped on the sh[oul]der. When we landed at Breslau [...] there were loud cries of 'Heil Hitler,' but the crowd was not allowed near – only officials & some children. The children presented flowers, which H: handed to an ADC, & he patted them on the cheeks. He seldom said anything. He is silent & slow in his movements when he is not making a speech.

Before he got into his waiting car [when they arrived in Breslau] he turned to an ADC, & took from a small cardboard box which the ADC held out a large white cachet or tablet. He then got into the car & stood in front of the front right-hand seat, & stood the whole of the 5 mile drive to the Public Hall, his right hand raised aloft, taking the salute in Hitler fashion, hatless, (tho' in uniform!) & turning gravely to right & left to answer the cheering of the crowds. On both journeys there was an unmistakably genuine yearning sort of look in their faces.

They followed him along with their eyes, as our car went slowly

negotiations should be kept in being. I tried to impress this upon your friend, Ribbentrop, in the early house of Saturday morning, when I had a pleasant conversation with him on my way back from the Office. Anthony Eden is doing very well, but he must have a little help from Berlin.

For the moment I feel that you can be of the greatest use where you are.'

past, as if they really did regard him as the saviour of Germany & the man who was doing his v. utmost for them. Many looked strained, & many fanatical (there is probably Polish blood in Silesia). The whole time I only saw 2 men who seemed wilfully to avoid giving the Hitler salute.

In the vast hall we proceeded to the tribune through a line of Black Guards & thousands of cheering & 'heiling' voices, & the usual children popped out of the ranks every now & again & handed H: bouquets. The Germans love this, & H: always stopped, took the bouquet himself, handed it to an ADC, & patted the child on the cheek. When we reached the platform the cheering went on for about 5 min. H: had not a single note or scrap of paper in front of him, but made a rousing demoguogic [sic] speech, lasting 50 min – most of it rubbish when analysed, but much to the taste of his audience (He is a great admirer of LlGeorge's oratory, see *Mein Kampf*, & has obviously modelled himself on him).

One thing he said was typical of the Nazi outlook – 'I am responsible to my conscience & to my people, but (*tonst*) to nobody else in the world'. As we flew back in the aeroplane, it occurred to me that this sort of sentiment must be much encouraged by his flying <u>all over</u> his own country, but <u>never</u> going outside Germany. In a way the rest of the world doesn't exist for him.

We had some apples & sandwiches on the return journey. Hitler again slept for a good part of it. We landed at Tempelhof after dark; & when H: passed me to get out of the 'plane he again shook hands in silence, with a caressing sort of pressure of the hand. He makes a favourable impression by his simplicity.

I forgot to say that after the speech we waited about 10 min while H: changed his clothes. It seems that he sweats v. heavily after the effort of speaking, so changes before doing a journey.

I also forgot to mention that I was in the car with him on both journeys through the streets of Breslau – he standing in front with the driver on his left, 2 Black Guards on the seats behind him, & von Ribbentrop, Ward Price & I on the back seat.

Behind us, & rather flanking us, were 2 cars loaded with S.S. men (Black Guards), & H: was never kept standing about longer than necessary. [...]

26 March – Kennedy to Barrington-Ward: *[...] I agree with you that unnecessary difficulties have been & are being created by France. On the other hand, do you know, one does understand the misgivings of neighbours of this country much more clearly than one did before, now that one has been here. And there is one point I would like to clear up. I did not mean to imply that one should have a policy which attempted to influence the internal politics of another country. I meant that my instinct was to say at once: 'This simply won't do. We can't deal with you – though we sympathize heartily with both your immediate & your ultimate aims – until you acknowledge that a Treaty cannot be and is not abrogated by this sort of action.' Had we all (including British public opinion) done this together at once, it would have discredited the authors of a policy which, when all is said & done, is in method similar to 1914 – an episode, mark you, which Germans still defend.*

However, we do seem to be taking a rather stiffer line now. I thought the leader in this morning's paper absolutely first-class....[389]

29 March   Yesterday afternoon I spent with some German friends, & in the course of it they told me that H: has spots in his throat – I think they said white ones – & that the doctor said they did not signify a serious illness – 'it w^d be too awful' she added 'if it were...' & then she stopped. Obviously she was going to say 'cancer', but either did not like to or did not know what the word was in English. They also told me that he sleeps v. little – hardly ever goes to bed before 2 or 3 a.m., generally working in the night. He can't stand smoke, having bn gassed in the War. Nobody smokes in his presence. Also he does not eat meat or drink wine.

I heard his final speech of this electoral campaign, sitting in the *Deutsches Operahaus* yesterday evening. A performance of 'Norma' was held up for the speech to be relayed to us. The audience listened in complete passivity. But that means nothing. They clapped at the end.

30 March   Looking in at a bookshop this afternoon I noticed an atlas which was open at 'Afrika'; & the former German colonies were all marked with '*Deutsch*' in brackets in front of the name – thus '*(Deutsch) Süd West Afrika*'.

I learned this evening that on Fri: March 13 the Passport Officer in the Embassy here (M^r. Forbes)[390] was ordered by London to destroy confidential papers. That shows how near war we were. Next day Ribbentrop was invited to London & the situation was eased.

I was told today by a reliable informant that the trouble with H's throat is simply over-strain, which leads to the formation of knots on the vocal chords. These have bn twice removed; but those organs are so delicate that they cannot stand a third operation – or at least if a

[389] 'A British Policy': 27 March 1936, p.15.

[390] George Arthur D. Ogilvie–Forbes (1891–1954): entered dip. service 1919; Counsellor in Madrid; Chargé d'Affaires in Madrid & Valencia 1935–7, in Berlin 1937–9, in Oslo 1939; Min. in Havana 1940–4; Amb. to Colombo 1944–8; kt. 1937.

third operation is carried out, the sufferer will probably lose his voice, & he may moreover develop cancer. [...]

1 April My impression is that the chief object of the peace proposals which Hitler put forward on March 7 was to ward off an allied blow for entering the demilitarized zone, & of those which he has put forward today (most appropriate of days!) is to allow the construction of forts in the Rhineland to proceed without hindrance.[391] And the 4 months which H: gives for negotiations carries him on to the end of July, i.e. to the date when the Olympic Games are to begin! He wants quiet & peace till they are over.

7 April Hotblack, who is a most intelligent Military Attaché, told me today that the Nazi authorities have instructed those who will be running the Olympic Games not to do any boosting of Nat-Socialism. This is a wise move; otherwise it w^d certainly be overdone. Householders on whom athletes wl be billetted have also bn advised not to be over attentive to their guests, but to give them one (family) meal during the course of their stay, & offer to show them the town, but otherwise let them go their own way.

19 Apr: Lunch at the French Embassy today, & after it M. François-Poncet spoke in an extraordinarily frank & interesting way about the Germans. They are a mixture of Slav, Germanic & Latin (Latin - Charlemagne & the Germans south & west of the old Roman limen or boundary), & people don't give enough attention to the Slav element as a rule, which makes the Germans extreme in depression & exultant in success – *Sehnsucht* [yearning] is more to them than *Besitz* [property]; they always must be yearning after something. This, combined with a Latin exactitude of mind & Germanic militarism makes them a formidable & unique people.

The Ambassador told us (Lockner,[392] [*sic*] of the A.P., & me) his personal experience on March 2, the day on which, he is sure, the Rhineland coup of March 7 was decided.

---

[391] When Hitler announced that German troops were in the process of re-entering the Rhineland he simultaneously offered a 'western' non-aggression pact for twenty-five years, the conclusion of the proposed air pact, bilateral pacts with Germany's eastern neighbours, and the willingness of Germany – under certain conditions – to rejoin the League of Nations.

[392] Louis P. Lochner (b. 1887): US journalist; staff, Associated Press of America in Berlin 1924–8, Chief of Bureau 1928–42; Pulitzer Prize 1939. See his *What about Germany?* (1943).

As a result of the publication of de Jouvenel's interview with Hitler in the *Paris-Midi*, Fran-Poncet was instructed by his Gov^t to enquire of Hitler whether he had definite proposals to make for the improvement of Franco-Ger: relations, & to add that they were ready to discuss <u>anything</u> except proposals which w^d be contrary to their existing obligations under the Covenant or to their friendships & treaties with other people.

He accordingly rang up Neurath early on Mon: morn^g (March 2), & Neurath answered 'I have an important Conference with the Chancellor at 11. Come now.' So Fran-Pon: went, soon after 10. They had a general but inconclusive talk, it being understood that the chief object of the visit was for the Ambassdr to ask for an audience of the Chancellor. Neurath said he w^d ask him at 11, & Fr-Poncet returned to his Embassy (quite close). Much to his surprise he got a ring almost at once, saying the Chancellor w^d be pleased to see him at once – 12 o'clock. So Fran-Poncet went down, the *Wilhelmstr.* again, this time to the Chancery. Hitler was in a great state of agitation. When the Ambassdr told him the only limits of discussn which had bn imposed by the Fr. Gov^t, H: asked at once 'Do your friendships include Russia? Can you change anything there? What we have already signed, we cannot change' answered Fr:-Poncet unequivocally; & he (Fr: Pon:) got the strong impression that at that moment Hitler made up his mind to go through with his project – just an impression, said Fr: Ponc: but a v. strong one – at that time he didn't know what the project was exactly, though he suspected that something w^d be done about Locarno & the Rhineland. He believes that if he had equivocated H: might not have gone through with the project in that form.

Hitler then tiraded against Russia for a quarter of an hour. Then they began to discuss Franco-German relations; & the upshot of it was that H: said he w^d let the Ambssdr know in the course of a few days what proposals he had to make. There followed the big denunciation & declaration of Sat^y, March 7.

Fr-Poncet agrees that it was hurried on & made <u>before</u> ratificatn of the Franco-Soviet Pact in the hope that it might prevent ratification. When Fr: Poncet, at the end of the conversatn, asked whether they sh^d issue a communiqué, H: said it w^d be difficult to word one in such a way as to suit them both. Fr-Poncet then proposed only a few lines, & H: agreed, but later, when Fr-Poncet saw Neurath again, at luncheon, N. begged him not to issue even that, as it w^d cause too much speculation. 'Mindful of the Hoare-Laval business' said Fran-Poncet to us, I agreed.

François-Poncet believes that the final definite decision was taken at 5 pm that afternoon, when H: & Neurath met the military chiefs. In the meantime Neurath was assuring the American & the Italian

Ambassdrs that no violation of the Locarno Treaty was being considered by the German Gov^t – 'I don't know' said Fr: Poncet 'at what hour Neurath began to lie'! i.e. he doesn't know exactly when Neurath knew that the re-occupatn of the Rhineland had bn definitely decided on. Orders to the Army were issued on March 4, & rec^d by the units in question on March 5, they began to move on March 6, & entered the Rhineland while Hitler was speaking on March 7.

Fr-Ponçet is a brilliant & most interesting talker – & v. ready to talk! When I was writing my message this evening, I remembered something he had said which w^d fit in well; but I was not absolutely certain about one point. So I telephoned to the Embassy to ask if I might see him for 5 min. just to check what I put in my message (he had invited me to come & see him any time) & he said I c^d come. I got there at about 20 min. past six, & didn't get away till a quarter past 7! He told me amongst other things that what finally decided him to give up business & politics & come to Berlin as Ambassdr was that he had a conversatn with Brüning, who was then Chancellor (1931); & Br: <u>had admitted that Germany had committed faults in 1914</u> – *avait commis des fautes*; & he (Br) was the only German he had heard admit that much. He felt sure that Brüning wanted a new Germany; & he (Fran-Poncet) thought, here is a great opportunity of bringing about the long-delayed rap-prochement with Germany. But he had not bn 3 months in Germany when he found that Brüning, though a most honourable man – or perhaps because he was that – was no match for the Nazis on one side or Hindenburg on the other. 'He fought with toothpicks' said Fr-Poncet 'while they, the Nazis, fought with bludgeons.' As for Hindenburg, *il se moquait de lui*. Brün: slaved night & day for weeks to get Hindenburg re-elected President against Hitler, & succeeded; & within a few weeks Hindenburg dropped him! But long before this he (Fr-Poncet) had come to the conclusion that Brüning did not represent the real Germany. Germany is now Prussia on a larger scale.

At the end of our talk the Ambssdr came all the way down the long staircase with me, still talking. He thinks there may be more trouble this summer.

22 Apr: At luncheon yesterday with Dufour[393] I met two members of the *Mitteleuropäische Wirkshaftstag,* [sic] Freiherr von Wilmowsky,[394] a

---

[393] Albert Dufour von Feronce (1868–1945); entered for. service 1919; Counsellor in London 1920–4, Min. 1924–6; U-Sec.-Gen. and Dir. of the Intl Bureaux section, LoN. secretariat 1926–32; Amb. in Belgrade 1932–3.

[394] Tilo Wilmowsky (b. 1894): brother-in-law to Gustav Krupp; arrested following 20 July 1944 attempt to assasinate Hitler; sent to concentration camp. See his *Warum wurde Krupp verurteilt?* (1950).

brother-in-law of Krupp v. Bohlen, & Dr Max Hahn.[395] The former
was a particularly attractive man.

They all dwelt on the still existing danger of communism in Ger, &
D: gave an interesting example of communists' methods. Some time
ago it was noticed that on the pavement at intervals was stamped or
painted 'Communism still lives.' The authorities were puzzled, as they
c^d not think how men c^d manage to paint all these inscriptions without
being seen. Watch was kept, & it was eventually discovered that two
men were going round carrying a v. heavy basket between them, &
occasionally resting it on the pavement, & every time they did so
'Communism still lives' was stamped upon it!

All three men, Dufour, Wilmowsky & Hahn clearly thought that
German expansion in Central Europe was the one thing that w^d
get trade expanding again; but I think they genuinely felt that as far
as they were concerned political domination was not necessary – all
they wanted was freedom to trade, removal of artificial hindrances.
They gave me the impression that <u>prosperity is waiting round the
corner</u>.

23 Apr: There is however absolute proof that the young generation
are being brought up to the idea that Memel, Danzig Vienna & even
Strassburg must eventually belong to Germany again. I was shown a
copy of the official educational magazine of the Party this morning (at
the Embassy), & in it are instructions to teachers to inculcate these v.
points into the minds of their pupils.

Stahmer,[396] of Rib:'s Staff, said to me this morn^g that the reason why
Hitler struck unexpectedly & without warning on March 7 was that
they knew the French Gen: Staff was contemplating action against
Germany in July! Just the same excuse as they gave for invading
Belgium in 1914. He explained to me solemnly that these things always
happen in the late summer, when the crops have been got in, & so
Hitler decided to act first, & to act without warning – because an offer
to negotiate w^d not only have been useless, but w^d have enabled France
to store the necessary oil for counter-action. The reason, acc: to him,
why the French Staff c^d <u>not</u> retaliate on March 8 was that they had
<u>not</u> got the accumulation of oil supplies necessary nowadays for
mechanized warfare.

[395] Albert Hahn (b. 1889): managing Dir. *Deutsche Effektenund Wechsel-Bank*; Hon. Prof.
of Economics, Frankfurt Univ. 1928.
   [396] Heinrich Stahmer: one of the 'advisers' in the *Dienstelle Ribbentrop* outside of the
Auswartige Amt; negotiated the military alliance with Japan in 1940; Amb. in Nanking
1940–3; to Tokyo 1943–5; captured 1945.

25 Apr: A cheerful luncheon at the Embassy. The Naval Attaché's wife (M^{rs}. Muirhead Gold),[397] [sic] next whom I sat, told me that Hitler had bn asked by a friend of hers where he looked when he was making a speech, did he look at the audience or into the distance beyond them? He had answered that he looked at 12 or 20 persons sitting fairly nearly in front of him, observed them pretty closely, & took his cue from them.

Phipps told me that a short time ago v. Neurath was v. keen to go to the Embassy in London, but now he doesn't want it.

(Young) Lord Jellicoe[398] was there, & told rather an amusing story about himself. He had bought a map of Berlin, which was evidently 3 years old at least, for wanting to get somewhere near the *Brandenburger Tor* he asked a policeman for the way to '*Stresemannstrasse*'. The policeman glared at him; so Jellicoe murmured something more in broken German, which saved him! The policeman saw that he was a foreign tourist & not a German Communist! & told him the way to the '*Hermann-Göring-strasse*', as the street has bn renamed by the Nazis. It was before *Stresemann-str* known as the *Budapesterstr*, & before that as the *König-grätzerstrasse*!

Now the *Eckener-allée* has just bn renamed, as the great airship-man has made himself obstreporous to the regime.

27 Apr: [. . .] I had a most interesting conversatn with Dr Gaus[399] this morn^g – the legal adviser of the For Ministry. He was at pains to explain to me that the despatch no: 46 of Dec 16, 1935 (Phipps to Hoare) does not convey a correct impression of what passed between Hitler & Phipps. Hitler did not turn down the proposal to start negotiations so flatly as Phipps reported. It was rather Phipps – acc: to Gaus – who was half-hearted about the whole business.

Gaus was not himself present, but is evidently kept closely & confidentially informed, & is himself an able, strong-headed & I sh^d say sincere man. He was apparently convinced himself that Hitler never meant to turn down the Air Pact.

Hitler did however doubt the usefulness of negotiating the Pact on the basis of bilateral agreements.

[397] Gerald Charles Muirhead-Gould (1889–1945): naval officer; Capt. 1931; naval Attaché 1933–6; commanded HMS *Devonshire* 1936–7; Flag-Officer-in-Command Sydney 1941–4; actg Rear-Adm. 1944; Flag-Officer-in-Charge Western Germany 1944–5.

[398] Christopher Theodore Jellicoe (1903–1977): naval officer; Lieut. 1930–1, Commander 1939, Capt. 1943, Rear-Adm. 1953; s. of 1st Earl Jellicoe.

[399] Friedrich Wilhelm Gaus (b. 1881): German diplomat; mb. of delegation to Brest-Litovsk 1918, Versailles 1919, Genoa 1922, Locarno 1925; Deptuy Dir. legal dept *Auswärtige Amt* 1921–3, Dir. 1923–43.

In any case, each interlocutor reported his own version, & this may be a case of honest mis-memory of exactly what was said on either side. I am surprised this does not happen more often after long dipl: conversatns. [...]

Gaus did persuade me of one thing, & that is that the Franco-Soviet Treaty is at least a technical infringement of the <u>Covenant</u>. It stipulates for action if unanimity c$^{\underline{d}}$ not be reached in Council. This is practical & sensible, & may be said to be a strengthening of the working of the Covenant in practice – but certainly it is against the procedure laid down – & therefore, Gaus argues, also an infringement of Locarno. (The British French Belgian & Italian legal advisers said it was compatible with Loc: Gaus thinks that when Sir W$^{\underline{m}}$ Malkin[400] said it was the others all agreed without further ado).

Note the fundamental quality for a diplomatist of being able to keep the thread of a conversat[io]n. Never losing hold of the points he wants to bring in even through the longest divagations. Make them at the right moment. Yet listen well.

29 Apr: Pinsent,[401] the financial expert of the Embassy, spoke to me in a most interesting & instructive way this morn^g about Colonies & raw material for Germany, & also about Schacht's[402] position. I've made a note on the former point elsewhere.

Germany has got herself into a frightfully difficult position. She <u>could</u> improve her economic position in one way by reducing import of raw material for rearmament, but that w$^{\underline{d}}$ almost certainly increase unemployment – & she cannot afford to do that. She c$^{\underline{d}}$ also improve her financial position in one way by allowing a much freer movement of capital; but the first thing that w$^{\underline{d}}$ happen w$^{\underline{d}}$ be that all the Jews w$^{\underline{d}}$ take their capital out of the country, where it is now locked up! In other words, they <u>cannot</u> allow freedom – economic or political.

30 Apr: Our Naval Attaché here (Capt: Muirhead-Gould) told me this

[400] (Herbert) William Malkin (1883–1945): lawyer & civil servant; entered FO 1911; Asst Legal Adviser FO 1914–25, 2nd Legal Adviser 1925–9, Legal Adviser 1929–45.

[401] Gerald Hume S. Pinsent (1886–1976): Asst Sec. Treasury 1931; Financial Adviser in Berlin 1932–9; in Washington 1939–41; British Food Mission, Ottawa 1942–3; Principal Asst Sec. Treasury 1944–6; Comptroller-Gen. Nat. Debt Office 1946–51.

[402] Hjalmar Schacht (1887–1970): Pres. *Reichsbank* 1933–9; Min. of Economics 1934–7; Plenipotentiary-Gen. for War Economy 1935–7; Min. without Portfolio 1939–43; arrested on suspicion of complicity in plot to assassinate Hitler, July 1944; interned in concentration camps until end of WWII; judged not guilty of war crimes at Nuremberg. See his *My First Seventy-Six Years* (1955).

morn^g that when the Germans first built submarines he had a rather sharp exchange with a German Naval Officer. Germany had only just recovered freedom to have submarines, & the officer told him they w^d have 50 (or whatever the number was) in 3 months. 'Then you must have started making them already' said our man 'Oh! no' said the German. Finally M-Gould, knowing perfectly well that submarines cannot be built in 3 months, told him he was lying!

The officer went away much incensed. Next day the Naval Attaché called at the Min: of Marine, & saw another officer, & he explained to him that all the parts of the submarines had already bn made separately, but that the submarines had not been ordered! & the assembly of the parts w^d only take 3 months. So, he said, his colleague had bn telling the truth!

I can understand Muirhead-Gould's feelings, but at the same time if he wants to extract information from the Germans, it is not a v. good start to call them liars! & I am not surprised that he now says they tell him nothing, & that all business is done through the German Naval Attaché in London & the Foreign Office. He moreover is told not to spy by the Admiralty. So he doesn't have much to do! [...]

1 May   There was to have been dancing out of doors tonight, on this day of official enjoyment, but going round about tonight I saw none – & heard bands playing marches but not foxtrots. They prefer marching to dancing here!

2 May   To-day I went to Potsdam with the Stahmers, & the question arose whether to have luncheon in Potsdam itself or go on to a *Schloss* in a Park, which has bn turned into a restaurant. Mrs Stahmer seemed to like that idea best, so I said we'd go on there (I was being host for luncheon), when the chauffeur intervened to say that the restaurant in the Park was run by a Jew. This settled the matter for Stahmer, who had by this time come up. It was impossible to go there! Our car, being one from Ribbentrop's office, had the Nazi pennant in front, so we c^d not be seen at the Schloss! Mrs S. indicated to me that she thought the whole thing was absurd; but Basil Newton, with whom I spent the evening, said that the chauffeur c^d have denounced Stahmer if we'd gone there, & might have, if he'd got anything against him. ...

6 May   Saw Ribbentrop yesterday. I had a polite message, asking if I c^d go round & see him at the *Kaiserhof*. I was rather surprised to get it, & still more surprised when I found that he apparently had nothing particular to say to me! He was just extremely affable, & we talked about people (he likes social gossip) & politics, of course. I had an appointment to see Breen at the British Embassy afterwards, & when I told him about Rib's affability, he said 'oh yes, I can tell you exactly what that is. They are saying, what has happened to Kennedy, he has quite gone over to the French camp since he has bn in Berlin – which they attribute to the influence of the Embassy – & they are trying to get you back'!

However, one or two interesting points did come out of my talk with Rib. He repeated the Nazi dislike of negotiating at Geneva, & he hinted moreover that if these preliminary conversatns went on too long Hitler might withdraw his proposals altogether. He pleaded once more for an Anglo-German accord, & asked what on earth stood in the way of it 'Want of confidence' I said.

Breen told me that he had himself heard Goebbels talking in a v. derogotary [sic] way about England the other day.

There is no doubt that our stock has gone down over this Abyssinian affair. Also Germans who go to London are not impressed by the signs of slackness which they see in the young men, & which, to give them their due, they have largely abolished here. The admiratn of G^t B^n & everything British had perhaps anyhow bn excessive, & now there is a reaction.

Breen says he thinks Hitler is definitely & genuinely anti-gas (in war), he having bn badly gassed himself. This does not mean that in a last extremity the German army w^d not use it, but Breen thinks that Hitler w^d refrain if he felt he could. [. . .]

8 May   Saw Arnal[403] at the French Embassy this morn^g, & urged vehemently upon him my policy of sticking to Locarno. LOCARNO STILL STANDS. We can't admit it is non-existent just bec: Germany says so.

At luncheon Hotblack made an interesting comparison between German barracks & British. Not only are the new Ger barracks far more comfortable than the average in England, but they are relatively even more comfortable by comparison with the conditions in which the men live in their own homes. In England a man lives in less comfort than the average of a working-man's home; in Germany in greater comfort. So recruiting is not nearly so popular in England as it might be if better relative conditions were created.

[403] Pierre Albert Arnal (b. 1892): entered *MdAE* 1920; U-Sec. Commercial Relations 1925–32; Counsellor in Berlin 1932–7; Head, LoN section *MdAE* 1937–40; Dir. Econ. Affairs 1940–4.

At the Holburns'[404] cocktail party von Strempel,[405] of the Foreign Ministry, told me that about a fortnight after I had got here (in Feb^y) the For: Ministry rec^d a despatch from Hoesch (Ambassdr in London) all about me! It seems that he said he & I had had many 'fruitful conversations'. How v. nice of him. He was indeed a charming & able man. von Strempel married his niece, just before his (von H's) death. von Str: told me also that Bismarck, who was in charge of the Embassy at the moment, had also written about me to the For: Ministry. It shows what a tremendous lot of trouble the Germans take about anybody connected with public opinion.

v. Strempel asked me <u>why</u> Hoesch was so much liked; & my private opinion of Bismarck. I said Hoesch was, to my mind, the model ambassador (& detailed reasons), & that Bis: was also popular, but a little too restlessly inquisitive.

10 May It seems to me bad dipl^y on the part of the Brit. Gov^t (& on Phipps' part if he did not try to dissuade them) to have pub^d the Brit: 'questions' just put to the Ger. Gov^t, arising out of Hitler's peace proposals. It was previously given out by *T.T.* – 'Dipl: Corrspdt's' notes, obviously prompted by the F.O. – that the questions w^d not be pub^d, anyhow at first. They <u>are</u> delicate questions, & it was explained that they (& the Press answers) had better not be 'shouted from the housetops'.

Quite right. But what does our Gov^t then do. Phipps tells v. Neurath, at the same moment as he presents the questionnaire, that it will be laid as a White Paper on the table of the H. of Commons next day & also pub^d in the Press.

Moreover Hitler is out of Berlin. Eden's despatch. Phipps is told to see Hitler. This being at the moment impossible, the publicatn of the contents is made before Hitler himself has bn officially informed of them, much less had time to consider them.

They are naturally annoyed about it here; & as our prestige has anyhow gone down yards as a result of the Abyssinian fiasco & tragedy, I'm afraid a spoke has bn struck, inadvertently, into the wheels of the negotiations.

[404] James Holburn (1900–1988): journalist, *Glasgow Herald* 1921–34; Asst Corrspdt & actg Corrspdt *The Times* in Berlin 1935–9, in Moscow 1939–40, in Ankara 1940–1, War Corrspdt for Middle East 1941–2, Corrspdt in New Delhi 1942–6, at UN headquarters 1946–8, Dip. Corrspdt 1948–5, Chief Corrspdt, Middle East 1952–5; Ed. *Glasgow Herald* 1955–65.
[405] L.S. von Strempel: German diplomat; Sec. Press Dept *Auswärtige Amt* in 1930s, responsible for Great Britain, the British Empire and Commonwealth, the Americas, Portugal and Spain.

I see that the Soc: Party in the H.oC. clamoured for immediate publicatn.

11 May   Yesterday I met that stranger in world politics, a Frenchman who understood & positively sympathized with the German point of view! & the tragedy is that he (M. Dubard, formerly Corrspdt of *l'Intransigeant* in Berlin) considers that Frenchmen & Germans will never harmonize, because their outlooks are fundamentally different. In particular, Frenchmen hold to *le droit*, the law; whereas Germans consider that what they call human rights, or sometimes *Das Leben des Volkes*, override Law. Law becomes a juridical technicality compared to these inherent rights – of which they themselves are the judges in their own case!

About the publication of the Brit: questionnaire – I was told at the Embassy this morn^g that what actually happened was that when Phipps presented it, in the morn^g (Thurs), he & von Neurath were in agreement that the terms sh^d be kept secret. Instructns to our Embassy on this point had bn v. strict – nobody to be told etc etc, so much so that I kept away from it, to avoid embarrassment.

Then at about 4 p.m. Phipps, to his surprise & regret, got telephonic instructions to tell the Ger: Gov^t. that the Brit: Gov^t. w^d like to publish after all, & w^d he so inform the Ger Gov^t, & ask their consent. So Phipps rang up Neurath, who agreed quite readily.

Quite a storm has bn raised here. The version told me on Fri: (8th) by the head of the Press Dept of the For: Ministry was not correct. He was v. angry, & made some bitter remarks, & distorted the story somewhat (see my entry of May 10). But the matter has bn bungled, chiefly by the F.O. (or Brit: Gov^t), & secondly by Phipps & Neurath, who might each in turn have protested against the sudden change of mind, but do not seem to have done so.

The German annoyance is probably being artificially exaggerated, but it must be remembered that the despatch of the questionnaire was continually being put off – about 10 days altogether – & they were on tenterhooks. When it came, it was stiffer than they expected, questioning their good faith – & in the meantime our prestige has gone down – over Abyssinia!

12 May   Had a short conversatn with that amusing talker M. François-Poncet, the Fr: Ambssdr. He was v. serious today however – the victory of militarism & dictatorship over the League of N. & democracy. '*La démocratie est bavarde*' he cried; & he said '*La masse va an fort. La masse est femme*'. He meant that the crowd follows a Mussolini or a Hitler; & the next thing we shall see is that the small nations will cluster round the strong men too.

He was most sarcastic about Lord Cecil & Prof: Gilbert Murray[406] & exclaimed '*Qu'ils jouent an billard, mais qu'ils ne passent pas la politique*'.

He entirely approved my view that it was a mistake of diplomacy to publish the British questionnaire. The leaders here have bn telling the public they stand well with England, & here comes a document which shows '*mépris*' for them & doesn't seem to believe what they say.

He told me that Neurath was putting it about that Phipps had told him (on the telephone on Thurs afternoon) that the Brit Gov^t <u>had</u> decided to publish the questionnaire next day.

14 May   The 'leak'. Breen told me today that Anthony Eden had decided to publish the Brit. questionnaire on Thursday because a 'leak' of it had occurred in a Brit: evening paper, from Berlin – at once. It was only handed in at 11 a.m. It sounds rather extraordinary. Breen said it was v. Strempel.

Breen also told me how much Simon had bn put off at the v. outset of his visit here, because when he got out of his aeroplane on *Tempelhofer-feld* he had bn greeted by sharply worded barks of command & strapping SS men had come to the salute! This almost shattered the miserable Simon! When he got to the Embassy he said something about 'the bottomless pit of hell had opened before him'. The poor fool has a horror of soldiers, I imagine. He voted against conscription in the War, I think.

15 May   Miss Whiskemann[407] [sic] called at the Office this morn^g, an intelligent & nice woman, of the *Manchester Guardian* type of mind. She studies German education, & fully realizes the appalling outlook of superiority & defiance to which the youth of Germany is being brought up.

18 May   Saw Sir E. Phipps for a few moments this evening; & I gathered that he now considers that sanctions w^d [be] n.b.g. [no bloody good] against this country. Franç-Poncet gave me that view also. So

---

[406] (George) Gilbert Murray (1866–1957): Regius Prof. of Greek, Oxford U. from 1908; Chm. LoN Union 1923–38; Pres. Intl Committee of Intellectual Co-operation 1928–40. See his *From the League to the U.N.* (1948).

[407] Elizabeth Wiskemann (1901–71): free-lance writer in Europe 1932–7; sponsored by Royal Institute of International Affairs to write book on Czechoslovakia (*Czechs & Germans*, 1938); Asst Press Attaché Berne 1941–5. See her *The Europe I Saw* (1968).

my mind is made up – unless I hear something in Prague or Vienna that makes me think differently.

Phipps also told me that before the coup of March 7 the F.O. were working out a new arrangement for the demilitarized zone about which they hoped to <u>make a bargain</u> with Germany.

Quite a good idea, but they were as usual too dilatory. I begged Leeper to hurry up about it, I remember (he gave me a hint of what was being planned when I saw him just before coming to Berlin).

20 May   Chat with Count Dembinski,[408] an attractive Pole, who declares that Danzig is the Singapore of Poland; & that if the Germans seize it, Poland will make war without thinking!

Then on to François-Poncet, who was as usual v. interesting. Of the Germans in general he said '*il n'y a pas de peuple où la sincérité est si liée au mensonge*'. Terribly true. They <u>are</u> sincere – but with 9 out of 10 there's an *arrière-pensée* '<u>if</u> circumstances change I can get out of this', or even they may not have the *arrière-pensée* at the moment; but, as Dembinski said to me, later they may persuade themselves that it is their <u>duty</u> to change their mind, even if it is against a treaty. National <u>interest</u> becomes national <u>right</u> in next to no time.

We both agreed that the personal animus existing between Eden & Mussolini is an unfavourable factor in the present international situation.

22 May   The famous Dr Schacht spoke to me with terrible bluntness this morn^g – it all came to this: Germany must have access to more raw material, & have it soon. The standard of living is going steadily down. Nothing can stop it except much freer world trade, esp: the acquisition by Ger of foodstuffs & raw materials. If it is not stopped, there will <u>inevitably be an explosion</u> – & the explosion, with the present regime in power, will take the form of war.

War, Dr Schacht admitted, w^d be no solution. It w^d in fact make things worse. But the only thing that c^d avert it was an increase of world trade.

An arrangement with G^t B^n sh^d be possible. Germany was ready to accept the primacy of G^t B^n, politically, economically & culturally in the world, he said; but she must come in as a partner, or there w^d be a conflict.

Germany, being a great manufacturing country, & short of foodstuffs,

[408] Bronislaw Dembinski (1858–1939): historian & politician; mb. Polish Diet 1919–22; U-Sec. of St., Ministry of Culture 1919–30; Prof. of History, Poznan U. 1923; Pres., Polish Fed. of LoN Societies.

must have a surplus of exports over imports (why only Ger, I asked? does that not apply to other manufacturing countries? Only to one or two, he said, & gave reasons, which I could not check).

He gave me a pamphlet he had written in 1926 called 'New Colonial Policy'. It was written during the 'borrowed boom' he said, & therefore it does not touch the now fundamental problem of a steadily diminishing standard of living. And now, he added, we are having another false boom, on money borrowed internally this time.

Germany <u>must</u> be able to sell where she must buy, & in her own *devisen*. This part of his argument was v. technical, & I will not try to reproduce it; but it led of course to his favourite theory that Ger must have colonies. He admitted that the former German colonies had never been much developed before the War, but then (as he fairly argued) Ger could sell elsewhere, & she cannot now, owing to the appalling econ: nationalism everywhere.

I pointed out the difficulties of re-transferring territories to Germany – hostility in the H. of Commons, wishes of local interests etc. I said I thought the present Conservative H. of Commons w$^{\underline{d}}$ never agree to it, & that a Socialist House, if it came w$^{\underline{d}}$ not agree to do it for Hitler.

I suggested that a start might be made, if Ger w$^{\underline{d}}$ re enter the League, by giving her Liberia to clean up, as Italy was going to clean up Abyssinia. He answered that Liberia was not big enough, & moreover was thickly populated. He agreed nevertheless that its transfer to Germany might be a contribution towards the solution of the problem; but what was really wanted was the development by Ger of a territory like Angola, which was very thinly populated & was very rich. He wondered whether Germany could not, for instance, lease half Angola from Portugal. He admitted that under Salazar Portugal was now developing its resources much better than they'd ever been developed before.

I thanked D$^{\underline{r}}$ Schacht for speaking to me with such frankness. He said it was easier for him to speak frankly to an unofficial person, & that he had heard from his son-in-law[409] that he c$^{\underline{d}}$ do so to me without his confidence being abused. I said I thought what he had told me seemed to be of extreme interest & importance, & asked if I might pass on the gist of what he had said to the Brit: Ambassdr. He agreed, if it was done discreetly. He said he did not object to his knowing what he had said, but that he naturally w$^{\underline{d}}$ not talk in that way if he had bn talking officially.

We had begun our conversation with a few remarks on current affairs. D$^{\underline{r}}$ Schacht said he was satisfied with the new arrangement by

---

[409] Dr Hilger von Scherpenberg of the *Auswartige Amt* Economic Policy Department married Inge Schacht in 1930.

which he shares his authority with General Göring, & he implied that it had one great advantage, namely that Göring & his immediate associates were learning a good deal about national economy which they did not know before.

I said that there were many rumours about a new Economic Peace Plan being prepared by Germany. He said he knew nothing of any such plan. 'And if the Gov^t were preparing one, I think I <u>would</u> know about it' he added. He considered that the Standstill arrangement was working well.

25 May That v nice Rente-Fink [sic] gave me the reasons today why Hit cannot edit & expurgate *Mein Kampf*. It all amounts to this – a prophet cannot say 'I was wrong'! & if he once began, where w^d he stop. All that was left in, moreover, w^d have additional weight. And people read it for <u>internal</u> policy, not foreign policy.

26 May Dembinski, the Pole, who has a v. nice flat here, travelled a year ago with Gen: Göring in Poland when the latter was on one of his shooting visits there. He says that Göring, M. Lipski[410] (the Polish Ambssdr in Berlin) & himself were in the same saloon in the evening & talked on well into the night. At one moment Göring's eyes began to close, & talking seemed to be an effort to him, so he retired to his sleeping-car, & ¼ hour later came back completely refreshed. C^t Dembinski says that he has '*des morphinistes dans la famille*' & that he recognized in G's looks the taker of morphia. G: is always supposed to have bn addicted that way, so this is probably true – or was à year ago. Since that episode G: has married. Some people say it has steadied him; but Dembinski says that '*le menage a bien de difficultés*'.

He says however that Göring is definitely nominated in Hit's political testament as his successor. Two abnormal men.

30 May Going round the *Festsaäle* of the *Schloss* here this morn^g with SDK our guide came to the portrait of Maria Theresa & explained that she was '*die schlimmste Feindin von Friedrich des Grossen'! Sie wollte Schliesien haben*' This was too much for me, & I explained to the party that she only tried to defend her own territory.

Yesterday we went round the other part of the *Schloss, die Wohnzimmer*, & I noticed that Kaiser Wilhelm, as well as having put in the

---

410 Jozef Lipski (1894–1958): entered dip. service 1922; 1st Sec. in Paris 1925; Dir. Ministry of For. Affairs 1925–34; Amb. in Berlin 1934–9. See his *Diplomat in Berlin* (1968).

bust of Fred:[erick] the Great over the mantelpiece of his Council room, had a medallion of him above his riding-saddled desk. He did himself – so the guide told me – have the bust of Schlieffen put into the Council-room. he also had his portrait as a Roman Emperor painted on the ceiling of the dining-room!

A lady in the other part of the *Schloss* asked the guide what there was to see in the *Wohnzimmer* part, & he replied '*Der Tisch*' on which he had signed the order for mobilization in 1914.

3 June Saw M. Mastny[411] the Czechoslovak Minister here this morn^g. Quite a shrewd old dip, who thinks it folly, as every prof: dip: that I have spoken to does, to keep on sanctions against Italy now that Abyss: has changed hands. He thinks it just possible – not probable that Musso: may come to an arrangement with Germany over Austria – i.e. give it up – & then between them they'll be an anti-League & <u>anti-British Empire</u> combination.

In any case, Mastny agrees that Hitler's first ambitions are towards Central Eur:, then probably eastwards, & finally overseas. He kept on talking of H's 'relative' sincerity, which is rather a good phrase – relative & temporary, I sh^d say!

I told him frankly I did not think Brit: pub: op: w^d sanction <u>active</u> steps by G^t B^n against Ger in Central Europe, though of course Czechoslovakia w^d have all our sympathy. I feel that above all we must not promise more than we can perform. He said he understood; but we must note that nevertheless an attack by Ger on Czecho: w^d cause 'a general conflagration'.

I doubt it.

4 June [...] In the afternoon Robin B-W & I went to see François-Poncet, who spoke for $1\frac{1}{2}$ hour, & was v. good, but unfortunately much of it was in English (for B-W's benefit) & he is not nearly so fluent or so amusing in English as in French.

Referring to the coup of March 7 he said that v. Neurath had <u>not</u> bn told what was intended on Mon: the 2nd – there was only a full meeting of the Cabinet on Wed^y 4th, & that Blomberg did not oppose the coup, though v. Fritsch[412] (the Cmdr of the Army) & some of the leading generals <u>were</u> against it.

[411] Vojtech Mastny (1874–1954): Min. in London 1920–5, in Rome 1925–32, in Berlin 1932–8. See his *Vzpomínky diplomata* (1997).

[412] Werner von Fritsch (1880–1939): German army officer; Lt-Col. 1922, Maj-Gen. 1930, Lt-Gen. 1932; C-in-C *Wehrmacht* 1935–8; forced to resign in February 1934 after being framed for homosexual acts; cleared by a military court; Col.-in-Chief, Twelfth Artillery Regiment 1939; killed in action on Polish front September 1939.

Fr-Ponçet says that Hit: is fundamentally a v. simple man – & he is something of a peasant too, with the suspicion & cunning of a peasant. He amusingly said that he uses v. Ribbentrop as Molière used to use his cook – he used to read her passages from his plays, to see whether they amused her or not – & H:'s foreign political messages & notes are prepared by the *Wilhelmstrasse* (For: Ministry), revised & toned by himself, & then read to Rib, to see what effect they have on him!

Fr-Pon says there are 3 *divisions blindées* in the Ger army – which are the spearhead of a modern attacking army. He is informed that one or two more are being formed.

9 June   At lunch with Vernon Bartlett today Segrue[413] the *N-C* Corrspdt here, made a good observatn when he said that in Ger & It eyes the League of Nations was an instrument for making permanent the status quo created by the war. Therefore our moral fervour against It over Abyssinia genuinely seemed to the Italians to be rather hypocritical. And Breen added that the great difficulty about the Peace Treaty was that we made such a song about the justice of it. If we had said frankly it was based on conquest the Germans, who appealed to the arbitrament of war, c^d not have had a grievance. As it is they can say, that is not our idea of justice. Make it a just peace.

Later an interesting talk with Pinsent (Financial Attaché) who said well about the L.oN. that its Covenant does not truly correspond to the mentality of nations to-day; & to take a falsified idealism as guide for our policy is dangerous.

He told me he thought Schacht was right in saying that the standard of living must go steadily down in this country under the present regime.

10 June   When I said goodbye to Stahmer yesterday he told me about having bn rec^d (as an ex-Service representative) by K. Edward; I asked him if he wore his SS uniform (all-black), & he said 'oh no, I went 'in Stresemann'.'! It seems that 'a Stresemann' is London trousers & short black coat, which Stresemann introduced to Germany! So the memory of the great statesman survives after all in the Nazi régime! even though '*Stresemann-strasse*' has been obliterated in favour of '*Hermann Göring-str*'!

Farewell talks with Dieckhoff & von Ribbentrop – both v. confiding, no doubt partly because am leaving. Dieck: told me the exact position

413 John Segrue (1883–1942): Corrspdt in Berlin, *Daily News* 1920–26, in Paris 1926–30, *News-Chronicle* in Berlin 1930–6, in Vienna 1936–8; died as prisoner of war in Upper Silesia 1942. See his *Farewell Austria* (1938).

in regard to the German reply to the Brit. questionnaire; & Rib: talked freely about the position of the Embassy here, & how out of touch they are with the people who really count. In which there is a good deal of truth, as one of them at least has admitted to me. Phipps hates the lot, & doesn't get on with them in the least when he does meet them. And they are too formal as to those with whom they'll deal.

von R: told me frankly that Ger w$^{\underline{d}}$ not negotiate 'within the present League of Nations'. He spoke in favour of making a beginning with the Air Pact even only betw: Eng & Ger. Create a crystallization point, & others will adhere. Something in that. I said I was in favour.

To Dieckhoff I developed my idea that Eden will eventually fall betw: two stools – tho' a Cons: he is pursuing a Soc: for: policy. That won't suit the Conservatives for ever. I said it also to Rib, & he thought I was right. [...]

VIENNA *14 June*   Was stirred from bed this morn^{g414} by the sound of a military march, so common in Berlin; & I got up to have a look. And instead of brown or black-shirted semi-soldiers I saw a top-hatted (!) procession. The leader moreover raised his 'cylinder-hat' as he passed the Legation; & I found out afterwards from Walford Selby that this was because he was the chief porter of the Legation. It was a religious procession – today being Corpus Christi Sunday – & later another longer one passed, made up not only of tophatted gents, but also of women, girls, boy scouts – & soldiers! Sort of maypoles were carried by the girls; & the pace of walking was so slow that the soldiers had to march in a slow-step with paces of about 12 in.! The pace of the soldiers being made for them by the children – so charming & so Austrian!

Yet bang opposite me was flying the (Nazi) Swastika! On a building which I found to be the German Legation.

How significant & how ominous!

15 June   Saw von Papen this morn^{g}, a most agreeable man. At the end of our conversatn I told him that there didn't seem to be much difference betw British views & his views about Austria.

The trouble is – does v. Papen speak for anybody but himself? He told me [he] had come here on the '100% understanding' that the Ger policy which had resulted in the murder of Dollfuss sh$^{\underline{d}}$ be abandoned, & that Ger sh$^{\underline{d}}$ work for an understanding with Austria & not for the absorption of Austria. In fact he had seemed quite hurt when I said

---

[414] At the British Legation.

that people in England thought that Ger was working for the absorption of Austria!

Is this not just another case of the inherent duplicity of Ger policy? A man in Vienna who is genuinely in favour of an understanding, but who does not represent the dominating faction in Berlin.

He is a R.C., & I sh$^{\underline{d}}$ suppose genuinely favourable to the Austrian outlook. I compared it favourable to the Nazi outlook, & he indicated that he agreed.

He said that the 40 000 Austr émigrés in Ger were a problem in themselves, & had a thousand connexions with Austria. If he heard of any of their machinations he always tried to stop them.

What, I asked, really prevents the rapprochement of Austria with Ger? I asked. Certain countries are working to <u>prevent</u> it, he answ$^{\underline{d}}$ – & indicated France & Italy.

I asked him if the Austrian problem were an internal problem for Germany? 'We are the same *Volkstum*', he answered '& the same *Kulturkreis*'. Austr had a great past in Ger history, & had still her part to play in the spread of Ger culture.

I mentioned certain influences behind Hitler, which seemed to have diff$^{\underline{t}}$ ideas about Austria from what he had. He seemed to admit it. 'It is a pity you are not in charge in Berlin' I said 'Well, I may go back there' he answered.

Finally, I observed that probably the great diff^{y} was lack of confidence, accentuated since the Rhineland. H: had said repeatedly he was not going to upset Locarno, & then suddenly did it. Austria no doubt thought the same course might be in store for her. He seemed to understand.

He declared however that Ger was really a religious country & that the present anti-rel: movement w$^{\underline{d}}$ die out.

He held my hand long at parting (typically German) & begged that we sh$^{\underline{d}}$ work for the same object – a better understanding between Ger & Austria.

16 June   Later in the day yesterday I saw the pol: head of the Austrian Foreign Ministry, Herr Hornbostel;[415] & he told me (& Reed) that v. Papen actually was approaching the Austrian Gov$^{\underline{t}}$ about getting on better terms with Ger: They, the Ger Gov$^{\underline{t}}$, would try to get something settled before answering the Brit: questionnaire. Told Walford Selby, who will see the French Minister today, & see if he has anything on the subject. Herr Hornbostel was frank to the point of casualness. A typically easy-going Austrian. A clever one, but I sh$^{\underline{d}}$ say not with first-

[415] Theodor Hornbostel: Dir. Political Dept, For. Ministry 1936–8; arrested 1938.

class judgment. At one moment he was heartily discussing with Reed whether the Austrian army w$^{\underline{d}}$ shoot if a German army came across the frontier! He was quite sure they w$^{\underline{d}}$, but he seemed to think the battle might only last a few hours.

Herr Ludwig[416] – head of the Press Dept of the Ministry – gave us quite a long address, in which he mentioned that the *hackenkreuz* (Swastika) had become fashionable in Vienna in the 80s & 90s, but the movement had died out. Now again, he maintained, the Nazi movement (in Austria) had sunk to about 10 per cent of the pop[ulation] (Reed says that is too low a figure, but Selby says it has admittedly become very feeble). Ludwig rather surprised me by mentioning as 'the two big questions of the moment' the restoration of the Hapsburgs & the position of P$^{\underline{ce}}$ Stharemberg[417] [sic] & his *Heimwehr*. It is generally admitted that although the present Gov$^{\underline{t}}$ is Monarchist they will not recall Otto[418] unless things are absolutely desperate. It w$^{\underline{d}}$ be a last move to rally the country. Reed thinks it w$^{\underline{d}}$ be a good one <u>in that respect</u>.

One phrase that Ludwig used struck me v. much. He said 'Austrian policy is *durchsichtig*' (transparent). I said at once what a contrast to that of the country I've just come from'!

It is a thing that has again impressed me on this visit – what a decent people the Austrians are, & how favourably their outlook compares with that of the north Germans! I have found moreover that they are bracing themselves together considerably, & there appears to be a firm spirit of resistance, apart from the army, which I was told had increased in value v. greatly during the last 3 years. There is a <u>natural</u> antagonism between the Austrians & the Prussians. There is more distinction betw them than I realized.

Another point which I hadn't sufficiently taken into account is the effect of the past over the present – the great past of Austria is everpresent to them. They are a proud though simple folk; & they want to play their part in the future of <u>Germanism</u>. They have moreover more spirituality than the Germans; but they don't seem to have that extraordinarily effective relationship between the led & the leaders.

British political stock does not, I regret to say, stand v. high, (as in Germany, the Abyssinian failure has sent it down), but they still look

[416] Eduard Michel Ludwig (b. 1883): head, Austrian Press Service 1920–36; interned at Dachau 1938–43; Deputy, National Assembly, 1946–58. See his *Österreichs Sendung im Donauraum* (1954).

[417] Ernest Rudiger Starhemberg (1899–1956): ldr, Christian Socialist Party & para-military *Heimwehr*; Vice-Chanc. & Min. of Security, & ldr of Fatherland Front until May 1936. See his *Between Hitler & Mussolini* (1942).

[418] Otto von Habsburg (b. 1912): deposed and exiled to Switzerland 1919; exiled to Spain, Belgium and U.S.

to us & remember with gratitude our help (esp: financial) in their most difficult days. And they still welcome our disinterested guidance. This is v. well given by Selby, I sh^d say.

Walford S's opinion is that we sh^d work for the greatest possible <u>econ:</u> union of Ger & Austria, but delay any <u>political</u> forcing of the pace. It will probably come, but it w^d be magnificent if it c^d be delayed until Nazidom has ceased to control the destinies of the Reich.

I saw a big statue of Goethe in the Ring – fine proof of the common <u>culture</u> of the two races.

In the *Ballhausplatz* (For: Ministry) I saw the room in which the Congress of Vienna was held – a white handsome room with 5 doors, one being supposed to be for each of the G^t Powers! so that none had to go in after the other.

I also saw the spot where Dollfuss was shot & died. Above it is now a little shrine, with a beautiful bust in carved wood of a weeping woman (? the Virgin Mary). Curiously enough this was given to him a little while before his death.

PARIS *18 June*   Had a nice talk with Sir George Clerk this morn^g. He gave me 3 points –

Train public opinion

Keep in the closest possible touch with France

Make up our minds what we (G^t B^n) can do & what we cannot.

He agreed that, within the democratic system, we must approximate our methods as far as can properly be done to those of dictatorships, so as to be able to hold our own against them.

[LONDON] *22 June*   Was told today that Baldwin is almost dithering – lost his confidence after the Hoare-Laval episode, & has now lost it even in the H.of C, where he usually feels at home.

Leeper much perturbed at the attitude of *T.T.* over Germany, with which I also cannot fully agree – a matter of tone & attitude rather than policy.

It seems that Phipps sent home the memo: I sent him after my talk with Schacht, & marked it important. He also let the F.O. have my covering letter.

He said the real question we had to decide in regard to our policy towards Germany was – which is most dangerous, Ger lean or Germany fat? i.e. the Germany of today or the Germany of 1914.[419]

GENEVA *30 June*   Luncheon today with Walters[420] (of the Secretariat) Lumley[421] being the other guest. He is Parl^y Pte Sec^y to Eden, & we had an interesting discussion at the beginning of luncheon about the fatigues of the For: Sec^{y}ship. He says Eden hasn't had a proper rest for two years, & they are trying hard to let him have it. He quite agreed with me that to get a right perspective was made extremely difficult by

---

[419] On this date Reginald Leeper recorded this conversation:

'Mr. Kennedy of 'The Times' lunched with me to-day on his return from Germany. Amongst many interesting things he told me, he laid chief emphasis on the following.

He regarded it as vitally important that the Secretary of State should seize the first available opportunity to state in the House of Commons in very firm and unmistakable language that we regard it as essential that the German Government should return an answer to the questionnaire we had sent at the earliest possible date; that we have shown from the very beginning a desire to enter upon those wider negotiations which had been foreshadowed in Herr Hitler's declaration of March 7th; but that until the German Government responded to the attempts which we had made, it was impossible to make the progress so desired.

Mr. Kennedy emphasised that the Germans were simply delaying and prevaricating, and he suspected that in September, at the Nuremberg party Congress, Herr Hitler would make a flaming speech announcing that he had put forward proposals for a 25 years' peace last March, but that the Governments of Europe had shown little desire to respond and had ignored the wider aspects of those proposals.

Mr. Kennedy has returned from Berlin with an entirely different outlook from what he had before he went. He criticised strongly the 'soft' policy of 'The Times' towards Germany, saying that it has created an entirely wrong impression amongst the Germans who are living, breathing and thinking only of German aggrandisement and are laughing at us as mere weaklings. He urged me to put forward this view as strongly as I could as coming from him who had seen with his own eyes what was happening in Germany; that it was of the greatest importance that the British Government should tell the Germans off as firmly and as sharply as possible at the earliest possible opportunity.'

On 4 July Vansittart minuted on this memorandum: 'According to the Times this morning, it seems to be in contemplation that the Germans shd be invited to a conference whether they reply [to the questionnaire] or not. I do not yet know whether this is authentic or not, but if it is, it will not be possible to meet Mr. Kennedy's advice, which is otherwise very good.

I cannot let this paper pass without drawing attention to the completeness with which, out of the very mouth of the strongest of our adversaries & critics in the Times itself, it bears out the F.O. against the Times, which has been a minor national disaster for years in the hands of poor Mr. Dawson. This is the conclusion of a long chapter, & I register it without surprise; for in any divergence of views on foreign policies between the Times and the F.O., one might always lay 100 to 1 on the F.O. and make money.' Public Record Office, FO 371/19907 – C4593/4/18.

[420] Francis Paul Walters (1888–1976): secretariat of LoN 1919–39, Deputy Sec-Gen. 1939–40. See his *History of the League of Nations* (1960).

[421] Lawrence Roger Lumley (1896–1969): Con. MP Kingston-upon-Hull E. 1922–9, York 1931–7; Gov. of Bombay 1937–43; PUS India & Burma; suc. 11th Earl of Scarborough 1945; kt. 1948.

the fagging effect of democratic methods. Foresight & freshness are almost impossible, & they are <u>essential</u> for big policy.

I had a nice $\frac{1}{2}$ hr's talk with A. Eden at the Carlton Hotel here yesterday morn[g]. He <u>was</u> tired, & <u>passive</u>; v. sensible, & <u>listened</u>, but no bubble – nothing creative about him, poor man. How c[d] there be? Moreover, he tried to fit big issues into 5 min frames – it can't be done. Nearly at the end of our talk (which was almost entirely about Germany) he said 'What about the Colonies? I am thinking of saying something pretty firm against any cession. What do you think?' I said 'That's a pretty big question. My impression is that some day we sh[d] come to an arrangement with the Germans about it'. He said he rather thought that too; 'But not Tanganyika. That won't do. West Africa, perhaps'. 'A Cabinet matter' I said 'isn't it? Better leave it in suspense'.

He was v. nice, regretted the talk had bn so short, & said he hoped to get me to come & dine one night. At the beginning he said (after a few preliminaries) 'I want to ask your advice about what to do next – & this before Lumley, his P.P.S., & Michael Wright, of the F.O. I attach [a] memorandum of what passed between us. Lumley said, by the way, that the For: Aff: Com[tee] of the H.oC. was developing into a v. useful body. It focusses parl[iamentar]y opinion on for: affairs. It focussed meeting against Simon, for instance, & helped to cause the Cab: reshuffle that dropped him.

I hope however the For: Sec[y] will not be expected to appear before it. (I must try to ask AE about it).

29 June:　Memorandum to Editor – Confidential *I had a talk with Eden this morning.*[422] *He asked me my impressions of Germany, which I gave him. My views are familiar to you so I need not repeat them. German foreign policy, as I believe, can all be included in the phrase that Germany will take what she can get. She has in truth two foreign policies – one which is tactical & varies very slightly from time to time, according to the immediate object to be attained, and in which the word peace is very prominent; and the other is aggrandisement, by force if necessary. All young Germans are being brought up in the belief that they are destined to dominate Europe; at the same time propaganda in favour of obtaining colonial territory is increasing. Not merely are Germans not encouraged to favour a conciliatory policy with other countries but they are brought up to be anti-internationalist. There is an extraordinary contradiction, at the same time, between individual Germans and Germans in the mass, and no doubt during the Olympic Games the German*

---

[422] ALK noted in the margin: 'One thing AE said was – 'I don't know why the French didn't mobilize on March 7' – showing that it was not he who dissuaded them. Later, in pencil he added: 'But I think E's remark was to mislead lead me.'

athletes will be full of good-will towards their foreign colleagues, and quite genuinely so. Nevertheless the book which all young German sportsmen are expected to read, 'Deutschkunde' [German Character] which preaches very different doctrines, will be kept in the background.

Turning to the question of British policy, Eden also made me do most of the talking. I suggested that if the Germans don't quickly reply to the British questionnaire it might be as well to reassert the Treaty of Locarno, minus the Rhineland Clauses (which must be regularised). That treaty is the only one in the world which has been concluded entirely on the new model of the League Covenant, i.e. not an alliance with or against any nation but a balance of armed force against any signatory which becomes an aggressor. Germany must either resume her place in it, or remain outside. Why should we negotiate a new treaty at her bidding?

On the other hand, we should be ready to negotiate the Air Pact, which I believe Germany is ready to do – especially if she can begin by bi-lateral negotiations with us. I am sure that Ribbentrop would be delighted to make a beginning like this, and I don't see why it should not be done.

In regard to the League let us go easy. No true collective system is possible just now. Germany is regarded as a potential aggressor by her neighbours without exception, and it is therefore inevitable that they should incline to bind themselves together. But this destroys the possibility of erecting a real collective system. It is again a system of opposing camps. Let us therefore not get mixed up in it more than we can possibly help. All this talk of 'League reform' is premature. There must be a new balance in Central Europe first.

Germany will expand. It is almost certain in the course of the next few years. We cannot stop her. We must not help her. Therefore we must keep as clear as we decently can while maintaining the League in existence – chiefly as a consultative body – and hope that some day Germany may become a genuine member, if she has another régime &/or has attained most of her European objectives.

Of course Germany has quite reasonable arguments in favour of her expansionist tendencies. She has a most inhospitable climate and poor soil and a most vigorous people. Self-determination, if it could be fairly applied in Europe, would certainly result in an increase of the number of Germans within the Reich. A good strip of Czecho-Slovakia would join it & possibly all Austria. I got the impression in Vienna that at the moment a majority of Austrians probably hate Hitlerism too much to wish to join the Reich now. Cultural & religious antipathies seem to be at least as strong as racial sympathy – which however will not prevent a majority from siding with the strongest at a critical moment.

In any case I do not see that we can either encourage or stop Germany in Central Europe; and I believe her domination there will at least bring greater all round economic prosperity than anything else could. Eden said he personally agreed with this (the point about prosperity).

Referring to colonies, I found Eden inclined to make a firm statement against the idea of their cession, though apparently not unwilling to come to some arrangement with Germany later on.

1 July   van Masdijk (who has come here from Berlin) spoke to me about the Austrian Royal family tonight. He knows Archduke Otto v. well. He says he is v. nice, v. clever, v. quick & also v. democratic. He is most keen to return to Vienna. He w^d like to be a sort of overlord over Austria, Hungary & Czechoslovakia – a scheme to which Masdijk says Benesh told him he might agree! I sh^d suppose only in the last resort.

The Archducal family apparently have no money whatever, & feed poorly & dress miserably. But the ex-Empress has brought them up v. well all the same. Perhaps it is the extreme poverty which has made Otto so democratic.

Viennese shops have offered to dress the Archduchesses gratis – they now wear cotton stockings & old shoes – but ex-Emp^{ss} Zita refuses.

GENEVA *2 July*   Lunched with M^r & Mrs Steer[423] today. He was our Corrspdt in Addis Ab: all through the Abyss^n business. He says that a settlement c^d have bn reached <u>with the consent of the Emp:</u> on the basis of the 1906 Anglo-Franco-It:^{n} Agreement, before the war began. Barton,[424] our Min:, 3 times over got the offer of Lake Tana. We (three countries) c^d no doubt have brought in the L.o.N. for the purpose of administrative reforms (cp: China).

Lumley said the other day, by the way, that the Galla tribesmen now want to be a Protectorate under the Brit: Empire!

Wright told me this evening t[hat] Eden had not had a free hand in the Cabinet. If he had, he said, we sh^d not have got into the present frightful position. He appeared to mean that E. w^d have gone right through with sanctions – he didn't like the Hoare-Laval proposals & doesn't like taking off sanctions now.

His (Eden's) object now is not to give the Central Eur: States the impression that we are abandoning them, but at the same time not to tie ourselves up with them. Is greater frankness possible? One does not want to say to Germany 'Go ahead'.

I think a new man preferably Winston C. wl have to come along who is not so entangled with all these Europeans. Eden can try again later.

13 July   A conversatn with Leeper at the F.O. today showed me, I

---

[423] George Lowther Steer (1909–1944): Special War Corrspdt *The Times*, Addis Ababa 1935–6, Spain 1936–7; Special Africa Correspondent *Daily Telegraph* 1938–9. See his *Caesar in Abyssinia* (1936).

[424] Sydney Barton (1876–1946): Consul-Gen., Shanghai, 1922–9; Min. in Addis Ababa 1929–37; kt. 1926.

think, the ineptitude of Vansittart – in a moment of crisis & diff^y not seeing the big things but spinning webs & being over clever.

A Locarno meeting had bn proposed (by Eden, Delbos[425] & van Zeeland)[426] for the remaining Locarno Powers at Brussels – but Italy has jumped in to say she will not come unless Ger: is invited too. (So my idea of saying to Ger – here we are, 4 of us still in Locarno, will you come in or not, is no longer feasible).

So now Vansittart has proposed (& Leeper takes it up eagerly) that we sh^d propose) a 7-Power meeting – the 5 Locarno Powers plus Poland & Russia.

'What are they to discuss?' I asked. 'Peace' says Leeper!! 'They must have a definite agenda' I said. It w^d be much better either to propose the discussn of all the German Peace proposals, or else set about negotiating a new Locarno.

But Vansittart's idea is this – the rump of the old Locarno is best, because after March we had Staff discussns, which make it a real thing. So let's stick to that, even if it is only Eng, Fr & Belgium. If we want to discuss a new Locarno, Ger wl demand as a preliminary that the Staff discussns sh^d be abandoned.

I see that; but we w^d all the same do better in my opinion, now, to get on with the new Locarno & include the Air Pact.

28 July – Kennedy to Dawson:[427] *Grateful as I am to you for having made my conditions of work on The Times so easy, I do not feel justified in going on in the present way; and after a good deal of anxious thought I have come to the conclusion that I want to live in the country for a while and write a book.*

I really do not feel up to daily and still less to nightly journalism just now. [. . .]

Writing a book in the country would be exactly right; and moreover it is just the moment to think out quietly what has gone wrong with our diplomacy – for something has gone completely wrong, – and work it out in a small book. I believe it might be useful. And there are one or two things that badly need saying about Germany, and I quite see that they can be said better in a book than in The Times I believe, as you know that while Hitler talks of peace he is preparing war, and I simply must say so.

[425] Yvon Delbos (1885–1956): French politician & journalist; Ed. *Radical* 1914; Min. of Justice & V.P. 1936; For. Min. 1936–8; Min. of Educ. 1939–40.

[426] Paul van Zeeland (1893–1973): Belgian economist, financier & politician; PM 1935–7; escaped to England 1940; Commissaire aux Repatries 1944; For. Min. 1949–55. See his *A View of Europe* (1933).

[427] Copy deposited in *The Times* Archive.

I also do not believe in the possibility of rendering the League of Nations politically effective at the present time. [. . .][428]

2 Aug: Gen: Sir John du Cane[429] (here on a visit at Abbotswood) does not think the African territories are worth fighting about. A good opinion. He has sound judgment.

He lunched with LlGeorge the other day. He says he was in brilliant form, but gave an account of a recent meeting (of LlG) with Baldwin, acc: to which the same cannot be said of Stanley B.

5 Aug: I'm not sure that L$^{\underline{d}}$ Halifax isn't <u>too</u> leisurely, as acting For: Sec^y. It is so difficult to know how to strike the golden mean! Two instances – A week ago in the H. of Lords he made a speech on the reform of the L. of Nations, which was completely academic & showed no sense of the urgency of the problem, whether the League can be reformed or not –

Now, I find that though in charge at this critical time, since Parl^t has gone into recess, he proposed to direct affairs from Yorkshire. He has however returned today, owing to complicatns about Spain.

16 October   Yesterday at luncheon with the John Walters I met a nice Spaniard of the regular Spanish intellectual type (Prof: Castiliejos?)[430] & his English wife. They gave us many instances of the combination of honour & horror which is found among the Span: communists the Communist Party, by the way, now being the <u>Conservatives</u> of the Left, that is, the gov^t Parties!

Passengers from an international express for Barcelona had to be

[428] Kennedy felt he could not ask for another long sick leave and therefore must resign. He offered to take leave without pay but Dawson replied that resignation would be better; they agreed that he would stay on until the end of October. The two of them appear to have had an increasing difference of opinion on Germany since Kennedy's return. On 12 July Dawson noted in his diary that 'The papers were all agog with a sudden (but not wholly unexpected) German pact w. Austria. I went to see Leo Kennedy about it ... A good business for what it is worth & certainly to be welcomed in public as I had some difficulty in convincing L.K.' Dawson Mss. 40, f. 105; and, on 22 July: 'Kennedy wrote rather a feeble leader about the Locarno meeting tomorrow...' ibid., f. 110.

[429] John du Cane (1865–1947): army officer; Lt-Gen. 1919, Gen. 1926; Gen. Officer Commanding-in-Chief, British Army of the Rhine 1924–7; A.D.C. General to King Geo. V. 1926–30; Gov. & Cmdr-in-Chief, Malta 1927–31; retd. 1931.

[430] José Castilliejo (1877–1945): Spanish jurist; Prof. of Law, U. of Madrid 1920–37; mb Intl Commiss. on Intellectual Co-Operation, LoN 1932–38.

deposited some distance outside the town; but the Communists saw to it that they & their luggage were transported into the town; & the men who did it w^d not accept a peseta!

Again, a doctor who was performing an operation in a hospital, & had others to do, was told by the Com^sts that he must come with them, as they had to search his house. He said he c^d not leave his patients, but w^d give them his keys, as he had nothing to hide.

When he got back to his home later he found all his papers disturbed – & 10,000 pesetas gone!

So he complained to the chief of the Militia. The man took it seriously, & said he w^d look into the matter. Next day the doctor had to go to the hospital again, & while there got a message to say that his money had bn restored, & 4 militiamen left in charge of it. This point was a grim joke – the D^r found his money on his desk all right, & 4 dead militiamen, seated in chairs, round the desk! They were the thieves, & the chief had had them shot!

In a village near Barcelona the Syndicalists had decreed that women also were to be communized, & the Mayor was to have first choice. He chose the doctor's wife. She accordingly went at once to see the Mayor, & invited him to have supper with her & her husband. He went – & they shot him dead, & made off in their car. (This happened, M^rs C: said, actually before the Civil War began. It was the sort of thing that was going on). Spain is v. local & individualistic.

The pictures of the Prado have been placed in the basement.

Pray God this won't be happening all over Europe before long!

22 Oct: Yesterday had a talk with Cadogan at the F.O. He agreed that diplomacy has failed in Europe. There is nothing to be done except to try to keep war out of this part of Europe.

30 Oct: To-day, my last day's work on *T.T.*, I went round to the F.O. & saw Leeper, & he greeted me with the words 'Well, you had your swan-song this morning'! – referring to the leader I wrote last night – on Spain – & Göring! I brought in a special last para to answer Gen. Göring's outrageous speech of the evening before. It wanted answering at once. GD took some persuading, because the leader, like the debate in the House, was on Spain – & he didn't like the two mixed up. However in the end he let me have my way.[431]

The F.O. are delighted. It seems that this morning Leeper asked Eden if he'd seen the leader in *T.T.*, & Eden said 'Yes, grand'.

[431] 'No Intervention': 30 October 1936, p.17.

That is v. satisfactory.

Eden was himself debarred by the rules of procedure in the House from speaking of anything but Spain last night. That seems foolish formalism, & w^d not be understood in Nazi Germany. As Leeper quite agreed, it was advisable to answer Göring at once. If the Gov^t couldn't do it in the House, they ought to have the use of the wireless to do it. . ..

'No Intervention'

For the reason already given the FOREIGN SECRETARY's speech had necessarily to be confined to Spain; but it may be as well, lest silence should be misunderstood in Germany, to express at once and without ambiguity the impression which has been made on public opinion in this country by the tone of GENERAL GÖRING's speech delivered in Berlin on Wednesday night. The General is usually considered to be the most powerful member of the German Government after the Chancellor himself, so that his remarks can hardly be dismissed as unimportant; and it is not too much to say that his outburst about stolen colonies and stolen gold was so grossly misleading as to be calculated to increase the obstacles to any sort of agreement between his country and Great Britain. The figures by which he supported his arguments were also quite inaccurate, as a note by our Diplomatic Correspondent indicates this morning. GENERAL GÖRING said that the British mandated territories formerly in the possession of Germany were stolen from her after 'an unfortunate war.' But the war was neither begun nor desired by Great Britain, and the territories have not in fact been annexed. Germany would be ready, the General continued, to pay for her raw materials with gold; but the gold too had been 'stolen' from her. Yet, as everyone knows, the amount of money paid in reparations by Germany was actually less than the amount she borrowed from Great Britain and the United States. This thesis of the General will nevertheless, in the ordinary course of German propaganda, be repeated by every troop-leader and labour camp leader in Germany throughout the winter, and imbibed as uncritically and as enthusiastically as they were by the Berlin audience on Wednesday. That way lies conflict, and not agreement, between Germany and Great Britain. It was not a happy introduction for the new AMBASSADOR

5 Nov.[432]   Pleasant discussion with Walford Selby in the Marlborough this afternoon. He agrees with the view that dipl^y has failed & is at present helpless. It can only wait in the hope that our rearmament will

[432] Recorded in pencil.

modify the situation in such a way as to make a new opening for it.

He says Germany reminds him terribly of before the War. Again they are throwing out hints that they & we c^{d} so easily dominate the old world if we stood together. [...]

1937

At the beginning of the year Kennedy's book, Britain Faces Germany, *appeared*[433]. *The new, cynical opinion that he had formed of Hitler and the Nazis during his stay in Berlin now crystallized. Hitler had gone over to 'gangsterism' in foreign affairs; his demands had grown steadily greater.*[434] *'It is probably true to say that he will always demand as much as he dares to demand.'*[435] *Thus, it was essential that Britain rearm and prepare to face war. If the Nazi system was to be made a scourge to humanity Britain would have to oppose it as it had opposed Napoleon, until his power to do harm was destroyed.*

But there was still time and there was still hope. A 'bold but simple' approach to Germany on the part of Britain (disentangled from both France and the League of Nations) could produce results: 'unless our democracy has lost its capacity for robust policy, or Hitler's better nature has entirely atrophied, a settlement is possible.'[436] *The fact that Hitler had appointed Ribbentrop, 'his right-hand man' as ambassador to Britain demonstrated his desire for an understanding. But of what might such an understanding consist? Kennedy's discussions with Schacht and others had convinced him that Germany desired a foothold in the colonial world for reasons of national prestige and that this gave Britain the opportunity to make Germany a partner in Africa in return for a settlement of differences in Europe. 'I believe it would be an act of true wisdom to give all the scope to its energies that is possible. The economic organization of central Europe, for instance, will probably never be accomplished except under German direction. And I do not think we have the right to say that this people is not fit to colonize.'*[437]

4 May Kennedy to Dawson: *[...] I'm extremely glad to know that generally speaking you agree with my conclusions. In point of fact I altered the sentence about 'drift' in proof. [...] My point is that the process of indoctrination now going on in Germany is taking them steadily, day by day, further away from us. The poison of* Mein Kampf *is fowling the atmosphere. What Hitler teaches at home and professes abroad are two different things. That's why I feel no agreement is worth the paper it's written on unless Hitler alters the general tone of his internal propaganda. I know* Mein Kampf *is not directed against us, but its teaching, diffused in a thousand forms, is stoking up the Germans to 'the maximum of*

---

[433] Jonathan Cape, 1937.

[434] p. 132.

[435] p. 144.

[436] p. 174.

[437] p. 173.

aggressiveness' – one of its many phrases of that sort. If there is one point on which we (you and I) differ, I think it is Mein Kampf *– I regard it as the most important & most dangerous book in Europe.*

    P.S. I hope to heaven you're right about the salutary effect of the period of silence! It looks, seen from the outside, as if Germany were drawing steadily further away from us and nearer to Italy. And those two hooligan Powers both have imperial ambitions.

LASTINGHAM *18 May* Had a couple of interesting days in London 'twixt Appley & here, going to the house-warming of the enlarged German Embassy on Thurs: night, 13th, & meeting lots of folk there & at the Travellers', where I was staying.

The lavishness of the Ger Emb was positively barbaric! Viands & other edibles everywhere, more than one could eat standing up! – unless one were accustomed to handle them between finger & thumb – & opened champagne bottles on every mantelpiece. One c^d not count the rooms that had bn opened, for they were on two floors of three houses! Yet no big fine room among them (we did not go into the dining-room). Very obviously 3 houses run together. The Germans whom I met – & who were v. plentiful – asked the natural question, what are you doing now? to which I replied as blithely as possible 'I've just written a book which you won't altogether like – but which aims at a settlement between England & Germany.'

F[ie]ld Marshal von Blomberg was the German hero of the evening. Ogilvie-Forbes told McClure[438] & me at the Club that he has bn having private interviews with Cabinet Ministers, as well as his advertised talks with Baldwin, Eden etc., & has made an excellent impression. Am not surprised, for he is a regular charmer.

A criticism which Lothian made to me of Eden was that when he saw German representatives he always saw them in the company of colleagues or secretaries (of his own). I think however that Eden is quite right to do this.

Hitler was wise to send Fld Mar^l Blomberg. Göring had bn by way of coming for the Coronation, & feelers were put out. Naturally they produced a cold response, so Göring (so Ld Swinton[439] told me the

---

[438] William (Kidston) McClure (1877–1939): joined *The Times* 1913; Rome Corrspdt 1915–20; British Embassy Press Officer, Rome 1921–39; kt. 1934.

[439] Philip Cunliffe-Lister (1884–1972): Con. MP Hendon 1918–35; PPS Bd of Trade 1920–1; Sec. of Overseas Trade 1921–2; Pres. Bd of Trade 1922–4, 1924–9, 1931; Colonial Sec. 1931–5; Sec. for Air 1935–8; Min. Resident W. Africa 1942–4; Min. of Civil Aviation 1944–5; Chanc. Duchy of Lancaster 1951–2; Commonwealth Sec. 1952–5; changed surname from Lloyd-Greame 1924, cr. Viscount Swinton 1935, Earl 1955. See his *I Remember* (1948).

other day at Swinton) went about swearing that if he wasn't to go to London <u>nobody</u> would go – H: was clever enough & brave enough to snub him by sending v. Blomberg.

I had a long talk with Lothian at the Club. He has recently bn to Germany where he saw both H: & Göring. He gave a fearsome account of what is in their minds – <u>threatening</u> London with bombing (hoping a <u>veiled threat</u> w<u>d</u> be enough) & threatening openly all neighbouring countries with German minorities with destruction, unless they allowed the minorities to attach themselves to the Reich. H: however w<u>d</u> still like a peaceful settlement with Britain, but it must contain the cession of colonial territory – the mandatory basis <u>not</u> excluded. <u>That</u> is promising.

Lothian said that Italy was envisaged as an ally against Britain but thought that there was nothing signed betw[een] the two countries – & not even a fundamentally good feeling. Norton (Vansittart's Sec^y) agreed (at the Ger Emb reception) with Lothian's view that Mussolini is much more unbalanced than Hitler.

Lothian regards H: as a <u>prophet</u>, first & foremost.

He spoke to me at some length of the importance of the Anglo-Am: guarantee to France in the 1919 Peace Settlement. He made out it was an essential element in it; & the U.S.A's failure to uphold it destroyed the whole balance of the Treaty of Versailles.

There is no doubt much truth in that; but it is also clear that Lothian, who as Ph: Kerr had so much to do with the Peace Treaty, is now a little ashamed of his handiwork, & makes what excuses he can for it.

McClure, of our Embassy at Rome, told me in the Club that when Simon paid a visit to Rome (alone) Musso: produced a Disarmam^t plan which included the moderate & controlled re-armament of Germany. M^cC asked Simon whether it could not be taken as a basis of discussion for a Dis^t Convention. Simon turned to him & said sharply that he <u>could</u> not sanction any re rearmament of Germany in the face of British public opinion.

We both agreed that real statesmanship, in the old sense of the term, resides rather in the dictators than in the democracies. They formulate long-distance policies & carry them through, & can up to a point defy ignorant public opinion.

PARIS *22 June* One more talk at the Brit: Embassy, this time with Sir Eric Phipps & in a different room – looking over the forecourt instead of the garden. Phipps is obviously much more in his *assiette* here than in Berlin, & he devoted most of his talk to the uselessness of trying to come to terms with the scoundrels & adventurers who are now running Germany. He instanced the Concordat as a Treaty which they had signed entirely voluntarily & had since broken in every particular. He is, I think, an R.C. – in any case Lady Phipps is – & he seems to think it w^d be positively immoral to make any sort of arrangement with them. Nevertheless he admitted that he himself had urged a rather unwilling F.O. to negotiate the Naval Agreement. To that he added that they were not in a position to build more than 33 per cent of our strength, & w^d not be for a v. long time.

He descanted at length on the decision of Berlin to postpone Neurath's visit on a flimsy excuse. He said that N. didn't want to come, & when he felt he couldn't give a point-blank refusal to our invitat^n he tried to make the condition that Spain sh^d not be a subject of discussion. I wonder then what he did think he w^d talk about? Phipps said 'you must have something in your bag if you go on a diplomatic journey,' & he had for that reason deprecated the visit which Simon & Eden paid to Berlin in 1935. And afterwards S & E had written to him to tell him that after having paid the visit they concurred in his opinion.

I expressed nevertheless my view that it was urgently necessary to reach a durable peace with Germany. So said he was convinced that Ger w^d not make war about Colonies. He said too – & this I much regretted – that by 'running after Germany' we should lose our real friends. I answered strongly that in the first place to offer to negotiate was not to run after, & secondly that really I thought France believed in our good faith sufficiently to trust us to negotiate with Ger without being disloyal to her & to other democratic countries. By all means let France come in, if she is not going to hamper & impede us at every turn, as she used to before.

Phipps's view is that Ger is getting into straits, & that we can beat them, & sh^d beat them, financially & in rearmament. I don't mind if we can do this without goading them into a war of desperation. That is the danger.

So difficult do the Germans find it now to get raw materials for armaments that they are turning more & more to Russia, & calling off the anti-Bolsh: campaign – so Phipps says. Our re-arm^t needs are absorbing some of the sources elsewhere, from which they used to draw.

Altogether a lively & interesting talk, in which I flatter myself we showed how to differ without ill-feeling. I did a good deal of arguing (on the lines of my book) which I haven't recorded. I believe I made a little impression on him, tho' not enough to convert him, I fear.

23 June Just back from a talk in his morning office with a French deputy of the Right, M. Paul Reynaud.[440] Short, dapper, dry, clear-headed little man, dealing with telephone calls all the way through our talk, & then resuming the conversation with me exactly where we had left off, without any reminder on my part. The chief point I wanted to make to him was, that if we (G^i B^n) made a separate approach to Germany it would not imply disloyalty to France, to democratic institutions, or to the League, but only a determination to get negotiatns going & not to be hampered by anybody, as we had bn on earlier occasions. I instanced the naval agreement that had bn negotiated between us & Germany, & which afterwards had bn recognized as generally beneficial. He said that an effort to get an understanding with Ger certainly might be made, esp: with the condition of better control of internal propaganda; but he begged that French feelings sh^d be more carefully nursed than they were on the occasion of the naval negotiatns. I agreed, & said that I was sure if France cared to join in she w^d be most welcome, as long as we were not kept back.

LONDON *15 July* [...Eden] & Neville Chamberlain get on well together, & between them they sometimes take decisions on for: policy without consulting the rest of the Cabinet – one of the reasons being that Sam Hoare is always ready to oppose AE on every occasion. He is an arrant, knavish politician, from all I hear!

28 July[441] Yesterday by chance met A.E. just outside the Ambassadors' entrance to the F.O. He greeted me by saying he had got my book (*Britain Faces Germany*) to read during his holidays – it was one of the two 'work-books' he was taking with him, the other one being Seton

---

[440] Paul Reynaud (1878–1966): Deputy 1919–24, 1929–40; Min. of Finance 1930–1, 1938–40, of Colonies 1931–2, of Justice 1932, 1938; condemned to life imprisonment by Vichy govt 1941; liberated 1945. See his *In the Thick of the Fight 1930–45* (1955).

[441] Although the records are not clear, it appears that Kennedy returned briefly to work at *The Times* following the publication of his book. Dawson noted in his diary on 14 July that he had been in the office 'wrestling inter alia with the British proposals for continued non-intervention in Spain on wh. Leo Kennedy wrote his first leader in this month's "comeback"'. Dawson Mss. 41, f. 105, Bodleian Library; on 8 August that 'I extracted a couple of leaders fr. Kennedy while he was still with us.' ibid., f. 117; and, on 9 August that there was a crisis over the German threat to expel Ebbutt from Berlin: 'I got Kennedy, who was surprisingly meek about this threat, writing about it ...' ibid., f. 118.

Watson's[442] *'Britain in Europe'*. I said 'That's v. nice of you – but do make it a real holiday'. The words sprang from me because he looked so tired – his eyes rather hollowed & nervous looking, face rather drawn, but he was full of 'pep'. He answered 'Yes, I'm damned tired. One gets stale, & then details fidget one.' I said 'you're not that yet, but holidays are really frightfully important'. He indicated complete assent, & seemed pleased that I was so emphatic. There is still a lingering devotion to the Northcliffian folly that one must have full steam up every minute of the day & every day of the year. Northcliffe did it no doubt, but in the end he blew up. In modern conditions occasional complete relaxation seems to me to be more necessary than ever.

Mentioning this evening to Orme Sargent how tired AE looked yesterday, Orme said yes, he couldn't be otherwise after this summer, coronation & all. He amusingly compared post-war with pre-war diplomatic parties. Before the War they w$^{\underline{d}}$ consist largely of minor Royalties, who now did not exist; & they & their Royal spouses & daughters w$^{\underline{d}}$ talk of a thousand agreeable things & make the evening a refreshment. Now all the representatives of foreign countries are the Prime Ministers or Foreign Ministers, & instead of gay chatter with a charming princess AE finds himself buttonholed after dinner by the Foreign Minister of Esthonia, who notes his every word, & will no doubt compose a long despatch on the subject, to take its place in the archives of Talinn! (have I got the Capital right?)

11 Aug   Got a good 'Right & Left' in the way of meals yesterday! Dinner with Tony de Rothschild,[443] after a luncheon with Ewer,[444] of the *Daily Herald*, earlier in the day. Ewer is not a v. interesting specimen of 'Red,' for he is too moderate & sensible altogether! In fact we hardly seemed to disagree at all! A v. nice fellow.

Tony's was a bachelor party – Sir Auckland Geddes,[445] Arthur Villiers,[446] another man & myself. Excellent wines – incl: '96 Port – over which we discussed much politics, esp: Sir Auckland & I, stimulated

[442] Robert William Seton-Watson (1879–1951): historian & publicist; founded *New Europe* in 1916; Masaryk Prof. of Central European History, U. of London 1922–5; Prof. of Czechoslovak Studies, Oxford U. 1945–9. See his *Britain & the Dictators* (1938).

[443] Anthony Gustav de Rothschild (1887–1961): Chm., Industrial Dwellings Society; Pres., Norwood Home for Jewish Children.

[444] William Norman Ewer (1885–1977): joined *Daily Herald* 1912; For. Ed. 1919–49.

[445] Auckland Campbell Geddes (1879–1954): politician, diplomat & businessman; Unionist MP Basingstoke 1917–20; Amb. in Washington 1920–3; Chm. Rio Tinto Co. & Rhokana Corp.; kt. 1917; cr. Baron Geddes 1942.

[446] Arthur Villiers (1883–1969): merchant banker; Dir., Barings Bank 1919–54.

by Tony. Sir A: was rather sarcastic when I suggested that the U.S.A. might have stopped oil going to Italy at the beginning of the Abyssinian trouble, if all the rest of us had done it. Roosevelt might have recommended them not to send it, but Sir A said he'd like to know what could have stopped Standard Oil from getting it there.

Sir Auckland was v. interesting about Spain, where he now has business connexions. He thinks that Franco will win, but will never be master of Spain, for his authoritarian system does not really appeal to Spaniards. He also said that the Italians are now cordially disliked, & are not much good for fighting. They are used on the lines of communications. Franco is £90,000,000 in debt to Italy & Germany, & has no means of paying them in full, though he pays what he can as he goes along. He is of course v. patriotic, & will not willingly part with an inch of territory to any foreigner. He w<u>d</u> like to recover Gibraltar for Spain.

HAMBROOK *27 August*   During the last 2 days have had interesting talks with the B[isho]p of Chichester,[447] & with L<u>d</u> Howard of Penrith.[448] The Bishop talked chiefly about the Church in Germany, & then I talked about our relations with Ger. The Bp thinks there is little that is promising in matters of the Church, but he sees signs of misgiving in high places at the isolation of the German Church. As they pursue a deliberate policy of isolation in international affairs, I am surprised at this. The Bp had evidently read my book with thoroughness, & we discussed many of its points.

I discussed diplomatic points with Esmé Howard, esp: relating to the L. of Nations, about which I want to write my next book. Lady Isa joined in always in the general pol: discussion. She & he have heard from Limburg-Stirum[449] who is the new Dutch Minister, who has just

---

[447] George Kennedy A. Bell (1883–1958): Dean of Canterbury 1924–9; Bishop of Chichester 1929–58; Chm. Church of England Committee for non-Aryan Christians, 1937; Vice-Chm. Christian Council for Refugees, 1938; Chm. Central Committee of World Council of Churches 1948–54. See his *Christianity and World Order* (1940). On 8 November 1934 he sent a brief letter to Kennedy to thank him for his assistance on the German Church issue: 'I cannot tell you how much I appreciate what "The Times" has done, and how deeply indebted the whole Church must be, especially the German Evangelical Church, not only for the reports from Berlin and Munich but for the leading articles. The leading article in "The Times" of October 12th was an extraordinarily opportune article, and I am sure made a deep impression coming just at that moment.' The letter has been inserted in the Journal.

[448] Esme William Howard (1863–1939): entered dip. service 1885; mb. delegation to Paris Peace Conf. 1919; Amb. in Madrid 1919–24, in Washington 1924–30; kt. 1916; cr. Baron Howard of Penrith 1930. See his *Theatre of Life* (1935).

[449] Johan P. Limburg-Stirum (1873–1948): Min. in Berlin 1927–37, in London 1937–9. See his *Voor U persoonlijk* (1986).

been in Berlin for a long term, that there is a <u>great deal</u> of discontent there. Lady Isa also said that the Franco people in Spain were fundamentally <u>not</u> well-minded towards us. I expect she's right. She knows the Spaniards well.

4 Sept: An interesting talk on the overwork of Ministers, at the Huxleys this afternoon. Besides Michael H: there was Mason, who has bn one of the Pte Sec$^{\underline{ies}}$ at the F.O. for some time. I used to see him when he acted in that capacity to Simon.

He said that Sam Hoare was much the most able & efficient, that he had served, at the technique of getting through the work – orderliness & expeditiousness of mind.

On the subject of relieving Ministers of unessential decisions Michael has an interesting proposition. He says that in America an incoming Min: appoints several <u>political</u> under Sec$^{\underline{ies}}$, one for each dep^t of his Ministry – & they are <u>executive</u>. For every good Civil Servant there comes a point where he cannot take a final decision, not because he doesn't know enough, or doesn't know his own mind, but because he feels that the <u>political</u> consideratns still have to be taken into account – & can only be taken into account by somebody representative of the Government. In the British hierarchy that does not happen until the point reaches the Parl^y Under-Sec^y – & I imagine he does not feel inclined to decide v. much without reference to the Sec^y of State. By having 5 or 6 of his own henchmen in the Office, the Sec^y of State would feel that his political & governmental point of view was being properly represented, & w^d leave the decision to be taken by them & the Civil Servant. Only in case of disagreement between the two w^d he expect the point to come up for decision by himself.

There seems a good deal to be said for this idea, which apparently works well in the U.S.A.

GENEVA *26 September*   Last night the new Assembly Hall of the League building was filled for the first time – I put it this way, because the formal opening is to be next Tuesday, when the Assembly will meet there for the first time. Yesterday evening the Aga Khan, this year's President, gave a big reception – a concert followed by a dance. 3000 people were there, & the Aga K (so his Sec^y told Grande) had ordered 5000 bottles of champagne – & last night one got the impression that they w^d not last the evening!

Trolley-load after trolley-load was being run along the corridors to the *Salles des Pas Perdus*, & still struggling guests were going short! & I looked round the tables afterwards, & there was not a scrap of delicacies to be had – only bits of chicken, which the knifeless & forkless guests were looking askance at!

The Hall is magnificent – splendid but simple. Such good proportions that it doesn't look as big as it is. It holds 2000. Pictures have still to be painted for parts of the wall, so it will not look quite so severe when completed. The lighting, like the lighting of all the rooms in the Palace – the only Palace, I suppose, to be built since the War? – is first-rate – it gives a daylight effect. The majority of the lights are invisible to the eye. And the acoustics were perfect – a nice triumph for British technicians, for that was one of the tasks confided to us. A very good inaugural concert was performed by the Orchestre Romand of Geneva, & everybody commented how excellently every note was heard – a 'Kleine Nachtmusik' piece by Mozart was a good test. Beethoven's Overture made a grand opening, & Stravinsky's Finale an impressive end. [...]

27 September   I heard Lord Cranborne for the first time this afternoon – as the grandson of my hero L^d S:[alisbury] I was keen to know how he spoke. It was in the 'Com^{tee} of 23' on the Far East; & L^d C moved, at the beginning of the debate, a Resolut [io]n condemning the Japanese aerial bombardment of non-military objectives. He looked v. nervous & fidgety before getting up, but delivered his speech in a firm, strong, clear voice – he had the TS on the desk in front of him, & more or less read it. There was no touch of emotion in his voice or manner as he denounced the massacres – I suppose the Cecils don't <u>feel</u>. It w^d have added greatly to the effect of his speech if [he] had himself shown some feeling, I thought. Insted, [sic], he broke into a smile almost directly he had finished.

It seems to me a mistake of tactics that this Resolution sh^d be passed by this Advisory Com^{tee}. I saw Walters, of the Secretariat, this morn^g, & urged just such a Resolution upon him, but I hoped it w^d be the whole Assembly that w^d pass it in the most solemn & impressive manner possible. That is all the League can do, but it is something.

Sunday, 17 October   Kennedy to Dawson:[450] [...] *am so glad you published*

---

[450] *The Times* archive. On 11 October Dawson had written in response to a letter from Kennedy: 'I shall be very glad to publish your letter, though I do not quite agree with it. I am not convinced that we should settle everything by just handing back the German colonies. On the other hand I am all for letting them have colonies – particularly in West Africa – as part of a general settlement and to show them that we do not regard them in this respect as being outside the pale. I thought that Leo Amery's letter was characteristically deplorable. ... Meanwhile our South African brethren are behaving

my letter about Germany and Colonies. Of course I agree with you that 'we should not settle everything by just handing back the Germany colonies;' but neither is it feasible to carry out a general settlement all at once, and this would be the biggest single contribution towards a general settlement – or resettlement, I would prefer to call it, because I do think it is very important to do it as an admission that the 1920 settlement was one-sided, and to regard this as an agreed and final settlement – so far as anything can be final. Change seems to be a law of history! And what we have got to do is to make the method of change less ruinous than a war of bombing.

I also fully realize the difficulty of handing even back to the League loyal and trustful black men! Articles in W. African papers on my book have shewn me something of their feelings.

LONDON *19 October* Was much struck at a cinema last night by the cheers of the audience for the Duke of Windsor. It was during the ordinary news reel. Neville Chamb^ln^ & the Queen (Elizabeth) – the King did not appear – got cheers; but much the loudest broke out each time that Windsor appeared – it was during his tour of factories in Germany. I think he probably appeals particularly to cinema audiences, & to down-&-outs! He is after all the chief of the down-&-outs! [...]

20 October Had a talk with Conwell-Evans, who is in close touch with Ribbentrop. He says Rib is being much criticized in Ger now – the toughs don't like him – but that he still retains the full confidence of Hitler & is not likely to be recalled.

He told me that when v. Neurath was invited to come here by the Brit. Gov^t^ in the spring, Rib: asked Eden what they w^d^ be discussing? Would the discussion, in particular, include colonies? To which AE replied 'We will tell you what we think about that.' This seemed to Rib: to preclude fruitful negotiation.

with even more humbug than we; for they seem to be supporting the German claim to colonies in general, while at the same time making it perfectly clear that they are not prepared to part with German South West – or indeed with Tanganyika, which they seem to regard as a sort of outpost of the Union. [...]'

1938

18 February[451] – Kennedy to Dawson: *[...] It is rather satisfactory to win the applause of a League fan*[452] *because the main trend of the article was rather favourable to the anti-collectivists – no coercion, no obligatory action etc. each nation must judge for itself. I am glad to see that Halifax said quite definitely in the H of Lords yesterday that it is not desirable to say precisely beforehand what we shall do in every case and that we shall be free to act as we think right in the circumstances – at the same time every country should know that what we do will certainly be in the general framework of Article XVI and the rest of the Covenant. But I hope Halifax does not suppose – as he seemed to imply – that Machiavelli is a back number on the Continent! He errs very greatly if he does!*

With things brewing up – more to come in Austria? I can and will finish off things here at our Legation in Prague. Being however somewhat short of funds I could not do much unless I came to an arrangement by which T.T. would at any rate pay for a return ticket for me.

Perhaps you will let me know what you think of either of these proposals and I will make my arrangements accordingly.

24 February Kennedy to Dawson:[453] *[...] I agree with you that Chamberlain is right; at this moment only the most direct methods have the slightest chance of success. And Anthony Eden's past is so obviously an obstacle to better relations with Italy. I do hope however that he will soon be back, a fresher man, and be swiftly re absorbed into the Cabinet! My fear is that Germany, Japan and Italy by their own volition are already in conflict with us, and that even Chamberlain's effort is coming rather late.*

Your two leaders were superb!

26 February Kennedy to Dawson:[454] *If the Labour people formally bring up again the question of the Foreign Secretary being in the H. of Lords, I wonder if you would give me a chance of doing a leader on the subject? It is one I feel so*

[451] On 3 February 1938 Dawson had noted in his diary that he had had lunch with Kennedy, 'who wants to work again. I suggested a definitely limited period, but he will be v. valuable this summer. I think we are in complete agreement about Germany, the League etc.' Dawson Mss. 42, f. 25, Bodleian Library. Kennedy then travelled to central Europe on behalf of *The Times* and returned to work on the editorial staff on 1 April.

[452] Dawson had sent him a copy of a letter from Gilbert Murray.

[453] Letter deposited in *The Times* archive.

[454] Letter deposited in *The Times* archive.

strongly about. There are so many arguments in favour of it, quite apart from the personality of Halifax, and of the absurdity and unpartiotic-ness of arguing that the man who is best qualified for the post cannot be allowed to do it because he is a peer!

2 March Yesterday morning in London about 10.30 I was turning out of Duke Str[eet] into King Str, & nearly ran into the P.M. & Mͬͫ Chamberlain, who were making the corner in the opposite direction! I had not seen Mͬͫ Ch: for 2 or 3 yrs; & she proved herself the perfect P.M.'s wife! Stopped at once – v. kind of her – remembered my name – mentioned it to Nev: (with whom I shook hands) – & proceeded to make some nice remarks, invited me to come to her (summer) receptions after Easter at 10 Downing Str, had almost thought of asking Sylvia & me to help her to entertain at her pre-Easter receptions etc. v. polite & friendly. He meanwhile stood aside. Looked in good trim – fighting trim.

GERMANY *12 March* In train from Nüremberg towards Czechoslovak frontier[455] – Had a most interesting talk with an old man in a tram this mornͫͦ, returning from the immense new stadium which Hitler is building outside (south of) the town of Nuremberg. 'All this seems a little exaggerated to you' he said, realizing I was British. I said yes, so he said that it <u>had</u> seemed so 'to us older men' too; but now he thought 'we must live into the new times. New times have "new needs."' He went on to say that they must choose between the new regime & Bolshevism. I said in England we thought there was a middle course. He thought democracy was failing in England '*Schottland is noch gesund*' he said, but England is too industrial. (Like so many foreigners, he declared I did not look like an Englishman, so I gave the usual explanation, that I was Scottish).

His idea that no compromise was possible between extremes was typically continental.

Later he of his own accord mentioned the coup d'état which has happened overnight in Austria, no doubt at German instigation, which

---

[455] Which explains why this entry is in pencil.

has put Seyss-Inquart[456] in Schuschigg's [sic] place.[457] He said that S's idea of a plebiscite at 5 days' notice was an expedient of the Vatican. 'Well' I said 'most Austrians are Roman Catholics, aren't they'[?] 'Yes' he said 'so they are here in Bavaria. And many have relations in Austria. Now however a lot of them will renounce Rom: Cath'cism in Austria, as it will cease to be the State religion.' 'Anyhow' I said 'we don't like these sort of goings-on in England. *Immer die Macht, die Macht, die Macht*'. 'You don't understand' he said, 'you are out of it all'. With that I had to jump out & catch my train. His last remark was partly prompted, I think, by the fact that by that time other people were listening. At first he seemed to me to show little sympathy with Nazi ideas.

I could detect no trace of excitement in my hotel or in the streets over the coup in Vienna – although by the papers it seems that German troops have bn asked for by Seyss-Inquart & may now be marching across the frontier. A certain number of Swastika flags were flying, but Goebbels had bn making a speech the night before, so I don't know whether they were still flying in his honour or on account of the coup. (Those) Masts near the hotel were already being taken down. However from the train I can see some flying, in townlets, which can hardly be in honour of Goebbels. Many folk here, as my tram-friend observed, have friends & relatives in Austria.

The old man in the tram obviously thought that justice was on the side of Germany, & I've no doubt that practically all of them think the same. Last night two different papers had exactly the same headline about Sch's proposed plebiscite – 'Unbelievable Provocation;' & this morn[g] I read that Sch's statement that he was invited to make a change of gov[t] 'in ultimatum form' is a lie, & that he left office on account of inner political forces.

---

[456] Artur Seyss–Inquart (1892–1946): Austrian Nazi; State Counsellor 1937; Min. of Interior 1938; Chanc. of Austria 1938; Lt-Gen. *SS* 1938; Reich Gov. of Östmark 1938–9; during the war served as *Reichskommissar* for Netherlands; hanged at Nuremburg for crimes committed in Netherlands.

[457] On 9 March Schuschnigg had announced that on Sunday 13 March he would hold a plebiscite on the issue of Austrian independence. The question that was to be asked was: 'Are you for a free and German Austria, independent and socially harmonious, Christian and united; for peace and employment, and the equality of all who profess their faith in the people and the Fatherland?'. On 11 March Germany presented him with an ultimatum to postpone the plebiscite. When he agreed they demanded his resignation, with the provisions that Seyss-Inquart was to succeed him, that two-thirds of the cabinet seats be allotted to Nazis and that unrestricted freedom be given to the Nazi party in Austria. Schuschnigg, fearing invasion, announced his resignation via radio at 7:30 p.m.; by 8:15 Seyss-Inquart announced that he had invited Germany to assist him in preserving order in Austria and that German troops were crossing the frontier. By the next day one-thousand German troops occupied Vienna.

These people will never hear the R-C Austrian view, & in any case they believe what they want to believe.

In <u>Strassburg</u> I felt I was in a Germanic town. The local people without exception, that I overheard talking among themselves, spoke that Central European German that one hears in Switzerland – v. closely resembling Austrian German, Tyrolese, Bavarian etc. It is a rather passive amorphous element which from time to time has bn dominated from Vienna or Paris, & in the future will be dominated more & more from Berlin.

I found Strassburg (Fr: <u>Strasbourg</u>) v. interesting as the place where two civilizations meet & <u>merge</u>. I was not there long enough to judge adequately, but the town seemed to be a good combination of German solidity, orderliness & cleanliness with French freedom & go-as-you-please. Each side of the Rhine is a strip of flat country, & beyond the strips, hills. I sh^{d} say the real geographic & racial frontier was the row of hills to the <u>west</u> of Strassburg – in other words, Alsace (Elsass) is more Germanic than French, though I believe Lorraine is truly French.

The Rhine, though he's an immense fellow, is not the frontier nowadays that he once was.

In Strassburg I counted 10 <u>local</u> papers in the German language at a newspaper kioske. There is a special smell about German towns – the streets – & Strassburg smelt German.

PRAGUE *14 March*   Prague does <u>not</u> smell German. Czechs are a drab-looking folk. Sober & hardworking, Basil Newton says – but also musical & artistic. Bourgeois.

Yesterday we had a long drive to Bohemia – the German part of the country, I mean. Beautiful, & very invigorating air, esp: at Marienbad & Carlsbad. We went past Lavy to C-bad, Marienbad & back by Pilsen – a rather gloomy looking place, where no doubt they need good beer to cheer them up. German villages better built & better kept than the Czech. But the <u>Bavarian</u> best of all – those that I passed in the train on the way here.

Basil Newton told me that on being appointed H.B.M's Minister here ($1\frac{1}{2}$ year ago) he went twice to the F.O. in order to get general instructns on the Brit: attitude towards Czechoslovak[ia]. Twice he was to see Eden, & was twice put off. He went round the Office trying to find somebody who could give him a line. Finally he got Orme Sargent to dictate to him a policy while he sat there!

This was kept back by S, to be endorsed by the For: Sec^{y}; & eventually Basil N: got an appointment with Eden which E. was able to keep. When B.N. went in, Eden had a copy of BN's instructns, & went through them with BN – but was evidently reading them for the first time. In other words, Orme Sargent's memorandum had not penetrated to him, or at least he had not had time to read it before.

Too rushed, no doubt.

BN also told me that Kirkpatrick,[458] who went to Berchtesgaden with L$\underline{^d}$ Halifax, said that L$\underline{^d}$ H: showed himself very realist – did not pretend to believe in collective security etc And two days ago, when Ribbentrop went to say goodbye to him – after the coup in Austria – H: spoke v. straight to Rib: It seems that Rib: had the impertinence to compare what Ger: has just done in Austria to what we had bn doing in Ireland. L$\underline{^d}$ H: said the comparison did not hold; it was rather as if we had tried to dictate to Belgium what Prime Minister they were to have. (Our conduct in the past to Ireland might, I think, justifiably be made a subject of comparison. L$\underline{^d}$ H: might have said that now we were negotiating freely on terms of equality with de Valera, & that we scrupulously kept the Treaty we had signed with the Irish Free State some time ago. Perhaps Lord H: did say this).

BN complains that the Brit. Gov^t, by 'taking note', formally, of Ger assurances, merely irritates the Germans & does no good. Göring has just announced that the Ger: troops in Austria are only there for the purpose of supervising the plébiscite & will be withdrawn when conditions are again stable. The Brit. Gov^t has instructed Sir Neville Henderson,[459] our Ambssdr in Berlin, to inform the Ger Gov^t that we take note of these assurances. BN says if he had bn consulted he w^d have suggested that this was a useless démarche. However the matter has (naturally) not bn referred to him.

15 March (Confidential)   BN showed me his despatch to HMG summing up his impressions after the German coup in Austria. He is against making any sort of promise of help to Czechoslovkia. He regards this place as unworkable. Its strategic position is hopeless now that the Austrian & German armies will form one. He thinks it will be much best if these people make the best terms with Ger that they can, & as soon as they can.

---

[458] Ivone Augustine Kirkpatrick (1897–1964): entered for. service 1919; 1st Sec. in Rome 1930–2; Chargé d'Affaires at Holy See 1932–3; 1st Sec. in Berlin 1933–8; Dir. For. Div. Ministry of Info. 1940; For. Adviser to BBC 1941, Controller of European Services 1941–4; Asst. U-Sec. FO 1945–8, Deputy U-Sec. 1948–9; PUS (German Section) 1949; UK High Commissioner for Germany 1950–3; PUS FO 1953–7; kt. 1948. See his *The Inner Circle* (1959).

[459] Nevile Meyrick Henderson (1882–1942): entered for. service 1905; Min. in Paris 1928–9, in Belgrade 1929–35; Amb. in Buenos Aires 1935–7, in Berlin 1937–9; kt. 1932. See his *Failure of a Mission* (1940).

17 March   Had a most interesting & really moving talk with Pres. Benesh in the Hradcany Castle yesterday afternoon. He is of course intensely desirous of getting some form of guarantee from G^t Britain for the independence of Czechoslovakia. He did not <u>beg</u> for it, or make any appeal to sentiment; but gave reasons on general grounds why it w^d be in our interest, in the long run, to give him one. He was particularly favourable to the idea of an alliance, which I said, at the beginning of our talk, w^d be the only way by which we could be definitely bound. This is all set out in the report on our conversation which I have dictated this morning, so I won't go over the ground again. Dr Benesh received me in his study in the magnificent Hradcany Castle, & then took me across to his library – a fine big room – to have tea. We spoke for 2 hours. He looked rather worn, as well he may be, poor man, in these days of ceaseless anxiety, & did not talk with the same vivacity as he used to at Geneva. Still, he brought out his arguments all right, & v. clearly. He was v. friendly, told me that I should come to Prague again & that it w^d always be a pleasure to him to receive me. He sent cordial messages to Steed, <u>&</u> Violet, also Harold Nicolson & Cadogan – whom I happened to mention, & whom we both used to see a lot at Geneva. I thought he seemed to cling to his English acquaintances, & to the memories of Geneva, when he played a leading rôle in what seemed to be a going concern.

He is clearly & naturally extremely anxious, & his face fell every time that I advanced an argument showing the difficulties of our giving a guarantee to Czechoslovakia. Pathetically, the one thing he wants is a British guarantee. I think the way we came in on Belgium's behalf in 1914 has made a profound & lasting impression on the Continent.

16 March   Memorandum on Conversation with Beneš:[460] *President Beneš began the conversation by questioning me on the British interpretation of Article 16 of the Covenant. I reminded him that the Prime-Minister had recently emphatically declared that he did not suggest that any article 'even Article 16' should be taken out of the Covenant, and said that I thought there was a general desire in England that it should stand in principle. This did not mean however that it would be regarded as either automatic or compulsory in its operation. We know that several other States (such as the Scandinavian) had said that they did not feel bound to join in Sanctions against any aggressor, and I thought that public opinion in England was coming to feel that its value now was that it gave us at least the full right, if not the duty, to take action against an aggressor; but that each individual State must decide for itself whether it would take action. This should still be a formidable deterrent to a potential aggressor, especially if the action contemplated by other States*

---

[460] A typewritten copy inserted in the Journal.

were air action. President Beneš said emphatically that he accepted and agreed with this interpretation of Article 16. Turning to the particular case of Czecho-Slovakia, I said that I regretted that the French Government was apparently pressing the British Government for an answer, yes or no, whether we would give definite guarantees beforehand to act on Article 16 to the Czecho-Slovak Government, or join with France if she assisted Czecho-Slovakia. I said that I thought it was next to impossible for the British Government to say yes or no. For one thing, being a parliamentary state, it would be impossible for any Foreign Secretary to bind a future Parliament to take action in a more or less unknown contingency. Parliament might refuse to vote the necessary supplies. On the other hand it seemed undesirable to say no definitely now, which would obviously only be an encouragement to Germany or any other possible aggressor. I said that of course we were bound to action in the case of an invasion of France, as we had what amounted to a Treaty of Alliance with France. A Treaty of Alliance was itself approved by Parliament and must of course be regarded as definitely binding for us.

I then asked President Beneš if he could give any reasons why he thought it was to the interest of the British Empire to give a guarantee to Czecho-Slovakia. He answered this question at some length which I may summarise as follows:

He began by dwelling upon the considerable material resources and industrial equipment of Czecho-Slovakia, the value of the Skoda Works and the geographical position. Czecho-Slovakia, being a salient into the heart of the new German Reich, would make an immense difference to Germany whether it was against her or in her power. Czecho-Slovakia was indeed a key position. It was a European fortress which, if it fell, would involve the fall of other countries; and once they had entered the German orbit they might be forced to take sides against us ultimately if another world war broke out.

Dr. Beneš then said that he had no doubt that ultimately the British and the French Empires – he was very emphatic that the French possessions in Africa were coveted by Germany – were on the list of Germany's ambitions. Apart from the material aims of Germany the President suggested that there was already an absolute conflict of methods and that it might be considered a cause worth making a stand for to prevent further triumphs from being won by the method of intimidation and violence. Dr. Benes used the striking phrase 'Czecho-Slovakia is only a little accident in the whole terrible world affair'. The whole gist of his argument was that we should find that we certainly had to make a stand against Germany some time, and he suggested that the sooner we made it the better. He believes that the economic and financial position of Germany is still weak; but if they succeed in dominating the resources of Central Europe their position will be immeasurably stronger.

I told him that these arguments seemed to me to be really very impressive, but that I felt that British public opinion would hardly accept the conclusion which they led to at once. We should be better prepared to give an unconditional guarantee if the Czech Government had first made a resolute attempt to come to an agreement direct with the German Government. Dr. Beneš said tersely 'agreement means surrender'. I said that this seems to me rather a startling view; and he modified it to the extent of saying that if he were joined in his negotiations by Great Britain and France it might be different. He might then reach a real agreement with Germany. He recalled at some length the method by which he had negotiated an Arbitration Treaty with Germany at Locarno with the full sanction and endorsement of Sir Austen Chamberlain & Monsieur Briand. He said it was the only way to negotiate with Germany. He could not trust her sufficiently to negotiate simply tête à tête. Her signature would mean very little. Germany could so easily raise some point of interpretation afterwards and charge Czecho-Slovakia with having broken the agreement; and she (Germany) would be her own judge whether the agreement had been broken or not. She would then act swiftly and without any warning, as she had in the case of Austria.

There was a definite hope, Dr. Beneš thought, if we could hold out against Germany for a few years longer without allowing her to increase her resources in Central Europe, that something like an internal financial and economic collapse might take place. He was absolutely certain, he said emphatically, that Germany's internal economic situation was steadily deteriorating. This was one more reason in his opinion for Great Britain to make a firm stand now. He thought Germany was not fit for a major war, and Hitler knew it; and therefore if we said we would come in he would not at this date commit any action which would bring us in. He returned again to the question of an alliance with us, which obviously he would very much desire. He said we had one with Belgium which was quite one-sided; so far as he was concerned he would certainly wish to make it reciprocal that is to say that he would feel his country bound to take part if it should be Great Britain which was attacked in the first place. Dr. Benes seemed to think that this year 1938 was likely to be the most critical post-war year. He considered that German nationalism was in an exalted state. 'Nazüsm is the last degree of German nationalism. After this, collapse.'

Speaking of the Sudeten Deutsche inside Czecho-Slovakia he dwelled upon the great freedom which was allowed to them – they are at this moment holding many meetings and writing many articles favourable to what Germany has done in Austria and entirely contrary to the feelings and policy of the Prague Government – and he said he could not possibly admit the right of Germany to protect them. It would give Germany the right of continual interference. He admitted the right of interference from outside countries through the League of Nations; and of course if Germany were in the League she would share that right with everybody else. He was prepared however on his own to do even more that [sic – than] had already been done for the Sudeten Deutsche.

Turning for a moment to the Berlin-Rome axis he said that a firm agreement between Italy and Great Britain might have a very far reaching effect. He thought that in the long run the arrival of Germany on Brenner would inevitably harm Italo-German relations; and if Italy took her place in the Anglo-French orbit it would also very probably bring in Jugoslavia, Hungary and other countries. He thought that the first reaction in Hungary to the Vienna coup was not at all favourable to

Germany; and he seemed to think that the Austrians themselves might a little later become distinctly troublesome to the Nazi Reich.

One of the things that President Beneš said was 'unlike Austria we will fight. We shall be massacred [sic] *but we will fight.' Although he never once as it were begged for British support, I could see that his whole mind was bent on getting some sort of guarantee from Great Britain. The idea of an alliance seemed particularly to appeal to him – and every time I said something implying that such a guarantee was improbable his face fell. He seemed in an anxious but nevertheless courageous frame of mind.*

PRAGUE *18 March*   Kennedy to Dawson:[461] *[...] For the sake of brevity my part of the conversation [with Beneš] is of course left out. We spoke for 2 hours, and I put to him all the arguments why Great Britain should not give any specific guarantee in this part of the world.*

On the other hand, as you know, I am convinced that Nazi Germany has a long-term programme which she is determined to carry out – however peaceful her declarations are between the bursts of action – and that she means both to break up this country and to challenge the British Empire. She is exaltée; and we are strong enough to meet her. The only question therefore for us, as I see it, is this – at what point are we going to cry 'halt'? Is Czecho-Slovakia good ground on which to make our stand? I am staying on here over the weekend and pursuing my enquiries into the Sudetendeutsche question – there is really no problem about it. They are certainly one of the best treated minorities in Europe, now.

Confidential Memorandum on Conversation with Benesh:[462] *After a few preliminary remarks about the Council of the League, as to which M. Benesh admitted that he now regretted its enlargement last year from 10 to 14 members, I drew the conversation to the Rothermere[463] campaign in England & U.S.A. in favour of a rectification of the frontiers of Hungary.*

M. Benesh said that it was doing a lot of harm, that it was embittering the relations of Czecho-Slovakia and Hungary, and that it was creating a certain amount of anti-British feeling in Czecho-Slovakia; but he admitted that there was actually a certain amount of justice in the Hungarian claim. He had not asked for the whole extent of the present frontiers at the Peace Conference.

But first of all, he said, remember that if there are 600,000 Hungarians in Czecho-Slovakia, there are over 200,000 Czechs & Slovaks in Hungary; also that the Hungarians in Czecho-Slovakia enjoy a social and political freedom which

[461] Letter deposited in *The Times* archive. Kennedy told Dawson that he has passed on 'the gist' of his conversation with Beneš.

[462] Deposited in *The Times* archive.

[463] Harold Sydney Harmsworth (1868–1940): proprietor, *Daily Mirror* 1914–31, *Daily Mail & Evening News* 1922–40; Sec. for Air 1917–18; cr. Baron Rothermere 1914, Viscount 1919.

neither Hungarians nor Czecho-Slovaks enjoy in Hungary; and the big estates have been divided up in Czecho-Slovakia but not in Hungary. The absolute system of rule in Hungary itself made a sharp antagonism between the two countries.

The first thing to bring about was a real spirit of conciliation between the two countries, so that negotiations on any subject could be entered into with some prospect of success. That was the first step, & Rothermere was making it more difficult.

There must be a sort of Central European Locarno. I said that it was clear that Great Britain could not be a guarantor; would he expect other nations to guarantee the pact? He said that he would not expect any definite obligation to intervene actively, but he would like a special and local affirmation by the Great Powers of the obligations that they had already undertaken in the Covenant of the League.

I said that this would really amount to a local application of the Protocol. He thereupon explained what he understood by the Protocol. He saw that there must be changes in Europe; he was absolutely against 'petrification', as he called it. He had always insisted – in spite of the protests of Poland and Rumania – that the Protocol must in no way be allowed to invalidate article 19 of the Covenant (which allows re-consideration of Treaties that have become obsolete). He said, speaking of the Boundary between Hungary & Czecho-Slovakia, 'I am convinced that a rectification of frontiers must come'; and added 'I am speaking to you now most confidentially and not as the Foreign Minister of the Czecho-Slovak Republic'. He said he could not publicly express these sentiments at present, but in a year or two it might be possible, if the agitation caused by the Rothermere articles had died down. He said that President Masaryk[464] *had often spoken about it to him.*

Benesh actually had his plan ready for the rectification of the frontier. The present boundary, he said, had been drawn so as to leave an important lateral railway on the Czecho-Slovak side. He would say to the Hungarians, when the time came, now you must build me another railway (i.e. pay for it) within the ethnic frontiers of Czecho-Slovakia, and then we will hand over to you that part of the country with the old railway which is inhabited by Hungarians. He also explained that there were a number of other small concessions which he would ask of Hungary, not that they were of great value, but because they would make the whole transaction appear to be a bargain, and thus be more acceptable to his own Parliament. Czecho-Slovak public opinion would, he felt sure, comprehend. England could help more than France. France was known to be biassed in favour of the Little Entente, but England could by diplomatic action in Buda-Pesth and in Prague push both States towards reconciliation.

The first thing was to create an atmosphere in which pacific changes would become possible. The position inside Hungary was strained, he thought, and the Hungarian government itself would recognise the wisdom of tranquillising public opinion.

---

[464] Tomas Garrigue Masaryk (1850–1937): Czechoslovak philosopher & politician; first Pres. of Czechoslovak Republic 1920–35.

18 March It seems that on the occasion of Hitler's famous interview with Schuschnigg in Feb[ruar]^y H: raved at Sch: for the whole day. He seems to have the power to be impassively calm or furiously angry at will.

19 March Yesterday I went to the headquarters in Prague of the *Sudetendeutsche*, to see one of their leaders (Sebekowsky). I was favourably impressed by the atmosphere of mingled informality & efficiency that pervaded the place. Hatless young men in pull-overs, but alert & obliging in a manly way.

One of them took me along to a room, where immediately afterwards Sebekowsky appeared. S: was attired in an ordinary new suit, possibly for my benefit. He was v. direct, answered all my questions simply, & made out a v. good case for the union of the *Sudetendeutsche* with the Reich.

BN was good enough to say yesterday that the account I had given him of my talk with Benesh – which he had already communicated to the F.O. – was v. useful to him yesterday aftern^n when he himself was rec^d by Pres: B.[465] He says the Pres: was more tired than he has ever known him. I'm afraid his anxieties are overwhelming. I do not foresee a long existence for his country. If he w^d compromise by letting the Sudetens join Germany, we (G^t B^n) might give him his guarantee, & Czechoslovakia w^d survive. But I don't believe he'll compromise.

Ward Price came here to luncheon yest^{day} (at the Legation) & one of the other guests was P^{ce} Lobkowitch[466] – the first a Nazi heart & soul, the second violently anti-Nazi. There was a battle royal! Both quite uncompromising & rich in overstatement. Ward Price's words most ominous, for he has arrived here straight from the Hitler entourage in Vienna. He accused Czechoslovakia of being about to plunge civilization into war because she was so obstinate about the *Sudetendeutsche*! Pretty stiff!

APPLEY *28 March* When I was in PARIS 3 days ago Sir E. Phipps gave me an illustration of the complete ascendancy of Hitler over his advisers. In Berlin (when Sir E: was ambassador there) he had to make a rather disagreeable communication to the Ger Gov^t He made it to v. Neurath,

[465] Newton reported the conversation to the Foreign Office in tel. No. 33 on 17 March 1938.

[466] Maximilian Lobkowitch (1888–1967): Czech diplomat; entered dip. service 1920; Sec. in London 1920–6; retd 1926; exiled to Britain 1939; Amb. in London 1940–7; exiled to U.S. 1947–67.

who took it quite calmly, but said he w^d like to take it in to Hitler, & would the Ambassador come in with him. So they went in together to the Führer; & when the Brit: Gov^t's message was conveyed to him, he raged. Whereupon v. Neurath raged <u>even more bitterly</u>! – & to end up with, when, later in the day, the Ambassador had to see v. N: again just to wind the incident up, v. N: was once more perfectly urbane & easy to deal with!

March 24 'Journey through Austria:'[467] Having had occasion to pass through Central Europe during the past week, a few travel notes, filled out in the freedom of a French train, may help to convey an impression of Austria ten days after Hitler's hammerstroke.

Vienna still looks like an occupied city, with soldiers and armed police in every thoroughfare, military motor cars carrying troops hither and thither, orderlies speeding along on motorcycles, and sentries standing armed and steelhelmeted outside the principal hotels. This was also the case at Innsbruck, where I spent one night, and where my brown shoes, when I put them outside my room to be cleaned, looked very modest and civilian in the long row of Wellingtons and bespurred elastic-sided boots of the German military and police officers who were the chief occupants of my hotel. And all the way between the capital and frontier one noticed mounted pickets, military camps and mechanized transport parks. But I was told (and I sought my information as far as I could from independent sources) that these German officers and soldiers are good ambassadors of their country. They certainly seemed to be enjoying themselves and to be perfectly friendly with the people, especially in the country districts. They have after all been taken from their garrison towns on business that is something between a military expedition and a picnic. Much of it is just a joy-ride for them, and in Vienna they are being sent round in motorbuses sight-seeing by companies. In the Tyrol I was told that they were getting much more fresh meat and butter than they had eaten for a long time. Nor did I see or hear of arrogance in their behaviour.

The dirty work, and there is plenty of it, is being done by the S.A. and S.S. men, whose duty it is respectively to track down Jews and political 'undesirables.' As an ordinary traveller one had little direct evidence of their work. Getting news on these matters in Vienna just now is rather like trying to describe scenery from inside a tunnel. But one heard horrible stories of the doings of these men from sources that were trustworthy. Certainly it is not believed that all the reported

---

[467] Typescript inserted in the journal, with a note that it was written in the train and that *The Times* had declined to publish it.

suicides are really cases of suicide. Political refugees and prisoners are often (there is every reason to believe) just shot down. They include some of the most honourable and patriotic men in Austria, whose convictions led them to back Schuschnigg and independence. I was told there was a list of just under 900 such, who had taken a more or less prominent part in suppressing the Nazi movement in the days of Dollfuss and Schuschnigg. They were marked men from the day Hitler crossed the frontier. For them there is no mercy. A foreigner who opposes Nazi-ism may be admitted to be an honourable opponent, but a man of German blood who opposes it is regarded as a renegade, a subnormal, a traitor to be destroyed like a rat – kept in a cage of just shot down. The hooliganism is, now at any rate, strictly organized and controlled. It is not promiscuous, and the ordinary citizen, provided he is not a Jew – they have ceased to be citizens – may go about his work as usual. And so may foreigners. I was provided by a thoughtful British Consul with a toy Union Jack which I sported in my buttonhole. I recommend this practice to travellers in Austria just now, but I ought to say that I was there for several days before I wore my proud emblem and was never once molested or inconvenienced in any way.

While Himmler's Black Guards (S.S.) are tracking down the politicians, the Stormtroopers (S.A.) are ruining the Jews. The usual practice seems to be simply to reduce them to penury and then to prevent them from earning any money – and they are usually not allowed to leave the country, even if they had the means. The position of these poor people is pitiable to the last degree, for the Stormtroopers seem effectively to have banished all feelings of mercy from their make-up and to be totally unmoved by the sight of physical agony or mental anguish. They carry out their orders with the impassive efficiency that must have been the chief qualification of torturers in the Middle Ages. Like most Germans, they have placed their consciences unreservedly in the hands of Hitler. I heard (from an entirely sure source) of Jews still at large who had implored their doctors to give them an overdose of morphia. It is of course a quite usual thing now for the partners in a mixed marriage to divorce and live apart if they have anything to lose, for to be married to a Jew or a Jewess is a disqualification for a job or even a pension. Other victims of the terror are monarchists. They share with Jews and Schuschnigg's men the nerve-racking experience of trying to settle down at night with the fear that when they are asleep they may be seized and carried off to prison or a concentration camp.

But though actual terrorization is selective there is a process of intimidation which is more subtle and more widespread. With a unanimity that cannot possibly be spontaneous every man, woman and child that one saw seemed to be wearing a swastika badge, and I gathered that practically everyone intends to vote in favour of Hitler and union in the plebiscite next month, because the mere fact of not voting would become known and would endanger a man's livelihood. I heard of one definite case of a supporter of Schuschnigg who was not on any account going to fail to vote for Hitler because he thought that if he merely abstained he might lose his pension. These considerations make it extremely difficult to judge how far the population is really behind the Anschluss. The whole country is smothered in swastikas. 'Aryan' shops everywhere show Nazi emblems and portraits of Party leaders. Copies of *Mein Kampf* crowd the windows of every bookshop. The Jews have been put out of business, and there is Reich German custom to be attracted. It is of course quite impossible to engage casual acquaintances in conversation on their political views; but from a few friends who were willing to talk I gathered that in all probability Austrians felt a mixture of sadness and relief – sadness because they are a proud people, and from being imperial they have now become subordinate; and relief because they are also rather a helpless people, and now at least they know where they are and that they have a powerful defender.

Moreover their original impulse after the War was certainly to join Germany; and to-day Hitler, besides making his impressive display of might, is also keeping well in the forefront the Socialist side of National Socialism. His lieutenants are, for the present at any rate, positively cultivating the Socialists of Vienna (who were of course the enemies of the Dolfuss [sic] régime). Soup-kitchens go round the poorer parts daily, and military motor lorries unload stores. In addition, the '*Kraft durch Freude*' movement has been started at once, and joy-riding parties are already leaving Austria for all parts of Germany. The Austrian troops must also be enjoying their popular parades in German town; so Hitler has at least brought immediate material satisfaction to a large proportion of the population, and they are all led to believe, with every prospect of justification, that industry will revive and unemployment disappear.

The whole of the Press, local as well as metropolitan, has been standardised with the most extraordinary rapidity and thoroughness. I made a point of reading as many provincial papers as possible. In hardly a single one did I find a piece of objective news, much less comment. They spoke at length of Goebbels' last speech of Bürckel's[468] latest ordinances; and devoted columns to the departure of a batch of workers on a '*Kraft durch Freude*' outing (with due tributes to the local brass band, which had learnt the Horst Wessel tune so quickly and so

---

[468] Josef Bürckel (1895–1944): Nazi politician; Min. to the Saar 1934; Commissioner for the Saar 1935–8; *Gauleiter*, Austria 1938–9, Moravia 1939–40, Lorraine 1940–1, *Westmark* 1941–5.

well). Even in the more important newspapers world events were only very briefly mentioned, and even then, whenever possible, were brought into relation with Nazi *Weltanschauung*. It must be almost literally true to say that every Austrian newspaper has become a propaganda sheet. I went to a cinema in Vienna and the whole of the news reel was taken up – ten minutes of it – with scenes of Hitler's entry into Austria and Vienna. During that time two Black Guards sat near the back of the stalls, presumably to see how the audience behaved; for they strode out as soon as the news pictures were over. (In two theatres which I entered Black Guards also stood at the back of the stalls). As it happened the audience at the cinema, which was a small one, gave no sign of approval or disapproval.

The whole Austro-German mind is being closed to outside influences. In another town I went to see a performance of one of Lehar's musical comedies. Even that opportunity was not missed to impregnate the right ideas. The programme, for which I paid 2d., contained an article headed 'Richard Wagner: Was is Deutsch' – apparently an extract from something that the great composer had written on the German mentality. In any case we were told in our programmes that the 'German people are those Germanic tribes who cherish their language and their customs on their native soil.' They may occasionally wander abroad and hear different ideas, but they derive their real mind from the 'inexhaustible variations of the old god-myths.' Much of the article was unintelligible to me; but the general gist of it was that Germans are a chosen people who need only to rely upon their pristine virtue and prowess.

If German influence is going to extend much further, it seems probable that the whole mind of Central Europe will be codified according to the dreadful gospel of Rosenberg, and that the ideas which we cherish in England will gradually cease to penetrate there at all. It is the present education of young Germans that is going to make understanding between our two countries so difficult; and it is not the least part of the tragedy of Austria that the genial spirit of the Viennese is being systematically drawn into the meshes of this never idle mind-machine.

LONDON *6 May*   At luncheon yesterday A.C. Temperley told us an excellent & most significant story about Gen: v. Reichenau,[469] who was the <u>political</u> general of the German army until quite recently (he is

[469] Walther von Reichenau (1884–1942): Chief of Staff, *Wehrmacht* 1933; Gen. 1935; Cmdr Seventh Army Corps 1935; Cmdr Army Group IV 1938; C-in-C Tenth Army 1939; Field-Marshal 1940; killed in air crash Jan. 1942.

temporarily in disfavour). Temperley & a Scottish general were sitting with von R & another German officer after dinner, in Germany, at the manoeuvres last autumn; & the Scottish general (Ironside)[470] challenged v. Reichenau to a bottle of whisky. They set to, & the Scotsman grew steadier & steadier, while v. Reichenau, unaccustomed to that particular beverage, grew garrulous & reckless. Finally they proposed a series of toasts, & one of them proposed 'England & Germany!' v. R: toasted all three of the others, & added the word 'Brothers'. 'England & Germany! Brothers!' – & the last time he said it, lurching forward a bit, he added 'For four years'!! ACT says that 'it will take them just about 4 yrs to train all the officers they need & get all the equipment they need. He does not anticipate a war in which the [British] army shall be engaged.

v. Ribbentrop, ACT says, is now anti-British. He was a failure in London, & has returned to Ger. soured.

On the occasion of the Austrian coup (in March) Vansittart thought Germany intended to attack us at once, & said so. ACT heard this from a sure source in the *D.[aily]T.[elegraph]*. office.

Eden received 6000 letters on the occasion of his resignatn. (L[y] Marjorie Beckett[471] told us that he got masses from New Zealand & Canada, as well as from the Brit: Isles).

Anthony Eden, acc: to ACT, was much influenced by the Opposit[n] when he was For: Sec[y] – unduly so. I always thought so too. But I've no doubt his argument w[d] be that he was trying to represent the nation & not merely a Party – not even the Nationalist Gov[t]. Neville Ch: undoubtedly represents more strictly the Go[t], & the result is a sharper cleavage in foreign affairs than before – but also more definite results. AE wasn't getting results. Since he left Nev: Ch: has brought off the Anglo-Italian agreement, the Anglo-French military pooling of resources & plans, & also the Anglo-Irish Settlement.

LONDON *12 May* Had a short talk yesterday with that mine of informatn on Ger: affairs, Conwell-Evans. He contradicts what Temperley told me about Ribbentrop – but both may be right. Rib: may

---

[470] Edmund 'Tiny' Ironside (1880–1959): Commandant Staff College, Camberley 1922–6; Commandant 2nd Div., Aldershot 1926–8; Commander Meerut Div., India 1928–31; Lieut. of H.M.'s Tower of London 1931–3; Quartermaster-Gen. India 1933–6; Gen. Officer C-in-C Eastern Command 1936–8; Gov. & C-in-C, Gibraltar 1938–9; Inspector-Gen. of Overseas Forces 1939; Chief Imperial Gen. Staff 1939–40; Gen. 1935, Field Marshal 1940; kt. 1919; cr. Baron Ironside of Archangel & of Ironside 1941. See *The Ironside Diaries 1937–40* (1962).

[471] Marjorie Blanche Beckett (d. 1964): daughter of 5th Earl of Warwick; m. William Gervase Beckett (1866–1937) 1917, Con. M.P. 1906–29.

have left London disillusioned & biassed against us, but have bn restored by his reception when he returned, as Foreign Minister, to present his letter of recall – so small are the great! Anyhow Con-Evans declares that he was immensely delighted with the honours paid to him & particularly with his $2\frac{1}{2}$ [hr] talk with L$^{\underline{d}}$ Halifax. Eden always treated him coolly, & once declined to see him – tho' I believe an ambassadr has a prescriptive right to be received.

Rib has got Weiszäcker[472] as his chief of the For: Min: in Berlin, & has sent here as Counsellor Kordt[473] – brother of his own *Chef de Cabinet*. Both are moderates & want an agreement with us – so Con-Evans says. He knows them v. well, & confides to me that Kordt is <u>not a Nazi</u>. He is liable to be spied upon by Bohle's men here, so one has to keep that pretty quiet.

13 May   Had 10 min. v. interesting talk with Harold Nicolson at The Travellers' this evening after dinner, in which he confided to me that he had given a tea to Henlein,[474] the *Sudetendeutsch* leader, whose sudden visit here for 48 hours has caused a big flutter of excitement. The man really comes, I feel sure, as Hitler's emissary; & he says his policy is to push for a plebiscite for (or against) autonomy, with the Czech Gov$^{\underline{t}}$; & if the Czech Gov$^{\underline{t}}$ refuses, as it certainly will, then he will push for it on an international basis – that is to say, with other countries (ourselves, France, Italy, Germany) keeping the ring, while the vote is taken. That w$^{\underline{d}}$ probably be refused by Germany.

However, as I agreed with Harold, it is a policy to work on & has a good deal to be said for it.

HN pretends to be very sorry for himself – the papers have got hold of this story, he appears as a centre of intrigue, rumour casts him for all sorts of roles (eg For: Sec$^{\underline{y}}$ in Winston Churchill's Gov! but he (HN) didn't say this) etc etc But what really bothers him is that apparently he may lose his seat at Leicester.

[472] Ernst von Weiszäcker (1882–1951): entered for. service 1920; Min. in Oslo 1931–3, in Berne 1933–6; *Staatssek., Auswärtige Amt* 1938–43; Amb. to Holy See 1943–5; sentenced to five years' imprisonment for war crimes 1949; released after 18 months under general amnesty. See *Die Weizsäcker-Papiere 1933–50* (1974).

[473] Theo Kordt (1893–1962): Counsellor in London 1938–39, in Berne 1939–45; Head of For. Dept of Chancellor's Office 1950–3; Amb. in Athens 1953–8.

[474] Konrad Henlein (1898–1945): founder & leader of Sudeten *Heimatfront* [Patriotic Front] which became *Sudetendeutsche Partei* 1933; *Reichskommissar* for Sudetenland Sept. 1938; Reich Gov. of Bohemia & Moravia May 1938; *SS-Obergruppenführer* 1943; committed suicide May 1945. See his *We Want to Live as Free Men among Free Men* (1983; transl. of 1938 ed.).

24 May   I think L^{d} H:[alifax] is doing v. well as For Sec^{y}. GD of course sees a lot of him; & H: seems to have shrewdness & serenity in good proportion. Nothing rattles him. He is v. sincere himself but entirely realizes that the present German leaders are not. GD says he says he won't believe their assurances until their [sic] fulfilled. At the same time he is of course extremely courteous to them. Last Sunday was a v. critical day over Czechoslovakia, so L^{d} H came back from Oxford, where he was present at an All Soul's celebration (as was also GD), & was busy most of the day. He did not however sit glued to the FO, but went for a walk in the Park for an hour after tea with Lady H. All v. good.

Sir Neville Henderson, our Ambassdr in Berlin, got so rattled last Sunday as to propose to H that he should evacuate the ladies of the Brit: Embassy & other members of the Brit: colony. He had apparently started to make arrangements already – acc: to the Reuter account – L^{d} H told him – 'as near as one can to an ambassador' as GD said to me – 'Not to be a damned fool.'

There is (naturally) a greater maturity about him than about Anthony Eden. [. . .]

25 May   Re Sir Neville Henderson's ordering of a special coach to take away from Berlin some of the ladies of the Brit: Embassy & Consulate, I heard yesterday that this precaution had a most salutary effect upon the German leaders, who heard what he had done just when they were deliberating whether they c^{d} safely make a coup in Czechoslovakia. It naturally conveyed the impression that the Brit: ambassador expected us to be involved if war broke out, & so had a strong deterrent effect upon them!

1 June   At luncheon today Palmstierna told me an extraordinary thing about Anthony Eden. When AE was For: Sec^{y} he went down to the aerodrome once to meet M. Sandler,[475] the Swedish For Min, & found him (Palm^{trna}) waiting for him too, of course; & AE said to Palm^{tna} 'You know my position in the Cabinet is not too easy; can't you drop a word to the Press about how well you (Sweden) & I get on at Geneva'.

This was somewhat feeble on AE's part, really. There <u>is</u> something rather pettifogging about him. He was always seeking the goodwill of

---

[475] Rickard J. Sandler (1884–1964): PM 1925; Min. of For. Affairs 1932–6, 1936–40; mb. Swedish delegation to LoN 1927, 1929, 1931–8; Pres. LoN Assembly 1934; Swedish rep. to LoN Council 1936–9.

the Socialists, & I suppose he thought that they w$^{\underline{d}}$ be v. pleased at his getting on v. well with that doughty upholder of the League, Sweden! It shows rather a lack of perspective. He has become too europeanized.

Palmstierna – who now that he is out of harness speaks even more freely than before – also told me that once at the earlier proceeding of the Non-Intervention Com^{tee} on Spain Grandi & Maisky[476] used the most outrageous language to each other; so he (P) got up & asked the Chairman if he might speak *hors de Protocol* – i.e. words not to be recorded – & having got his leave then proposed that the speeches of Grandi & the Soviet ambassdr sh^{d} be expunged from the minutes of the meeting – saying 'it will go all round the world' (in dipl: reports). Grandi agreed at once; Maisky wldn't at first, but later agreed to, after P: had taken him aside. Palm$^{\underline{na}}$ says the standard of diplomacy has gone down, & so many diplomats have no diplomatic instincts.

That was an anecdote to Grandi's credit. Another one he told me was that Grandi 'leaked' to the Press once, & when what he had said was reproduced in the Swedish Press he complained to Palm$^{\underline{na}}$ about the leakage! P: answered him – 'oh well, we all know where it came from'. (This was after a meeting of the Non-Intervntn Com^{tee}).

4 June Last Wed[nesda]$^{\underline{y}}$ (1$^{\underline{st}}$) I also had an interesting talk with L$^{\underline{d}}$ Hardinge of Penshurst, whom I went to see in his rooms in Down Str. As is the way with public men who have a great career behind them he spoke chiefly of the past; but we did discuss one or two problems of today, & I was v. glad to find that our views were in close accord.

He told me privately that twice when he was ambssdr in Paris he had turned down the proposal to have an alliance with France. He thought that successive Brit: Govts had bn much too allied to Fr: policy as it was, & that we might have played a remarkably useful & influential part if we had bn more detached.

Germany is not ready for war now, but will be later – unless a strong oppos[i]t[io]$^{\underline{n}}$ developes [sic] inside Ger to policy by war-making or war-threats, which he thought was possible. [...]

Hearing that I had bn staying in Prague with Basil Newton, he asked me what sort of a man he was. I told him – quiet, very cool, with I thought a shrewd judgment – 'that's a very good thing, he said'. [sic] He seemed to like the <u>coolness</u> most of all. cp: Talleyrand '*surtout, pas*

[476] Ivan Mikhailovich Maisky (1884–1975): Russian diplomat; Counsellor in London 1925–7, Amb. 1932–43; Deputy For. Min. 1943–5; arrested during anti-Jewish purge of 1949; imprisoned 1949–53.

de zèle.' Being <u>detached</u> – having his own feeling under strict control, but <u>understanding the feelings of others</u>. Europeans are moved more by their feelings than by their mental processes.

17 June   It is little known that last Whitsun tide we v. nearly had another weekend crisis, this time caused by Italy. Mussolini has got tired of waiting for the recent Anglo-It^{n} Agreement to come into force. It does so when It: troops are being substantially withdrawn from Italy [sic – Spain]. When he signed, Musso: thought that moment was near; but since then the Catalans, with help from across the French frontier, have revived, & the end of the War seems as far off as ever. Therefore we have not yet recognized Italian Empire over Abyss^{nia}.

So on Sat. June 4 Ciano asked Ld Perth[477] to come & see him & in Fascist tones told him that either G^{t} B^{n} must recognize Abyss: now or else the whole Agreement w^{d} be off. Perth took it quietly, but at the same time regarded it as serious; as Ciano's language was menacing. He sent his account by despatch – not telephone or telegram. Halifax received it on Monday July 6 – & has <u>taken no notice of it</u>.

In the F.O. they were at first v. excited about it, talked of calling in Winston Churchill to the Gov^{t}, said Eden was right after all etc etc However, now all is calm again – for the present anyhow. Example of the value of <u>delay</u> & masterly inactivity.

I was shown a private letter yesterday from Halifax to GD on the subject of our (*TT's*) attitude in the Czech-German dispute. He regards our advocacy of a plebiscite as being at least rather premature & embarrassing the negotiatns betw: Benesh & the Sudetens. He indicates that he may come to supporting the idea of a plebiscite himself; but asks us to go slow.

I quite see that in <u>negotiation</u> the idea of a plebiscite may better be kept in the background. But I hope & think our articles may have helped by showing the Germans that we in G^{t} B^{n} have an open mind & want to see <u>justice</u> done. They were beginning to think that we were completely on the side of Czechoslovakia, bec: our dipl^{y} has always spoken of a solution 'within the framework of the Cz-k State' – i.e maintaining the present boundaries, which is of course the <u>Czech</u> view. We are by way of acting as mediators, therefore we sh^{d} be impartial, & in a plebiscite Sudeten Germans c^{d} vote for remaining inside the Cz-k State, if they did wish to.

18 June   Freiherr v. Rheinbaben[478] came to PHS yesterday evening, &

---

[477] Eric Drummond suc. as 16th Earl Perth 1937.

[478] Werner Karl von Rheinbaben (1878–1964): German diplomat & politician; *DVP* deputy 1920–30. See his *Auf dem Monte Verità* (1954).

I had a frank talk with him. He is a decent fellow. He was one of Stresemann's close adherents, but has now by force of circs: become a Nazi. I said I was sorry to hear it, as feeling here was becoming daily more anti-Nazi, tho' not necessarily anti-German.

He was interesting about the technique of for: pol: in Germany. The big decisions, he said, had <u>always</u> bn taken by the Head of the State – the Kaiser before the War, & now more than ever by Hitler. The public did not know enough to exercise any control under any system, & have not good political judgment. Hitler listens to advice, but trusts his own flair. Ribbentrop's influence is that he sees all the foreign ambassadrs etc & reports what they say to Hitler <u>just as he likes</u>. (Hitler, I believe, seldom reads written reports. He prefers verbal reports). And foreign envoys do not often see Hit: for personal interviews.

Thus the impatience of the Nazi hotheads over Czechslkia will not influence H, who sees the diff: between Cz: & Austria. Rheinbaben thinks that H: wl go slow. More by tone & gesture than by words he implied that Hit: considered that eventually Czslkia wl fall into his hands.

Himmler, Rheinbaben said, is the one man that Hitler has to listen to – being head of the secret police.

20 June   Ref: to L<u>d</u> Halifax's letter to GD (see June 17), GD showed me the draft of his reply in the office late last night (he has bn in Yorkshire). I suggested one or two alteratns, wh he made. It defended our view firmly.

I saw Conwell Evans yesterday afternoon on his return from Berlin. He found Ribbentrop still v. eager (in C-E's opinion) for an understanding with Britain. He had 4 hrs' talk with him.

Hitler, it seems, is devoting himself almost entirely to architectural matters just now – rebuilding of Berlin etc: An excellent sign!

23 June   Yesterday I had a short talk with L<u>d</u> Howard of Penrith at The Travellers. In discussing diplomacy he insisted on the great importance of remembering the characteristics, temperament etc of the people with whom you were dealing. English people were often not v. good at that. But if you were trying to get the same thing from different kinds of foreigners you ought to go about it in a different way with each.

29 June   Yesterday at M<u>rs</u> Chamberlain's afternoon reception at 10

Downing Str I said to L^y Maud Hoare[479] that I feared Cabinet Ministers got no opportunities now for real rest & recuperation as they were never in Opposition! Only too true, she said, 'we are hanging on by our eyelids' – physically, she meant, not politically! I said I admired all the more the amplitude of the address which Sir Sam had delivered to Reading Univ: when he was inaugurated as Chancellor. She was v. pleased & said she w^d send me a copy of the address in book form.

Mrs Chamberlain has done up 10 Downing Str beautifully, & opened it up too, for I gathered that she had had new windows put in the small corner room looking towards Carlton Ho:, which now makes a charming boudoir for herself. All the chair coverings etc seemed to me to be in excellent taste & all to go well together.

She has moreover coerced the authorities into letting her have some good pictures for the walls – e.g. a Turner or two. The furniture however, though good class, is still not really good.

15 July It has bn interesting to receive (GD from Halifax) a long F.O. memorandum arguing against the holding of a plebiscite among the Sudeten Germans. We (*T.T.*) had advocated it, hence this counterblast, evidently by Vansittart. In a private note by Halifax to GD the former says that the memo: is 'not necessarily our last word' but that the arguments it contains merit, he thinks, serious attention. Wisely put!

Van makes out quite a good case, but rather overstates it. One sentence actually is to the effect that 'the wishes of the inhabitants are what matter least.'! He means, I should in fairness add, in a practical way – from the practical point of view.

7 September 1938 Telephone Message: Mr. MacDonald (Prague) to Foreign News Editor.

Lord Runciman asked me to see him today. He & all members of the mission have been, he said, shocked and dismayed by the final paragraph of The Times *leader today.*[480] *He called it unhelpful & unnecessary, & also highly dangerous in*

[479] Maud Hoare; m. Samuel Hoare 1909; d. of 6th Earl Beachamp.

[480] 'Nuremberg and Aussig,' 7 September 1938. Dawson noted in his diary for 6 September that he had had 'an extremely arduous afternoon & evening – Leo Kennedy was there rather reluctantly prepared to write on the Czech crisis wh. was obviously coming to a head & produced an article wh. I had to get him to re-write at the last minute. Even so it ventilated rather crudely the idea which we had often [illeg] before, of a secession of the Sudeten fringe in Germany & there was a lot of hurried revision to

the present delicate stage of the negotiations. I must say that both he & the other members of the mission seemed very much upset by it. They thought of issuing a special communiqué disavowing the leader but heard that the Foreign Office had already issued a statement in London.

From the Prime Minister's office came similar messages of dismay. The Sudeten-Germans, too, are very much upset by it & both sides say it is a sign of British bad faith, an attempt (they say) to force a precipitate action by the Sudeten Germans.

I need not go into all the theories of British policy that have been woven around the leader already, but Lord Runciman's final words were that its effect had been most disturbing in a difficult day 'It has caused us a black day,' he said.[481]

'Nuremberg and Aussig'

The message which our Prague Correspondent sends this morning shows that the Czechoslovak Government are now ready to go very far indeed in meeting all reasonable demands. There is no difficulty about allowing the Germans – and all the other nationalities – full equality of status with the Czechs ... according to our Special Correspondent, 'very far-reaching concessions' are now to be made towards 'full self-government' for the German areas. ... The whole plan is one for the removal of grievances, and for the greater participation of Sudeten Germans (and other minorities) in the government of the country.

No Central Govt would still deserve its title if it did not reserve in its own hands Defence, Foreign Policy, and Finance. There does not appear to be any dispute about this principle in the minds of the Government or of HERR HENLEIN; and, if the Sudetens now ask for more than the Czech Government are apparently ready to give in their latest set of proposals, it can only be inferred that the Germans are going beyond the mere removal of disabilities and do not find themselves at ease within the Czechoslovak Republic. In that case it might be worth while for the Czechoslovak Government to consider whether they should exclude altogether the project, which has found favour in some quarters, of making Czechoslovakia a more homogeneous State by the secession of that fringe of alien populations who are contiguous to the nations with which they are united by race. In any case the wishes of

be done at midnight.' Dawson Mss. 42, f. 132, Bodleian Library. A plate in *The History of the Times* vol. II (between pages 930 & 931) reproduces Dawson's 'corrections' to Kennedy's draft leader. The authors of the *History* never refer to Kennedy by name, but only as 'the leader-writer'. Their argument that the decision taken in 1923 not to have a Foreign Editor left *The Times* without an 'expert', thus placing 'the conduct of foreign affairs, even when a situation of extreme delicacy was reached, in the hands of the Editor unassisted by a specialist' (p. 931) is preposterous.

[481] A copy of this message is in volume 12 of the 'Press Cuttings Book', where Kennedy has noted that 'There were other reasons. Riots etc.' The leader as I originally wrote it contained fuller & franker arguments in favour of an offer of secession by the Czech, Govt. to the Sudetens, but GD wdn't have it in that form, so I had to re-write the last half of it after 10 p.m.)

the population concerned would seem to be a decisively important element in any solution that can hope to be regarded as permanent, and the advantages to Czechoslovakia of becoming a homogeneous State might outweigh the obvious disadvantages of losing the Sudeten districts of the borderland.

17 Oct We were told an interesting thing by the F.O. yesterday (M.H. to RB-W) in connexion with the Hungar^n appeal to the '4 Munich Powers' over the Czechoslovak-Hungary frontier question. The neg^{tns} having broken down at Komarom the Hung^n Gov^t appealed to G^t B^n, Fr: Ger: & Italy. The F.O. quickly received a message from Musso: suggesting a 4-Power meeting at Venice. A few hours later it rec^d a second message, cancelling the first! Musso: had heard from Hitler, & so it was off! The second message explained that the Venice meeting was just a Hungarian proposal wh: Musso: had 'passed on'!

I find I have made no notes at all during all the terrific Czechoslovakia crisis we have passed through. The pace was too furious. I shall have to rely on the Cutting-book to refresh my memories. There is just one small episode of the earlier phase, in the summer, which I'll jot down, as illustrating a method of informal, very informal, dipl^y in these democratic days! S: & I were lunching at the Ritz with P^{ce} & P^{css} Lobkowitch, & M. Mazaryk (the Czech Minister) was there. Before luncheon I was talking with Lady Forres,[482] & I c^d see *he* wanted to talk to me, but privately. He came up, but L^y Forres did not give us the chance of a private talk before we all went in to luncheon. Then Mazaryk slid alongside & we walked together into the restaurant, during which brief interlude he managed to blurt into my ear 'Plébiscite, damn, damned plébiscite' – a sort of obbligato of oaths & the word plébiscite, which I perfectly understood. For in *T.T.* we had twice put forward the suggestion of a plébiscite for the Sudeten areas of Czchslkia, much to the disgust of the Czechs.

It was incidentally this suggestion of ours that evoked a private letter from Ld Halifax to GD (in June or July it must have been – see Cutting-book) in which he begged us not to pursue the proposal of a plébiscite, as they (the Brit: Gov^t) were trying another solution. But in this letter he added that he personally by no means ruled it out as an ultimate solution. It was this opinion of his which encouraged us (*T.T.*) to put forward the proposal of secession in Sept, when obviously Runciman's efforts were failing. By that time feelings were running so

[482] Jessica Forres (d. 1972): daughter of William Harford JP; m. Stephen Williamson (1888–1954) 2nd Baron of Glenogil (cr. 1922); businessman; Chairman of Lobitos Oilfields Ltd, Anglo-Ecuadorian Oilfields Ltd (d. 1954).

high that separation without a plebiscite seemed the only solution, as L$^{\underline{d}}$ Runciman himself came to agree.

We also knew in a roundabout way that Neville Chamberlain was ready to consider secession. He had attended a luncheon given by Lady Astor to some American journalists in the summer, at which one of them had asked him whether he would consider that solution – & he had answered in the same common sense way as L$^{\underline{d}}$ Halifax, that he w$^{\underline{d}}$ not refuse to consider it. This was quite private & confidential, of course, as was L$^{\underline{d}}$ Halifax's letter – but they fortified us in putting forward our proposal – before Hitler proposed it.

I think that Chamberlain's only mistake in the whole business was the tactical one of not saying anything about it in public until Hitler faced him with it at Berchtesgaden. Then he accepted it at once. It looked like capitulation to a dictator.

Incidentally however this caused Hitler to make a miscalculation. Our proposal in *T.T.* (on Sept 7) was vigorously disowned by the F.O. Press Dep$^{\underline{t}}$ (Leeper, prompted, if he needed prompting, by Vansittart no doubt), & the repudiation of secession as a solution was taken up by all the Press in chorus. Hitler therefore supposed that Chamb: w$^{\underline{d}}$ not agree to it when he put it to him. He told him this in subsequent conversation.

I believe Hit. hoped for a refusal, which w$^{\underline{d}}$ have given him an excuse to invade Czchslkia, which he was longing to do. It w$^{\underline{d}}$ have bn in the name of self-determination, so he would have, & could have, counted on the passivity of the democracies of France & G$^{\underline{t}}$ B$^{\underline{n}}$. Daladier in any case, though willing to fight, felt quite unable to.

LONDON *21 October*   I heard last night that the reason why Hitler made such a sour speech at Saarbrücken a week ago (& so soon after the Munich Agreement) was that he had just rec$^{\underline{d}}$ a letter from L$^{\underline{d}}$ Halifax expressing the hope that when Germany got into the Sudeten country there w$^{\underline{d}}$ not be a repetition of the cruelties & persecution of individuals which followed the occupation of Austria. That was why Hitler talked about our being 'governessy'. To be gentle is in his eyes to be soft. He sees no difference between the two.

25 October   Yesterday had luncheon with L$^{\underline{y}}$ Marjorie Beckett, who said that masses of people were still urging Anthony Eden to come out as a rival leader to Chamberlain. Most of them however are Libs & Socialists; & as Queenie B: said, 'Anthony is a Conservative.' AE is however obviously much tempted; but refrains, as, although he has no opinion of Nev: Ch: in foreign affairs, he feels it w$^{\underline{d}}$ be disloyal to turn against him. I said I thought that was the right attitude. Wait. No doubt his stock is going down a little, but he must be patient. Chamberlain won't last for ever; then a leader will be needed, & he can come out as strongly as he likes. He does of course understand foreign temperaments, esp: the German, much better than Nev: Ch:

Nev: Ch: on the other hand, as I heard from GD later, in the evening, has a perfectly clear idea of his own programme. He means to get on with Italy first, & more or less leave Germany alone until early next year, & then bring up the question of colonies in a bold & comprehensive manner. Roughly he divides African territories into two categories – those which can or will be able to govern themselves, & those which will not. The former must go their own way, without disturbance e.g. Rhodesians. The latter consist of the Central African territories, & would include Tanganyika. He will propose a European condominium for these, of which Germany w^d be a member. And the various members will individually administer separate regions. G^t B^n w^d for instance certainly continue to administer Kenya. Germany w^d preferably be allotted interior territories but, if she accepted any such international scheme at all – I've no doubt she w^d insist on Tanganyika as well.

'German' S.W. Africa would be made over outright to S: Africa, with special compensation to Germany.

3 Nov: I met with Conwell-Evans yesterday after luncheon, about to report to 10 Downing Str, after a visit to Germany. He evidently acts as unofficial sleuth – & a good man too, for the job. He is always v. secretive, but he told me that he had found German opinion still definitely favourable to Chamberlain, & growing less favourable to Hitler. Esp: the mothers – they find their children are taken right away from them & made over to the State, probably to be used as cannon-fodder. [...]

10 November Kennedy to Dawson: *Just a line to say that I am not going to write an introduction to the Penguin book on* Mein Kampf. *When the proofs came I found that the book was an undiscriminating anti-Hitler production, definitely Leftist, and made up of motley quotations from extremist Nazi literature. I hope however that Penguin may now publish my own book 'Britain Faces Germany' in their series. I have also been asked by Wilson Harris*[483] *to do an article on Hitler for the* Spectator, *which I should like to do.*

[483] (Henry) Wilson Harris (1883–1955): Ed. *Spectator* 1932–53; Ind. MP Cambridge U. 1945–50. See his *Life So Far* (1954).

22 November Yesterday at a nice luncheon with Alex: & L^y Theo Cadogan. Mazaryk was present; his spirits seem to be irrepressible, & he made many of his jokes to Sylvia – next to whom he sat – some of them pretty coarse. He is going to retire, but live in London – & one of his more harmless jokes was that everybody was being exceedingly kind to him & offering him a bed. 'I am being offered beds all over London' he said to S: 'but apparently nothing in them'! In point of fact he has taken a flat. [. . . .]

LONDON *30 November* AE thinks too much of consequences – is too much of the calculating politician. L^y Marjorie B: was here yesterday, & told us of all the people he saw one after another on the subject of his going to USA. Quite a private journey, to deliver a lecture, & only for a fortnight. But apparently he has discussed every possible consequence reaction & effect before he could make up his mind to accept the invitatn. I said to L^y Marjorie 'Why can't he make up his own mind what is right, & do it'. She was rather inclined to agree. I said he'd never be a leader unless he did.

7 Dec: [L^y Theo Cadogan ...] told me that she & her Alec often had AE quietly to dinner, & sometimes Cranborne too, whose advice AE always likes to have & usually follows. She said that AE, esp: lately, was frightfully nervy; most fidgety; can hardly sit still, & crumbles his bread & lets the crumbs fall on the floor, & even dropped butter on to the floor! And when he went in to have a talk with Alec Cadogan after dinner he did not sit down at all but spent the whole talk walking up & down.

I said that this might be just that AE was so high-strung; but [L^y Theo] said, tho' certainly he is highstrung, he does not seem to have quite the stamina for the heavy responsibilites of a statesman. She thinks he lacks physical solidity. He cannot put things aside. He worries. [. . .]

16 December Had a conversatn with Ld Londonderry 2 days ago at L^dery House – he having invited me to come one day after my letters to *T.T.* about Mein Kampf. He was extremely pleasant, but is to [sic] rambly to be impressive in what he says. He flits lightly from point to point. However, from his Cabinet experience & knowledge of the German leaders some of his opinions are interesting – e.g. he does not believe that the German Air Force is as efficient as they like to think. Also, his impression of Göring – that he is a sportsman, in the literal not the moral sense of the word. He is extremely keen on shooting & also on animal life, & L$^{\underline{d}}$ L: evidently found that a great bond of union. He had however recently written him a v. strong letter on the way Germany is treating the Jews, & pointing out how impossible it had made his (L$^{\underline{d}}$ L's) post$^{\underline{n}}$ as a friend of Germany. He said they were leading straight to war etc, but, just as in his conversatn, the force of the letter seemed to me to be spoilt by its diffuseness (about 10 pp altogether).

Göring had not yet replied (3 wks since the letter was written).

Lord L: spoke once or twice of the admiratn he felt for men who had started from nowhere & reached the positions where they now where [sic] – by contrast with his own 'pampered life' – a phrase 2 or 3 times (But they have no scruples, & he has) which he used.

He said that during the first National Gov$^{\underline{t}}$, when MacD was P.M. & Nev: Ch: Chancllr of the Exchequer, Nev: Ch: was absolutely single-mindedly frugal, determined to restore the nation's finances, & brushing aside every demand of himself & the other two Service Ministers. One unfortunate result was, that during the Rhineland crisis of 1936 both Baldwin (by then P.M.) & Nev: Ch: got an exaggerated idea of our weakness in defence. Hitler was bluffing (as I know well!) but we did not stand up to him as we might have. And when the Germans began to rearm in earnest, instead of making a bargain with them at once, as we might have, our only idea was to re-arm too.

7 Jan: Saw Cadogan again at the F.O. yesterday. He has become more fluent than he used to be – this, combined with his habitual directness, makes him most informative & helpful. I think & hope that he now feels he has shaken off Vansittart![484]

He is just off to Rome with the P.M. & L$^{\underline{d}}$ Halifax. He said he believed Hitler still thought that the democracies were 'on the run,' but that Musso: was shrewder & better advised. Hitler doesn't hear anything except what a few v. biased people (like Ribbentrop) tell him.

17 January Two days ago (on Sunday evening) GD saw the P.M. immediately on his return from Rome. GD was struck by how fit he looked – bronzed & very vigorous – although he had a v. strenuous visit, & the long journey both ways with a night in the train. GD had bn talking about this to the mutual friend of himself & the PM – Sir Horace Wilson[485] – & he says that they agree that one thing that keeps Chamb: fresh is his absolute immunity from worrying or brooding. He makes up his mind what is the best <u>immediate</u> thing to do, & does it with all his might, to the exclusion of doubts & alternatives.

GD had a v. interesting conversatn with the P.M. on Sun [day], in which he (PM) said that he preferred dealing with Musso: to dealing with Hitler, as 'Mussolini is a reasonable being & Hitler is a fanatic'. ('Neurotic' w$^{\underline{d}}$ be still nearer the mark?) Musso: scouted the idea that either he or Hitler was contemplating a *coup*, in N. Africa, Ukraine, or anywhere else. Hitler however probably meant to go on until he had got rid of <u>all</u> Jews out of Germany. Musso: told Nev: Ch: that he (himself) <u>needed</u> peace to consolidate his position at home. I reminded GD that this was <u>exactly</u> what Musso: had said to <u>Austen</u> Ch: about 10 yrs ago – since which Abyssinia had happened! Though in point of fact Musso: did have 10 years of consolidation before he invaded Abyssinia. GD told me that he had said to Nev: Chamberlain 'You

[484] Cadogan replaced Vansittart as PUS at the FO in January 1938. Vansittart was 'kicked upstairs' – or pushed aside – to the position of 'Chief Diplomatic Adviser', a position that was created expressly for the purpose of removing him from the headship of the FO.

[485] Horace John Wilson (1882–1972): Asst Sec., Ministry of Labour 1919–21, PUS 1921–30; Chief Industrial Adviser 1930–9; PUS Treasury & Head of Civil Service 1939–42; kt. 1924.

have evidently impressed your personality on the Italian people;' & Chamb[n] had answered 'Yes, I believe so. Mussolini himself grew steadily more friendly during the visit; & the people clapped Halifax & me wherever we went. Halifax was an ideal companion for the occasion, & made a great impression as the type of English Christian gentleman'.

I think Nev: Ch's great service has been to make the desire for peace articulate where it had not been articulate before i.e. in Germany & Italy. I put this into the leader I wrote on Sun: night.[486] Also Chamb: now feels (after this visit) that he is free to make a personal appeal to Musso: at any moment.

As showing how GD & I co-operate in producing leaders I'll attach the typed questions which I gave him to take to Nev: Chamb: when he went to see him.[487] GD apparently read them out one by one when he got to Downing Str.

This was my copy of my questions – & I have scribbled on it, some notes before he took them some after he had got back.

Here are also notes which GD wrote at Hever on Sunday morning for the leader which I was to write on Sun: evening. I used some of them near the beginning of the leader & some near the end. Some I did not put in – such as the hit at Garvin[488] 'To placard the situation as 'no worse' is to conjure up risks which never existed.' 'No Worse' had been Garvin's top headline over his main article, on the Rome visit, in Sun: morn[g]'s 'Observer.'[489]

I had been in favour of having the leader on Sat[y] morning. I could & should have written on just the same lines on Fri: night – but of course the fact that GD saw the P.M. on Sun: made it possible to write with much more assurance & authority. That probably counter-balanced the fact that for the public it was 48 hours late, & all the Sunday papers had had their say first.

That is always a question. Each case has to be settled on merit.

'Return From Rome'

The benefits ... of a visit which was not made for purposes of negotiation have been largely psychological; but so, in part, are the troubles of Europe.

---

[486] 'Return from Rome': 16 January 1939, p. 13.

[487] 'Is it about right to say that neither side scored, or wanted to score? Are further specific negotiations contemplated? What might be regarded as the gains of the visit (even if impalpable)? Is one of them that Mussolini pledged himself specifically to peaceful methods?

[488] James Louis Garvin (1868–1947): Ed. The Observer 1908–42.

[489] Kennedy noted: 'I tore up these notes inadvertently'.

And it is emphatically of practical as well as spiritual value that the BRITISH PRIME MINISTER has once more impressed himself upon the peoples of the world as an architect of European peace. The visit to Rome, it must be remembered, had its origin in a cordial invitation from SIGNOR MUSSOLINI, given and accepted when he and MR. CHAMBERLAIN were playing memorable parts in the prevention of war at Munich. To refuse such an opportunity to confirm his personal contact with the leader of the Italian people would have been to reverse the whole of MR. CHAMBERLAIN's policy. It would also have been to repudiate the ordinary dictates of common sense. The BRITISH PRIME MINISTER by his successive visits to the Continent has made the desire for peace articulate where it was not articulate before. That in itself is no mean achievement.

7 February   Yesterday I went to Londonderry Ho: to have a talk with Lord L. He is extraordinarily pleasant – more attractive than impressive! Really slow in the uptake sometimes. But he told me about his recent exchanges with the PM, which is always interesting, & about the visit he proposes to pay to Göring in March – which sh^d be _more_ interesting. We also discussed the speech he is going to make at the Primrose League tonight.

Talking of relations with Germany, I put into his head the possibility of trying to get Ronald Lindsay to go there on a special mission when he has done with Washington (which wl be in July). Lord L. rather liked the idea, & seemed inclined to put it to the P.M. [. . . .]

28 March   K. Buday[490] brought me a special message from the P.M. of Hungary, who is a friend of his (Count Teleki)[491] – that in a vital international crisis Hungary w^d never be against us (G^t B^n). From the rest of our conversatn, I have inferred that the rider sh^d be added 'If we can help it'!

1 April   Cadogan, whom I saw on Thurs:, also thought that C[oun]^t Teleki w^d only be on our side if he c^d manage it! This I told to Buday, confidentially, when I saw him again – gave him luncheon at The Travellers'. He was v. indignant, & said that Knox,[492] our Min: in

[490] Kálmán Buday: See his *The International Position of Hungary & the Succession States* (1931).

[491] Pál Teleki (b. 1879): Hungarian politician & geographer; P.M. 1920–1; Min. of Worship & Public Instruction 1938; P.M. 1939–41.

[492] Geoffrey Knox (1884–1958): entered dip. service 1912; Counsellor in Madrid 1931; Chair, Saar Basin Governing Commission 1932–5; Min. in Budapest 1935–9; Amb. in Rio de Janiero 1939–41; kt. 1935. See his *The Last Peace & the Next* (1943).

Budapest, must have grossly misinformed the F.O. Buday got quite excited when I told him about the statement wh Chamberlain was going to make in the afternoon – on help for Poland. He declared that Hungary <u>might</u> come in too – ought to anyhow – <u>he</u> w^{d} do his best. And he has flown off to Budapest today to try to influence Ct Teleki!

4 April　Great row over our leader of Apr 1, on the nature of our guarantee to Poland for her 'independence', given by Nev: Chambl^{n} in the H.oC. on Fri: March 31.[493]

I had seen Cadogan the day before (Thursday) & wrote the leader entirely on the lines of our talk & of what he told me. Possibly GD & I between us put a shade too much stress on the <u>limitations</u> of the guarantee, & too little on its <u>implications</u>.[494] But surely of all blunders the worst is to allow more to be read into a guarantee than is intended.

In any case GD went to see Halifax yesterday, & Halifax told him the following – On the Sat^{y} morn^{g} (the day of the appearance of my leader) he (L^{d} H) went to see the P.M. at 10 Downing Str [eet], & as he came in the P.M. put down *T.T.* with the words 'I've just been reading the leader in *T.T.* & that's just what I meant'. Halifax agreed that it was just about right. But a little later came furious expostulations from the Polish ambassdr, & the F.O. a little bowed to the storm & indicated that one or two of our phrases were 'a little unfortunate.' e.g. 'We do not guarantee every inch of Polish territory' & 'The key word is not integrity but independence.' (GD put in 'not integrity.' I had not mentioned integrity, but agreed to the insertion. In any case it was Cadogan himself who told me that the Gov^{t} had proposed the words 'integrity & independence', & prided himself on the fact that the F.O. had persuaded them to drop out the word 'integrity'. I had of course reported that to GD).

'A Stand For Ordered Diplomacy'

The Prime Minister's statement in the House of Commons yesterday was one in which every word counted. It should be read and re-read if its exact implications are to be appreciated correctly. That however is by no means to suggest that it was ambiguous or obscure. When every allowance has been made for its reticences it is seen to be a bold and definite challenge to

---

[493] 'A Stand for Ordered Diplomacy': 1 April 1939, p. 15.

[494] Dawson noted in his diary on 31 March: 'Leo K writing the leader after a great deal of discussion & diplomatic, parliamentary notes etc. all requiring a lot of revision (& excision).' Dawson Mss. 43, f. 53, Bodleian Library.

methods of diplomacy – if indeed the name has been applicable – which have recently shocked the conscience of the world. This Nazi violence of method has created an intense conviction – among the democratic countries particularly – that international dealings will degenerate into the habits of the jungle if differences between a larger and a smaller nation continue to be settled, as they have been settled on four or five recent occasions, mainly by reliance upon the threat or the use of brute force. The historic importance of the British Government's declaration is that it commits them to stand for fair and free negotiation. The new obligation which this country yesterday assumed does not bind Great Britain to defend every inch of the present frontiers of Poland. The key word in the declaration is not integrity but 'independence.' The independence of every negotiating State is what matters...

Recent issues have been decided in a manner which was orderly only because resistance was known beforehand to be vain, and reasonable only in the sense that reason preferred acquiescence to war. In every case except one, it may be admitted, there has been something to be said for the actual settlement that was reached; and MR. CHAMBERLAIN's statement involves no blind acceptance of the *status quo*. On the contrary, his repeated references to free negotiation imply that he thinks that there are problems in which adjustments are still necessary. The stand which Great Britain and France are making is simply for a return to decent and normal methods of diplomacy. The leaders of countries that have had to negotiate with HERR HITLER in the past have been systematically vilified by all the apparatus of the totalitarian Press and wireless, browbeaten in personal interviews, intimidated by the tramp of armed men which has actually accompanied negotiation, and then driven, like BENESH, into exile, or flung, like SCHUSCHNIGG, into a house of detention, there to have his health undermined by long and solitary confinement. Such behaviour by the FÜHRER of a great European State is a reversion to the habits of pre-Christian days and is utterly incompatible with civilized standards. The process of bullying and despoiling must be stopped. The relative strength of nations will always, and rightly, be an important consideration in diplomacy. But the elementary rights and liberties of small States must be maintained. Independence in negotiation must be restored to the weaker party. That is the essence of yesterday's declaration.

April 4   Memorandum to the Editor:[495] *[...] Forbes, who is an exceptionally steady man, sends the following report from Berlin with a covering message to say that it is undoubtedly 'sensational' but he would not send it without having confirmed it, as he says, from many sources. The report, which comes direct from the German War and Air Ministries, declares that Hitler has become obsessed with a hatred of England and is laying plans for a lightening attack 'without warning and without an ultimatum' on the British Fleet. Forbes adds that he has nothing to show that such an attack is imminent but – allied with other reports – it is being taken*

[495] From 'Miscellany book'.

*seriously here. The movement of ships are being kept quiet and the services generally
have been asked to take precautionary measures. (4) At last something more cheerful.
Beck*[496] *today gave a clear assurance that Poland would march against Germany
immediately if Great Britain were attacked. Halifax explained our obligation to
France and said that in our view an attack on Belgium, Holland or Switzerland
would be an attack on England: what would Poland do in such case: Beck said he
would have to think about it; certainly Poland would honour immediately their
obligation to France.*

5 April   Yesterday we had luncheon with the Dilkes;[497] M̲ͬ̄ͦ̄ D. is a
daughter of Sir W̲ͫ̄ Seeds,[498] our Ambssdr in Moscow − & they told us
that when Litvinoff heard about our article (see last entry) he informed
our Ambssdr that it showed that England was not in earnest & that
her guarantee was not good enough; so he did not care to continue
negotiatns for a similar Pact between G̲ͭ B̲ͫ̄ & the USSR.

We heard last night in PHS from our Berlin Embassy, via the F.O.
that Hitler is half crazed by the arrangement between ourselves &
Poland, & has bn thinking of a sudden air-dash against the British
Navy! This, sensational as it sounds, was reported by Ogilvie-Forbes,
our Chargé d'Affaires in Berlin. It seems that the Brit: Navy (& no
doubt, fear of a blockade) is absolutely on Hit:'s nerves. It was this
information which must have prompted L̲ͩ Stanhope's rather jovial-
bellicose 'let em-all-come' speech on the Ark Royal at Portsmouth last
night. He said they had all their anti-aircraft guns manned; & I daresay
the Fleet were rather hoping the German air-force <u>would</u> come over
like a mad-dog, & be shot down.

No doubt they'd do some damage; but it w̲ͩ dish Hitler.

I feel that if our leader had bn extra-provocative instead of extra-
tranquillizing, it might conceivably just have set Hit: off in his present
mood. I've always said to GD − remember we're dealing with a
neurotic, & it's as important to be calm as to be firm. He has quite
agreed.

LONDON *26 April*   Ref: back to entry of Apr 5 − I had dinner last night

[496] Jozef Beck (1894–1944): Mil. Attaché in Paris 1922–5; *Chef de cab.* to Marshal Pilsudski
as Min. of War 1926–29; Min. without Portfolio 1929–32; Deputy P.M. 1930–2; U-Sec.
of St., For. Affs 1930–32; Min. of For. Affs 1932–3, 1933–4, 1934–5, 1935, 1935–6, 1936–
9; mb. LoN. Council for Poland, 1931–9; escaped to Rumania 1939, interned 1940, died
in internment 1944. See his *Dernier rapport* (1951).

[497] John Fisher Wentworth Dilke (1906–1944): son of Sir Fisher Wentworth, 4th Bt
Dilke; husband of Sheila.

[498] William Seeds (1882–1973): entered dip. service 1904; High Commissioner, Rhineland
1928–30; Amb. in Rio de Janiero 1930–5, in Moscow 1939–40; kt. 1930.

at the Rum$^{\underline{n}}$ Legation, & there had quite a good talk with L$^{\underline{d}}$ Stanhope, who came up & talked with me in most friendly fashion. I referred to his Ark Royal speech, & he told me that it had been suggested to him that he might say a few words about the 'empty seats,' because they were all there to thank the cinema people for what they had done for the Fleet, & it seemed a bit ungracious that so many seats sh$^{\underline{d}}$ not be occupied. He admitted he might have put it differently; but claimed that the speech had had a good effect in Berlin. I said I wished a few more speeches were being made of the same sort. It had however given rise to a multitude of rumours, one of which was that the whole thing had bn a put-up job between himself & the P.M. 'Far from it' exclaimed Stanhope! Anyway there were 17 admirals as well as the First Lord on the Ark Royal; so the Ger: airmen rather missed a chance!

Discussing Hitler, I mentioned that he slept in the aeroplane when I flew with him, & was reported to sleep v. little at night – & Stanhope said that that was also the case with Ramsay MacDonald.

After dinner last night L$^{\underline{d}}$ Halifax (without knowing it!) had my modest little pencil of my pocket diary to annotate a despatch that had bn brought round during dinner. I was talking to Jebb,[499] of the F.O., & Halifax asked him for a pencil; & he, not having one, turned hurriedly to me!

I also had some talk with L$^{\underline{d}}$ Sempill,[500][sic] Rex Leeper, L$^{\underline{d}}$ Lloyd, & Rum[ania]$^{\underline{n}}$ Foreign Minister, M. Gafencu.[501] [...]

Winston Churchill was somehow the big man of the evening. He seemed to be talking in a v. interesting way at dinner, with everybody near him listening to him. Then after dinner M. Corbin had a long tête-à-tête with him, as did others. He rather spoilt things at the end of the evening however, by standing opposite M. Gafencü & making him a little farewell speech – I heard remarks about how his (M: G's) personality had impressed itself upon all who had met him, & much more in that style, delivered with a slight smile of self-consciousness which entirely spoilt its effect. One or two representatives of the Press were standing near (Graves, Gordon-Lennox & I had just bn talking

---

[499] Hubert M. Gladwyn Jebb (1900–96): entered dip. service 1924; FO 1929–54; pvt. Sec. to PUS 1937–40; FO delegate to Ministry of Economic Warfare 1941–2; Head of Reconstruction Dept 1942–5; Asst U-Sec. 1946–9; Permanent Representative at UN 1950–4; Amb. in Paris 1954–60; kt. 1954; cr. Lord Gladwyn 1956. See his *The Memoirs of Lord Gladwyn* (1972).

[500] William Francis Forbes-Semphill (1893–1965); engineer & aviator; Pres. Royal Aeronautical Society 1927–30; suc. 19th Bt. Semphill 1934.

[501] Grigore Gafençu (1892–1957): journalist & politician; founded *Revista Vremei* 1919, *Timpul* 1927; mb. of Nat. Peasant Party; For. Min. 1938–40; Min. in Moscow 1940–2; exiled to Switzerland 1941–5; sentenced in absentia by communist government to 20 years imprisonment for high treason. See his *The Last Days of Europe* (1944).

to M. Gafencu, & after finishing his speech Winston turned to us & shook hands with us!! All slightly operatic.

I was glad to see that Ld Halifax did not look at all unduly fagged or strained.

17 May   Rubido-Zichy, from BudaPest, looked in this morn^g^. I was right to see him. He wanted to tell me what Buday had so often told me, that Hungary doesn't at all like the Germans, & wants to remain on as good terms with us as she possibly can.

He is going on from here to Brussels, & expects to be rec^d^ by Otto of Hapsburg, who he obviously regards still as his lawful sovereign. But he says their plight is now pitiable. Even when they have a guest to luncheon all they can offer him is soup, rabbit-pie & some cabbage! The Germans have cut off all their income from Austria, so they have to rely on the proceeds of their properties in Hungary. What they seem to resent even more than the cutting off of their Austrian revenues is the cutting out of their names from the *Almanac de Gotha*! Rubido-Zichy was himself v. indignant about this. They are still the oldest Royal House in Europe, he said.

6 June   Reception at St James's Palace yesterday evening in connexion with London House, the home here for students from overseas. It is fine to stroll through rich, well-furnished rooms, hung with good pictures, with a Guards string band playing in one of them, & meeting nice people all along the route! also the windows were wide open on the Mall side & one looked out into the summer night. We met Palmstierna, P.K. Hodgson,[502] L^y^ Leconfield Ld Bessborough & others. I had quite a good talk with L^d^ B, who did me the compliment of saying that he always made a note of what I said was going to happen, as so far my prognostications had always proved correct! This time he asked me if we were going to pull off an agreement with Soviet Russia, & I said 'just.' [....]

20 June   Yesterday GD gave me the draft of the address which Ld Halifax is to deliver in 10 days' time at the annual dinner of the RIIA. L^d^ H: had sent it to GD for suggestions, & GD passed it to me. I have

[502] Patrick Kirkman Hodgson (1884–1963): pvt. Sec. to Duke of York 1926–33.

made some (herewith).[503] It will be interesting to see if Halifax takes up any of my points.)

30 June In Lord H's speech, as delivered last night, there was still nothing about propaganda or Lord Perth; but it had definitely bn gingered up & the slight error about Poland had bn rectified.

I find that Ld Halifax showed it to a lot of people beforehand – e.g. to Ld Trenchard,[504] whom I met in PHS with GD, & also next day as it happened at 10 Downing Str (Mrs Chamberlain's reception). He (L^{d} T) is sending us a letter backing up Ld Halifax. He said something to GD to the effect that L^{d} H's ideas delivered in his own (L^{d} T's) rough language might have bn best of all! Ld T. is Kitchener-like in appearance, but has a quite genial manner, which I think K.oK.[505] [sic] had not.

The P.M. looked well & buoyed at his reception (on the 28th).

4 July Last weekend (Sunday was the 2nd) the F.O. expected a German coup in Danzig. Ld Halifax took every possible step, to warn the Ger. Gov^{t} that this w^{d} involve war with us as well as Poland, incl: the summoning of the Dipl: Corr spdts of the chief newspapers to the F.O. on Fri: evening. He gave them the outline of his attitude, v. stiff, which duly appeared in the Press next morn^{g}; & I also remember hearing a stiff reminder of the Brit. attitude on the BBC on Sat^{y} night (when I

[503] 'Very sound indeed, of course, and full of good arguments but they would get across better if he could put a kick into them.

There is a lack of the telling phrases of last year's address e.g. 'There are various kinds of change, from the convulsion of the earthquake to the slow development of the forest tree'.

In 1938 he said – 'We have no wish to cramp legitimate developments or to encircle any nation with a ring of potential enemies'. It seems to me it would be well worth while boldly to recall this sentence with particular emphasis on the opening words 'We have no wish'. The explanation he now gives of why we have done it will be all the more effective.

Last year he also said 'The best propaganda you can do for the British people here and throughout the Empire is to give them facts, as objectively as you can'.

This seems to offer a good entry for explaining the work of Lord Perth, which is not mentioned, but which would fit appropriately into a discourse at Chatham House.

On p. 1, Poland is included in the list of nations to whom we have given unilateral pledges, but Beck made a point of saying that the pledge was reciprocal.'

[504] Hugh Montague Trenchard (1873–1956): Chief of Air Staff 1919–29, 1st Marshal of the Royal Air Force 1927; Comm. Metropolitan Police 1931–5; Chm. of the United Africa Company 1936–53; kt. 1918; cr. Viscount 1936.

[505] Horatio Herbert Kitchener (1850–1916): army officer; Min. for War 1914–16; cr. Earl Kitchener of Khartoum 1914.

was at Hambrook), which was no doubt communicated to them by the
F.O.

On Sat^y L^d H: himself went off to Eton to see one of his sons play
cricket against Winchester.

He seems to have scored another victory over Hitler. H: undoubtedly
planned to annex Danzig in April (?or May), & we checked him then.
Now he seems to have bn checked again. There have been great
demonstratns by Nazi semi-soldiers, & fiery speeches, but no declaratn
of actual union with Germany.

H: may branch off into Slovakia & Hungary?

POSTSCRIPT

15 Oct: 1939   In a conversatn the other day [...] L$^{\underline{d}}$ Halifax said he thought this war was chiefly one between the home fronts, & w$^{\underline{d}}$ be won or lost at home. After the War the chief thing w$^{\underline{d}}$ be to have a negotiated peace, not an imposed one.

GD communicated above to me. I said I was sure L$^{\underline{d}}$ H: was absolutely right. We must have an <u>agreed</u> peace. Thereafter we must try to do what we did last time, only a damned side [sic] better. There was no statesmanship in our foreign policy between the two Chamberlains – Austen & Neville.

7 Nov: 1940   [convers with Benes ...] In the earlier part of the conversation – which I began by reminding him of our last talk, in March 1938, in the Hradchany [sic] Castle at Prague – he pulled out of his pocket a map of CzechoSlovakia showing the territorial concessions made to Germany. The map looked as if it had been in & out of his pocket ever since! & for some time Benesh spoke with earnestness & a trace of bitterness about those tragic days. No recrimination, however. He told me that three times Russia had offered to help him if he w$^{\underline{d}}$ fight – & he had always answered, I cannot & will not fight unless Eng. & France fight with me. It was quite new to me that Russia had offered to come in. But Benesh said he knew that <u>Bonnet</u> had assured <u>Germany</u> beforehand that France would <u>not</u> fight!

Benesh does not blame us, England – who had no treaty, unlike France – for not fighting, but says that Germany was then nothing like so well prepared as she was a year later. In particular, she had not accumulated the stores of oil, & was not so well organized economically.

After Munich, he knew the CzechoSlovak Republic was doomed. He prepared forthwith his speech of resignation, but held on a couple of months while he prepared the 'conspiration' – as he called it – for the days when CzechoSlovakia was under German domination – now! that is. And he is acting today on the lines he then planned, & is in <u>daily</u> contact with the plotters inside Czecho-Slovakia. He has got, I think, an uncanny foresight. [....]

APPENDIX

1932

2 January: 'Prohibition in Finland'
12 January: 'A Prince of Ethiopia'
13 January: 'M. Laval Resigns'
14 January: 'President Hindenburg's Position'
16 January: 'France & Lausanne'
21 January: 'Advice to Europe'
23 January: 'The French Chamber on Reparations'
29 January: 'Reparation Meetings'
30 January: 'Shanghai'
9 September: 'The Territorial Army'
19 September: 'The British Statement'
22 September: 'Equality of Arms at Geneva'
5 October: 'Public Opinion and the Lytton Report'
14 October: 'Hungarian Policy'

1933

24 January: 'A New League Committee'
25 January: 'M. de Jouvenel's Mission'
27 January: 'Sir John Simon at Geneva'
4 March: 'The Prime Minister for Geneva'
9 March: 'To Geneva via Paris'
11 March: 'On to Geneva'
15 March: 'The Hitler Revolution'
17 March: 'A Draft Convention'
20 March: 'The Meeting in Rome'
24 March: 'Account Rendered'
27 March: 'Peaceful Revision'
4 May: 'Two Schools of Diplomacy'
8 May: 'Germany at Geneva'
13 May: 'A Breathing Space'
15 May: 'Herr Rosenberg Departs'
16 May: 'A Challenge to Peace'
27 June: 'Offence and Defence'
17 July: 'The Four-Power Pact'
18 July: 'Sir John Simon's Holiday'
19 July: 'Troubles of a Socialist Republic'
24 July: 'Hitlerism'
28 July: 'Herr Hitler's Responsibility'
29 July: 'Fascism of the Left'

1 August:	'Mr. Henderson's Job'
4 August:	'1914 & 1933'
11 August:	'Changes in Diplomacy'
5 September:	'Limitation of Arms'
6 September:	'The Nazi Rally'
11 September:	'Queen Wilhelmina'
12 September:	'Austro-German Relations'
16 September:	'A Turning Point'
20 September:	'Austrian Discords'
22 September:	'Supervision of Armaments'
23 September:	'Changing Austria'
26 September:	'Geneva Meetings'
28 September:	'Arms And Germany'
4 October:	'Herr Dollfuss's Escape'
5 October:	'Conservatives & Disarmament'
6 October:	'British Principles Affirmed'
9 October:	'German Aims & Arms'
16 October:	'The Break-up'
17 October:	'Sir Austen Chamberlain's Birthdays'
18 October:	'The Two Cases'
19 October:	'Anglo-German Civilities'
20 October:	'A Socialist Success in Norway'
25 October:	'The Fall of M. Daladier'
26 October:	'A Necessary Postponement'
27 October:	'The New French Govt'[506]
31 October:	'A Scandinavian Conference'
3 November:	'An Unwarranted Expulsion'
4 November:	'Obligations of Peace'
7 November:	'The Tallest Poppies'
8 November:	'The Disarmament Debate'
13 November:	'A Vote of Censure?'
14 November:	'Herr Hitler's Case'
15 November:	'A British Initiative'
21 November:	'A Conservative Success in Spain'
23 November:	'The Issue in Europe'
25 November:	'The Next Stage'
28 November:	'The Turn of M. Chautemps'
29 November:	'Three Possible Courses'
30 November:	'Security in the Air'
2 December:	'German Workers' Clubs'

---

[506] 'Written on incomplete information. I left at 11:30 prime minister, & Casey put the final touch at 1.30 a.m.' All footnotes in appendix are A. L. Kennedy's and are reproduced as they appear in the Clipping-Books.

4 December:	'The German Church'
5 December:	'After the Spanish Elections'
7 December:	'Italy & the League'
11 December:	'M. Avenol's Visit'
14 December:	'Foreign Policy in the Lords'
15 December:	'Disarmament by Diplomacy'
19 December:	'Poland at Home & Abroad'
20 December:	'Frontiers & the Aeroplane'
22 December:	'Disarmament & Revision'
23 December:	'Revolt in the German Church'
30 December:	'President Roosevelt on World Peace'

1934

2 January:	'A Frontier Dispute Settled'
5 January:	'Sir John Simon in Rome'
9 January:	'A Conflict in Germany'
22 January:	'Another Useful Council'
25 January:	'Austria & Germany'
27 January:	'Better Neighbourhood'[507]
30 January:	'The year One'
31 January:	'Hitlerism in Action'
1 February:	'A Bold Advance'
3 February:	'The German Reply to Austria'
6 February:	'The Crisis in France'
7 February:	'The British Plan'
8 February:	'Confusion in Paris'[508]
9 February:	' "Vive Doumergue!" '[509]
13 February:	'Civil Strife in Austria'
15 February:	'International Understanding'
16 February:	'A Diplomatic Journey'
17 February:	'The Austrian Tragedy'
20 February:	'Austrian Independence'
21 February:	'Dimitroff'[510]
26 February:	'Conflict in the German Church'
27 February:	'Whither Austria?'
28 February:	'Moral Disarmament in Practice'
2 March:	'Emperor Again'
6 March:	'The Eden Mission'
9 March:	'Appeasement in Austria'

[507] 'Begun at 10.30 pm, on receipt of the news'.
[508] 'Middle para. Rest written by Casey'.
[509] 'Middle part by Casey'.
[510] 'The Dimitroff leader produced quite a crop of supporting letters, & notices in other papers.'

13 March:	'Suspense in Spain'
15 March:	'Disarmament Again'
19 March:	'The Rome Protocols'
20 March:	'An Unsettled Conflict'
21 March:	'Two General Görings'
22 March:	'Imperial Defence'
26 March:	'M. Doumergue's Task'
5 April:	'The Way of Agreement'
17 April:	'German Armaments'
19 April:	'A Breakdown'
23 April:	'M. Titulescu on His Travels'
27 April:	'Rearmament Regulated or Unregulated?'[511]
30 April:	'The New Spanish Cabinet'[512]
1 May:	'Japan and China'
2 May:	'May-day Contrasts'
4 May:	'The Outlook of France'
7 May:	'The Mind of Germany'
9 May:	'The Arms Outlook'
11 May:	'Modernizing China'
14 May:	'Another Council To-day'
16 May:	'Support for M. Doumergue'
17 May:	'From the Practical to the Ideal'
18 May:	'A Good Initiative'
19 May:	'A Debate on Foreign Policy'
23 May:	'Russia & the League'
25 May:	'The Builder of a Nation'
28 May:	'A Critical moment'
29 May:	'Turkey & the Straits'[513]
30 May:	'The German Case'
31 May:	'A Debate on Realities'
1 June:	'Suspense at Geneva'
5 June:	'Arms & Security'
8 June:	'The German Church'
11 June:	'A Further Chance'
13 June:	'One Dictator to Another'
15 June:	' "Affection & Friendship" '
16 June:	'Dictators' Discussions'
20 June:	'A Catalonian Dispute'
21 June:	' "Critics & Carpers" '

[511] 'This leader caused annoyance at the F.O. (Vansittart) as it propounds a policy unwelcome to them. (Their one idea is to keep in with France).'
[512] 'Some of above by Graves.'
[513] 'Written by me instead of Graves, who was out to dinner.'

25 June:	'The Policy of M. Barthou'
26 June:	'Lord Reading on Versailles'
28 June:	'Air & Empire'[514]
29 June:	'Italy & the Tirolese'
2 July:	'Purging a Party'
6 July:	'A New Japanese Government'
7 July:	'M. Barthou's Visit'
11 July:	'M. Barthou Returns to Paris'
12 July:	'Dr. Dolfuss & the Terrorists'
14 July:	'A British Interest'
17 July:	'Solving a Spanish Dispute'
18 July:	'Norwegian Fishing Limits'

1935

27 February:	'A Pleasant Visit'
4 March:	'Sir John Simon for Berlin'
4 April:	'The British Role'
18 April:	'The Geneva Verdict'
26 May:	'An Opportune Visit'
24 June:	'From Paris to Rome'
25 June:	'Intolerance in Germany'
27 June:	'Talks in Rome'
29 June:	'Batsman & Bowlers'
1 July:	'M. Laval in Control'
2 July:	'Mr. Eden's Statement'
3 July:	'Well Done South Africa!'
5 July:	'Abyssinia & Europe'
8 July:	'A League for Peace'
10 July:	'Naval Programmes'
12 July:	'British Foreign Policy'
15 July:	'Italy, Abyssinnia, & the League'
31 July:	'Geneva To-day'
2 August:	'Britain & Abyssinia'
3 August:	'Agreement at Geneva'
7 August:	'An Untimely Proposal'
8 August:	'Investigation of Walwal'
10 August:	'A Misleading Analogy'
14 August:	'A Mission for Peace'[515]
15 August:	'Cricket To-day'
20 August:	'The Cabinet to Meet'
22 August:	'To-day's Cabinet'

[514] 'GD's idea.'
[515] 'Written after a talk with Eden.'

23 August: 'The Cabinet's Decision'
27 August: 'Air Raid Precautions'
29 August: 'Two Cabinets Meet'
30 August: 'A Stricken King & People'
2 September: 'The Abyssinian Concession'[516]
4 September: 'The Council Meets'
5 September: 'At Geneva'[517]
6 September: 'The Council & Italy'
10 September: 'A Diplomatic Manoeuvre'
12 September: 'A Momentous Speech'
14 September: 'A Decisive Speech'
17 September: 'Germany & the Crisis'

1936

10 September: 'German Claim to Colonies'
11 September: 'Independence for Syria'
12 September: 'Franco-Polish Friendship'
14 September: 'Last Day at Nuremberg'
15 September: 'The Council of the Little Entente'
16 September: 'Strike Fever in France'
21 September: 'The Assembly To-day'
24 September: 'A Socialist Victory in Sweden'
24 September: 'The Struggle for Madrid'[518]
1 October: 'The Czechosolvak Germans'
5 October: 'Minor Activities of the League'
8 October: 'Inside Madrid'
9 October: 'No Intervention'
12 October: 'Dr. von Schuschnigg's Autocracy'
13 October: 'New Government in Hungary'
15 October: 'Unity in Defence'
16 October: 'Belgian Policy Reconsidered'
20 October: 'Poet & Ambassador'
21 October: 'British Obligations'
23 October: 'London Talks To-day'
26 October: 'Italy & Germany'
27 October: 'A Victory for Moderation'
30 October: 'No Intervention'

[516] 'Following a leader by GD, written 2 days before on the main issue.'
[517] 'A poor hurried thing!'
[518] 'A short leader by me converted into a first by Braham.'

1938

4 August:	'Idealism in Practice'
4 August:	'The Last King of Poland'
8 August:	'Lord Runciman at Work'
9 August:	'Empire Interchanges'[519]
11 August:	'Minorities in Rumania'
13 August:	'Palestine After the Visit'
15 August:	'Tortured Spain'
5 September:	'Negotiations Continue'
6 September:	'Forty Years a Queen'
7 September:	'Nuremberg & Aussig'
12 September:	'Suspense'
13 September:	'Herr Hitler's Speech'
15 September:	'A Bold Initiative'
17 September:	'The Prime Minister's Return'
19 September:	'A New Advance'
20 September:	'Prague & the Plan'
22 September:	'The Second Visit'
27 September:	'The Issue'
29 September:	'The White Paper'
30 September:	'Agreement at Munich'
3 October:	'An Overshadowed Assembly'
5 October:	'Other Claims on Prague'
6 October:	'President Benesh Resigns'
10 October:	'Czechoslovakia To-day'
11 October:	'A Famous Cricket Leader'
13 October:	'A French Ambassador for Rome'
14 October:	'Redrawing the Frontier'
15 October:	'Hungary & Slovakia'
17 October:	'Arms & Policy'
21 October:	'Hungary & Slovakia'
24 October:	'Mediation in Spain'
25 October:	'Rights & Responsibilities'
26 October:	'German Refugees in Czechoslovakia'
2 November:	'An Agreement to be Completed'
3 November:	'Italy & Spain'
5 November:	'New Frontiers'
15 November:	'King Carol's Visit'
17 November:	'A Treaty Completed'
19 November:	'Baltic Birthdays'
21 November:	'Queen Maud of Norway'
23 November:	'Another Link with Portugal'

[519] 'Written impromptu!'

24 November:	'Duration of Test Matches'
25 November:	'King Leopold in Holland'
29 November:	'Mr. Chamberlain for Rome'
30 November:	'The New Czechoslovakia'
1 December:	'Independence Day in Iceland'
3 December:	'A Proper Protest'
7 December:	'The Franco-German Declaration'
9 December:	'The Belgian Government Carry On'
13 December:	'Memel & Europe'
15 December:	'A Bold Italian Innovation'
17 December:	'Italian Claims'
19 December:	'Cold over Europe'
20 December:	'Mr. Chamberlains's Survey'
23 December:	'A Pause in Spain'
28 December:	'A Quarter of a Million'
29 December:	'Relief for St. Helena'

1939

2 January:	'Into the New Year'
4 January:	'M. Daladier's Journey'
6 January:	'History Perverted'
10 January:	'The Visit to Rome'
13 January:	'Reform in Hungary'
16 January:	'Return from Rome'
18 January:	'Home Via Geneva'
20 January:	'Mr. Lloyd George's Speech'[520]
23 January:	'The League Council Ended'
24 January:	'The Nazification of Memel'
27 January:	'The Kaiser Looks Back'[521]
30 January:	'Chile's Misfortunes'
4 February:	'A New Rumanian Ministry'
7 February:	'Tragic Exodus from Spain'
8 February:	'Leisure of Nations'
10 February:	'The End in Sight'
13 February:	'Bilingual Belgium'
15 February:	'Recognition?'
16 February:	'Grotius Commemorated'
20 February:	'Towards Peace in Spain'
22 February:	'A Business Cabinet in Belgium'

[520] 'As much GD's as mine, almost.'

[521] 'A short leader on above was first written by somebody else, which I thought rather washy. And I thought we were missing an opportunity. So GD suggested treatment as above, by me.'

22 February:	'Ash Wednesday'
24 February:	'Lord Halifax on War & Peace'
25 February:	'Recognition on Monday'
28 February:	'Recognition'
1 March:	'Recognition Endorsed by Parliament'
4 March:	'Central Europe'
10 March:	'The Belgian Crisis'
11 March:	'The Strong Hand in Slovakia'
14 March:	'Czecho-slovakia Again'
15 March:	'Czecho-slovakia Destroyed'
17 March:	'The New Protectorate'[522]
18 March:	'Britain & Europe'
20 March:	'Reactions to Germany'
21 March:	'The President's Visit'
23 March:	'The Case of Memel'[523]
24 March:	'Return to Normal'
25 March:	'Common Ideals'
27 March:	'A Fresh Start?'
29 March:	'Changing Another Frontier'
30 March:	'Back to Diplomacy'
1 April:	'A Stand for Ordered Diplomacy'[524]
3 April:	'Colonel Beck's Visit'
4 April:	'Democracy Vindicated'
6 April:	'President Lebrun Re-elected'
8 April:	'Neighbours of Germany'
26 April:	'Questions & Facts'
27 April:	'Great Britain & Rumania'
1 May:	'Germany & Poland'
4 May:	'Poland & Russia'
6 May:	'Poland's Case'
9 May:	'Russia & the Balkans'
11 May:	'Britain & Russia'
12 May:	'Britain Speaks'
15 May:	'Aggression & Defence'[525]
20 May:	'British Foreign Policy'
22 May:	'The Meeting at Geneva'

[522] 'Much of these leaders is being projected nightly into Germany by the BBC.'

[523] '... apparently the Memel leader pleased Downing Str v. much, acc: to GD.'

[524] 'This leader, with its slight qualification of the support offered to Poland, has caused annoyance in the F.O. & an outburst of lectures at our expense in other papers – notably the D.T.

In point of fact I had a talk with Cadogan on the subject the day before writing it – but then GD & I made up our own minds.'

[525] 'Considerably amplified by B-Ward – it was originally written for a second leader.'

23 May:	'The Berlin Ceremony'
24 May:	'An Alliance that Endures'
25 May:	'Progress with Russia'
27 May:	'Cricket in Full Swing'
29 May:	'A State Coach for the Governor'
31 May:	'Hungarian Cross-Currents'
1 June:	'M. Molotoff's Speech'
6 June:	'Spain for the Spaniards'
7 June:	'To Liége by Water'
7 June:	'A Landmark in Rumanian History'
9 June:	'Lord Halifax's Speech'
10 June:	'Yugoslavia & Rumania'
13 June:	'The Dual Policy'
17 June:	'Uneasy Bohemia'
22 June:	' "Imperium et Libertas" '
24 June:	' "Intolerable Insults" '
26 June:	'Arms & Social Services'
28 June:	'Japanese Threats'
29 June:	'From Tientsin to Tokyo'[526]
29 June:	'A Reply to Hitler'
30 June:	'Where Britain Stands'
5 July:	'The Talks with Russia'
7 July:	'Migration for the Tirolese'
10 July:	'The Baltic Difficulty'
11 July:	'Britain & Danzig'
12 July:	'After the Statement'

[526] 'Rest by Graves [ie after 'four suspected Chinese gunmen'].'

INDEX

A biographical note can be found on the page in which each person is first mentioned in the text of the journals.